TRIACASTELA `27` 20.7km `238`

Fonfría
Alto do Poio
Padornelo
Hospital
Liñares
N-120
A-6

PALAS DE REI `30` 26.1km `254`

Rosario
Vilar de Donas
Portos
Eirexe
Ligonde
N-547
Hospital
Gonzar
Toxibó

SANTIAGO `33` 20.1km p.279 `270`

Catedral
A-9
Monte Gozo
San Marcos
Villamaior
Labacolla
rio Labacolla
Aeropuerto
N-634
Amenal
N-547

O'CEBREIRO `26` 30.1km `226`

GALICIA
La Faba
Herrerías
Ruitelán
LEÓN
Vega de Valcarce
San Fiz
Trabadelo
Vilar
Pradela
Moral
Pereje
Dragonte
③ ② ①
p.225

PORTOMARÍN `29` 22.9km `248`

(rio Miño)
Villachá
Paradela
Momientos
Ferreiros
Morgade
Leimán
C-535
Mercado de Serra
Barbadelo

ARCA `32` 22.2km `266`

Santa Irene
Xen
Salceda
N-547
Calle
As Barrosas
ARZÚA

VILLAFRANCA `25` 30.7km `216`

rio Cúa
Valtuille
Pieros
A-6
Cacabelos
N-120
Camponaraya
PONFERRADA
p.221
Campo
Embalse de Bárcena
MOLINASECA

SARRIA p.247 `28` 25.0km `242`

Aguiada
Calvor
Furela
Samos
Montán
San Xil
Renche
① ②
TRIACASTELA

RIBADISO `31` 26.4km `260`

N-547
Castañeda
Boente
MELIDE
A CORUÑA
LUGO
Casanova
San Xulián
PALAS DE REI

A PILGRIM'S GUIDE TO THE

Camino de Santiago

St. Jean · Roncesvalles · Santiago

—

The Way of St. James

The ancient pilgrim path also known as *Camino Francés*

John Brierley

*A Practical & Mystical Manual
for the Modern Day Pilgrim*

6th EDITION

4

© John Brierley 2003, 2006, 2007, 2008, 2009, 2010

First published as A Pilgrim's Guide to Camino Francés in 2003
This new fully revised 6th edition published in 2010.
ISBN 978-1-84409-192-8

British Library Cataloguing-in-Publication Data.
A catalogue record for this book is available from the British Library.

All photographs © John Brierley 2010
Cover and author photograph by Gemma Brierley
All maps © John Brierley 2010

Printed and bound in the European Union

Published by
CAMINO GUIDES
An imprint of Findhorn Press Ltd
305a The Park
Findhorn
Forres IV36 3TE
Scotland
Tel: +44(0)1309-690582
Fax: +44(0)131-777-2711

Email: info@findhornpress.com
www.findhornpress.com
www.caminoguides.com

CONTENTS:

[A] ACKNOWLEDGEMENTS:

This guidebook has been a lifetime in the making and a decade in the mapping. It is an ongoing journey with many deep valleys and high peaks. Countless individuals have crossed this path and each one, in their own way, has helped to shape it. This is no less true today as I finalise this latest update of the original guide. So, apart from my earlier mentors and helpers, I want to thank the many Friends of the Way *Amigos del Camino* and the various associations whose voluntary efforts to waymark the route means that, today, we only need the barest details to get us safely to our destination.

And a special thanks to pilgrims who took the time to feedback comments and suggestions, many of these have now been incorporated in this latest guide. Just before an earlier edition went to the print, I received an email asking why I was endorsing 'cheap' air travel to and from Santiago when it was so costly on the environment. Details have been included on how you can offset damaging greenhouse emissions and travel carbon-neutral, whether this be by air, rail or bus. My conscience is also clear because I know that walking the caminos can be a powerful catalyst for positive change so that the means (of getting there) fully justifies the end (expanded awareness). A central tenet of these guides is that pilgrimage starts the moment we become conscious that life itself is a sacred journey, carrying with it the responsibility to act accordingly.

And finally, I thank you, fellow pilgrim, for travelling the path with me. Let us remind each other that every step is a prayer – for good *or* ill – so let us manifest goodwill in all our thoughts, words and actions.

Buen Camino John Brierley

NOTE TO THE 6th EDITION:

The route still remains largely unchanged since the previous edition was published in 2009 but the addition of several new hostels and cafés en route has helped to relieve some of the pressure on facilities. Some existing hostels have also witnessed an upgrading of the facilities offered particularly the addition of washing *and* drying machines, the latter can be a real boon in wet weather. This smaller and lighter edition makes it even easier to carry in your pocket.

The biggest change continues to be the rise in the number of pilgrims travelling the camino – now breaking through the 100,000 ceiling (outside Holy Years) for the first time in modern history. Inevitably this puts a strain on resources and some hostels at bottleneck locations were *completo* by noon, before they were officially due to open! This is no reason *not* to go during the extended summer period but we may need to be more flexible on where we sleep and have enough energy in reserve to search out alternatives if necessary. The one piece of advice that I would pick out from the first edition and underline is simply this, *'There are no guarantees in the life of a pilgrim and we are well served by developing an attitude of gratitude for all learning experiences found along the path.'*

A snapshot of modern Spain has been included at the end of the historical sketch to provide a cultural and political context for pilgrims visiting Spain for the first time. As an aide-mémoire essential Spanish *Español* words are shown in italics with the exception of camino that has now become effectively anglicized. A self-assessment questionnaire has also been included to help formulate and, hopefully, answer some of the deeper questions that often bubble to the surface when we clear space and head off along a path of enquiry.

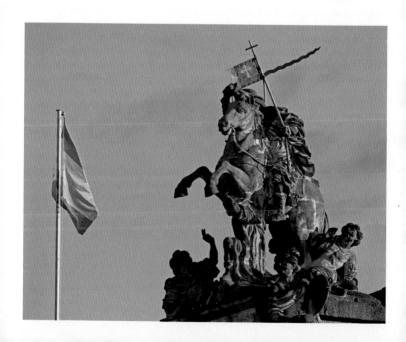

INTRODUCTION:

Welcome to The Way of St. James *el camino de Sant Iago*. Unlike the many other routes to Santiago de Compostela, the waymarking on the French Way *camino francés* is now very extensive. The familiar yellow arrow *flecha amarillo* will become a source of great comfort to you along the way – popping into view just when you think you are lost. This said, an accurate map and guidebook is useful to help you plan your itinerary and excursions and to put you back on the path when your mind wanders and your feet follow!

I generally found guidebooks were either too big (and full of information that I could gather elsewhere along the way) or too small (with inadequate data). There was also a wide variation in the distances provided, exacerbated by the total absence of details of the start and end point for measurements, 'Burgos 12 km' is meaningless without specifying *where* in Burgos – the new pilgrim hostel is 7.8 km from the start of the city environs, a very long way at the end of a day's walk! But what inspired me to write *another* guidebook was the almost universal absence of any reference, yet alone waymarks, to the *inner* path.

I urge you to find a spiritual purpose for taking this journey. If you have difficulty with this term, find one more meaningful to you, and check out your local bookstore – you'll find a wealth of literature on the subject. The words 'spiritual purpose' produced 62 million suggestions on my web browser, while 'significant journey' threw up 45 million – so you get the idea! But attend to this promptly so that you have time to mull over your motivation *before* you travel. The strategy is not to feel pressurised to follow any particular 'way' – you will know when something rings true for you – learn to trust your resonance. Some suggestions are listed in the bibliography.

I have endeavoured to find a balance between the *inner* and *outer* journey by paying equal respect to both. That is why these guides are subtitled *a practical and mystical manual for the modern day pilgrim*. That we might find a place to lay our weary head at the end of the day but also, and crucially, that we might feel supported and encouraged to dive into the mysteries of our individual soul awakenings, without which all journeying is essentially purposeless. Along every path of enquiry there comes a point that requires a leap of faith, where we have to abandon the security of outdated dogma handed down to us over millennia. When we reach that point we have to let go of the safety of the familiar and dive into the unknown, with nothing but our faith to support us.

The traditional pilgrim way is on foot. You can also obtain a certificate of completion *compostela* by going on bike or horseback but you may miss some of the beauty of the outer landscape and the spirit of the inner journey. Pilgrimage takes the time it takes. Travel alone if at all possible – this way you are more likely to meet the local villagers and shepherds and absorb their wisdom and local lore. You will learn the native language as you go and you will also meet other fellow pilgrims along the way. But above all, you may meet your *Self* and find that you are never alone – and that is surely a primary purpose of pilgrimage, perhaps of life itself.

This guidebook is dedicated to the awakening of human consciousness. It was born out of a mid-life crisis and the perceived need for a time to reflect on the purpose and direction of life. We have a sacred contract, a divine function and reason why we came here. Pilgrimage provides an opportunity to delve deeper into that purpose and the time to re-orientate our life towards its fulfilment. We have been asleep a long time, but alarm bells are ringing for young and old and there are signs that we are collectively waking up. There is a new yearning to break free from our self-imposed imprisonment. This is eloquently captured in the words of Christopher Fry in *A Sleep of Prisoners:*

> Thank God our time is now when wrong
> Comes up to face us everywhere,
> Never to leave us till we take
> The longest stride of soul folk ever took.
>
> Affairs are now soul size.
> The enterprise is exploration into God.
> Where are you making for?
> It takes so many thousand years to wake,
> But will you wake for pity's sake?

May your journey be blessed along your chosen path – rough or smooth, long or short – whichever route you take, know that you are loved and your destination is assured. God speed *Ultreya!*

[1] Preparation – A Quick Guide:

• **When?** Spring is often wet and windy but the route is relatively quiet with early flowers appearing. Summer is busy and hot and hostels often full. Autumn often provides the most stable weather with harvesting adding to the colour and celebrations of the countryside. Winter is solitary and cold and some hostels will be closed.

• **How long?** The route is divided into 33 stages each one corresponding to an average days walk – but find your own pace and overnight at intermediate hostels as required. Clear the decks and allow some spaciousness into your life – 5 weeks is ideal but join or leave the route to fit in with your schedule.

[2] Preparation – Outer: what do I need to take *and* leave behind.

• Buy your boots in time to walk them in before you go.
• Pack a Poncho, Spain can provide downpours at any time of year.
• Bring a hat, sunstroke is painful and can be dangerous.
• Look again if your backpack weighs more than 10 kilos.

What *not* to bring:
• Get rid of all books (except this one – all the maps you need are included.)
• Don't take 'extras', Spain has shops if you need to replace something.
• If you want to deepen your experience, leave behind:
  – your *camera* – you'll be able to live for the moment rather than memories.
  – your *watch* – you'll be surprised how quickly you adapt to a natural clock.
  – your *mobile phone* – break the dependency and taste the freedom.

[3] Language learn it now, *before* you go.

[4] •Pilgrim Passport, •Protocol & •Prayer

• Get a *credencial* from your local confraternity – and join it.
• Have consideration for your fellow pilgrims and gratitude for your hosts.
• "May every step be a prayer for peace and an extension of loving kindness."

[5] Preparation – Inner: why am I doing this?

Take time to prepare a purpose for this pilgrimage and to complete the self-assessment questionnaire. Start from the basis that you are essentially a spiritual being on a human journey, not a human being on a spiritual one. We came to learn some lesson and this pilgrimage affords an opportunity to find out what that is. Ask for help and expect it – it's there, now, waiting for you.

Whatever you do – for heaven's sake don't forget to start.

[B] BEGINNING – *Before you go*: This section has more detailed notes on preparation. Once you have finalised your packing consider cutting out these pages along the dotted line to leave extra space for your *credencial* or other personal papers – every ounce needs to be accounted for!

When to go? If you like peace and quiet, the **spring** months of March and April will provide few other pilgrims and tourists. Hostels will be opening and flights and ferries should be operating, at least on a limited basis. You will be accompanied by early spring flowers and cool conditions for walking, although the nights are likely to be cold and rain plentiful, especially in the mountain areas and Galicia. Pack additional wet gear and warm fleeces.

The **summer** months can be very hot and accommodation, even water, in short supply. July and August are bedlam and, if this coincides with a Holy Year (any year when St. James' Day, 25th July, falls on a Sunday) it can turn into a nightmare for those wanting an introspective time. These 2 months alone account for almost half of all pilgrims arriving in Santiago for the whole year. May, June and September are also becoming very busy.

The **autumn** season from late September through October often provides more stable weather than spring, the fierce heat of summer is over, the snow hasn't yet arrived and most hostels are still open. If you are an experienced walker, the depths of **winter** can provide some of the most mystical experiences. There may be fewer flights and many hostels will be closed, but I have never wanted for a bed or floor to sleep on at this time of year. Costs will be lower and you'll have much of the camino to yourself. Bring warm waterproof clothes and remember that daylight hours are restricted, so the daily distance that you can cover is reduced.

The **weather** in northern Spain, particularly Galicia, is very unpredictable. The **summer** months may see temperatures soar to over 32 Celsius (90 Fahrenheit) and the nights are often uncomfortably warm. Sun protection is vital, especially on the high plateau *meseta* much of which has no shade of any kind. Plenty of water is essential to replace fluids lost through physical exertion and the heat. In **winter** the higher ground can be blocked with snow with temperatures dropping below freezing. At the shoulder seasons, you can expect anything in between.

The worst weather I ever experienced was in May when it rained non-stop in Galicia for 9 days, accompanied by fierce storms and low temperatures – by contrast, early November was warm and dry. So be prepared for any eventuality. **Daylight hours** can be important when planning each day's stage. In the summer you have all the hours God made and certainly more than you could walk! In mid winter, your daylight is reduced to 8 hours.

When does everyone else go? The following graphs might help your decision. Whilst clearly not everyone arriving at Santiago will report to the pilgrim office or collect a *compostela* the following figures give a good indication of general trends. 80% of all pilgrims arrive in Santiago via the *camino francés* (down from 95% 5 years ago) and 41% arrive in the 2 months of July and August.

The number of pilgrims has increased tenfold over the past decade with 114,026 pilgrims from 138 nationalities collecting a compostela during 2007. Note that these figures relate only to pilgrims arriving by foot, bike, horseback or wheelchair. Others arriving by road, rail and air are counted in millions.

The first graph shows the number of pilgrims collecting a compostela for the 12 years up to 2007. Holy Years (in yellow) greatly increases the number on the route and the next one could push the figure to ¼ million for the first time in the modern history of the camino. After the Holy Year of 2010, the next *Año Santo Jacobeo* will not be until 2021.

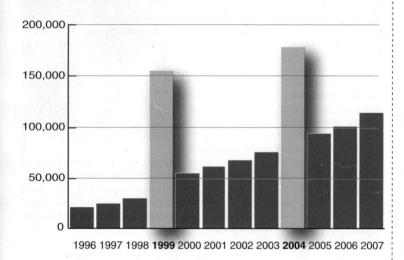

The next graph is based on monthly figures during 2007. January has the lowest number of pilgrims arriving in Santiago at 350 with 27,140 arriving during the month of August.

How long does it take? This depends on many factors such as level of fitness, which varies between individuals and within individuals (your biorhythms don't just affect mood swings!). When you add in variations in weather, detours (planned and otherwise) and different motivation and time constraints all this results in a heady mix of possibilities. I once met a manic pilgrim in Finisterre who had just arrived from Seville. He had walked 1,000 kilometres in a staggering 19 days that's over 50 km per day! He just had time to proudly show me his *credencial* to 'prove' the fact, before heading off down the hill again! It appears that many people allow completion of the journey in the minimum time to become the main focus. You are the only one who can evaluate your purpose and, if sporting achievement is yours, so be it, but it is unlikely to be a pilgrimage.

Statistics are limited, but my sense is that most people take 4 weeks to walk the entire *Camino Francés*. This fits (just) into a month-long holyday period with a day either side to fly in and out. These 30 days represent something of a minimum and would require averaging 28 kilometres a day with no detours, no rest days, no strains or sprains and no alternative travel plans. By the time you have found a bed, had a shower, massaged your feet, washed your socks, had a meal… there will be little time to attend mass, meditate, write-up your spiritual journal, reflect on your purpose…

Find your own pace but the one described here will allow you to reach Santiago *gracefully* in 5 weeks. This allows for an average of 24 kilometres a day for 33 days with 2 rest days. I like the idea that I walk one day for every year that Christ lived on earth. It connects me to a bigger picture and slows the pace to allow the inner alchemy of introspection to work. Pilgrimage takes the time it takes – 6 weeks (40 days and 40 nights) invites a deepening of the experience and would allow for the inclusion of the pilgrimage to Finisterre returning to Santiago via Muxía (see *Camino Finisterre*) and still provide time to integrate lessons and insights learnt along the way. Others start along one of the waymarked routes that commence further back in France (see map inside back cover) and there is even a route that commences in St. Petersburg in Russia! However, many people work within a 2-week framework and so will need 2 or 3 trips to complete the entire camino. The commencement of daily budget flights from the UK to midpoints such as Santander and Valladolid make access to Burgos and León an easy option and rail and bus connections within Spain are reliable and inexpensive.

In reality we have all the time in the world, but most of us don't believe it (especially our employers, employees, partners and peers). Come back to the 'real world' is a phrase that is often heard – and where, in heaven's name, might that be? And even if we know we have all the time there is if we are honest, perhaps we are afraid to take the time to reflect on our life and its direction. I know people who have cleared the decks and opened up a whole summer for pilgrimage, only to return within days, terrified of having time to contemplate their lives and the changes that any soul-searching might prescribe. Pilgrimage, like life, is experienced on many different levels. What makes sense for one may seem strange to another. We each have our reason for going. Whatever you do, don't put off starting as it might prove to be a major turning point in your life.

How to get there – *and back*: (See **map** on inside back cover for airports and ferry terminals). Note that schedules and prices are liable to change and reduced services can be expected during the winter months.

Carbon Neutral Travel: All travel has an impact on the environment; none more so than air travel. We can, however, minimise the damaging emissions of greenhouse gases by offsetting the amount produced in what is effectively a carbon sink. <www.climatecare.org> will calculate the amount of emissions produced by air, rail or car from your departure point and what you would need to contribute to offset this. A return flight London to Santiago will produce 0.33 tonnes of CO_2 – rail reduces this by around 2/3^{rds} but the stakes go up if you're coming from the west coast of the USA or Canada where you produce 2.04 tonnes (based on 80% seat occupancy). Carbon offsets don't solve the whole problem but help orientate us towards finding solutions. The key aspect here is about raising awareness – not about producing guilt trips. In these harsh economic times the cancellation of flights by airlines that haven't enough passengers booked to make the flight economic is a worrying and increasing trend – stay flexible!

From the UK by Air: The easiest way to get to St. Jean de Pied de Port is to fly to **Biarritz**. Ryanair has a direct service from London & Birmingham. Easyjet also fly into Biarritz from Bristol and London. These schedules usually allow time to catch the airport coach (regular departures; journey time ½ hour) to Bayonne *Baion* rail station in time to get the mountain railway to St. Jean. The scenic rail journey takes 1½ hours with a 5 minute walk into the town centre. Alternatively consider taking a taxi direct from the airport to St. Jean, a distance of 55 km and check out any other passengers with scallop shells who might share the cost or contact Express Bourricot ✆ +33 559 373 628 a pilgrim travel company adjoining the pilgrim office in St. Jean who will collect. **Bilbao** with rail or bus connections to Bayonne (or Pamplona for Roncesvalles) has direct flights from London with Ryanair, EasyJet, Clickair, BA & Iberia. Easyjet also flies Bilbao from Bristol. Other access points along the camino with direct Ryanair flights from the UK include **Madrid**, **Valladolid** and **Santander** with easy onward bus or rail connection to Burgos or León. Easyjet fly London to Oviedo (Asturias) with easy access to León. **From Ireland by Air:** Ryanair fly direct Dublin and Shannon to Biarritz also to Madrid and Santander. Aer Lingus fly Dublin to Bilbao. Iberia has an extensive service to regional airports.

Bus: National Express / Eurolines have a direct London to Bayonne daily service that takes 23 hours. **Rail:** Raileurope / Seat61 show several through-fares London to Bayonne (via Paris Nord) via TER taking around 10 hours. **Ferry:** P&O sail Portsmouth to Bilbao – journey time 36 hours. **Car Hire:** It is very competitive *within* Spain and this makes a good option for onward travel especially when car sharing. However, a pick-up in one country with a drop-off in another is usually prohibitively expensive.

From the rest of Europe: There are extensive and inexpensive rail and bus connections from all parts of Europe. The budget airlines have also extended their networks within Europe – check out appropriate sites.

Returning from Santiago: Increased services by rail, bus and air have made departure from Santiago easier and in some cases cheaper than previous years. Travel costs vary widely but increasing competition between national and budget airlines has helped to minimise the hike in oil costs. Generally the sooner you commit to going the cheaper the ticket – but staying flexible on a return date can sometimes be rewarded with a last-minute promotional fare. Galicia has 3 international airports at Santiago, A Corunna & Vigo although a question mark now hangs over whether Galicia can justify 3 airports in such close proximity.

•**Air** *Ryanair* fly direct from Santiago to London Stansted, Liverpool, Frankfurt, Rome, Valencia, Barcelona and Madrid. *Click-air* fly Santiago to Barcelona and from La Corunna and Vigo direct to London Heathrow. *Vueling* fly direct to Paris and *Air Berlin* have flights to major destinations throughout Europe from Santiago via their hub in La Palma Majorca. *Aer Lingus* fly Santiago – Dublin (summer schedule) and *BA* and *Iberia* and other major airlines offer regular services throughout the year via connecting airports in Spain, mainly Madrid.

•**Rail** – you can book online through Spanish rail network RENFE (in English) www.renfe.es/horarios/english or Rail Europe www.raileurope.co.uk/ •**Bus** you can book online with Alsa / National Express for connections throughout Europe www.nationalexpress.com (click on Spanish services). •**Ferry** The advantage of sailing home is that you get a chance to acclimatise slowly – Santander & Bilbao offer regular sailings to the U.K. Check with Brittany Ferries (Santander - Portsmouth) and P&O (Bilbao - Plymouth). •**Car Hire** If you can find other passengers to share the cost then this is often a relatively cheap and convenient way to travel on to such places as Santander or Bilbao and flying or sailing home from there.

TRAVEL NOTES:

Pilgrim Passport *credencial* and Protocol:

In order to stay at pilgrim hostels and to receive a *compostela* (certificate of completion of pilgrimage to Santiago) you need to provide proof that you have walked the route (at least the last 100 km from Sarria). This is done by having a pilgrim passport *credencial* impressed with a rubber stamp *sello* primarily by the wardens *hospitaleros* in the pilgrim hostels but you can also have it stamped at cathedrals, churches, hostels, bars and town halls along the way.

You can obtain a pilgrim passport or record before travelling from the Confraternity of St. James in London or possibly from a local Confraternity in your country of origin (see useful addresses at the back) alternatively you can obtain a *credencial* on arrival at the pilgrim office in St. Jean Pied de Port / Roncesvalles (or Sarria as a last resort). Every effort should be made to join and support the work of the Confraternities who do so much to prepare and maintain the route and its facilities. Apply in good time (an internet application may speed processing.)

Pilgrim Hostels:

Pilgrim hostels *hostales, refugios* or *albergues de peregrinos* are reserved exclusively for pilgrims on the camino. They are provided throughout the route at convenient 10 – 20 km intervals (frequently less, never more) and all are on, or immediately adjacent, to the camino. This includes youth hostels *albergues juvenil* that are generally available to pilgrims holding a *credencial*. Accommodation is usually in bunk beds with additional overflow space on mattresses *colchonetas* on the floor *suelo*. **Bedbugs** are still causing spasmodic problems in a few pilgrim hostels. They live in mattresses, feeding at night, so until the hostel is chemically treated the problem remains but can break out again at any time. Carrying a pillowcase and regularly shaking out all bedding are useful preventative measures. If affected you will need to wash or tumble dry *all* clothes at highest settings for 2 hours and possibly take anti-histamines.

Hostels are generally open from April (Easter) through to October. Many now stay open all year (subject to closing for holidays such as Christmas or maintenance) but even those listed as closed may be open and vice-versa – be prepared for the unexpected. With increasing demand new hostels are opening every year and existing ones extending their season and the greater problem is finding accommodation in the summer rather than the winter! Names and telephone numbers have been included for emergency use (busy wardens will not thank you for idle requests) and to aid pilgrims travelling off-season to establish whether or not a hostel is open. It is generally not possible to book pilgrim hostels in advance.

Albergues generally fit into one of 6 main categories as follows: (the shortened form appears on the maps).

[1] *Muni.* **Municipal** hostel *albergue municipal* a basic hostel with limited facilities owned and maintained by the local authority. The warden *hospitalero/a* often lives next door. In this category are the Galician government hostels *albergues Xunta de Galicia*.

[2] *Par.* **Parish** hostel *albergue parroquia* these are generally owned by the local diocese and run by the parish priest. Some offer a regular pilgrim mass and they tend to be more informal and relaxed than municipal hostels and some offer a communal meal with blessing.

[3] *Conv.* **Convent or Monastery** hostel *monasterio o convento* (*mosteiro* in Gallego) it is often difficult to differentiate between a monastery (community of monks) and a convent (community of nuns) as the Spanish word *monasterio* or *convento* applies to both. *Convento* on its own is a monastery (monks) while *convento de monjas* (nuns) is a convent! The atmosphere in each is often markedly different so check the details provided.

[4] *Asoc.* **Association** hostels are owned and run by local Spanish or other national confraternities, sometimes in conjunction with the local authority. They tend to be particularly well equipped for the needs of the pilgrim and are generally staffed by former pilgrim volunteers.

[5] *Asoc.**(star) **Network** hostel *red de albergues* are private hostels that have formed themselves into a loose association. They are often owned and maintained by an individual but are increasingly being handed over to a management group, engendering greater confidence in ongoing availability. They have a similar sense of brotherhood / sisterhood as in confraternity hostels and often provide additional facilities, such as washing / drying machines, internet access, dinner and breakfast.

[6] *Priv.* **Private** hostels *albergues privado* are similar to the network hostels (above) but with no overall code or regulations. They tend to be more flexible than other hostels (commercial realities) with a full range of facilities and many have washing *and* drying machines and more flexible opening hours.

Opening Hours: vary but are generally cleaned and ready again from around midday to welcome pilgrims. A few still open later although private hostels tend to open earlier. Many hostels have a policy of holding places for those travelling by foot until around 18:00, cyclists not being admitted until after that time. Hostels generally close their doors and turn off lights around 22:00. The morning routine will find early-birds discreetly, or noisily, leaving their beds from 05.30 with the main rush hour between 06:30 and 07:30. Most hostels close for cleaning at 08:30 when the last stragglers will be sent on their way.

Any special arrangements, such as the provision of breakfast, will generally be notified on arrival but it is good practise to scan any notice boards. Opening times for tourist offices and museums are generally from 10:00–13:00 and again after *siesta* from 16:00–19:00. Shop hours are generally a bit longer. Note that many public buildings, including churches, are closed on Mondays.

Warden *hospitalero/a* every hostel has at least one person whose job it is to ensure that the place is open at the appropriate time in the day and doors are locked and lights turned off at night. Resident *hospitaleros* are generally voluntary, live in the hostel itself and have probably walked the route in previous years and therefore know the needs of their fellow pilgrims. Non-resident wardens will live locally (often adjoining) and can provide reliable local information such as where to shop, restaurants, times of Mass, etc. Non-resident wardens are generally on hand between 16:00 and 20:00 to allocate bed spaces, collect the overnight charge and to stamp *credenciales*.

Facilities and levels of cleanliness vary widely, but hot showers are now standard everywhere. Don't forget that hot showers do not mean limitless hot water. If you are last in a group early in the afternoon, the water may have run cold. Conversely if you are last in during the evening it may have heated up again! There is a welcome increase in the number of hostels now providing automatic washing machines *lavadora* rarer but often more practical is the addition of a dryer *secadora* (not to be confused with the less useful spin-dryer *centrífuga*) – it can rain for days on end and a *secadora* can make an big difference to personal comfort. Most hostels provide a kitchen with cooker, pots, pans and (some) basic cutlery and the majority have a sitting room or lounge that often serves as the dining area.

Standards – earlier versions of this guide had a 'scallop shell' grading system but standards and facilities offered are changing constantly so grading can often set up false expectations. Galicia is trying to introduce a rating system with 2 stars** awarded to hostels which have a bed to shower/ toilet ratio of 10:1 or less (that's considered good!). However, you will find an objective note of facilities offered at time of going to press which includes the number of bed spaces and the number of rooms available. Simple division will indicate how many roommates you are likely to be sharing with – up to 120 beds in one dormitory! **Gratitude** for mercies small and large is a trait to be developed by all genuine pilgrims. This is nowhere more apparent than in the offering and acceptance of a place for the pilgrim to lay his or her head. Tired at the end of a long day or caught out in a storm *tormenta* any port may well induce a feeling of profound gratitude for the humblest of abodes and the most casual of welcomes – this is entirely as it should be.

The best way to establish the standard of a hostel is from the welcome you receive at the door and from comments made by fellow pilgrims in the *pilgrim guest book*. There is a generally held, and erroneous, belief that all true pilgrims must stay at the pilgrim hostels. Mediaeval pilgrims used every available accommodation regardless of whether or not it was an official *hospital de peregrino*. Indeed, medieval merchants and inn-keepers were dependent on the custom of the pilgrims for their livelihood and it is no different today. Yes, by all means stay in the recognised hostels and meet up with fellow pilgrims and share news, but don't become reliant solely on these hostels. Spread your inner and outer wealth!

If the hostels are full **alternative accommodation** is generally available in the immediate area. These also vary widely in facilities offered and priced (generally per room – not per person) accordingly. The Spanish tourist board categorises all 'official' accommodation and 'r' in each category denotes *residencia* (no dining facilities beyond breakfast). In practise the main defining feature in cost is the number of stars awarded. The cost of accommodation also varies between seasons (add 25% during peak holidays) and regions (add 25% in cities). Some smaller hotels and hostels, particularly in rural areas, offer a pilgrim discount but ask at reception *before* booking.

During off-season the price of a room can often be less than that officially displayed. At the lower end (from €15) we find simply beds *camas* and guesthouses known variously as *fondas*, *hospedajes* or *hospederías* without any star category. Moving up the scale (from €25) are *pensiónes* and *hostales* with one or more stars and the smaller rural *hoteles*. In the middle bracket (from €40) are up-market B&B's usually presented at a high standard and known variously as rural houses *casa rural CR*, rural tourism *turismo rural TR* or agricultural tourism *agrícola turismo AT*. Then come the hotels from 1 star in rural areas *(from €25) up to 5 stars in the city (€150+)*.

Costs: allow a basic €25 a day to include an average €5 for overnight stay at a municipal hostel (€3 in Galicia) and the remainder for food and drink. Some hostels provide a communal supper (dependent on the warden *hospitalero*) for a small contribution and many have a basic kitchen where a meal can be prepared. Alternatively most locations have one or more restaurants to choose from and many have a special 'pilgrim menu' for a fixed price of around €10. If you want to indulge in the wonderful gastronomy of Spain and sample its finer wines then expect to double this basic cost. A few parish hostels still use a donation basis with the underlying philosophy: *leave us what you can and if that is only your prayers that will be sufficient.* We must be careful not to abuse this trust in our individual circumstances – unless you are a genuine mendicant, plan to leave at least 5 euros towards basic costs of maintenance. Private hostels average around €9 per night but often provide additional facilities such as internet access, washing / drying machines and dining facilities (supper and breakfast at nominal extra cost).

Payment: all pilgrim hostels, most small pensions, rural B&B's *casa rurales* and local shops operate on a cash only basis. That being said, even the smallest town and many of the villages have automatic cash dispensing machines *cajeros automáticos* that accept most international bank debit or credit cards. Traveller's cheques are difficult to exchange and also rely on inconvenient bank opening hours. Consider settling your bill the night before if you plan an early departure.

Eating out: A basic pilgrim menu or *menú del dia* starts from around €9. Once you go off the set menu costs rise out of all proportion. *Tapas* (small snacks available from many bars and cafés throughout the day) or the more generous *raciones* are appetising but expensive. Vegetarians have a really hard time as Spain, which is firmly carnivorous, has little understanding of the needs of the *vegetariano/a*. Vegetable soup is often made on meat stock and don't be surprised to find chunks of ham in your cheese omelette unless you are *very* specific! Breakfast equates to *café* and *croissantes*. Another cultural challenge posed to northern European and North American pilgrims are meal times. Lunch *almuerzo* (or simply *comer*) is the main meal and rarely ends before 15:00 and dinner *cena* doesn't usually start before 20:00. It helps to think laterally (*tapas*), to speak clearly (*en español*) and to prepare meals of your choice and time in the hostels from provisions bought in the local shop *mercado*.

Respecting nature: Litter has increased in recent years along the camino. Discarding tissues after urinating is particularly offensive. If you feel the need to (re)use tissues please bin them appropriately or consider using a urinating device for women hikers – *www.sheewee.com*. There are many practises that allow us how to live lightly on the planet – essentially *'walk the path so that no one can tell that you have passed by.'* A rewarding discipline is to collect some rubbish along the way each day with the intention of leaving the path *better* than you found it. If a sense of superiority arises, visualise yourself cleaning up the mess that you left behind at other times in your life when you were, perhaps, less aware. It only requires a small number of conscientious pilgrims to eliminate the problem. You might also like to try a psychic cleansing after experiencing any negativity in your own thoughts or in any interaction that you witness en route that is unloving. Simply shake out the negativity from your mind and invite loving thoughts to replace them. These simple practises will help to keep both the physical and psychic environment clean.

Respecting fellow pilgrims: facilities such as showers and kitchens have a limited supply of hot water and utensils and overall facilities, especially during the summer months, can be stretched. Be aware of your own needs but also of the needs of others and try and find a balance that feels right. If you have arrived early and bagged the best bed keep an eye on who comes in later – if you are on a bottom bunk and someone arrives late with a damaged knee you could move to a top bunk. Observe your reactions but don't judge yourself. There is already enough guilt in the world to engulf it and we certainly don't need more! Awareness is the starting point for change.

PREPARATION – *OUTER:*

Physical – what shape is the body in? Any reasonably fit person can accomplish this journey without undue stress. Some years ago I walked from Seville to Santiago (1,000+ km) with a Japanese grandfather who celebrated his 80th birthday en route. However, if you have recently had an illness or are otherwise concerned about your state of health then go and have a medical check up. It takes the body a few days to adjust to the regular walking with full backpack. Give body, mind and soul time to acclimatise. Don't push yourself at the beginning – remember that most injuries, such as strained tendons and blisters occur in the early days.

It is always advisable to put in some physical training before you go. I would be surprised if more than 10% of pilgrims actually act on this advice. If you are one of the 90% who haven't then *please* heed the advice to take the first week slowly. I know many pilgrims who have had to deal with the mental, let alone physical, anguish of having to pull out of the pilgrimage because they did too much in the early days. Lightweight walking poles, if used properly, can greatly reduce wear and tear on the body. If you don't have a pair (one in each hand creates better balance and is twice as effective) consider buying a set. They are likely to prove a good investment for this walk – and future ones!

A related matter is the weight you carry, both your backpack and body weight. If you are 2 stone overweight and are going to be carrying an additional 2 stone on your back, the resultant stress factor is likely to show up in cracks, literally, in the body (1 stone = 14 pounds = 6.4 kilograms). While you will inevitably lose weight on the journey, try and reduce before you start out. Pilgrimage is a great metaphor for life. What are you carrying that is unnecessary? *"From contentment with little comes happiness."* African proverb.

Equipment and Clothing: (Think quality not quantity)

Your pilgrimage starts at the planning stage. So start by invoking the highest for your journey and bring awareness to what you buy. There is so much exploitation of human and natural resources supported by our unconscious consumerism. Become informed and use your voice and money to support those companies who genuinely try to make a positive difference in the world. To walk a pilgrim path for peace in gear produced from exploitative business practises or oppressive regimes is not congruent – we must make very effort to *walk our talk*.

What to bring? You will bring too much; everyone does! Be prepared to give away, leave behind or post back items you don't need and notice which option you choose, why and at what stage of the journey. Aim to carry no more than 10% of body weight with an upper limit of 10 Kilos (22 lbs). Whatever you carry your knees and feet will absorb most of the shock and will be the first to buckle if you carry more than essentials. Buy materials that are essentially: (a) lightweight and non-bulky (b) that wick away moisture from your skin (c) are easy to wash and quick to dry.

Essential equipment from the feet up includes:

walking shoes / boots: They should provide good ankle support, be breathable, lightweight and yet have strong soles for the rough ground you will encounter. Heavyweight boots are not necessary but consider trail shoes with waterproof lining if travelling in the winter season. **Sandals** or other lightweight shoe for use in the evening while your boots dry out and have a chance to breathe.

socks: bring several pairs as it is a good idea to change socks and massage your feet half-way through the day (even if you don't think they need it).

trousers, skirts and shorts: for most of the year shorts are ideal and your legs will dry out much more quickly than fabric if you walk into a rain shower. Rural Spain remains very traditional – a sarong is ideal for women to wrap around bare legs when visiting churches, etc., and also cool and easy to wash and dry.

fleece: a lightweight fleece is useful – you will need to increase the thickness the closer into winter that you plan to travel. If you intend travelling in mid-winter you will need proper thermal clothing and a sleeping bag for the subzero temperatures that you may encounter, particularly on the higher ground where you can expect snow and ice.

waterproofs: even allowing for obvious seasonal changes the weather in northern Spain, particularly in Galicia, is notoriously unpredictable (see Weather). There are many lightweight rain and wind-proof jackets and trousers, Paclite® by Burghaus are ideal, but expensive. A cheaper option is a plastic poncho that covers not only the body but the backpack as well. This can be rolled out during rain showers and the loose fitting nature of the poncho means you don't get *too* much build up of sweat as with most tight fitting plastic or nylon garments.

hat: in the summer months your main consideration will be protection from the sun. Wear a wide brim hat to protect your head and neck and any other exposed areas. Sunstroke can be painful and, in extreme cases, dangerous.

rucksack: 50 litres should be ample, avoid large capacity bags (70 +litres) as you may be tempted to fill it with unnecessary items. An essential element is the waist strap that must allow you to adjust and carry the weight on your hips – *never* off your shoulder. You will need dry bags (not plastic bags which can actually pool water!) to ensure dry kit at the end of a wet day. If you are not using a poncho then a backpack cover is also recommended for heavy downpours.

sleeping bag: essential for all pilgrim hostels. If you are travelling in the summer months a lightweight 1 or 2 season bag will suffice. A zip will allow you to open it up in very hot conditions. Most hostels, especially in the mountain areas, have blankets.

first aid: All hostels are obliged to carry first aid boxes and there are innumerable chemists *farmacia* along the way. However, some essentials should be carried with you. While prevention is better than cure, unless you are well seasoned you will get blisters! Each to their own, but *Compeed*® is readily available, easy to apply and acts as a second skin. Whatever you bring apply it as soon as you feel a hot spot developing (don't wait until it has developed into a full blister). Many make the mistake of loosening shoes to relieve the pressure but this can aggravate the friction – the cause of the problem in the first place. Make sure your footwear fits snugly.

Other essentials are plasters and antiseptic ointment for cuts and pain relief tablets such as Paracetamol for toothache etc. and Ibuprofen for relief of muscular pain. Bring a high factor sun protection and apply regularly or, alternatively try P_{20}® by Riemann which binds to the skin and only needs to be applied once each day. You will also need lip protection and after sun lotion. Be sure to bring an adequate supply of any prescribed medication, e.g. inhalers for asthmatics, as these may be difficult to obtain en route without prescription. Elasticised tubing can help support a sprained knee or ankle.

For the **homoeopathically** inclined, essentials might include: Arnica for muscular sprains and bruising, Calendula for cuts and Combudoron for insect bites. For those using chemically based products, bring equivalent treatments.

toiletries: Apart from the usual take a small scissors with needle and thread for draining blisters and essential repairs.

water container: many people prefer carrying two ½ litre bottles rather than a bulkier 1 litre that can be harder to pack and unpack. **Water is essential** and evidence supports the view that a minimum 2 litres a day can significantly reduce fatigue, blisters and other common ailments of long distance walking as well as avoiding dehydration. There are drinking fonts *fuente* **[F]** all along the way – fill up at every opportunity especially in high summer when drinking fonts can dry up. You may notice a marked difference between the quality of water in and around the main cities with their chemical additives, so empty and refill from the purer waters of the mountains and rural villages whenever possible.

Optional Extras:

walking poles: while not essential, they are highly recommended and will greatly reduce the impact on your body (around 25% if used properly). They will steady you over rough patches and may create confidence when facing the innumerable dogs that dot the countryside. Take two to avoid becoming lopsided and try and get ones with the handles angled to avoid wrist strain. Most pilgrims opt for a wooden staff collected along the way and that is certainly better than nothing.

sleeping mat: very useful if you want the freedom of experiencing life under the stars and increasingly necessary if you are travelling in the busy season as it allows you more options – there will always be a floor somewhere! *Therm-a-Rest*® is the most comfortable but is heavier and more expensive than a basic foam-style mat.

cooking utensils: many hostels have basic kitchen equipment. However, if you intend cooking regularly it is advisable to bring your own utensils and cutlery. A small plastic container with lid will make it easier to carry soft fruit (such as tomatoes) and sandwiches.

camping equipment: there is no need to carry a tent; however, if you enjoy and are experienced in the outdoors you will know what to bring. Campsites en route are few and far between and most hostels don't have facilities for tents.

books: be *very* selective as books add enormously to weight and you'll be surprised how little time you have for reading. Try bringing something inspirational and uplifting that you can read over again such as a compendium of your favourite poems. Historical notes and more detailed information on the many artistic treasures to be found along the way are often issued free of charge from tourist offices or as part of the price of an entry ticket.

camera: a *compact* camera may allow you to share some of your experiences with friends and family on your return. But don't forget that you can't photograph an *inner* experience, so don't set up a disappointment for yourself! A well-known travel author, writing in *The Times* states, 'Photographing local people is selfish. It takes much and gives little.' The camera not only creates a physical barrier but also insulates the photographer from the reality of the experience. I have taken several thousand slides for this guidebook and regret any offence I may have caused – but perhaps they will suffice for your purposes also.

binoculars: a *compact* set will enable you to pick out the detail of some of the many fine monuments and buildings along the way. It might also help to identify alternative paths and help pick out directional signs, etc. I would prefer to take a pair of binoculars to a camera, but better still:

monocular: weighs less than half that of a pair of binoculars. It is easy to use, won't go out of focus and fits easily into a pocket. It might be a compromise for leaving behind the camera and binoculars.

mobile phone: leave it behind – your experience, and that of your fellow pilgrims, will be greatly enhanced by doing so. Break the dependence.

A checklist with Spanish translations is provided on the next page to help strengthen your vocabulary and assist you to buy or replace items along the way.

This is not necessarily a recommended list, as this will vary through the seasons. Highlight your essential items and then tick them off as you put them into your backpack. (see also *Basic Pilgrim Phrases*).

Checklist:	*Lista:*
Clothes:	*Ropas:*
hat (sun)	*sombrero*
sunglasses	*gafas de sol*
shirt(s)	*camisa(s)*
T-shirt(s)	*camiseta(s)*
travel vest	*chaqueta de viaje*
jacket –	*chaqueta –*
waterproof	*chubasquero*
breathable	*transpirable*
underpants	*calzoncillos*
shorts	*pantolones cortos*
trousers	*pantalones largos*
handkerchief	*pañuelo*
socks	*calcetines*
Shoes:	*Zapatos:*
boots (mountain)	*botas (de montaña)*
shoes (walking)	*zapatos (de andar)*
sandals (leather)	*sandalias (piel)*
Size:	*Tamaño:*
larger	*mas grande*
smaller	*mas pequeño*
cheaper	*mas barato*
more expensive	*mas caro*
model	*modelo*
Essential documents	*Documentos esenciales:*
passport	*pasaporte*
pilgrim record	*credencial de peregrino*
wallet / purse	*monedero / cartera*
cash	*dinero en efectivo*
credit card	*tarjeta de crédito*
travel tickets	*pasaje de viaje*
diary	*diario*
emergency addresses	*dirección de emergencia*
phone numbers	*números de teléfono*
Backpack	*Mochila*
rain cover	*protección de mochila*
sleeping bag	*saco de dormir*
towel	*toalla*
water bottle	*botella de agua*
penknife	*navaja*
Toiletries:	*Artículos de tocador:*
soap	*jabón*
shampoo	*champú*

tooth brush	*cepillo de dientes*
toothpaste	*dentífrico*
hair brush	*cepillo de pelo*
comb	*peine*
sink stopper	*tapón de fregadero*
shaving cream	*espuma de afeitar*
razor (blades)	*maquinilla de afeitar*
face cloth	*guante de aseo*
sun cream (lotion)	*crema solar (loción)*
after sun cream	*leche solar (after sun)*
moisturiser	*crema hidratante*
toilet paper	*papel higiénico*
tissues	*pañuelos de papel*
sanitary pads	*salva-slips*
tampons	*tampones*

First Aid Kit: *Botiquín*

painkiller	*analgésico*
aspirin / paracetemol	*aspirina / paracetamol*
plasters	*esparadrapo*
blister pads	*apósito para ampollas*
compeed-*second skin*	*compeed-segunda piel*
antiseptic cream	*crema antiséptica*
muscular ache (ointment)	*pomada para dolores*
musculares	
homeopathic remedies	*remedios homeopáticos*

Medicine (prescription):   *Medicina (prescripción):*

asthma inhaler	*inhalador para el asma*
hay fever tablets	*medicina para las alergias*
diarrhoea pills	*pastillas para la diarrea*
other (doctor)	*otros (médico)*

Accessories: (optional)   *Accesorios: (opcional)*

walking poles	*bastones de caminar*
pilgrim shell	*concha de peregrino*
monocular	*catalejo*
binocular	*prismáticos*
camera	*cámara*
torch	*linterna*
wrist watch	*reloj de pulsera*
alarm clock	*despertador*
poncho	*poncho*
sleeping mat	*esterilla*
clothes pegs	*pinzas para la ropa*
clothes line (cord)	*cuerda para tender ropa*
cutlery	*cubiertos*
knife	*cuchillo*
fork	*tenedor*
spoon	*cuchara*
mug / cup	*taza / vaso*

LANGUAGE *LENGUAJE:*

The Spanish are proud of their national identity and language, particularly in rural areas. It is a matter of extreme discourtesy to assume that everyone will automatically speak English. To walk into a shop or to stop and ask directions in anything other than the native language of the area you are travelling through is clearly insensitive. It behooves pilgrims to have at least a few basic phrases and to make the time to learn and use them. English is **not** widely spoken in the countryside. Ideally get a language CD a month or two *before* you travel and spend a few minutes each day practising this lovely lyrical language – the third most widely spoken in the world. Be sure to take a small dictionary and phrase book with you. Below you will find some basic pilgrim words and phrases that may not be included in a general phrase book.

As all place names and directions will, of course, be in Spanish (or Galego when in Galicia) all maps have been prepared accordingly. Some common phrases and words have also been scattered around the text as a reminder that you are a guest in someone else's country. For the real novice, I have included words that have a similar resonance between English and Spanish. This should enable you to more readily bring to mind the required word, even if it isn't exactly *exactamente* the word that a professional translator might have used. An example is vigilance! with the Spanish counterpart *Vigilancia!* One might more properly use the word danger *peligroso* but this bears no resemblance to the English word at all. For those of you who are *elocuente*, please *omitir* the following section *sección!* Spanish is placed in italics immediately following the English word or phrase. You will make progress if you follow these fundamental conventions *convenciónes fundamentales*:

Nouns are either masculine or feminine. Most are obvious, some are not. Trial and error is a way forward, with words ending in *e* favouring the masculine and those in *a* the feminine. The *el* or *la*, plural *los* or *las* and add *s* or *es* at end of the word. The man *el hombre,* the men *los hombres,* the woman *la señora,* the women *las señoras.* **Vowels** are articulated at the end of the word. Melide, pron: Meh-**lee**-deh. U is pronounced as in oo – one *una* pron: **oo**-na. **Emphasis** is on the penultimate syllable unless otherwise denoted with an accent. Nájera, pron: **Ná**-kher-a *not* Ná-**kher**-a.

Consonants are similar to English excepting: 'c' is pronounced th as in then. Centre *centro* pron: **then**-tro – 'd' at the end of a word is pron: th as in path. You *usted,* pron: *oo-***steth**. Note here the emphasis is on the last syllable, an exception to the rule! – 'g' and 'j' have a guttural kh sound similar to a Scottish loch: urgent *urgente* pron: *er-***khen***-tay* or garden *jardín* pron: *khar-***deen** (note emphasis on last syllable because it has an accent) – 'h' is always silent. Hotels *hoteles* pron: *oh-***tel***-es.* –'ll' is pronounced with a yeh sound / full *lleno* pron: **yeh***-no.* –'ñ' is pronounced as in onion / tomorrow *mañana* pron: *man-***yahn***-ah.* –'qu' is pronounced as in k for key / fifteen *quince* pron: *keen-***thay.** –'v' falls between v and soft b sound / journey *viaje* pron: *bhee-**a**-khay.*

Verbs are more complex but follow 3 basic forms: [1] those ending in **-ar** as in *hablar* to speak. I speak *hablo,* you speak *hablas,* he/she speaks *habla,* we speak *hablamos,* you all speak *habláis,* they speak *hablan.* [2] those ending in **-er** as in *comer* to eat. I eat *como,* you eat *comes,* he/she eats *come,* we eat *comemos,* you all eat *coméis,* they eat *comen.* [3] those ending in **-ir** as in *vivir* to live. I live *vivo,* you live *vives,* he/she lives *vive,* we live *vivimos,* you all live *vivís,* they live *vivan.*

Basic Phrases: so here are a few simple phrases to get you going. A new language can't be learnt in a day; but it is really important that you *try* whenever the opportunity arises – everyone loves a tryer.

Greetings / *Saludos*

Yes / *Sí* No / *No*
Please / *Por favor* Thanks / *Gracias*

How are things? / *Qué tal?* Have a good trip / *Buen viaje*
Hello! How are you? / *Hola! Cómo está?*
Good day / evening / night *Buenos días / Buenas tardes / noches*
What a splendid day / *Qué día mas espléndido!*
Goodbye! Until later / *¡Adiós! Hasta luego*

Welcome / *Bienvenida*

What's your name? / *¿Cómo te llamas?* My name is ... / *Me llamo ...*
Where do you live? / *¿Dónde vives?* I live in London / *Vivo en Londres*
Are you English? / *Eres Inglés(a)* I'm Irish / *Soy Irlandes(a)*
I'm single / *Estoy soltero(a)* I'm married / *Estoy casado(a)*
I have 2 sons / *Tengo dos hijos(as)* I have no children / *No tengo hijos*
I'm here on holiday (pilgrimage) / *Estoy aquí de vacaciones (peregrinación)*

Excuse me! / *¡Disculpe!* Pardon? / *¿Perdone?*

What did you say / *¿Cómo dice?* It's not important / *No importa*
Do you understand? / *¿Entiende?* I don't understand! / *¡No entiendo!*

I speak very little Spanish / *Hablo muy poco español*
Do you speak English? / *¿Habla usted Inglés?*
How do you pronounce that? / *¿Cómo se pronuncia eso?*
Please write it down. / *Escríbamelo, por favor*
What does this mean? / *¿Qué significa esto?*

Where is it? / *¿Dónde está?*

Here / *Aquí* There / *Allí*
On the left / *a la izquierda* On the right / *a la derecha*
Outside the bank / *Fuera del banco* Beside the cafe / *Al lado del café*
Near the centre / *Cerca del centro* Opposite the market / *Enfrente del mercado*

Where are you going? / *¿A dónde vas?*
Where is the pilgrim hostel / *¿Dónde está el albergue de peregrinos?*
Where are the toilets / *¿Dónde están los servicios?*
Where can I change some money? / *¿Dónde se puede cambiar dinero?*
Where do I get the taxi to the airport? / *¿Dónde se coge el taxi al aeropuerto?*
How do I get to the centre of León? / *¿Cómo se va al centro de León?*

What time is it? / *¿Qué hora es?*

It's midday / *Es mediodía* Five past one / *Es la una y cinco*
Ten past two / *cuatro y dos* Half past three / *Tres y media*
Quarter past four / *cuatro y cuarto* Twenty to five / *cinco menos veinte*
Quarter to six / *seis menos cuarto* Five to seven / *siete menos cinco*
Today / *Hoy* Yesterday / *Ayer*
Tomorrow / *Mañana* Day after tomorrow / *Pasado mañana*
Last week / *la semana pasada* This month / *este mes*
Next year / *al año que viene* Every year / *todos los años*

What day is it today? / *¿Qué día es hoy?*
Lunes / Martes / Miércoles / Jueves / Viernes / Sábado / Domingo
What is today's date? / *¿Qué fecha es hoy?*
It's April 10th / *Estamos a diez de abril*
Saturday, September 25th / *sábado, veinte cinco de septiembre*

spring / *primavera*	**summer** / *verano*
autumn / *otoño*	winter / *invierno*

enero / febrero / marzo / abril / mayo / junio / julio / agosto / septiembre /
octubre / noviembre / diciembre

Room / *Habitación*
Do you have any vacancies? / *¿Tienen alguna habitación libre?*
I'd like a room for one night / *Quería una habitación para una noche*
There's a problem with the room / *La habitación tiene un problema*
It's too hot (cold) / *Hace demasiado calor (frío)*
There is no hot water / *No hay agua caliente*
Where can I wash my clothes / *¿Dónde puedo lavar mi ropa?*

Doctor / *Médico*	**Dentist** / *Dentista*

I need a dentist (doctor) / *Necesito un dentista (medico)*
Where is the health centre? / *¿Dónde está el centro de salud?*
I have blisters / *Tengo ampollas*
I have a tendinitis / *Tengo tendinitis*
My leg/knee/foot/toe hurts / *Mi pierna / rodilla /el dedo del pie me duele*
My ankle is swollen / *Mi tobillo está hinchado*
My lower back is in spasm / *Mi espalda tiene una contractura*
Where is the pharmacy? / *¿Dónde está la farmacia?*

Food / *Comida*	**Menu** / *Menú*
breakfast / *desayuno*	lunch / *la comida*
savoury snack / *tapas*	dinner / *cena*

meat / *carne*	**fish** / *pescado*
beef steak / *bistec*	trout / *trucha*
fillet steak / *filete*	salmon / *salmón*
pork / *cerdo*	sole / *lenguado*
lamb / *cordero*	hake / *merluza*
veal / *ternera*	prawns / *gambas*
chops / *chuletas*	squid / *calamares*
ham / *jamón*	mussels / *mejillones*
chicken / *pollo*	seafood / *mariscos*

vegetables / *verduras*	**(tomato) salad** / *ensalada (de tomate)*
desert / *postres*	fruit / *fruta*
sandwich / *bocadillo*	cheese / *queso*
red wine / *vino tinto*	**white wine** / *vino blanco*
water / *agua*	milk / *leche*

I am hungry / *Tengo hambre*
What time is dinner (breakfast) / *¿A qué hora es la cena (el desayuno)?*
Is there a vegetarian restaurant? / *¿Hay un restaurante vegetariano?*
What's today's menu / *¿Cuál es el plato del día?*
Do you have a menu in English / *¿Tiene un menú en Inglés?*
This food is cold (too hot) / *La comida está fría (muy caliente)*
Where can I find a shop to by food? / *Dónde puedo encontrar una tienda para comprar comida?*

Train / *Tren*   **Bus / *Autobús***
Have you a timetable? / *¿Tienen un horario?*
What time do we get to León? / *¿A qué hora llegamos a León?*
How much is a single (return) ticket? / *¿Cuánto cuesta el billete de ida (y vuelta)*

I want to cancel my reservation / *Quería anular mi reserva*
When does the museum open? / *¿Cuándo abre el museo?*
When does the bus arrive at Arcos? / *¿Cuándo llega el autobús para Arcos?*
When is the next train to Bilbao? / *¿Cuándo sale el próximo tren para Bilbao?*

Shoes / *Zapato*   **Size / *Talla***
I take size 8 / *Calzo el cuarenta*
footwear / *calzado*   shoelace / *el cordón*
shoemaker / *zapatero*   shoeshop / *zapatería*

Clothes / *Ropa*   **Size / *Talla***
I take size 40 / *Mi talla es la 40*
Have you a bigger (smaller) size? / *Tiene una talla mayor (menor)*
big / *grande*   small / *pequeño(a)*
(See under check list for other items)

Books: (limited)   ***Libros: (cupo lim.)***
spiritual texts   *textos espirituales*
inspirational quotations   *citas inspiradoras*
poetry   *poesía*
phrase book –   *libro de frases –*
  Spanish   *Español*
  French   *Francés*

Map / *Mapa*   **Plan / *Plano***
option / *opción*   crossing / *cruce*
castle / *castillo*   church / *iglesia*
chapel / *ermita*   cathedral / *catedral*
wayside cross / *cruceiro*   drinking font / *fuente*
bridge / *puente*   rise or height / *alto*
park / *parque*   town square / *la plaza de la ciudad*
town centre / *centro de ciudad*   ruins / *ruinas*
river / *río*   street / *calle* (written c/)
sun rise / *salida del sol*   sun set / *puesta del sol*
waymarking / *indicador*   yellow arrow / *flecha Amarillo*

THE CAMINO – PAST, PRESENT & FUTURE

The Past – *The Changing Course of History*

•Pleistocene Age c. 1,000,000 B.C.

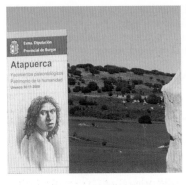

The earliest human remains ever discovered in Europe are to be found on a small hill directly on the camino (see stage 12 – Atapuerca). So we follow in the footsteps of our ancestors who have been accorded the scientific name *Homo Antecessor* and dated to over 900,000 years B.C. In recognition of the unique part Atapuerca plays in our understanding of the way of life of the first human communities the site was accorded World Heritage status by UNESCO in 1998.

•Late Paleolithic period c. 10,000 B.C.

During this period we see the arrival of hunter-gatherer clans *Homo Sapiens* from central Europe. They settled along the northwestern fringes of Spain in the Cantabrian mountains where we can still find some of the best examples of their rock art in the cave dwellings at Altamira. These have been described as the 'Sistine Chapel of the Paleolithic period' and led the site to be added to the UNESCO World Heritage list in 1985. (The caves are situated 30 km west of Santander.)

•Megalithic period c. 4000 B.C.

This period is best known for the building of great *mega* stone structures sometimes referred to as Dolmens or Mamoas. They are the early 'cathedrals' of our ancestors and were aligned to the winter solstice sun and connected to sun worship. Some of the best examples can be found along the *camino* in Galicia. This megalithic culture was deeply religious and left a powerful impact on the peoples who followed.

•Early Celtic period c. 1,000 B.C.

Central European Celts settled in northwestern Spain and Portugal, inter-marrying with the Iberians and giving rise to the Celtiberian tribes. Remains of their Celtic villages *Castros* can be seen dotted around the remote countryside, especially in Galicia, but examples also exist along other parts of the camino. These fortified villages were built in a circular formation usually occupying some elevated ground or hillock. The extensive mineral deposits of this area gave rise to a rich artistic movement and bronze and gold artefacts of this period grace many museums.

•Early Roman period c. 200 B.C.

The Roman occupation of the Iberian peninsular began around the 2nd century B.C. The Romans were attracted by the rich mining potential of the area. Decimus Junius Brutus was the first Roman general to break the fierce resistance of the Celtiberian tribe known as the Lusitani who occupied the area around the Miño valley. Brutus fought his way to the end of the world *finis terrae*, a place of immense spiritual significance at that time.

•Early Christian Period c. 40 A. D.

While there may be no historical evidence to support the contention that St. James preached in Galicia, there is some anecdotal testimony to that effect. It appears that some years after Christ's crucifixion St. James sailed to Galicia (probably Padrón and Finisterre) and commenced his ministry amongst the pagan population there. It is reasonable to assume that he and his followers would have known about the importance of Finisterre as one of the foremost places of Druidic ritual and initiation. It was common practice for the early Christian church to seek out such sites on which to graft its own message. It appears that St. James' mission met with only limited success and he returned to Jerusalem where he was summarily beheaded by Herod in 42 A. D. Following his martyrdom, St. James disciples brought his body back via Padrón in order to be buried at World's End *Finis Terre*. The legendary Queen Lupa conspired with the Roman Legate based at Dugium (present day Duyo in Finisterre) to destroy St. James body and that of his disciples (see *A Pilgrim's Guide to the Camino Finisterre*). In a story reminiscent of the Biblical Red Sea flight into freedom, they managed to escape with the bridge over the river Tambre collapsing just after they had passed over. Libredon (now Santiago) was not far away and it was here they finally laid St. James body to rest. This period marks the beginning of the San Tiago story in Spain but the mists of time grew over these remarkable events, until they finally disappeared from collective memory.

•The Middle Ages c. 476 – 1453

The decline and fall of the **Roman Empire in Spain** was hastened by the barbarian invasions and the arrival first of the Franks and Suevi tribes and then of the Visigoths from Gaul, although their chaotic influence was felt most acutely in Toledo. Incessant internal squabbles resulted in one faction seeking, rather unwisely, support from the Muslim community in Morocco, who duly obliged, arriving in rather larger numbers than anticipated! Islam had spread at breathtaking speed across northern Africa and less than 80 years after Muhammad's death in Medina in 632 the Moorish conquest of the southern Iberian peninsular, spearheaded by Tariq of Tangier in 711, was virtually complete.

The relatively benign rule of the Moors (the name given to the Arab and Berber settlers from Morocco) appears to have been much more favourable than life under the Visigoths. The latter had initiated the first expulsion of Jews from the peninsular while the Moors allowed complete freedom of religious and artistic expression. Indeed the ***western Islamic empire***, centred at Córdoba, was amongst the most tolerant and enlightened administrations to be found anywhere in the known world. *Mozarabic* was the name given to freely practising Christians under Moorish rule and this period saw a great flowering of the sciences, art and architecture in Spain. Some of the finest example of the

Mozarabic style (Christian churches built using the typical Moorish horseshoe arch) can be seen at San Miguel de Escalada near León and at Santo Tomás de las Ollas in Ponferrada.

While this period was not without resistance to Muslim domination, alarm bells began to ring when they advanced northwards and in 778 Charles the Great *Charlemagne* crossed the Pyrenees to stop their advance at Zaragoza and greatly upset the volatile Basques by breaching the walls of Pamplona on his return (having given assurances that the town would not be damaged) setting in motion the famous battle of Roncesvalles and the defeat of the rear-guard of the army under the command of his nephew Roland. This in turn spawned the epic poem of chivalry *La Chanson de Roland*. The story of El Cid a century later has a similar chivalric vein (see under Burgos).

The Santiago story re-emerges in 813 when a shepherd named Pelayo was drawn to a field in Libredon by a 'bright light' or star. Thus we have, the field *compos* of the stars *stella* of Saint James *Sant Iago*, which gives us *Santiago de Compostela*. Other accounts suggest the name comes from the Latin for burial *componere,* as there was evidence of a Roman cemetery on this spot built over earlier Celtic remains. Either way, the Bishop of Iria Flavia (Padrón) *Theodomirus* seized the moment and 'confirmed' the discovery of the tomb of the Apostle and so the story of St. James was resurrected in perfect timing to spearhead the re-conquest *reconquista* of Spain for Christianity, starting with the battle of Clavijo in 844 to the decisive victory at Las Navas de Tolosa in 1212 and each time St. James appeared at the crucial moment to turn the tide of battle.

Thus we have the image of St. James the Moor-slayer ***Santiago Matamoros***, depicted as the knight in shining armour astride a white charger decapitating Moors with his sword. On the strength of these successes, St. James became the patron saint of Spain, a position that he enjoys to this day. The first written record of pilgrimage to Santiago also belongs to this period when Bishop Gotescalco journeyed here in 950 and in 1072 Alfonso VI abolished tolls for all pilgrims travelling up into Galicia through Val Carce.

Between the 12th and 14th centuries Santiago de Compostela grew in importance and prestige, at times even eclipsing the pilgrim routes to Rome and essentially taking over from the pilgrimages to Jerusalem once the crusades had collapsed and the Holy Land was lost to the Christian cause and no longer accessible. It is remarkable that tens of thousands of pilgrims chose to suffer the hazards of this route every year during the Middle Ages. A combination of the relative accessibility of the route and the miracles associated with the relics of the Saint beneath the magnificent cathedral were certainly contributing factors in its popularity. The *Camino de Santiago* was now firmly established and from this period we see the gentler image of St. James the Pilgrim ***Santiago Peregrino*** portrayed all along the route with staff, bible, wide brim hat to keep off the sun and scallop shell *concha*. The *concha* survives as the single identifying symbol of the pilgrim to Santiago, hence the term *concheiros* to distinguish them from *romeros* and *palmers* which were applied to pilgrims going to Rome and Jerusalem respectively. One of the great exponents of the camino in the 12th century was Pope Calixtus II who instigated the privileges of the Compostelan Holy Years. It was at this time that the French priest Aymeric Picaud from Parthenay-le-Vieux near Poitou travelled the pilgrim road. He recorded his experiences in detail in 5 volumes that became known as the ***Codex Calixtinus*** in honour of the incumbent Pope. Book 5 is known as the Book of St. James *Liber Sancti Jacobi* and is essentially the first travel guide to the camino dividing it into 13 stages commencing at Saint-Michel by St. Jean Pied de Port.

The increasing activity gave rise to many religious and chivalrous orders dedicated to the protection of the pilgrim and the furtherance of the aim of the Crusades to re-establish Christianity now diverted away from the Holy Land and specifically towards Spain. While there has been extensive research into the Camino de Santiago and the background events that helped to shape the physical route we walk today, its esoteric heritage is less well documented. For many, the Knights Templar with their links to the contemporary Western mystery tradition became a corner stone in this 'hidden' heritage of the camino. Their secret initiation rites and Gnostic (as opposed to literalist) interpretations of biblical events coupled with their rising influence throughout the Western world, became a threat to the power base of the Papacy and the Catholic Monarchies and led to their eventual downfall. Pope Gregory and King Philip of France joined forces and on Friday 13th October 1307, **Jacques de Molay**, the Grand Master of the Order, and the majority of the Knights Templar were arrested and subsequently put to death. The legacy of this massacre lives on in our collective folk memory as the reason why Friday 13th is considered unlucky. With the demise of the Knights Templar there disappeared one of the original protectors of both the outer pilgrim pathway and its inner mysteries. One of the best preserved Templar castles lies directly on the camino at Ponferrada (pictured).

Much of the property and commanderies of the Knights Templar along the camino were transferred to the **Hospitallers of St. John** who already had a strong presence in Spain. This illustrious order influenced the development of many of the towns and cities we travel through today, such as Pamplona, Burgos, León, Santiago, not to mention the many villages and hamlets that maintained pilgrim *hospitals* to house and protect the pilgrims that travelled this route and the many other caminos that snaked their way across Spain to Santiago. In this way the caminos provided a framework for the re-emergence of Catholicism throughout Spain.

•The Catholic Monarchs 1479 – 1808

Spain's 'Golden Age' sprang from the union of Isabel I of Castile and Fernando V of Aragón. Isabel *la Católica* is widely regarded as the most influential ruler in Spanish history. She oversaw the *reconquista* and the collapse of Islam and Moorish rule in Iberia. More notoriously, Isabel instigated the Inquisition and ruthlessly stamped out all 'heretical' sects, expelling the Jews from Spain in the process. She then set about financing and promoting the 'discovery' of the new world and the plunder of its ancient riches. 1492 marked both the Discovery of the Americas by Columbus and the final re-conquest of Granada under her rule. She must have regretted marrying off her daughter, Catherine of Aragon, to Henry VIII but would, no doubt, have been pleased that her grandson Charles V became Holy Roman Emperor and married, rather more fortuitously, Isabel of Portugal. This deft move added the considerable wealth of Portugal to her overseas dominions and an already impressive list of assets.

The only surviving (legitimate) child from the marriage of Charles and Isabel acceded to the throne in 1556 becoming Felipe II of Spain (and Philip I of Portugal) and effectively the first King of a united Hispanic peninsular. This marks the high point of Spanish influence abroad. Things began to go downhill from here on, starting with the ill-advised Spanish support of Mary Queen of Scots claim to the English throne and the ensuing ill-fated Armada in 1588. The power and influence of the monarchy continued its downward spiral over the next century and in 1700 Felipe V came to the Spanish throne, starting the War of the Spanish Succession between the Bourbon dynasty of France and Charles of Austria whose claim to the Spanish throne was supported by the British. Spain suffered badly in this long drawn out dispute, losing Gibraltar in the process.

•The Peninsular War and the First Republic 1808 – 1810

Events turned from bad to worse with the arrival of Napoleon's army in 1808 and the abdication of King Carlos IV. Spanish resistance was supported by British troops under Sir John Moore and the French were finally ejected and in 1810 a newly formed Parliament *Cortes* prepared a constitution. This first effort at parliamentary rule was short lived and was quickly followed by the Carlist Wars and a series of military coups lasting for another century.

•The Franco Years 1936 – 1975

In 1936 General Franco seized power leading to the one of the bloodiest civil wars in history. The Republican northeast enlisted thousands of volunteers in the International Brigade but was no match for the Nationalist army in the southwest under Franco that had the support of Nazi Germany and Fascist Italy. The ensuing carnage on all sides is hauntingly portrayed in Pablo Picasso's painting *La Guernica*. Monuments to the dead of the Civil War are found all along the camino.

•Modern Spain 1975 – 2005

Franco's carefully groomed successor, Admiral Carrero Blanco, was assassinated by Basque separatists in 1970 and on Franco's death in 1975, King Carlos nominally succeeded and appointed political reformist Adlofo Suárez to form a government. This proved widely popular with the people but the liberal approach of Suárez was not supported by the military. The Suárez government drew up a new constitution and in 1978 Spain became a full democracy under a cumbersome and decidedly expensive system of self-rule with its 17 autonomous communities *autonomías* (the larger ones are subdivided into provinces) which each elect representatives to the central government based in Madrid. The camino passes through 4 of these *autonomías* viz: Navarra, La Rioja, Castilla y León (Burgos, Palencia and León provinces) and Galicia (Lugo and la Coruña provinces). The only hiccup in this progress towards democracy was a military coup in 1981 but Spain regained her composure and democracy was swiftly re-established and the Franco years put firmly behind.

In 1982 the socialist party (PSOE) won a sweeping victory under Felipe González who successfully steered Spain into full membership of the EEC in 1986. In 1996 the populace gave the conservative José María Aznar, leader of the right wing *Partido Popular* (PP), a narrow mandate and in the 2000 general election Aznar and the PP were returned with a resounding majority. But in November 2002 the oil tanker Prestige ran into a storm off Finisterre and the ensuing ecological catastrophe sank not only the livelihood of scores of Galician fisherman but, in due time, the right wing government as well. The disregard for the environment displayed by the President of Galicia and the Spanish environment minister resulted in a popular cry up and down the country of 'never again' *nunca mais*. It only took the government's deeply unpopular support of the invasion of Iraq coupled with the retaliatory Madrid bombings in March 2004 to put the socialist's back in power under the youthful leadership of José Luis Rodríguez Zapatero. The new government set in motion an immediate change in foreign policy and, more controversially, a sudden but decisive shift from a conservative Catholic to a liberal secular society that led to a newspaper headline, 'Church and State square up in struggle for the spirit of Spain.' And seemingly immune to all these social and political upheavals, the camino quietly goes about her gentle spirit of transformation.

The Present: *Breakdown and Breakthrough:*

Two centuries of rampant materialism have resulted in a spiritual aridity unparalleled in human history. Statistics reveal a collapse in church attendance matched by a significant fall in the numbers entering the priesthood. Recent surveys indicate that Spain, until recently seen as a deeply religious society, now has less than 20% of its population actually practising Catholicism.

Yet here is the rub – in this same period the numbers entering the Camino de Santiago have soared and the pilgrim figures have risen tenfold in a decade. How do we interpret these trends? There seems little doubt that there is a great thirst for genuine spiritual experience and a deep desire to refresh and enliven our religious life. It has been suggested by a leading Christian moderator that we have become bored and disillusioned with the religion we have been fed since childhood and this is leading to a collapse of formalised religious practice.

A Future Perspective: *A New Age of Pilgrimage:*

There are many explanations for the anomalies and sweeping changes confronting us today. Each of us will read the signs and interpret these to develop our own future scenarios. I favour the emerging concept of a new and unprecedented flowering of human consciousness that is so positive and profound that we have no collective idea where it will lead us. We have become so spiritually dehydrated that we are now desperate to drink directly from the Divine Well itself and our thirst will no longer be slaked by drinking from a substitute or tainted source. We are awakening to a new spiritual age – one less dependent on an outer authority and more attuned to the God within. Conjecture is rife, but we cannot deny the statistics that point, on the one hand, to collapse and, on the other hand, to renewal. While the death of the old can be alarming the birth of the new is always exciting. Something is undoubtedly 'astir in the land' and what we are witnessing is, perhaps, a collective emergence to a new spiritual reality directing our lives.

Of course, the more cynical might point to tourism, now the single largest industry in the world, as the reason for the sudden rise in the interest in the

Camino de Santiago. Truth is relative and human nature such that we each will tend towards a theory that reinforces our individual belief systems. Today, Santiago flourishes as a centre of both tourism and pilgrimage, but the ancient path itself is less susceptible to commercialisation. *El Camino* is rousing itself from centuries of slumber and its potential to exert a positive influence on the changes confronting us at every turn along the way is enormous. The spirit of St. James and the camino is alive and well and ready to assist each one of us in formulating a new and positive future quite unlike anything we have manifested in the past. 'Time for Change' is Barack Obama's platform – ours too.

PREPARATION – *INNER*: *Why am I doing this?*

A majority of those setting out on the *Camino de Santiago* give a religious or spiritual reason for going, yet few appear to undertake any conscious inner preparation for the journey. It is so easy to allow the demands of our secular life to rob us of time for such preparation. We take our tired bodies and neglected souls and dump them at the start of the camino and trust that all will be well. And of course, all will be well and our physical and spiritual muscles will become rejuvenated – it's just that warm-up exercises can speed our rate of recovery and maximise the benefits. A pilgrim travels on two paths simultaneously and must pay attention to both. When we place ourselves on the pilgrim path we sow the intention to stretch and expand soul consciousness so that we can lift ourselves out of the mundane in order to journey back to God or whatever name we give to that nameless Source from whence we came.

And how, in this busy secular world of ours, do we prepare for such a journey? A useful guideline is to spend at least as much time on inner preparation as general logistics. This way we balance the inner and outer realities and give equal account to both. Spirit seeks to inform all those who sincerely ask the deeper questions behind our existence. These questions may arise from some crisis; diagnosis of a life threatening disease, death of a loved one, loss of employment, marital breakdown or just deep dissatisfaction with life for no apparent reason. All of these events can awaken in us a desire to understand the context as well as the content of our lives. Existential loneliness will not disappear by finding or replacing partners, changing jobs, moving house. Of course, in discovering who we are these outer circumstances may change but it is our ability to see the changing dramas of our life, and the life of others around us, against a larger backdrop that will bring a united purpose to all our journeying.

We all have different psychological, spiritual and emotional needs and pathologies. While pilgrimage can be a way of breaking through resistances (releasing blocks and realising insights as to what prevents us being all that we are) it is wise to start off with a relatively balanced state of mind. If you feel you need psychotherapy, counselling or other help, seek it. It will be disturbing enough when previously dearly held belief systems start to break down. A mental and emotional check up might be useful, even necessary, before you start embarking on an inner quest.

When asked to describe a personal experience of the sacred, an overwhelming majority refer to a time alone in nature, 'A sunrise over the sea; animal tracks in fresh powder snow; a walk under the full moon'. It was not the sun or the moon that created any shift in perception but they acted as a reflection of a larger perspective, a distant memory of something holy – something bigger than, and yet part of, us. This is where the camino can provide such a powerful reminder of the sacred in our lives and the desire to reclaim our spiritual inheritance.

As we set out towards the fabled city of Santiago we need to be mindful, as *A Course In Miracles* suggests, that the true temple is not a structure at all. Its true holiness lies at the inner altar around which the structure is built – yet the real beauty of the inner temple cannot be seen with the physical eye. An emphasis on beautiful structures can be a sign of unwillingness to exercise spiritual vision. As we walk through the *landscape temple* that is the *camino* and through the towns and cities spread out along the way we pass some of the most physically striking religious buildings to be found anywhere in this world. But let us not confuse the messenger with the message and help each other to also search out that elusive *inner altar*.

Risks: Apart from the obvious precautions, especially in the larger towns and cities, it is hard to conceive of a safer environment within which to reflect on life and its direction. The people along the camino have been welcoming pilgrims for centuries. The needs of medieval pilgrims were looked after by *hospitallers*, today they are called *hospitaleros* which is a much more welcoming word than the English equivalent of warden. And this distinction goes to the heart of the camino. Countless millions have walked this path with a high purpose in mind and many of these seekers return to serve the ongoing needs of the pilgrim. That elevated intentionality and goodwill is embedded in this route and available to each of us as we pass along it.

There are of course exceptions to every rule. We live in a fearful world and this is nowhere more obvious than in Spain where military and armed police presence is noticeable everywhere you go and many homes have guard dogs. However, we need to put crime in perspective and realise that our privilege to have the freedom, time and money to be able to walk a pilgrim path can be resented by a tiny minority who see pilgrims as a legitimate target for rich pickings. We need to remind ourselves that an attack is really a cry for help and calls for understanding and a loving response, not a counter-attack. If you find yourself becoming fearful for yourself or your belongings, you might find the following words of *William Ward* a source of encouragement:

> To laugh is to risk appearing a fool
> To weep is to risk being called sentimental
> To reach out to another is to risk involvement
> To expose feelings is to risk exposing your true self
> To place your ideas and dreams before a crowd is to risk their loss
> To love is to risk not being loved in return
> To live is to risk dying
> To try is to risk failure.
>
> But risks must be taken
> Because the greatest hazard in life is to risk nothing.
> The people who risk nothing may avoid suffering and sorrow,
> But they cannot learn, feel, change, grow or really live.
> Chained by their servitude they are slaves who have forfeited all freedom.
> Only a person who risks is truly free.

SELF-ASSESSMENT *INNER WAYMARKS*

This self-assessment questionnaire is designed to encourage you to reflect on your life and its direction. View it as a snapshot of this moment in the ongoing journey of your life. In the busyness that surrounds us we often fail to take stock of where we are headed and our changing roles in the unfolding drama of our life story.

You might find it useful to initially answer these questions in quick succession as this may allow a more intuitive response. Afterwards, you can reflect more deeply and check if your intellectual answers confirm these, change them or bring in other insights. You can download copies of this questionnaire from the *Camino Guides* web site – make some extra copies so you can repeat the exercise on your return and again in (say) 3 months time. This way you can compare results and ensure you continue to follow through on any insights that came to you while walking the camino.

❐ How do you differentiate pilgrimage from a long distance walk?

❐ How do you define spirituality – what does it mean to you?

❐ How is your spirituality expressed at home and at work?

❐ What do you see as the primary purpose of your life?

❐ Are you working consciously towards fulfilling that purpose?

❐ How clear are you on your goal and the right direction for you at this time?

❐ How will you recognise resistance to any changes that might be necessary?

❐ When did you first become aware of a desire to take time-out?

❐ What prompted you originally to go on the camino?

❐ Did the prompt come from something that you felt needed changing?

❐ Make a list of what appears to be blocking any change from happening.

❐ What help might you need on a practical, emotional and spiritual level?

❐ How will you recognise the right help or correct answer?

❐ What are the joys and challenges in working towards your unique potential?

❐ What are your next steps towards fulfilling that potential?

How aware are you of the following? Score yourself on a level of 1 – 10 and compare these scores again on your return from the camino.

❐ Awareness of your inner spiritual world

❐ Clarity on what inspires you and the capacity to live your passion

❐ Confidence to follow your intuitive sense of the right direction

❐ Ability to recognise your resistance and patterns of defence

❐ Ease with asking for and receiving support from others

MAP LEGEND *OUTER WAYMARKS*

This guidebook provides you with essential information in a concise format. The maps have been designed so you can instantly see how far it is to the next café or place of interest etc. without having to scale the distance. All pilgrim hostels are clearly shown (with the number of bed-spaces in brackets) and the location of alternative accommodation is also provided. Distances on the maps correspond to those in the text and are generally spaced at around 3 km intervals corresponding to approximately 1 hour of walking at an average pace. For clarity and accuracy each stage begins and ends at the front door of a clearly specified pilgrim hostel.

Waymarks: Thanks to the voluntary efforts of the various associations and 'friends of the way' – waymarking is now so thorough that we need only the barest information to get us safely to the end of each stage along the way. If you get 'lost' it is invariably because you have let your mind wander and your feet have followed! – stay present and focused especially at points shown with an exclamation mark [!]. If you find yourself temporarily off-course be careful when asking directions as locals are not generally familiar with the waymarked paths but may direct you along the public roads – it is often best to re-trace your steps until you pick up the waymarks again. A sun-compass has been provided on each map as an aid to orientation. In all cases where there are alternative routes I have recommended 'the path less travelled' – my criteria is always to minimise the amount of time spent on asphalt which is so hard and tiring underfoot.

Should you become lost you will find a **'sun compass'** to help re-orientate you. Even in poor weather we can generally tell the direction of the sun so, for example, if you are walking from St. Jean to Roncesvalles you are heading south/west and the morning sun will be on your left (east). At midday the sun will be straight ahead (south) and by late afternoon it will be on your *right>* (west). If you find yourself in the late afternoon with the sun on your *<left* – stop and re-assess as you may be following some other track *back* to St. Jean. Those of us who decide to leave our wristwatch at home the sun will also become our natural clock. It
is surprising how quickly we get to know the time of day by the length of our shadow and our body will ring an alarm bell when it is time to eat or drink. The sun can also help us shift our human egoic tendency of self-aggrandisement towards greater humility by realising the relative insignificance of our physical existence. We like to identify ourselves as being at the centre of the universe and say that the sun rises in the east because that is our experience but it is entirely wrong – it is of course the earth turning on its axis that turns us towards the sun in the morning and away from it at night. This is more than mere semantics. The idea that the sun was the centre of our solar system was a heresy as Galileo discovered to his cost.

Familiarise yourself with the map symbols and note: [1] the **recommended** route follows the most natural pathway and is indicated by a line of yellow dots – symbolic of the yellow arrows that will be your friendly guide throughout the journey. Distances along this recommended route are shown in **blue.** [2] **Alternative** routes that are mostly by road are marked with **grey** dots symbolising the greyness of the asphalt and distances provided are also coloured **grey** and the text appears on a grey background. [3] **Alternative** scenic routes (sometimes with local waymarks only) are shown with green dots indicating the natural landscape they travel through and the text appears on a green panel. [4] **Detours** are shown with **turquoise** dots and the text appears on a turquoise panel.

Each day's stage is measured from the front door of one albergue to the next, i.e. daily distances are between sleeping accommodation. Intermediate hotels or hostels are also shown, those directly on the route in a solid panel and those *off* route with a border only. The number of available beds is also shown [in brackets]. The maps have been designed to show relevant information only and are therefore not strictly to scale – instead accurate distances are given between each point marked on the map and this corresponds to the text for ease of reference. Distances in between these points are shown bracketed in the text as follows: **[0.9 km]** plus **[0.3 km]** add up to the boxed figure in blue $\boxed{\text{1.2 km}}$ Note <left means *turn* left (left) means *on* your left – right> *turn* right etc.

[?] Indicates an option – recommended routes always follow the less travelled tracks so as to minimise the time spent on asphalt. The main (N-*National*) roads are shown in red, symbolic of their added danger and volume of traffic. Every effort has been made to minimise exposure to these 'red' routes and extra care is needed on the few stretches where they simply cannot be avoided. [!] Indicates either a dangerous stretch of road, a steep descent or an area where the waymarks are not clear. Use the 'sun compass' to help orientate yourself through cities and other poorly waymarked areas.

Text and place names on the maps are generally in Spanish *Castellano*. However, on entering Galicia, place names are provided in *Galego* unless they appear 'on the ground' in Spanish. The Church of St. John may, therefore, appear as *Igreja San Juan* or *Igrexa San Xoán*. Villages in Spain, particularly Galicia, tend to straggle without any defined centre and even the local church is frequently located outside the actual town. Distances are usually measured to the albergue or other clearly defined feature, such as a drinking font **[F]** *fuente*.

Contour guides are shown for each day's walk. This will give you a thumbnail sketch of the day's terrain and help you prepare for the uphill stretches and anticipate the downhill ones. They are drawn to an exaggerated scale to emphasise steep inclines.

Equivalent distances are given for each stage adjusted for height using the common factor of 10 minutes for every 100 metres climbed and then applied to the slower (leisurely) pace of 20 minutes per kilometre. For example: Total (cumulative) climb during the day of 600 metres is equivalent to an extra 3 kilometres (time and energy expended) calculated as follows: 600 (metres) ÷ by 10 = 60 (minutes). 60 ÷ 20 (minutes per km) = 3 (km).

Based on the following chart a very fit (fast) walker can accomplish up to a *maximum* of 40 *adjusted* kilometres in an 8 hour day. This drops to 35 km for an average walker and 25 km for a leisurely pace.

Fitness Level	kph	minutes/km	25km	30km	35km	40km
			The above distances (kilometres) will take the following time (hours)			
Fast walker	5 kph	12 min's/km	5.0	6.0	7.0	8.0
Average pace	4 kph	15 min's/km	6.3	7.5	8.6	—
Leisurely pace	3 kph	20 min's/km	8.3	—	—	—

Average pace depends on many other factors, apart from gradient. Awareness of the following additional factors will help you plan your itinerary.

Time of day will also affect your speed and endurance. Ideally start each day early and either (a) plan to finish by lunchtime or (b) plan a midday stop, rest in the shade, and continue on when the worst heat of the day is over.

End of day pace will produce the biggest variations. On the longer stretches, and especially if the day has been hot, you may find your pace slowing considerably and you should allow *half* the normal pace (*double* the time) in calculating whether to continue onwards.

Traversing cities along the route. The more time you spend on the quiet country sections the greater is likely to be your vulnerability to the noise and bustle of the cities. If you are travelling as a solo contemplative pilgrim you might plan your itinerary to walk through the city on the relatively traffic free Sunday or during siesta times. Waymarking in cities has to compete with consumer advertising, traffic lights and other distractions, so allow time to retrace steps if you take a wrong turning.

Traffic can be dangerous and draining. Spanish driving is no safer than in any other country (some would maintain it's worse!). Regarding the energy drain often experienced as a result of the noise and air blast or suction, especially of large articulated trucks, it can help to understand the dynamics of subtle (and not so subtle) energy. One way of working with this is to try 'singing' into the roar as it passes you by. As you hear traffic approaching, start humming your favourite tune. As it draws nearer raise your volume until, at the moment of passing, your roar matches that of the vehicle's engine. This is one simple method of, at least, dispersing any possible negative inner and outer vibrations! You can also use the sudden roar of a car passing at speed (or the sudden bark of a dog) as an alarm call – a rude awakening and reminder of your purpose for being on pilgrimage. Whatever reaction you have, try and stay focused and shake out any negative or angry reactions immediately they arise.

Senda: These modern gravel paths represent a sort of soulless modern 'autopista for pedestrians'. They are shown on the maps on a grey path (as opposed to earth brown) to denote their confusion between path and road (being neither one or the other). They run alongside the public road and are 'softening' with time.

Future Scenarios: Over the past few years, bus loads of tourists on 'pilgrim' holidays have begun to appear along the route. Some, doubtless well meaning charity organisations also organise bus tours that threaten to overload the capacity of the camino to cope gracefully. I have recently been forced off the path by 4 wheel drive 'pilgrim safaris' from a UK adventure holiday company – a humbling but not particularly edifying experience! *Mickey Mouse* dressed as a pilgrim complete with staff has already appeared around Sahagún, one of the worst effected areas. Perhaps León will develop a pilgrim theme park that might, ironically, reduce numbers on the camino itself. We need to stay vigilant and give feedback to local authorities, travel and charity organisations of any concerns we might have and remind ourselves that, during the medieval period, the camino was able to cope with twice the present number of annual pilgrims.

42

Map symbols used in this guide:

Total km   Total distance for each day's stage

Adjusted for climb (100m vertical equivalent to additional 0.5km)

(850m) Alto ▲   High point of each stage / contour line

◄ 3.5   Distance between points (3.5 km approximates to 1 hours walking)

→ 150m > / ^ / <   Interim distances – 150 metres turn right / straight on (s/o) / left

Path or track (brown symbolising earth)

Secondary road (green symbolising quiet country lane)

N-11   Main [N] road (red symbolising added danger)

A-1   Motorway (blue conventional motorway colour)

Recommended path (minimising asphalt)

Alternative road route

Alternative scenic route (less waymarks, local signage, GR etc.)

Optional detour to point of interest

Railway / Station

National boundary / provincial boundary

River / stream

Sea or river estuary / woodland

Church / chapel / wayside cross

Option point / extra care needed

Café bar / Drinking font (*Fonte, Fuente*)

Tourist Office / Manor house

Windmill / radio mast

Ancient monument / Viewpoint

Hospital / post office

Petrol station

Airport / bus / rail station

Pilgrim hostel (*Albergue*) / Youth hostel (*Juventude*)

Hotel / Pension

Country B&B (*Casa rural*) / country mansion (*Quinta*)

Ⓐ Ⓗ Ⓒ   *off* route accommodation

[32]   Number of beds (usually bunk beds in pilgrim hostels)

Muni.   Municipal hostel

Xunta   Galician government (Xunta) hostel

Conv.   Convent or monastery hostel

Par.   Parroquial (church parish) hostel

Asoc.   Association hostel

Priv. (*)   Private hostel (private network with star *)

Town plan

(Pop. – Alt. m)   Town population and altitude in metres

City and suburbs (grey) with historical centre (brown)

33 STAGE SUMMARY – ROUTE MAPS & TOWN GUIDES

St Jean Pied de Port – Santiago de Compostela 796 km (494.6 miles)

ST. JEAN PIED de PORT: The ancient capital of the Basque region of Basse-Navarre retains a delightful medieval atmosphere in its narrow streets. The Basque language has also been preserved so signs and place names may appear in French or Basque (and across the border in Spanish or Basque). This attractive town nestles in the foothills of the Pyrenees at the 'foot of the pass' *pied de port* to Roncesvalles (Ronceveaux in French). A population of 1,500 serves the many tourists, hill walkers and pilgrims that converge on this small enclave in the summer months. Activity gravitates towards the central square *Place du-Gaulle* where the efficient tourist office (0559-370 357) is located along with a range of hotels and cafés where you can wine and dine amongst the traffic fumes or…

Explore the historic walled town where the pilgrim office and hostels are located. St. Jean Pied de Port has become the principal gateway to the camino and the traditional starting point for pilgrims from all over the world with the exception of those in Spain, where the main starting point is Roncesvalles (for the whole route) or Sarria in Galicia which is just over 100 km from Santiago and the minimum distance required to qualify for a compostela.

**Porte St. Jacques
and Municipal Pilgrim Hostel**

A basic tour starts with a visit to the medieval *rue de la Citadelle*. This is a continuation of the Way of St. James through France *Chemin de Saint Jacques* and part of the camino itself. From this ancient cobbled main street there are several access points to the old ramparts. Towards the top end of the street you will find a museum with artefacts from the Camino de Santiago displayed in the 13th century Prison of the Bishops *La Maison des Evêques* adjoining the pilgrim office (see below). At the very top of the town is St. James Gate *Porte St Jacques* through which pilgrims arriving from Le Puy, Vezelay and Paris, via Ostabat, enter the town (World Heritage status).

From the *Porte St Jacques* a steep climb up takes you to the imposing Citadelle with a fine view over the old town and the Pyrenees over which you will pass tomorrow. A steep climb down on the eastern boundary (269 steps!) brings you to the narrow Porte de l'Echauguette that opens onto the river Nive and the 14th century Church of Our Lady at the End of the Bridge *Notre Dame du Bout du Pont*. A fitting place, perhaps, from which to bless the beginning of your journey and that of your fellow pilgrims who will pass under her protective arch *Porte Notre Dame* on the way out in the morning. From the church you can take a peaceful 1 km circular detour up river, past the wooden footbridge, to the Roman bridge *Pont Eyeraberri*. Cross over and return via the Pelota court *Frontón* and the rue d'Espagne back to the Porte Notre Dame (See town plan).

Pilgrim Passport – you can obtain a *Carnet de Pelerin* or *Credencial del Peregrino* from the welcoming pilgrim office *Accueill* (0559-370 509) at 39, rue de la Citadelle which is open most of the day (closed lunch) and late into the evening. It will provide general information on the first leg of the route, some idea of local weather conditions and can check availability of accommodation at the municipal pilgrim refuge and alternatives (L'Esprit du Chemin opposite). The pilgrim travel company, Express Burricot (559 373 628) adjoins.

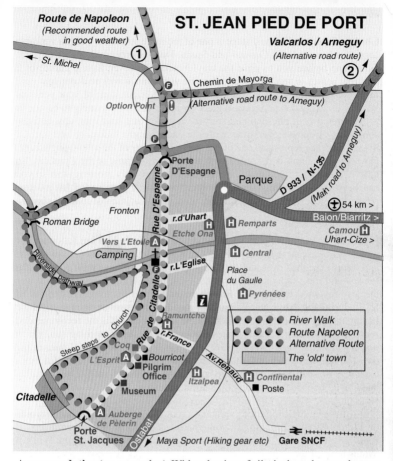

Accommodation (see town plan): Wide selection of pilgrim hostels, guesthouses and hotels. If you want to stay away from the noisy main square try any of the increasing number of guesthouses offering beds in the old town. Telephone code for France 0033. •Auberge de Pèlerin open all year with 24 beds in 2 rooms and all facilities. This municipal hostel is located just inside the Porte St Jacques at 55 Rue de la Citadelle at the top of the town. (check availability at the *Accueill*). The ever-popular •L'Esprit du Chemin (Huberta & Arno 0559-372 468) at No. 40 opposite the pilgrim office offers pilgrim dinner, breakfast and a picnic lunch for the next day. Just below at No.36 is •Au Chant du Coq (0674-310 283) with range of prices based on the number of beds in each room. At the lower end of town 21 rue d'Espagne is •Le Chemin Vers L'Etoile (Eric 0559 372 071) under new management with plans to increase the 25 places to 40 during 2010. •Gîte d'Étape Etchegoin (0559-371 208) Rue d'Uhart 9 where dormitory rooms are also available. The only hotel in the old town is •Hôtel Ramuntcho** (0559-373 517) centrally located on the corner of rue de Citadelle, 24 with pleasant dining room where you can eat *al fresco* on the balcony. •Hôtel des Remparts** (0559-371 379) Place Floquet,16. •Hôtel Etche Ona** (0559-370 114) Place Floquet,15. •Hôtel Central** (0559-370 022) Place de Gaulle and at the top end of the square (and price bracket) •Hôtel Des Pyrénées*** (0559-371 897). •Hôtel Itzalpea (0559-370 366) Place du Trinquet,5 and just behind, •Hôtel Continental*** (0559-370 025) Av. Renaud (on the way in from the rail station). A stroll around the town will reveal an equally wide selection of restaurants and bistros to suit all pocket and tastes.

Choice of routes: This first stage is one of the more strenuous and is a veritable baptism of fire into *El Camino* and Spain. Don't worry; millions of pilgrims have gone before you to pave the way! You do, however, have a choice of 2 different routes to reach Roncesvalles and your choice will be dependent on 2 main considerations: [a] prevailing weather conditions and [b] your personal level of fitness and experience. Whichever route you take is likely to be taxing as we stretch both physical and spiritual muscles that have, perhaps, become somewhat atrophied over time with our increasingly sedentary and secular lives. This stage represents one of the steepest ascents of the whole pilgrimage. However, the climb is rewarded with the great panorama of the Pyrenees. So have all your gear, food and water prepared for an early morning start so you can sleep soundly during the night holding your inner purpose for this journey, rather than your worldly goods, clearly in mind. If that purpose remains obscure – ask for clarity.

[1] Route de Napoléon: 25.1 km, adjusted for climb 32.0 km (allowing for a cumulative ascent in the day of 1,390m equivalent to an extra 6.9 km of time and effort expended over and above that required for a level walk). This is the longest and most arduous route but the most beautiful and spectacular. It was the way favoured by the great French general to get his troops in and out of Spain during the Peninsular War and by medieval pilgrims anxious to avoid the bandits hiding in the trees surrounding the lower route. It is the recommended route in good weather and it makes the most of the early morning sun, which doesn't penetrate into the Valcarlos valley (alternative route) until later in the day. The steep climb up onto the high plateau is rewarded with wonderful views back over St. Jean de Pied Port. The last section up through the Col de Bentartea and Col de Lepoeder is entirely on natural pathways.

[1a] A little known (and used) variant on route [1] is the GR65 from Mayorga on the outskirts of St. Jean. This alternative adds 1 km to the recommended route that it rejoins at the 1,000m contour close to the Pic d'Orisson. While it avoids most of the asphalt section of the D428 it is poorly waymarked and it is easy to get lost along the remote mountain paths. If you are an experienced hill walker and want to use this route obtain the IGN 1:25 map 1346 OT available in St. Jean or any good map shop – otherwise stick to the main route.

Likewise, unless you are an experienced hill walker, you should not tackle the recommended route: [a] in winter when daylight hours are greatly diminished and weather more extreme, or [b] during any other season if the weather looks bad or is forecast to deteriorate. Note that during late autumn and early spring there are frequent snow showers and these can obliterate the waymarks. At any time of year hill fog can cause poor visibility. Fog should be distinguished from early morning mist, which usually burns off in the first few hours long before you reach the high plateau and have to leave the relative security of the road. If you are unsure or anxious, enquire at the pilgrim office as they have access to local weather forecasts and regular updates. Guidebooks are duty bound to sound cautionary notes! Be sensible, but know that any reasonably fit person can cover the ground and is likely to have a peak experience in so doing. Remember to take food and water with you, as there are no facilities (beyond Orisson) and drinking fonts are few and far between. If the weather is very unsettled then it might be preferable to stick to the rigours of the N-135.

[2] Valcarlos route: 24.0 km, adjusted for climb 28.9 km (allowing for a cumulative ascent in the day of 990m, equivalent to an extra 4.9 km). Charles Valley *Valcarlos* was the way chosen by the Holy Roman Emperor Charlemagne to get his troops in and, somewhat disastrously, out of Spain. You cannot avoid the main road completely, but you can save 6 km of it before Arneguy and a further 10 km of it after Valcarlos. This alternative route runs parallel to the main road and follows country lanes into Arneguy. However, the waymarking is not so clear and there are several side roads that could delay you unless you stay alert and vigilant. 6 km after Valcarlos a path leaves the road and climbs directly to the Ibañeta pass through a mixture of pine and beech trees. This is a very steep pathway but it eliminates the innumerable bends on the main road.

[2a] A variant on route [2] is to follow the main road all the way to Roncesvalles 27.5 km, adjusted for climb 32.0 km (allowing for a cumulative ascent in the day of 890m equivalent to an extra 4.5 km). The road route is the longest and goes through the villages of Arneguy and Valcarlos with their shops, bars and hotels. However, this is a main route into Spain and is designated an N *(nacional)* road and is not recommended. Today, the road carries an ever-increasing amount of tourist traffic and is noisy and dangerous particularly in wet or windy conditions. Note that apart from the noise and danger of traffic it can also be very chilly in the early morning, as the sun does not penetrate the deep-sided valley until later in the day.

Preparations for next day – Outer: As you will need to leave early in the morning to get to Roncesvalles, you should shop for lunch the evening before as there are limited facilities on both routes and shops won't be open when you leave at first light in the morning. The rue d'Espagne has several food outlets including *Alimentacion* (opposite patisserie *Barbier Millox*) and a supermarket *Le Relais des Mousquetaires* on the corner of the rue d'Uhart and just before Porte d'Espagne is the *Boulangerie Iriart* (opens around 7 a.m.) Fill your water flask before you leave town and top up as you pass drinking fonts en route.

Preparations for next day – Inner: Take time now, again, to reflect on the purpose of your pilgrimage. Try the church for some quiet space or take a walk along the river. Look again at your personal journal or self-assessment notes and ponder on the journey of your life that has brought you this far – reflect on your purpose for now. You may yet meet Jesús Jato, but in the meantime you can walk with his words in your heart *El Camino es tiempo de meditación interior, no itinerario turístico.*

REFLECTIONS:

❐ **Personal Journal:** *"... The stress of arriving at St. Jean combined with the urge to begin the pilgrimage resulted in a false start. I walked for several hours before I realised that my mind was anywhere but present to the sacred journey I was embarking on. I had fallen straight back into my familiar mode of active doing and the simple act of Being was lost to me. In my haste and confusion I had forgotten to pause and to dedicate this first leg of the journey to my purpose – 'to find and inhabit that place within me that touches God'. Tears welled up from deep within me at this prompt from my guides, 'Start anew' they urged...*

...It was hard to retrace my steps but I knew that it was meaningless to continue in this frame of mind. Lost in the busyness of both past and future, I had forsaken the present, the only place I could find what I was looking for. I write these notes on a tiny balcony directly above the camino with the church tower just visible against the darkening sky. Tomorrow I will follow my inner guidance and start afresh..."

❏ **A journey of a thousand miles begins with a single step**. *Lao Tzu*

MAP 01 *796.0 km (494.6 miles) to Santiago de Compostela*

> *[1] Recommended route (weather permitting)*
> *Via Route de Napoléon / Col de Loepeder / Port de Cize*

ST. JEAN PIED-DE-PORT (Pays Basque) – RONCESVALLES (Navarre)

▬▬▬	Path / Track	--- ---	12.4	--- *49%*
▬▬▬	Quiet Road	--- ---	12.7	--- *51%*
▬▬▬	Main Road	--- ---	0.0	
Total km	**Total distance**		**25.1 km** (15.6 miles)	

Adjusted for climb   32.0 km (accrued ascent 1,390m = 6.9 km)
Alto ▲   High point: Col de Loepeder 1,450m (4,757 feet)

[1] **Recommended *Route de Napoléon*:** A strenuous uphill walk is rewarded with stunning views in all directions (provided we are spared the hill fog). The first part, as far as *Huntto*, is through steeply wooded countryside that gives way to open hill and moorland, interspersed with some woodland (mostly beech) on the Spanish side. While the uphill section will stretch the cardiovascular muscles, injury is more likely on the steep downhill stage into Roncesvalles when mind and muscles will be tired – stay very focussed.

The Practical Path: While we start with one of the more demanding walks of the entire route, you will doubtless be full of energy and the sense of adventure ahead. Don't let euphoria force a pace in these early days that you and your feet have not adequately trained for – walk lightly and easily within your physical capabilities. The hospitals and health clinics of Logroño, only 160 km away specialise in treating foot and leg injuries sustained by over-eager pilgrims some of whom are forced to abandon the journey at this early stage. If you are with a companion(s) then find your own walking speed and don't allow yourself to be forced into someone else's stride. You can always catch up later and in the meantime you will make new friends and experience the rich camaraderie that develops along the way. For general emergencies (medical, police etc.) phone 112. **Intermediate accommodation at:** Huntto (5.6 km) and Orisson (8.0 km) with café/restaurant.

❏ **The Mystical Path:** A sharing from the heart can be reflected in a simple smile. If the eyes are the windows of the soul, then words are often the blinds that shut out the light. Will your physical sight reveal the collection of hand crafted

☎ 948-760 225 La Posada
RONCESVALLES/*Orreaga*
(Pop. 30 – Alt. 960m)

Ⓐ → 4.0 **Albergue** ← 1.5
Conv.[120] *Itzandegia*
Casa Sabina ☎ 948-760 012

→ 4.1 **Ibañeta**
Alt. 1,055m

Don Simon

Col de Lepoeder 4.1 ► *1,450m*

Orzanzurieta

Col de Bentartea 1,340m

N-135

Camino 3.4

• K.58

Frontera / Fuente 1.6 Ⓕ

España
France

Pic de Leizar Atheka

Gañecoleta
Puente 3.2 →

← *mountain hut*

• K.63
Ⓕ

Cruceiro 3.6 †

Valcarlos Mun. [10]
Albergue / Centre 3.3
Ondarolle ●

Ⓐ Ⓕ Ⓗ **VALCARLOS**

1,100m
Pic D'Orisson 3.8 ►▲

GR 65

S
Coucher du soleil **W**

Lever du soleil

Ⓐ ← 2.4 **Albergue**
Orisson Priv.[18]
☎ 0681-497 956

E

† *Table d'Orientation*

ARNEGUY
Ⓓ ← 3.0 **Option**

● *Ventas*

Hunto 2.0 Ⓗ
Ferme Ithurburia Priv. [16]
☎ 0559-371 117

D-933
Oncorone →

3.6 **Puente**

Etchebestéa 3.1 ►

① **Route de Napoleon***
**in good weather*

② **Route Valcarlos**

†

● **Lasse**

R. Nive

Saint-Jacques

● St. Michel

● Caro

Ancien chemin de

rue de Mayona

Ⓟ 1.4 **Puente**

Porte d'Espagne / Option Ⓟ 0.5

(Pop. 1,600 – Alt.170m)
ST.JEAN PIED DE PORT

†

Biarritz / Bayonne ✚

ℹ *Tourisme* ☎ 559 370 357

R. Nive

Albergue 0.0 → Ⓐ
Muni. [24]

↓ *Ostabat*

crosses by the remote boundary marker and will you stop awhile to reflect on the truth behind this symbol? What else will your awareness reveal to you along the way that you can share with your fellow pilgrims when you reach Roncesvalles?

❏ **Personal Reflections:** *"... The deep sense of peace that surrounds me is in stark contrast to the stress I felt when I first set out. It had taken me awhile to realise it was All Saints Day – an auspicious start to my journey and a moment of tenderness as I recalled burying my father in Spanish soil on this very day all those years ago. I record these thoughts in the silence of my own company, surrounded by empty chairs and empty tables. I am the only pilgrim in this enormous building but I am not alone as the ancient Celtic prayer reminds me, 'Christ before me. Christ behind me. Christ all around me. Christ within me."*

Fauna and flora: Take time to take in the magnificent natural landscape that surrounds you. Watch out for the Griffon Vultures that soar in the mountain thermals alert for any signs of a sheep or other animal about to expire and become its staple carrion. These majestic birds have a wingspan up to 2.5m (8 feet) and there are 1,800 pairs in the region, the biggest concentration in the world. We will also see a variety of birds of prey including the Kite and Buzzard or the smaller and swifter Sparrow hawk and Falcon. This area is an important flight path for many species of migrating bird, all of which has spawned an ornithological information centre at Ibañeta. You may also encounter a rare Pyreneean chamois or wild horse on the hill and almost certainly see many of the hill ponies running free (distinguishable by their neck halters). The black-faced sheep roaming the high pasture are *Manech* bred for the quality of their milk and its award winning *Ossau Iraty* cheese. Depending on the season, you will see many varieties of wild flowers of every hue and colour including orchids, violas, narcissus and the ubiquitous pale blue irises that carpet the path all along the camino from here to the 'end of the world' at *finis-terre*.

Leaving the pilgrim office and central albergue in St. Jean we turn down the cobbled rue de la Citadelle passing the pilgrim office and the parish church and pass through the archway and over the river Nive. This is the lowest point of the first stage at 170m above sea level. By this afternoon we will have climbed to 1,450m through the Col de Lepoeder! *(As we look back from the bridge we will find the Virgin and Child watching over us as we take our first steps on the journey).* Proceed up the cobbled rue D'Espagne to:

| 0.5 km | **Porte D'Espagne** Option *Opción* [?] Ancient gateway to Spain and the point at which we decide which route to follow. Drinking font *Fuente* [F] (left). *For the alternative road route via Valcarlos and Puerto de Ibañeta continue up for 100m past the school and turn right> into Chemin de Mayorga. This avoids the busy roundabouts in St. Jean. The Chemin de Mayorga is also the access point to the variant [1a] via the GR65 (see route map).*

For the **recommended way** via Route de Napoleon over the Col de Lepoeder continue straight on passing [F] (right) – fill up if you haven't already. Ignore signs to St. Michel and continue up into the Chemin de Saint Jacques (*Jondoni Jakobe Bidea* in Basque) along the minor road D-428 veering <left at Villa Etchea Kalavainea and continue up to grove of chestnut trees at junction:

| 3.1 km | **Etchebestéa** (no sign) but here the road from St. Michel (Stage I of the Codex Calixtinus) joins from the left. *This was the ancient route taken by pilgrims coming from France.* Keep straight on uphill on the asphalt road (ignoring any woodland paths) to:

2.0 km **Huntto •Ferme Ithurburia** (0559-371 117) Where Mme. Ourthiague offers a variety of meal options and accommodation with 20 bed spaces. Shortly afterwards **[0.3 km]** turn <left onto grass track to rejoin road **[1.1 km]** with **[F]** (right) and viewing table and rest point (left). Continue along asphalt road for **[1.0 km]** to:

2.4 km **Orisson •Auberge*** (0681- 497 956) a network* hostel run by Jean- Jacques Etchandy and his family. **[F]** left. Open all year with 18 beds in 2 rooms. No kitchen but bar and restaurant with panoramic viewing platform. *[Note that the next albergue is: Roncesvalles – 17.1 km].* We now break through the 1,000m level to arrive at:

Auberge d'Orisson

3.8 km **Pic D'Orisson** (1,100m) with its statue of the Virgin *Vierge d'Orisson / Vierge de Biakorri* (left 100m) set against an impressive backdrop of the surrounding mountains and valleys. *(Note Marian shrines to Our Lady appear all along the route and are one of the most common symbols of devotion on the camino).* Nearby are the ruins of the ancient Chateau Pignon and this remote area once had a medieval pilgrim hostel. Continue on the asphalt road to the turn off (right) to Arneguy D-128 **[1.7 km]**. Keep straight on/left here for another **[1.9 km]** and turn off right> by memorial cross [!].

3.6 km **Cruceiro** a modern wayside cross and memorial leads us onto a rough grass track that cuts through a gap in the ridge ahead (Pic de Leizar Atheka and the Col de Bentarte). We *must* leave the road at this stage. *(If the weather has deteriorated and you are not confident of proceeding, your options are: return to Auberge Orisson, St Jean or take the D 128 to Arneguy. In an emergency there is a tiny mountain hut 50m (right) just through the gap ahead).* Pass through the gap in the ridge **[0.5 km]** (mountain shelter right) onto a woodland path turning <left at wire fence **[0.6 km]** along a heavily eroded gully passing a stone marker (No. 199) to a cattle grid **[0.5 km]** that marks the Spanish border.

1.6 km **Frontera [F]** *Fontaine de Roland* (left) cross over the cattle grid into Spain with a stone border marker (ahead left) confirming that we are now in Navarre. *(Don't stray onto the GR10 the long-distance route over the Pyrenees from the Atlantic to the Mediterranean that crosses the path down to the left)* continue up right> on the GR65 to pass the ruins of an ancient border post (left). The camino now continues in a gentler climb through scattered woodland (mostly beech) up along a wide track until we reach the highest point at:

4.1 km **Col de Lepoeder (1,450 metres)** from here we have our first view southwards over Navarre with the roof of the abbey at Roncesvalles and the town of Burguete in the valley below. **[?] Option:** *(If you are tired or it is getting late (dusk) and/or it is wet and slippery underfoot, you can take the less steep (but longer) option by turning right> downhill on the asphalt road to Ibañeta 4.0 km and a further 1.6 km to Roncesvalles).* Otherwise, keep straight on over the road to the pathway that drops steeply down [!] through magnificent beech woods *bosque de Irati* one of the largest remaining beech forests in Europe, around the conical hill of Alto Don Simón to:

4.0 km **Roncesvalles** [Orreaga] with •**albergue**, 2 hotels, the monastery, collegiate church, bookshop, museum and tourist office (see details overleaf).

ST. JEAN PIED-DE-PORT – RONCESVALLES
(Pays Basque)   (Navarre)

[2] alternative road route *Via Valcarlos and the Puerto de Ibañeta*
Preferred option in bad or deteriorating weather.

▬▬	Path / Track	--- ---	7.3	--- *31%*
▬▬	Quiet Road	--- ---	11.4	--- *47%*
▬▬	Main Road	--- ---	<u>5.3</u>	--- *22%*
Total km	**Total distance**		**24.0 km** (14.9 miles)	

◣ Adjusted for climb   28.9 km (accrued ascent 990m = 4.9 km)
Alto ▲ High point: Ibañeta pass 1,055m. (3,460 feet)

The Practical Path: This is another strenuous uphill climb with less open views but more shelter from wind and rain in the woodland areas. While providing the security of the main road with shops and hotels along the way (Arneguy and Valcarlos) it also contains the hazards and noise of traffic and the harsh asphalt that is so tiring underfoot. Note that almost half the journey is directly on or parallel to the busy National Route N-135. **Intermediate accommodation at:** Arneguy (8.5 km) and Valcarlos (11.8 km).

The variant [2a] is not recommended as it follows the main road all the way to Roncesvalles and you will have asphalt underfoot for the entire distance of 27.5 km (32.0 km when adjusted for the cumulative ascent of 890m). Note: many pilgrims inadvertently take this option as they miss (a) the turn-off right> onto the quieter country lanes just outside St. Jean (b) the scenic routes (green dots) in Arneguy and the turn-off <left above Valcarlos onto the woodland path.

Leaving the albergue / pilgrim office in St. Jean turn down the cobbled Rue de la Citadelle passing the parish Church of Our Lady at the End of the Bridge *Notre Dame du Bout du Pont* and out under the archway, over the river Nive and proceed up the cobbled rue D'Espagne to:

0.5 km **Porte D'Espagne Option** [?] The alternative road route via Valcarlos is recommended in bad weather. It is no less strenuous but the woods provide some shelter from rain and wind although the sun doesn't penetrate into the valley until late in the day. To access this route continue up for 100m past the school and turn right> into Chemin de Mayorga (signposted) to join the main road to Pamplona *Pampelune* on the D-933 (the N-135 once you cross the border into Spain).

1.4 km **Puente** [!] (1.9 km from the centre / albergue) as you leave the suburbs behind the main road takes a sharp left hand bend *down* to a slip road (right) [!] **Be Vigilant** *Vigilante*. Here, barely visible from the road and identified by a **3t** sign (3 tonne weight restriction) with red and white posts, is a short slip road to a concrete bridge over the river Chapitel (sometimes called petite Nive). Many pilgrims plod on along the main road, oblivious of this quieter parallel route.

You now continue on quiet lanes that wind their way up and down the pleasant rolling countryside parallel but away from the dangerous N-135. Veer <left at T-junction **[0.5 km]** continue and turn sharp <left at hairpin bend **[1.9 km]**. We now continue along a steeply undulating road for **[1.2 km]** down towards the main road over stream (bridge to the N-135 left) with sign to Oncorone right:

3.6 km **Puente** Turn up right> (sign Oncorone) and then down <left and up

again! to finally emerge onto the first short stretch of track where you cross the border into Spain at the modern shopping development *Venta Xabi*. **[F]** (right) and cafe (left). Continue straight on through the carpark (don't cross the river) and take the delightful riverside path all the way into Arneguy and:

3.0 km   **Arneguy / Option**. Several hotels and restaurants in Arneguy including •**Clementia** H**(0559-371 354). Continue straight on along the main road *or* turn <left over the bridge (back into France!) and take the quieter scenic route via Ondarrolle (recommended). Cross the bridge and turn immediately right> up along the far bank of the river all the way into Ondarolle **[2.6 km]** and turn down right> to re-cross the river and take the steep path up **[0.7 km]** to:

3.3 km   **Valcarlos** *Luzaide* •**albergue** municipal hostel located below the main square. Continue past the public toilets and turn <left on the main road. **[F]** and pilgrim monument opposite the church, which is dedicated to St. James. The church contains the first of many statues to the Saint as slayer-of-the-Moors *Santiago Matamoros*. Other accommodation: •**Maitena** Hs* (948-790 210) adjoining the square and •**Casa Marcelino** Hs (948-790 063). The village takes its name from Charlemagne, who camped here on his return home and to lick his wounds after the defeat of his army rearguard and the death of Roland at Ibañeta. **[F]** (right) as you leave the town **[0.5 km]**. Stay on the main road for another **[2.0 km]** and take a new turn off down <left (km.61) for **[0.7 km]** into:

3.2 km   **Gañecoleta** (no facilities) cross the river and take the riverside path cross back again up to the main road **[1.3 km]** continue up past (km.58) and take the slip road <left **[2.1 km]** to leave the main road for the last time.

3.4 km   **Camino** after **[0.4 km]** leave the track and take the narrow footpath up right> as it winds through beech and hazel woods for **[2.2 km]** to join the main road beside a house & dog kennels *Casa Borda Guardiano*. Leave the road again after 90m and turn <left and continue through pine plantation for **[1.5 km]** to:

4.1 km   **Puerto Ibañeta** (1,055m) formerly the site of the Church and Hospice of San Salvador built in 1127 to serve pilgrims to Santiago and moved shortly afterwards to Roncesvalles. The pass now has a modern chapel and a stone monument to Roland (*Song of Roland* fame) to mark the point at which the wail of his horn *Oliphant* was heard, too late to be rescued by Charlemagne. There is also a bird observation post with information on the many species and flocks of birds that use this pass on their migrations. Turn <left down by the side of the observation centre along the path again for the remaining **[1.5 km]** through the beech woods to:

1.5 km   **Roncesvalles** *Orreaga*

•**Albergue [1]** run by the collegiate church (948-760 000) and located in a somewhat austere Gothic building on the main road. Originally a medieval pilgrim hospital it was subsequently changed to a shop and exhibition centre and more recently converted back to form the main pilgrim albergue. Open all year (volunteer wardens in the summer months) with 120+ beds in 1 dormitory! limited shower and toilet facilities located in the basement with small kitchen and dining area. Additonal albergue due to open in 2012.

Albergue Roncesvalles

Admission to the pilgrim hostel and a very practical (small) pilgrim passport *credencial del peregrino* can be obtained from the collegiate pilgrim office with entrance under archway at the front of the main building. Open 10:00–13.30 and 16:00–19:00. If you arrive late and the dormitory is full they may open an overflow room with an additional 20+ beds in a room adjoining the pilgrim office; so stick around and look tired! The former youth hostel is now under renovation to provide additional pilgrim accommodation (due in 2012). **Other accommodation:** •**Casa Sabina** Hs (948-760 012) and •**La Posada** Hs (948-760 225) – both are adjacent to the monastery on the main road. *Next accommodation: Burgete (3.0 km) next albergue Zubiri (22.2 km).*

RONCESVALLES 'valley of thorns' (*Orreaga* in Basque) is still cloaked in its medieval atmosphere and provides another gateway to the camino. This is the major entry point for Spanish pilgrims travelling up via Pamplona and was one of the earliest and most revered pilgrim refuges connecting the Augustinian's with the care of the Santiago pilgrims. Since the 12th century it has received, *'All pilgrims... sick and well. Catholics, Jews, pagans, heretics and vagabonds...'* this open hospitality continues today with one judicial agency offering the opportunity to walk the camino as a way of purging offenders of their misdeeds in lieu of a custodial sentence – finding self respect engendering a reformed life (details of this inspiring *last chance* concept can be found at www.oikoten.be).

The Royal Collegiate Church of Saint Mary *Real Collegiata de Santa María* was built at the behest of the Navarrese King Sancho the Strong *Sancho VII el Fuerte* but was not consecrated until 1219 (after his death). It houses the beautiful 14th century statue of Our Lady of Roncesvalles *Nuestra Señora de Roncesvalles* and runs a bookshop with pilgrim literature, maps and souvenirs and an interesting museum which includes the fine enamel / silver relic known as Charlemagne's chessboard *ajedrez de Carlomagno*. Adjoining the church is the cloisters *claustro* rebuilt in the 17th century after they collapsed under snow! Access is via an inconspicuous door opposite the bookshop. Off the cloisters is the splendid 14th century *Sala Capitular* with its evocative 13th century mausoleum housing the tomb of Sancho VII and his wife Clemencia. The iron chains that Sancho broke in the defeat of the Moors at the famous battle of *Navas de Tolsa* in 1212 are located here and appear in the crest of the Government of Navarra. There is a small admission charge for the museum and cloisters.

Beside the Hostal La Posada is the 12th century Romanesque chapel of the Holy Spirit *Capilla de Sancti Spiritus* otherwise referred to as the *Silo de Carlomagno* and reputed to be the burial place of the slaughtered rearguard of Charlemagne's army and a medieval pilgrim burial site. Adjoining is the tiny 13th century Gothic chapel of St. James *Capilla de Santiago* whose re-positioned bell (from the chapel at Ibañeta) once guided pilgrims through the swirling mists often experienced around the Ibañeta pass. Adjacent is a monument commemorating the battle of Roncesvalles and the death of Roland in 778.

Lying at an altitude of 950m, Roncesvalles has a resident population of less than 100. The helpful Turismo (948-760 301) is located in an old mill *antiguo molino* behind Casa Sabina. Pilgrim mass Mon-Fri at 20:00, Sat & Sun 19:00 and festival days 18:00 in the *Iglesia de Santa María* with a special blessing for all pilgrims of any faith (check times at the pilgrim office). A simple pilgrim dinner is obtainable after mass (book *before* 18:00) at either the Casa Sabina or La Posada and provides an opportunity to meet other pilgrims and share experiences.

PROVINCE OF NAVARRA: A fiercely independent mountainous region, its turbulent past has been influenced most notably by the French. Charlemagne's army damaged the walls of Pamplona despite an assurance that the city would not be harmed and so the Basques subsequently massacred the rearguard of his army at Roncesvalles in retribution – but break no promises here and you will find a generosity of spirit and loyalty second to none. The hospitality of this region is graphically captured in the writings of many foreign authors, notably Ernest Hemingway who stayed for extended periods in Burguete and Pamplona. Fighting bulls and horses are bred in the hills and trout from the mountain streams and local game make up much of the cuisine of this area. Pork products find their way onto most menus with *chorizo* predominating (pork sausage marinated in various local spices, especially paprika) and often found in stews and soups. Vegetarians *vegetarianos* have a hard time here but on the lowlands further west we find widespread asparagus *espárrago de Navarra* and the bright red peppers *pimientas del piquillo* often stuffed with olives and other non-meat delicacies and eaten as snacks *tapas* along with the ubiquitous Spanish omelette *Tortilla de Patatas* made with thinly sliced potato and onion. The Navarrese love a sense of occasion and this is no more apparent than in the running of the bulls held during the festival of San Fermín in Pamplona in early July (to be avoided like the plague if you are on a solitary pilgrimage).

REFLECTIONS: *"I am doing the camino once again, looking for something I left behind or perhaps never found. It's like coming home."* Notes from a returning pilgrim from New Mexico recorded in the Pilgrim book in Roncesvalles. What are your reflections for this opening day?

_____
_____
_____
_____
_____
_____
_____
_____
_____
_____
_____
_____
_____
_____
_____

❐ **Whatever you can do, or dream you can; begin it.**
Boldness has genius power and magic in it. *Goethe*

MAP 02 *770.9 km (479.0 miles) to Santiago de Compostela*

RONCESVALLES – LARRASOAÑA

▬▬▬	Path / Track	--- ---	24.9 ---	91%
▬▬▬	Quiet Road	--- ---	1.0 ---	4%
▬▬▬	Main Road	--- ---	1.5 ---	5%
Total km	**Total distance**		**27.4 km** (17.0 miles)	

◣ Adjusted for climb   28.7 km (accrued ascent 270m = 1.3 km)
Alto ▲ High Point: Alto de Mezquíriz 955m (3,133 feet)

The Practical Path: Take care not to over extend yourself on these first few days of your journey. This second stage leads downhill across the fertile plain of the río Erro that flows southwards to join the río Ebro that we will meet in Logroño. The Alto de Erro forms the ridge that separates the Erro from the Arga river valleys. There is good woodland shade and plenty of drinking fonts along this delightful section of the camino 91% of which is natural pathways running more or less parallel to the N-135 which it crosses at several points. Close gates *cierren el portillo* as you pass through and be careful of the steep descent into Zubiri – the exposed rock makes it very slippery, particularly in wet weather. *An alternative for the next 3 stages is: [1] Roncessvalles – Zubiri 22.2 km [2] Zubiri – Pamplona 22.1 km [3] Pamplona - Puente la Reina 22.0 km.*

Note: If you are feeling tired and it is getting late in the day when you reach Zubiri consider staying here and plan staying in Pamplona the following day. It is a further 5.5 km to the hostel in the more traditional and popular pilgrim halt in Larrasoaña – allow 2 hours for a slower 'end of day pace'. **Intermediate accommodation:** Burguete *Auritz* (3.0 km) – Espinal *Aurizberri* (6.5 km) – Gerendian *Biskarreta* (11.8 km).

❐ **The Mystical Path:** Will you notice the *Pasos de Roldán?* The largest of these boulders is said to represent the footsteps of Roland – whose footsteps do *you* follow? Other legends have this melancholy place as another scene of Roland's failed attempt to summon Charlemagne to his rescue. Perhaps, in the silence of your own heart, you may still hear the wail of the Oliphant – symbol of that clarion call to be rescued from a world of pain and suffering that can only end in death and decay. Will you rest awhile at the old pilgrim well and hear a different horn break the woodland silence, a harsh and urgent note of warning from the fast moving traffic – a reminder to pilgrims that we travel now at a slower pace; one that allows time and awareness to expand.

P
A
C
El Camino ☎ 948-304 250

0.2 Albergue *Muni.[80]*

Puente **5.3** ►

LARRASOAÑA *(Pop. 200 – Alt. 500m)*

Esquirotz

Illarratz

Fabrica

Osteritz

H

ZUBIRI *(Pop. 500 – Alt. 520m)*

P
A

◄ **0.3** Albergue *Muni.[46]*

Puente de la Rabia **3.6**

río Arga

☎ 609-736 420 *Zaldiko Priv.* *[24]*

Embalse de Eugui

Venta del Puerto *(Ruinas)*

Alto de Erro **4.5**

▲810m

N-135

● **Paso do Roldán**

F

2.0 Linzoáin

río Erro

Gerendiain/*Viskarret* **3.4**
C

La Posada Nueva

1.9 Alto de Mezquiriz

955m

Casa Rural
C

Espinal/*Aurizberri* **3.5**

N-135

F

río Urrobi

O

Puesta del Sol

S

N

Salida del Sol

E

río Urrobi

*Loizu***** H

Burguete/*Auritz* **3.0** ►

H *Burguete*

Pensión Iturrialdea H

camino Canonigos

Cruceiro†

(Pop. 30 – Alt. 960m)

RONCESVALLES /*Orreaga*

A ◄ **0.0** Albergue

† *Alt. 950m*

❑ **Personal Reflections:** "…a blister has already formed on my left foot to balance the bruise on my right shoulder. Was it arrogance or absent-mindedness that made me ignore the advice to stop and tighten my shoelaces and backpack – 60 seconds of adjustment would have prevented the friction and saved days of unnecessary suffering. I have become so conditioned to travelling in the fast lane, always trying to get somewhere in the shortest possible time, that I forget that the present moment contains the only time there is to actually act – all else is psychological time leading to stress …and unnecessary blisters."

Leaving Roncesvalles albergue continue down the N-135 veering off right> at the camino information signboard **[0.2 km]** onto woodland path parallel to the main road (14th century pilgrim cross on far side) and rejoin road at the outskirts of Burguete **[2.0 km]** and continue for **[0.8 km]** through suburbs to:

3.0 km Burguete *Auritz* a traditional Navarese village at the start of which we find •**Hotel Burguete** Hs** (948-760 005) where Ernest Hemingway used to stay (it still has the piano bearing his signature 25/07/1923). The sombre central square is overshadowed by the *Iglesia de San Nicolás de Barri (a Saint closely identified with the camino and protector of pilgrims; but alas no help to the wise women of the area that were classified as witches and burnt at the stake here in the 16th century.)* Café Frontón serves breakfast to the throng of pilgrims arriving from Roncesvalles (if there are queues consider going on to Espinal or Viskarret), public toilets adjoin. Other central accommodation •**Jaundeaburre** Hs*(948-760 078) •**Pensión Iturrialdea** P*(948-760 243) and on the far side of town the up-market •**Loizu** H***(948-760 008).

100m past the square turn right> [!] down beside the *Banco Santander* and over the river Urrobi onto a wide farm track. At far end ford a small stream to enter a delightful woodland path to join a new asphalt track [F] left down into:

3.5 km Espinal *Aurizberri* another traditional village with the parish Church of Saint Bartholomew *Iglesia de San Bartolomé* (left) as we enter and café/bar in the central square (right). Continue along main street passing •**CR Errebesena** (948-760 141) & •**CR Haizea** Hs (948-760 399) **[F]** (left) and turn off <left **[0.3 km]** onto quiet road which merges into a track and continue for **[1.6 km]** up through young forestry plantation, climbing steps into mature beech woods at the high point 955m and finally down through open fields to:

1.9 km Alto de Mezquiriz (Alt. 930m) cross N-135 [!] by stone plaque to the Virgin and Child and continue on the path down steeply through beech woods running above and parallel to the main road (path has been resurfaced and can be slippery when wet so watch your step [!]). Cross the río Erro on stepping-stones before finally crossing the N-135 into:

3.4 km Gerendiain *Viskarret/Bizkarreta* ancient hamlet and beginning of stage II of the Codex Calixtinus with the 13th century

Church of St. Peter. Café Juan is in the square opposite casa rural •**La Posada Nueva** CR (948-760 173) also •**Refugio Sorogain** Aterpeak (948-392 025). On leaving village there is a deceptively good shop (left) after which turn <left onto path and <left again where path meets road through dense woodland and after **[1.2 km]** cross over N-135 again and continue for **[0.8 km]** into:

2.0 km **Linzoáin** pass pelota court **[F]** (right) and climb steep narrow defile (recently concreted) into dense mixed woodland. This delightful shaded woodland path continues along a ridge and the *Pasos de Roldán* until we meet:

4.5 km **Alto de Erro** (Alt. 810m) crossover N-135 to camino information signboard (left) and into woodlands passing a former pilgrim inn *Venta del Puerto* (now a ruin and cattle shelter) and descend steep rock outcrop **[!]** (dangerous in wet weather) to:

3.6 km **Puente de la Rabia** medieval bridge over the Río Arga *so called because of the legend that any animal led 3 times around the central arch would be cured of rabies. This is also the likely site of a former leprosarium. Chapels and hospices dedicated to San Lazarus were often located at the entrance or exit to towns along the way.* We will cross the river Arga many times over the next few days until we finally leave it at Puente la Reina.

If you are feeling strong *fuerte* continue to the albergue in Larrasoaña (5.6 km) further on. The busy N-135 bypasses this latter historic village which is quieter and more in keeping with the spirit of the camino. This would also allow you more time the following day to explore the historic city of Pamplona before proceeding, perhaps, to Cizur Menor (see next stages). If you are feeling tired or it is late in the day then turn right> over the bridge into the industrial town of:

Zubiri •**Albergue** [1] *Zaldiko* (609-736 420) private hostel in terraced brick house between the bridge and church. Open all year with 24 beds in 4 rooms and all facilities + small patio. Continue past the church and turn right> on main road to •**Albergue** [2] on the left 100m. Basic municipal hostel located directly on the N-135 in a former school building. Open all year with 46 spaces (2 dormitories) the basic facilities have additional showers and toilets in porta-cabins at the rear.

Albergue [1] Zaldiko

ZUBIRI: A small industrial town with a population 500 whose main street is the busy N-135. It serves the adjacent Magna plant *Magnesitas de Navarra*. The limited facilities include a welcoming grocery shop, bank and panadería centred around the parish Church of St. Stephen *San Esteban* with **[F]**. Other accommodation: Adjoining the bridge •**Pensión Zubiaren Etxea** (948-304 293) opposite albergue Zaldiko is •**Pensión Usoa** P*(948-304 306) and on the main road •**Hostería de Zubiri** Hs (948-304 329) and •**Pensión Goika** P*(948-304 067).

Albergue [2] Municipal

From the medieval bridge *Puente de la Rabia* continue up concrete path **[F]** (left) and continue over a stream to climb above the bleak Magnesitas industrial complex (down to your right) and through the hamlets of Ostériz, Ilarratz and Esquirroz (**[F]** and covered rest area) and along the Arga river valley to:

5.3 km **Puente Larrasoaña** medieval bridge. *(If you stayed the night in Zubiri and do not plan to visit this historic pilgrim village keep straight on for Pamplona).* Turn right> over the bridge and past the 13th Century Church of San Nicolás and veer <left into the village square with town hall and:

0.2 km **Larrasoaña** •**Albergue** a popular municipal hostel (948-304 242) open all year with 42+ places (28 beds in one dormitory and remainder on mattresses

colchones in small rooms upstairs). The basic facilities include a small open patio at rear and an additional 40 beds (on 2 floors) in a converted nearby outbuilding that is brought into service during busy periods. The extensive church porch also provides a 'floor and roof' in times of need. A warm welcome can be expected from the energetic mayor *alcalde*, a friend of the Way of St. James *amigo del Camino de Santiago*. I walked much of the way to Santiago with him in previous years and know he has first-hand experience of the needs of fellow pilgrims.

Albergue Larrasoaña

Other accommodation: Pensión •**El Camino** P* (948-304 250) at the far end of the village in c/San Nicolás, 16 (350m past the main square) also serves as a popular pilgrim meeting point with café-bar and restaurant Casa Salgado serving pilgrim *menú* and breakfast from 07:00. At the other end of town are •**El Peregrino** P* (948-304 554) and •**Bidea** P* (948-304 288) c/San Nicolás, 100. Casa Elita, a small food shop is also located in this area.

Pension El Camino & pilgrim Bar

Pension El Peregrino

LARRASOAÑA: This quaint town (population 200) has retained its close links with the pilgrim's Way. An important pilgrim halt in medieval times with 2 pilgrim hospitals and a monastery (no longer evident) it achieved the status of *Villa Franca* (a settlement of pilgrims arriving from France). Today it continues to welcome pilgrims and provide hospitality in its various hostelries.

REFLECTIONS: *"Worrying is praying for what you don't want."* From the pilgrim book in Zubiri.

_____
_____
_____
_____
_____
_____
_____
_____
_____
_____
_____
_____
_____
_____
_____
_____
_____
_____
_____
_____
_____
_____
_____
_____
_____
_____
_____
_____
_____
_____
_____
_____
_____

❐ **I am not a human being on a spiritual journey.**
I am spiritual being on a human journey. *Spiritual maxim*

MAP 03 *743.5 km (462.0 miles) to Santiago de Compostela*

LARRASOAÑA – CIZUR MENOR

▬▬▬	Path / Track	--- ---	9.2	--- *44%*
▬▬▬	Quiet Road	--- ---	2.8	--- *13%*
▬▬▬	Main Road (city)	---	8.9	--- *43%*
Total km	**Total distance**		**20.9 km** (13.0 miles)	

Adjusted for climb   22.7 km (accrued ascent 360m = 1.8 km)
Alto ▲   High Point: Monte Miravalles 700m (2,296 feet)

The Practical Path: The first half of this section is a tranquil walk crisscrossing the río Arga. The latter half is along busy main roads leading into and through the city of Pamplona. There is plenty of shade along the tree-lined river banks and a number of drinking fonts along the way. Be prepared for the noise and bustle of city life after the relative calm of the camino. City folk are forever in a rush, so tread warily amongst the traffic and watch your wallet. Pilgrims have reported items stolen from the suburbs of Trinidad de Arre onwards – 'Trust in God, but tether your camel,' feels like balanced advice. Pamplona is also a beautiful city and the camino runs through its historic heart – so you can soak up some of the lively atmosphere and its major buildings by just walking the waymarked route. Many pilgrims make an overnight stop here so they can visit the cathedral, museums and art galleries and explore Pamplona's medieval streets and sample some of its famous cafés and tapas bars. **Intermediate accommodation:** Akerreta (1.2 km) – Trinidad de Arre (11.2 km) – Villalba (12.0) – (Huarte 13.2 km, 2 km *off* route) – Pamplona (15.8 km)

❐ **The Mystical Path:** Will you notice the ancient stone cross with the delicate relief of St. James as pilgrim atop the scallop shell? It stands sentinel over the magnificent medieval bridge, gateway to this historic city. The sightless eyes have watched countless thousands of pilgrims wend their wary way over these self-same arches. And what of the invisible eye that sees beyond space and time, gateway to the inner realm of spirit. One path is full of distraction, distortion and decay. The other leads to the real world where only truth is visible. Which world you see depends on which you are looking for.

❐ **Personal Reflections:** *"... So many contrasting sensations – the quiet of the countryside, the bustle of the city, the warmth of the sun, the cool of the rain, the perfume of the wild flowers, the acrid smell of burning rubbish, the bright red of the ubiquitous poppy, the dull grey of asphalt road. I sit supported by my rucksack and watch the wild grasses and wheat stalks swaying in the wind. My lunch is laid out before me like a royal feast with local cheese and freshly baked bread acquired from a travelling baker's van. I feel an overwhelming sense of*

Roncal ☎ 948-183 885 **Priv.[50]**Albergue 2.8 Ⓐ
(Pop. 700 – Alt. 480m) **CIZUR MENOR**
St. Juan Asoc.[27] → Ⓐ

Ⓗ *Nekea*
**Cizur
Maior**

A-15

N-111

río Sadar   río Arga

A-15

N-240

*Universidad
de Navarra*

Cruce 2.3

PAMPLONA
(Pop. 190,000)

Amaiur Udal Ikastola

*Parque
Ciudadela*

*Parque
Tacoñera*

N-240

Juvenil YHA Ⓙ

Plaza de Toros ○

San Cernin

Seminario †

*Plaza
Castillo*

Ⓐ 2.2 **Albergue** *Jesús y María Asoc.[114]*

PA-30

Catedral

Jardinería →

Puente Magdelena

2.4 **Cruce**

Albergue 2.0

Burlada Ⓗ **Burlada**

PA-30

Ⓐ**Huarte**

*Monte
Miravalles*

Ⓗ *Obelix*
Villava

3.1 **Albergue** *Trinadad de Arre Conv.[36]* Ⓐ

—**Tuñél**

PA-30

Arleta
Monte Nerval

Ⓕ 3.8 **Parque** *(Fuente)*

† **Zabaldica**

Ⓕ **Parque** *(Fuente)*

Puente Irotz (Iturgaiz)

Irotz †

río Arga

N-135

Illurdotz ○

3.1 **Zuriáin**

río Ulzama

N-121

S   W
Sunset

Sunrise
E

N

Akerreta 1.0 Ⓕ
Akerreta ☎ 948-304 572 Ⓗ

LARRASOAÑA (Pop. 200 – Alt. 500m)

Ⓐ 0.0 **Albergue** *Muni.[80]*

Puente 0.2 →

*well-being and, somewhat self-consciously, say out loud that beautiful grace
with which to bless the richness of this day and my simple meal:*

> *The silver rain, the shining sun, the fields were scarlet poppies run
> And all the ripples in the wheat are in the food that I do eat
> So when I sit for every meal and say a grace, I always feel
> That I am eating rain and sun and fields were scarlet poppies run.*

If you have been staying in Larrasoaña return to the medieval bridge:

0.2 km **Akerreta** turn right> to climb up to the tranquil hilltop village of:

1.0 km **Akerreta** •Hotel (948-304 572) well restored Basque house. Continue
downhill through open country to rejoin the river Arga before crossing into:

3.1 km **Zuriáin** Here we join the N-135 for **[0.6 km]** turning off <left
(signposted Illurdotz). Re-cross the river Arga **[0.3 km]** and continue right>
between group of houses (dogs) and abandoned buildings climbing up a narrow
quarry path overlooking the Arga valley. The path drops down again through the
hamlet of Irotz and across the river again over the medieval stone bridge *Puente
de Iturgaiz / Irotz* **[1.6 km]** turning <left along the river bank with rest area **[F]**
and up to Zabaldika with 13th church (off route right) turn <left onto track that
bypasses this tiny hamlet and cross over the N-135 **[1.3 km]** to:

3.8 km **Parque** picnic site with toilets and **[F]** turn up right> onto steep track
(eroded) that skirts *Monte Narval* entering tunnel **[1.9 km]** under the busy
ring road PA-30. From here you climb around the side of pine-covered *Monte
Miravalles* Alto 495m **[0.4 km]** to join a disused road that drops down to the
magnificent medieval bridge over the río Ulzama (tributary of the Arga) just
above a weir and here we enter the suburbs of Pamplona in Villava **[0.8 km]**:

3.1 km **Trinidad de Arre** •Albergue
monastery hostel *Hermanos Maristas*
located behind the basilica church Convento
de la Trinidad adjoining the bridge. Check-
in first at the front reception – no urgency,
there has been a pilgrim hospital here since
the 11th century! Open all year with 36 beds
(3 rooms) and all facilities in this quiet
location adjoining the river with peaceful
gardens. There are shops and restaurants
close by in the suburb of Villava. *[Next
Albergue – Huarte 2.5 km (2.0 km off route)
or Pamplona centre 4.6 km].*

Albergue Trinidad de Arre
Río Ulzama

Note: for the next 9.7 km (until you reach Cizur Menor on the western outskirts)
the camino winds through the busy city of Pamplona (population 190,000) a
vibrant university city built around the historical old town at its centre. The
recommended route will bring you past most of the main sites and is generally
well waymarked but you need to be extra vigilant for the yellow arrows which
now appear on every conceivable surface such as lampposts and pavements
but have to compete with many other signs. You also need to watch out for the
fast moving traffic and your belongings – petty theft has always been a problem
in our unequal society. Medieval pilgrims were sometimes murdered for their
satchels and sandals!

Turn <left over the bridge at Arre and continue along Calle Mayor in Villava to the Town Hall **[0.5 km]** *Casa Consistorial* (flags) and café Paradiso.

Detour: 2.0 km to the albergue at Huarte (not waymarked). Directions: opposite the *Café Paradiso*, turn left past the Frontón and continue straight over road and pedestrian bridge (río Ulzama) by Plastico Brello. Veer right and join the main road that runs along the Río Arga [0.4 km]. Don't cross the road bridge but turn left (sign Uharte) and follow the road (and river) all the way into Huarte up the wide main street to the main square. •**Albergue Huarte** located behind the church (right hand side of main street) new municipal hostel (Tel: 948-074 329). Open all year with 60 beds (10 rooms) and all modern facilities. Return the same way to pick up waymarks again at Villava.

Albergue Huarte

Continue s/o through the busy suburbs of **Burlada** for **[1.9 km]** with various modern hotels and cafés, •**Obelix** P*(948-126 056) •**La Buhardilla** Hs (948-382 872) •**Hotel Villava** H***(948-333 676). Watch out [!] for waymarks veering diagonally right> by Banco Pastor into C/Larrainzar (neumaticos sign) up to main road (traffic lights) with garden centre

| **2.4 km** | **Cruce** Cross over to garden centre *Jardineria Arvena*. |

For an **alternative road route** turn <left and immediately right> up into Av. de la Baja Navarra passing the huge cross and edifice of the Seminario Diocesano (whose student accommodation is sometime made available to pilgrims during vacations) and turn right> into and through Parque de la Media Luna to rejoin the recommended route at the cathedral which is clearly visible at this stage.

For the **recommended route** veer right> and make your way over the pedestrian crossing by garden centre turning <left into c/ Burlada, a quiet road that runs parallel to the river Arga and crosses over it at the evocative 12th medieval bridge *Puente de la Magdalena* **[1.4 km]** which has become a traditional symbol of the camino. [*Note:* Turn left over bridge for 200m to •**Albergue** *Casa Paderborn* located by the river at Playa de Caparroso, 6. (Tel: 660 631 656) operated by a German confraternity. 24 places in 5 rooms with good facilities.]

Albergue Casa Paderborn

To proceed directly to the city centre veer right> over bridge, cross the tree-lined Playa Caparroso veering right> around the old city walls entering this historic city over the drawbridge and the splendid Portal de Zumalacárregi **[0.5 km]** also called Portal de Francia – a reminder that Pamplona has always opened its doors to pilgrims coming from France since mediaeval times. (Note: immediately inside the city walls there is an option to turn up sharp <left along the ramparts and viewpoint and veer right into the shaded square Plaza San

José to the Cathedral of Santa María la Real). An austere Gothic structure with a neoclassical façade. If you are staying the night in the adjacent albergue you can leave your backpack there and return to visit the interior which is much more satisfying than the stark edifice. The 15thC alabaster mausoleum of Carlos *El Noble* and his wife Leonor adorns the main nave but pride of place is the beautiful south door *puerta preciosa* ascribed to Master

Pamplona Cathedral
Plateresque Cloisters

Esteban who also carved the south door *Puerta de las Platerias* in Santiago Cathedral. The beautiful cloisters, with their fine filigree stonework, adjoin the diocesan museum (site of the original Roman citadel). Pamplona's new pilgrim hostel is only 100m down off calle Curia:

The main route (from Portal de Francia) continues s/o into calle Carmen (*antiguo Rua de los Pergrinos*) to the cross of 5 roads [**0.2 km**]. To continue through the city centre turn right into c/ de Mercederes or turn <left into c/Curia to visit the cathedral and pilgrim hostel [**0.1 km**].

Pamplona Albergue
Jesús y María

| 2.2 km | Albergue Pamplona's pilgrim hostel is part of the austere 17thC Jesuit church of *Jesús y María* on calle Compañía (closed December, January & during San Fermín festival in early July). 114 beds built into the side naves with all modern facilities. Good location from which to explore the old town.

Other accommodation: In the old city around San Saturnino is a wide selection of small and inexpensive hotels and pensions (check with the tourist office for current listings and see town plan for locations) these include: •**Lambertini** P* (948-210 303) c/Mercadore, 17. •**La Viña** P (948-213 250) c/Jarauta, 8 •**Pensión Eslava** P* (948-221 558) c/Eslava, 13. •**Escaray** P (948-227 825) c/Nueva, 24. In c/San Nicolás are: #5 •**Pensión Otano** P** (948-227 036). #13 •**San Nicolás** P* (948-221 319). #24 •**Don Lluis** Hs (948-210 499), and #12 •**Aralar** Hs (948-221 116). In c/San Gregorio (an extension of c/San Nicolás) are #2 •**La Montañesa** P* (948-224 380) and #5 •**Dionisio** P* (948-224 380).

At the far end of c/Mayor (behind the Convento Recoletas) is •**Hotel Eslava** Hr** (948-222 270) which overlooks the tiny *Plaza Virgen de la O* and forms part of the old city walls and leads directly into the spacious Parque Traconera. In the top price bracket is the modern 4 star Tres Reyes on our route out and the newly refurbished 5 star •**La Perla** H (948-223 000) on Plaza del Castillo (Hemingway used to stay here). During the hectic summer months additional pilgrim accommodation *may*

Calle San Nicolás

be available at: •**San Saturnino** (city centre) – •**Catholic Scouts** (Puente de la Magdalena) – • **Seminario Diocesano** on Av. de la Baja Navarra – •**Ikastola Aimur** sports hall at calle Fuente del Hierro (on way out of the city near the University of Navarre) – •**Albergue Juvenil** the youth hostel in the southern suburbs at calle Gorabe, 36 (beyond the football stadium near Milagrosa).

Pamplona Detours: [1] If you are a Hemingway *aficianado* take a trip down the Paseo Ernest Hemingway to a statue of the author outside the bull ring *plaza de Toros*. His novel 'The Sun Also Rises' published in 1926 made *Sanfermines* popular among foreigners so that today it has become one of the best-known fiestas in Spain. Records suggest the festival was started in the 13th century but may have pre-Roman origins and some legends suggest that San Fermín himself was martyred by being dragged

San Fermin – Souvenir shop

by bulls thorough the streets. Alcohol is probably the biggest cause of injury and death today despite rule 6 that states, 'it is not allowed to enter the route in a state of drunkenness or under the effects of drugs'. Return via *calle Estafeta* the famous street through which the bulls run as part of this world-renowned *Encierro* that takes place during San Fermín from July 6th to 14th when the city goes wild, beds are impossible to find and everything costs double.

Detour [2] just off the calle Estafeta is Pamplona's main square *Plaza del Castillo*, a huge open space with covered arcades shading the shops, bars and cafés. Don't miss the magnificent and sumptuous *interior* of the art deco café Iruña. Bar Txoko (top corner - gets the last of the evening sun) has splendid tapas. From the square it is a short walk to the Romanesque Church of St. Nicholas situated half way down the bustling and evocative *c/San Nicolás*

Plaza del Castillo

full of inexpensive *pensiónes* and *tapas bars* or head back to the camino via c/Chapitela into the Plaza Consistorial with the splendid ornamental façade of the town hall dominating the square.

Detour [3] If you want to visit the Museo de Navarra turn down right behind the town hall into c/Santo Domingo and at the far end is the classical facade of the medieval pilgrim hospital, now the Navarrese museum with Roman artefacts from the first century. Head back to the camino and at the start of c/Mayor we arrive at the geographical centre of Pamplona at San Saturnino a 13th century fortified church also called San Cernín and formerly the main pilgrim hostel on the upper floors. If you

Pamplona Town Hall
Plaza Consistorial

are staying in Pamplona this is a good place to take your bearings. Just in front of the church (in the paving slabs) is a plaque marking the well from which San Saturnino baptised the first Christians in the city. The helpful tourist office (948-206 540) is nearby (200m) down c/Campana in Plaza de San Francisco at the corner of c/Eslava (see city plan).

PAMPLONA with an ever expanding population (currently around 200,000) is a vibrant university city that retains its close historical connections with the camino and whose patron Saint is San Fermín. The Roman general Pompaelo reputedly founded the city in the first century B.C. Its long and dramatic history has been closely linked with pilgrims, many of who were enticed to settle in the city under special status. This migration often created petty jealousies between the native inhabitants and the favoured settlers, resulting in the development of separate districts, which later became fortified as open hostilities raged between the inhabitants and their differing cultures. In 1423 King Carlos conceded the Privilege of the Union,

Pamplona Cathedral
Calle Curia *(pilgrim hostel right)*

which extended the special status to all parts of the city and began an era of cooperation. Several other towns and cities along the Way such as at Estella (stage 5) followed a similar pattern of agreement and development. Pamplona marks the beginning of stage III of the Codex Calixtinus.

You could easily spend a day here exploring the many interesting monuments and museums, or… from the cathedral / pilgrim hostel continue back down the c/Curia (opposite the entrance to the cathedral) which leads into c/Mercaderes and up past the Iglesia San Saturnino into the narrow c/Mayor which opens out into the Plaza Recoletas (right) and Iglesia de San Lorenzo (left) with its chapel to the patron saint of Pamplona, San Fermín.

Museo Diocesano

Here we cross over the busy street into c/Bosquecillo alongside the Parque de la Taconera (right). At the busy junction of Av. de Pio XII and Av. del Ejército veer <left diagonally over the junction (pedestrian crossings) and through the relative calm of the park that surrounds the historic star-shaped citadel *ciudadela* (left). Halfway round the park watch out for arrows that veer off right> over the c/Vuelta del Castillo into c/Fuente del Hierro •**Fuente del Hierro** P* (948-178 270) and follow this wide tree-lined modern thoroughfare to:

| 2.3 km | **Cruce** Junction of c/Fuente del Hierro with c/de Iturrama. The school campus of Amaiur Udal Ikastola (right) makes its sports hall available for groups and possibly individual pilgrims to sleep in during the summer months. For additional hotels in this modern area of Iturrama veer right off the main camino and follow the connecting road for 300m that curves around between 2 playgrounds and links up with Av. Pio XII (the Clinica Universitaria and hotel

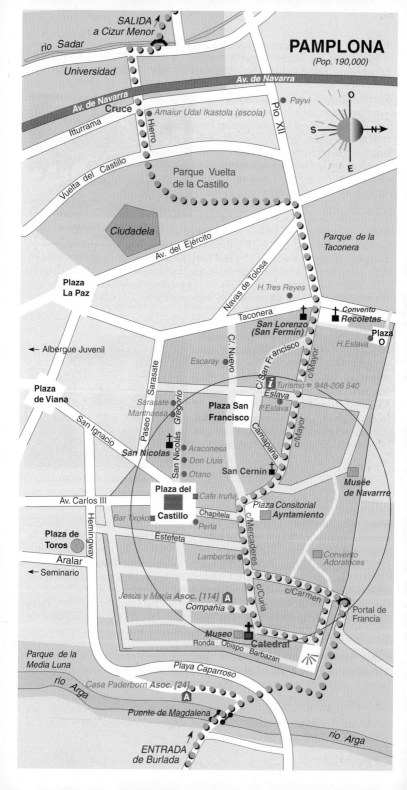

Blanca are visible at this next junction). There are a number of small *pensiónes* in this city area including •**Payvi II & Payvi III** P* (948-278 508) Av. Pío XII, 30 (adjoining petrol station) and •**Pasadena** P* (948-177 650) Av. Pío XII, 32.

Continuing on from Fuente del Hierro-Iturrama roundabout, pass under the busy Av. de Navarra ring road along the university campus. Here on the left **[0.7 km]** we can receive 'accreditation' from the university by having our credenciales stamped by the porter. Continue to the roundabout veering right> along main road and <left across the stone bridge over the Río Sadar **[0.3 km]**. Continue straight on over the Río Elorz **[0.4 km]** the railway line and the A-15 autopista

Pedestrian Bridge
Río Sadar

and uphill along the main road for **[1.4 km]** into Cizur Menor and the to church of St. John the Baptist (left) and: •**Albergue** [2] *Sanjuanista* run by the Knights of St. John (Joaquin Mencos 600-386 891) adjoining the first church on the left as you enter the town. Open June to September with 27 beds (3 rooms) and basic facilities.

2.8 km Cizur Menor crossroads.
•**Albergue** [1] *Roncal* (Maribel Roncal 948-183 885) located just up from the crossroads (below the church of San Miguel). Open all year and run by the dedicated Roncal family with 50 beds (5 rooms) with all facilities including a garden offering tranquillity – very popular and fills quickly during the summer season.

Albergue [1] Roncal
Cizur Menor

Note: If the albergues are full your options are [a] retrace your steps and find accommodation in Pamplona or its suburbs (a local bus service connects from here to the city centre). [b] Head over to Cizur Maior to the ultra modern 4 star hotel •**AC Zizur Mayor** (948-287 119) or the more modest •**Hostal Nekea** (948-185 044) Travesia San Francisco, 1 (Directions: head uphill past the church and take the flyover (autopista) [1.0 km] to the hotel or turn left up the main street to the far end to hostal Nekea [0.7 km] a total of 1.7 km from Cizur Menor. From this point the quickest way back onto the camino is to take the road to Galar) or [c] continue on to the albergues and casa rurales in Uterga 12 km.

Cizur Menor an affluent dormitory town of Pamplona. It was formerly a commandery of the Order of St. John of Jerusalem and also provided a pilgrim hospice dedicated to Our Lady of Forgiveness *Nuestra Señora del Perdón*, who was, and remains, much venerated in this area. Occupying an elevated site is the 12th century Romanesque church dedicated to the archangel Saint Michael *Iglesia de San Miguel Arcángel*. There are several restaurants (often closed in during week days) a bar and a chemist.

REFLECTIONS: *"The camino already feels like a real pilgrimage and has developed a deeper significance than when I began. I am stronger and have more courage than I thought. I have already been given many blessings and gifts..."* Notes from an Australia pilgrim recorded in Pamplona albergue.

❏ **Be the change you want to see in the world.** *Mahatma Gandhi*

MAP 4 *724.9 km (450.0 miles) to Santiago de Compostela*

CIZUR MENOR - PUENTE LA REINA

▬▬▬	Path / Track	--- ---	17.1 ---	*90%*
▬▬▬	Quiet Road	--- ---	1.5 ---	*8%*
▬▬▬	Main Road	--- ---	0.4 ---	*2%*
Total km	**Total distance**		**19.0 km** (11.8 miles)	

▲ Adjusted for climb   20.7 km (accrued ascent 350m = 1.7 km)
Alto ▲ High Point: Alto de Perdón 790m (2,590 feet)

The Practical Path: A short stage *(add 5.1 km from Pamplona centre)* with few trees and therefore little shade. Ahead of us lie a range of hills and we have a steep climb up to pass through the middle of the wind turbines *parque ecológico* visible on the skyline ahead at the Hill of Forgiveness *Alto del Perdón*. As we ascend there are wonderful views back over Pamplona and to the south the conical peak of *Higa* at Monreal is clearly visible, behind which are the Sierra de Leyre and the Somport Pass through which the *Camino Aragonés* joins the route at Eunate. As we crest the summit the view west over the Arga valley opens up with the villages we pass through now visible ahead. Be careful on the steep descent – it is easy to twist an ankle on the loose boulders. **Intermediate accommodation** (distances from albergue [1] in Cizur Menor): Zariquiegui 6.2 km – Uterga 12.3 km – Óbanos 16.7 km – Eunate 17.4 km (off route).

❏ **The Mystical Path:** Will you see the beehives? Each home to thousands of bees that collect nectar from the almond blossom and other flowering trees and plants that grace this fertile plain in the springtime. In the winter all is laid bare and the hives lie dormant waiting a time of renewal. Each season dresses the physical landscape in its different hues – what is the season of your *inner* landscape? Is it time to sow new seeds, a time of growth, of harvest or a time of reflection in the deep rich soil of the soul? The seasons turn in an endless cycle of life. After the dark of the winter solstice comes the light of mid summer day and in between these high and low points are the spring and autumn equinoxes when light and dark are perfectly balanced. Have we got the balance right in our life between the busyness of the ego and the beingness of spirit?

❏ **Personal Reflections:** *"... I saw her ahead on the road to Cizur Menor, a diminutive figure walking alone into the dusk. We were both making for the hostel unknowing that Maribel Roncal had closed it that year to take a well-earned rest. Dusk turned to nightfall as we contemplated our options. She was a young mendicant carrying no money and accepting only whatever charity*

☎ 948-340 220 Santiago Apostol *Priv.*[100]*

A

río Arga

PUENTE LA REINA
(Pop. 2,500 – Alt. 350m)

Padres Reparadores Conv.[100]

Albergue [1] 4.4 ➤ A 2.3 **Albergue [1]**

A *Jakue Priv.*[38]*
☎ 948-341 017

N-111

A-12

Arnotegui †

C *Casa Ossés*
■ **ÓBANOS**
A *Juan Irisarri Priv.[36]*
1.8 **Albergue**

Eunate 2.5 † A

Camino Aragonés

† 2.6 **Muruzábal**

Albergue 3.7 ➤ A **UTERGA**
Camino del Perdon Priv. [18] † *Muni.[2]*

▲

Puesta del Sol **O**

S

Alt. 790m ☼
Alto del Perdón 2.4 ← *monumento peregrino*

Salida del Sol

● *Fuente Reniega*

E

Zariquigui Priv. [16] A
Iglesia / Fuente 3.6 ➤
ZARIQUIEGUI

A-12

Galar ●

Guenduláin (Ruinas)

Cruce 2.6 ➤

Ⓗ *Nekea*

Cizur Maior

Fuente Románica ●

Ⓗ *AC Zizur Mayor*

Roncal Priv. **Albergue** [1] 0.0

CIZUR MENOR
(Pop. 700 – Alt. 480m) ■

N-111

she received along the way. She accepted a simple pilgrim meal at the bar but refused to take any emergency cash. I was the one imprisoned by my fears – my wallet thick with euros and credit cards. She was free, fearless and with an unshakable belief in the goodness of her fellow human beings. Her courage and trust leave me deeply humbled and with a profound sense of unease at my own doubts and limitations…"

Leaving albergue [1] in Cizur Menor turn right> at the crossroads (if coming from Pamplona continue s/o) and veer right> opposite medieval well, down past the pelota court [F] and continue through modern housing estate to a dirt road which threads its way all the way up to the village of Zariquiegui (below the wind farm on the horizon). The path winds through open arable fields to:

2.6 km **Cruce** cross asphalt road to Galar visible on a knoll up to the left. (*It was over this very ground that Charlemagne's Christian forces defeated Aigolando's Muslim army in the 8th century. Today a more peaceful spot is hard to imagine as we leave the city behind us*). Further on the path crosses a stream as we begin a gentle climb (bypassing the ruins of Guenduláin palace in the woods to the right – visible once we have cleared the trees) to:

3.6 km **Zariquiegui** prominent Church of Saint Andrew *San Andrés* with Romanesque doorway and **[F]**. 50m up the street opposite •**Albergue** (Tel: 948-353 353) pilgrim hostel opened in 2009 with 16 beds. No shop or bar in the village so you would need to buy food in Cizur if you plan to stay. Continue up steeply towards the wind turbines and just below the ridge is the ancient spring (dry) *Gambellacos* **[2.2 km]**. *Fuente Reniega (renouncement). A medieval pilgrim reached this spot dying of thirst. The devil, disguised as a pilgrim, offered to show him a spring if he would only renounce God. The pilgrim refused and St. James himself miraculously appeared revealing the spring and quenching his thirst with water in a scallop shell. Today, the well is dry (a sign, perhaps, of the spiritual aridity of our times) but we can look back over Pamplona and the Pyrenees beyond them and reflect on our own journey to this point. The hum of the wind generators above remind of us the possibilities of creating another, more sustainable future.* A final climb **[0.2 km]** and we reach the summit:

2.4 km **Alto del Perdón** (altitude 790m) featuring a wrought iron representation of medieval pilgrims, heads bent to the west wind. An information board gives a brief outline of this area and the ecological project (renewable energy) it fosters. Looking ahead are the villages we will pass through spread out below lining the route westwards. The conical peak of Monte Arnotegui with hermitage atop is situated overlooking Puente de la Reina and is just visible ahead on the horizon. Descend [!] carefully over the loose stones and through the scrubland to the rich red earth, vineyards and almond trees below. Here the path winds along a delightful ridge running parallel to a quiet country road that you join at:

3.7 km **Uterga [F]** •**Albergue [1]** directly opposite the fountain is a basic municipal hostel in the main square. Open all year with 1 bunk bed for 2 with floor space (supposedly) for 2 more in 1 very small room with shower & toilet off. No kitchen or other space but well maintained (keep it that way if you are staying). •**Albergue [2]** *Camino del Perdón* (Ana Calvo Cano 948-344 661) modern private hostel also on c/Mayor and open all

Uterga – Albergue [2]

year with 18 beds + private rooms. Lounge area, no kitchen but bar & restaurant with pilgrim menu. *[Next Albergue: Óbanos – 4.4 km]*. If all else fails, the Gothic parish church has a wide porch and the **[F]** in the centre offers pure fresh water (you might want to empty out the chemical residue from the water of Pamplona and refill here). The quiet country road continues to:

2.6 km **Muruzábal** Church of St. Stephen *San Esteban* with statue of St. James and **[F]** in the main square with bar and chemist.

Detour Eunate (recommended): This short detour will add 2.8 km to the direct route (around 1 hour including brief stop at Eunate). Directions: at the entrance to the village (opposite the town hall) turn <left past the church and around the back of the houses where the road turns down <left (Eunate is now visible ahead) onto a wide farm track passing a small *Ermita* before crossing the main road onto a tree-lined avenue to **Eunate church.** The beautiful 12th century Romanesque Church of Santa María de Eunate (see photograph below) is one of the jewels of the camino.

2.5 km **Eunate Church and Hostel.** The church has been linked with the Knights Templar who long defended the pilgrim on the route to Santiago. There is a striking similarity with the church at Torres del Rio (see next stage) with its octagonal form, modelled on the Holy Sepulchre in Jerusalem, and its unadorned interior, a feature also associated with the Knights. But, uniquely, Eunate has a splendid freestanding outer porch with delicate twin pillars that surrounds the church. (Closed on Mondays, but its setting and external cloister is still worth the visit). It has been suggested that Eunate was also a burial place for pilgrims who had succumbed to the gruelling physical hardships experienced along the route. Standing on its own in the simple beauty of the countryside it evokes a powerful reminder of our own journey back to our spiritual source and Home. Guardians *Mariluz* and *Jan* lovingly tend the church and provide taped background Gregorian chant and a pilgrim stamp from their private house adjoining that also acts as a traditional pilgrim refuge •**Albergue** – small private hostel with basic facilities and accommodation for around 8 pilgrims. Continue to Puente la Reina past the albergue through the picnic site to the main road [1.0 km]. *(An alternative here is to take the road to Óbanos, a distance of 1.1 km from this point, which is clearly visible up ahead and join the waymarked camino from there)* – or turn <left and continue past the road to Arnotegui and turn <left onto track [1.5 km] veering off right [1.6 km] over river to central Albergue [0.3 km]. Total distance from Eunate for both options is 4.4 km.

| 4.4 km | **Puente la Reina - Central Albergue [1]** |

For the direct route to Óbanos from Muruzábal continue along the main road turning right> as you leave the village to follow the path parallel to the secondary road, under the new bypass, to the village of Óbanos clearly visible on the pronounced rise ahead of you. Make your way through its sleepy winding streets resplendent with their armorial crests emblazoned in the stone facades for to:

| 1.8 km | **Óbanos Plaza and Albergue** opposite the imposing parish church [F] and shaded cloister in this historic village. Here the noblemen of Navarre met in the 14th century in an effort to limit the power of the monarchy. Their motto translates loosely as 'Liberty for people and country.' The impressive neo-Gothic Church of St. John the Baptist *San Juan Bautista* has a splendid retablo and statue of St. James. The skull of St. William is also housed here in a silver reliquary giving zest to the mystical play enacted here every few years: *The Mystery of Óbanos. Legend has it that William (Guillaume) Duke of Aquitaine, killed his sister Felicia in a bout of fury at her refusal to return to court duties after her pilgrimage to Santiago. Riddled with remorse and in repentance Guillaume also took the pilgrimage to Compostela and renounced his nobility for a life of poverty, penitence and prayer. He lived the remainder of his life in the hermitage of Arnotegui just outside the village.*

•**Albergue** private hostel (Juan Irisarri 676-560 927) prominently situated on the corner of the main square at San Lorenzo, 6. 36 beds (3 rooms) and all facilities with rear patio and lounge with open fire in the winter. Casa rural •**Osses** CR (948-344 261) c/San Guillermo, 3. Bar & restaurant Ibarberoa (in street behind the church) and shop (not obvious) in the square. Continue down the hill out of Óbanos across the main road along a track through fields joining the main road at hotel and albergue [2] Jakue for the final stretch to:

Plaza Óbanos & Albergue

| 2.3 km | **Puente la Reina** •**Albergue [1]** Convento adjoining main road as you enter the town at c/Crucifijo, 1. Monastery hostal run by the Padres Reparadores (948-340 050). Open all year with 100 beds (12 rooms) in recently renovated building with all facilities and extensive rear garden. The route from Óbanos brings you directly to this original pilgrim hostel [1] (where the distances in this guide are measured to). It is conveniently situated opposite the

Albergue [1] *Padres Repardores*

Church of the Crucifixion *Iglesia del Crucifijo*, which has undergone no less than 3 name changes and been administered by 3 different Orders. Originally known as the Church of St. Mary of the Meadows *Iglesia Santa María de las Vegas* under the auspices of the Knights Templar, when that order was outlawed it was looked after by the Order of the Hospitallers of St. John and became the Iglesia Santo Cristo. Today, it is named after the unusual 14th century 'Y' shaped Gothic crucifix brought here by medieval pilgrims from Germany. It is now under the care of the Padres Reparadores in the seminary opposite (linked by a stone arch). To access the town, pass under the arch and continue over the busy N-111 to explore the main street *c/Mayor*. Additional bars and restaurants are located along the tree-lined square that flanks the N-111 (see town plan).

•Albergue* [2] Jakue the reception pavilion is the first building you come to on entering town and part of the 3 star hotel •**Jakue** (948-341 017) who have reserved the basement area as a pilgrim hostel. Open March-Oct with 40 beds (2 main rooms but bunk beds arranged in small cubicles). Unusually for an establishment with a restaurant they provide all facilities with good kitchen, dining and lounge area. The lack of outside window space

Albergue [2] *Jakue*

is compensated by the addition of a sauna and library and an excellent buffet breakfast. Adjoining the hotel on the main road we can find a modern pilgrim statue erected to mark the joining of the Navarrese and Aragonés routes.

•Albergue* [3] *Santiago Apostol* (José Luis 948-340 220) a large network hostel* at the far end of town with access lane directly across from the medieval pilgrim bridge. An industrial style building on an elevated site, 1.1 km from albergue [1] including the 400m track up to it, but convenient for leaving the next day. Open all year with 100 places (60 in large dormitory remainder in 4 rooms of 10

Albergue [3] *Santiago Apostol*

each). No kitchen but bar and restaurant serving dinner and breakfast.

The town has all facilities including a convenient post office *correos* on the N-111 close to its junction with the c/Mayor. *Perhaps this is the time to send back home all those extra items that you realise that you no longer need?* A **tourist office** (948-340 845) is located by the medieval bridge. **Calle Mayor** is the well-preserved main street retaining its age-old atmosphere and site of the impressive **Iglesia de Santiago** with its 12th century facade and portico and a gilded statue of Santiago Peregrino adding some colour to the sombre interior. The other church is **Iglesia San Pedro Apóstol** close to the pilgrim bridge with its image of Nuestra Señora del Puy otherwise known as Our Lady of the Bird *N.S del Chori – a reference to the lovely legend of a bird regularly washing the face of the statue when it was kept in a niche on the bridge*. **Other accommodation:** •**El Peregrino** H** (948-340 075) adjoining the Hotel Jakue at the entrance to town on the main road. •**Bidean** Hs (948-341 156) c/Mayor, 20, offers comfortable rooms in delightfully restored house directly on the camino in the centre of town. There are several bars and cafés along the Paseo de los Fueros (N-111) and shops and restaurants on c/Mayor.

PUENTE LA REINA (Gares) *Puente de Arga* renamed Queens Bridge *Puente la Reina* in honour of its benefactor Doña Mayor, wife of Sancho III. She commanded the magnificent Romanesque bridge to be built to support the safe movement of the increasing number of medieval pilgrims who joined the route at this stage from both the camino francés and camino aragonés. The bridges' six arches span the Arga that has now swollen to a powerful river since we first crossed it back at the Puente de Rabia in Zubiri. Charlemagne is reputed to have stayed in this town after his victorious battle against the

Monumento al Peregrino

Moors back in Cizur. With a population of 2,000 it straddles the busy N-111 linking Pamplona with Estella and has a frequent bus service to both.

Estella

Convento Comendadoras

F

N-111

c/ San Pedro

Iglesia de San Pedro

Paseo de los Fueros

c/ Cerco Nuevo

c/ Mayor

c/ Cerco Viejo

A [3] Santiago Apostol

Iglesia de Santiago

H *Hostal Bidean*

c/ Mayor

Correos

C

c/ Crucifijo

N-111

Seminario

Iglesia del Crucifijo

A [1] Padres Reparadores

PUENTE LA REINA

Hotel***Jakue **H**
[2] *Albergue Jakue* **A**

Pilgrim Monument

Eunate

Obanos

REFLECTIONS:

❏ **Practise random acts of loving kindness and acts of senseless beauty.**

MAP 05 *703.6 km (437.2 miles) to Santiago de Compostela)*

PUENTE LA REINA – ESTELLA (Navarra)

▬▬▬	Path / Track	--- ---	18.6 ---	*85%*
▬▬▬	Quiet Road	--- ---	3.3 ---	*15%*
▬▬▬	Main Road	--- ---	0.0	
Total km	**Total distance**		**21.9 km** (13.6 miles)	

Adjusted for climb 23.4 km (accrued ascent 300m = 1.5 km)
Alto ▲ High Point: Alto Villatuerta 510m (1,673 feet)

The Practical Path: Another peaceful stage along gently rolling farmland and vineyards with few trees and little shelter. Some fine examples of Roman roadway between Cirauqui and Lorca and a glorious 85% is on natural tracks. The first section is a steep climb on a heavily eroded path before descending into Estella. **Intermediate accommodation** distances from albergue [1]: Mañeru 4.8 km – Cirauqui 7.8 km – Lorca 13.5 km – Villatuerta 18.2 km.

❏ **The Mystical Path:** Will you pause a moment to look upon the ancient stone cross atop the rise and reflect at the speed with which the motorised traveller now whizz past it? Can you see the beauty of the stonemason's craftsmanship that fashioned it, and the deeper meaning behind the symbol? In the rush of modern life we miss so much of true significance. Where else might we take time today to pause and ponder the waymarks Home?

❏ **Personal Reflections:** *"... I started today with the intention to give and receive loving kindness. Here I am less than 2 hours later seething with rage. Someone has stolen items from my rucksack. I note with rising indignation that my new water container has also gone. In this moment of anger I become both judge and jury, condemning my fellow human being to hell and damnation. Where have the loving thoughts I invoked at daybreak gone? Can I bring them back? It is easy to act in a loving manner when the sun is shining and body and kit are together. But can I bring myself to love in adversity? ..."*

Leaving albergue [1] pass under the connecting arch of the Iglesia del Crucifijo and the Padres Reparadores and continue over the N-111 into the narrow and historical c/Mayor. Past the Iglesia de Santiago (right) **[0.4 km]** to cross the famous XIIth century pilgrim bridge **[0.3 km]** (albergue *Santiago Apostol* is up the track straight ahead). Turn <left over the bridge and cross the main road to the Nun's Neighbourhood *Barrio de las Monjas* with its convento Comendadoras del Espíritu Santo **[F]**. Rejoin the Río Arga and pass under new road bridge and along a dirt track before striking off right> uphill along a steep ravine to pass the XIIIth century site of the Monasterio de Bogota before we crest the top at 470m **[3.9 km]** *(at this point there are fine views back over the Río Arga valley)* then down to the roundabout at Mañeru with **[F] [0.2 km]** to:

Luquín

Option 3.7 →

IRACHE

AYEGUI

ESTELLA
(Pop. 13,000 – Alt.426m)

Turismo ☎ 948-554 011

A-12

Albergue [1] 3.7
Muni. [110]

S.Miguel

Zarapuz 3.0 →

*albergue de peregrinos
medieval (ruinas)*

N-111

río Iranzu

Novaleta

río Ega

VILLATUERTA
La Casa Mágica Priv.[30]*

4.7 Puente

NA 132 Tafalla ←

La Bodega del Camino Priv.[36]*

Albergue 5.7 →

(Pop. 450) **LORCA**

*puente
medieval*

Alloz →
Embalse

acueducto

río Saldo

Urbe (ruinas)

puente romano

(Pop. 500) **CIRAUQUI**
Par. [12] **Albergue 3.0**
505m

O

*Puesta
del Sol*

S

N →

MAÑERU C

Rotunda 4.8 →
Alto 470m

*Salida
del Sol*

E

Monasterio Bogota (ruinas)

N-111   A-12

*Convento Comendadoras
del Espíritu Santo*

A *Santiago Apostol Priv.*[100]*

río Arga

(Pop. 2,500 – Alt. 350m)
PUENTE LA REINA
Albergue[2] *Central* **0.0 →**
Padres Reparadores **Conv.[100]**

4.8 km **Mañeru Roundabout.** Tranquil village linked with the Knights Templar and Order of St. John whose influence in this area was considerable in the Middle Ages. Church of St. Peter, bar, shop and casa rural •**Isabel** (948-340 283). The sleepy meandering streets lead to the cemetery via the street of the 'inevitable' *calle Forzosa* from where a view opens up of the next life… or our next destination, Cirauqui. We now start to pass through vineyards, interspersed with olive trees. The peaceful path winds its way up into:

Pilgrims approaching Cirauqui

3.0 km **Cirauqui Plaza** (*Zirauki*) a medieval hilltop village, beautifully preserved with narrow winding streets and houses bearing armorial crests and ornate balconies and fine village square. Church (restored) of *San Román* with multi-lobed doorway and Church of St. Catherine *Santa Catalina* both dating from the 13th century. •**Albergue** [1] Basic parish hostel with 14 beds in one room and small kitchen-dining area. The ancient building is accessed on the right just before entering the square off this traditional street with supermercado 50m

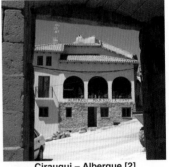

Cirauqui – Albergue [2]

(right) •**Albergue** [2] *Maralotx* private hostal opposite the church in Plaza San Roman at the very top of this tranquil village (678-635 208) with 28 beds (+ individual rooms) with all facilities, dinner and breakfast available.

Leave the village through an arch from the main square and out on to one of the best examples of **Roman road** on the camino continuing over a single span Roman bridge to cross over the N-111 and A-12 (Will *they* last 2,000 years?) onto a dirt track. The path now takes us gently downhill through open farmland running parallel to the new autopista (left) which we pass under onto the N-111 and back again under the A-12 to take a quiet country road to pass modern aqueduct turning <left over the famous medieval stone bridge (now restored) that crosses the Salt river *río Salado*. Aymeric Picaud, in his epic journal written in the 12th century warns pilgrims not to drink from its deadly waters. It was here that he encountered Basques preparing to skin any pilgrim's horse that might

drink from the river and die – his own horse falling victim to the Basques! Veer <left through an underpass (thoughtfully finished with attractive local stone) and up into the village of:

5.7 km **Lorca** 12thC St. Saviours Church *San Salvador*. This quaint village is the site of a former pilgrim hospice with connections to the monastery at Roncesvalles and now boasting 2 private hostels •**Albergue** *La Bodega del Camino** c/Placeta, 8 (Miguel 948-541 162) network hostel* with 36 places (bunk beds in dormitory + private rooms) + popular restaurant in this restored stone

Lorca – Albergue [1]

building at the far end of the village and •**Albergue** *Lorca* c/Mayor, 40 (José Ramón (648-541 190) with 14 places in 4 rooms (no kitchen). The route from here follows a track alongside the main road through farmland passing the site of an ancient pilgrim hostel *Hospital de peregrinos de Arandigoyen* founded in 1066, before taking a tunnel under the town bypass into the modern suburbs of Villatuerta (café right) to cross the medieval bridge.

4.7 km **Villatuerta Puente** A new hostel opened in 2009 in a medieval building 80m beyond the bridge (signposted). •**Albergue** *La Casa Mágica* (Simone & Miguel 948-536 095). 30 places, well equipped kitchen, covered yard for relaxing and massage and healing available. Bar / restaurant *Lara* on the main road (400m off route). Just over the

bridge is the 14th century Church of the Assumption **[F]** with raised flagstone surround and views back over the route from Lorca and towards Monte Jurra to the south. Note: Alternative (original) Route via Zaraputz begins at the church.

Before Estella was founded in 1090, early pilgrims travelled directly to the monastery at Irache via Novaleta, Echavarra and Zaraputz to the south. This route still exists and is marked as part of the GR 65 that also serves as an alternative route to Los Arcos via Luquín (see next stage). The route is now well waymarked and makes a delightful alternative route. Consider this option if you have walked the camino francés before or if you are travelling with

Zaraputz <left arrow

a companion and want to experience walking alone and the joy of meeting up again at the end of the day to share your individual insights. This short section may provide the confidence to take other optional routes later on. This alternative route is still virtually unused in comparison to the constant stream of pilgrims on the main camino.

Turn left around the side of the church and s/o at T-Junction onto track and first waymark **[0.1 km]**. The path now drops down at side of factory and under access road to the village of Novoleta **[1.6 km]** and under A-6 motorway **[0.4 km]** over river **[0.5 km]** where the track now climbs steeply for **[0.4 km]** to:

3.0 km **Zaraputz** ruins of the 15th century pilgrim hostel occupying a lovely elevated site (440m). Continue over a pedestrian bridge **[0.7 km]** climbing again to ridge (515m) where the first views of Estella open up ahead. The path curves around a valley and up again to cemetery **[1.4 km]** turn <left off asphalt road **[0.4 km]** and turn right> just before farmyard and cross over old road **[0.4 km]** into Holm oak woods. The path now drops down through woodland for **[0.8 km]** to route signpost:

Medieval pilgrim hostel – Zaraputz

3.7 km Option signpost with choice of routes: [a] continue by remote path direct to Luquín / Los Arcos (described in next stage) or [b] take the route to Estella / Monjardín by continuing under the A-6 to next option sign **[0.4 km]** (left for Monjardín or right for Irache **[0.5 km]**. The albergue at Ayegui is **[1.2 km]** or the main albergue in Estella an additional **[1.5 km]** (see map).

The main waymarked route now bypasses the ruins of the ancient hermitage of St. Michael *ermita de San Miguel arcangel* (all that remains of an extensive pilgrim hospital here, its artefacts dating from the 11th century are now in the Navarra museum). Continue along track, down steps beside the main road to rest area **[F]** and onto path that winds down to a pedestrian bridge over the rio Ega past *Camping Lizarra* and on down to riverside park and the 14[th]C Gothic Iglesia del Santo Sepulchro (left) with the Convento Santo Domingo behind it. Continue through the underpass (N-111) into the c/la Rua and:

3.7 km Estella •**Albergue** [1] *Assoc.* hostel (Luis Navarro 948-550 200) administered by the local pilgrim association and conveniently located at the entrance to the town at the beginning of the c/de la Rúa (the noisy N-111 is to the rear) with 114 beds spread tightly over 3 floors and large overflow dormitory next door. All facilities and well-equipped modern kitchen with extensive dining area, breakfast is available and a small patio to rear provides some open space. Several new hostels now relieve the pressure on bed spaces at this previous bottleneck. La Aljama also on c/Rua has a pilgrim menu.

Albergue [1] Municipal *(Above)*

•**Albergue** [2] *paroquial* new parish hostel on ground floor of modern residential building in c/Mercado Viejo with 28 beds and all facilities. •**Albergue** [3] ANFAS (society for the support of mentally handicapped – Ainhoa 948-554 551) at c/ Cordeleros 7 with 34 beds. For either hostel cross the bridge opposite albergue [1] and head s/o along c/Asteria and at 2nd crossroads (250m) – for albergue [2] turn up left into c/Mercado Viejo and the hostel is on the right after 100m (opposite Decora Hogar). For albergue [3] continue s/o uphill along c/Asteria and veer right to modern buildings 150m. The other 2 hostels are the opposite end of town on the way out in Ayegui. •**Albergue Juvenil** [4] *Oncineda* 300m *off* the route (right) at first roundabout in c/Monasterio de Irache (948-555 022). Open all year with 120 places in modern building with all facilities (meals available) and set in quiet wooded site.

•**Albergue** [5] *polideportivo* municipal albergue (948-554 311) left of the camino beyond the 2nd roundabout at the far end of town (1.6 km from albergue [1]) part of the Ayegui sports hall *Polideportivo.* Open all year with 70 beds and 100 mattresses. Pilgrim dinner and breakfast are available from the canteen.

Albergue [5] *Polideportivo* - Ayegui

Other accommodation: •**San Andrés** P*(948-554 158) plaza de Santiago is popular with pilgrims (as is nearby first floor restaurant *Casa Nova* on C.Fray Wenceslao) •**Cristina** Hs*(948-550 772) at c/Baja Navarra, 1 (between the main square and c/Mayor). •**Fonda Izarra** (948-550 678) c/Caldería, often booked out by migrant workers and better known for its pilgrim menu. •**Apartamentos Gebala** (606-980 675) Plaza Fueros, 31 has a special pilgrim price (ideal for small groups). In the modern industrial area near Ayegui are •**El Volante** (948-553 957) c/Merkatondoa, 2 and •**Hostal Area-99** (948-553 370) at no 32. Further afield is •**Yerri** H** (948-546 034) Av. Yerri, 35 out past the bullring on the western outskirts. In the upper price bracket directly on the camino on the outskirts of Estella (3.7 km from albergue [1]) is the modern hotel •**Irache** H*** (948-551 150).

Estella (Lizarra) with a local population of 15,000 is a vibrant town with lots to do and see. Estella is big enough to provide reasonable facilities and yet sufficiently compact to easily explore its wonderful historic buildings, museums, interesting churches and its varied restaurants and bars (perhaps a good place to take a day's rest). 200m past the albergue is Plaza San Martín with its graceful fountain and the helpful *Turismo* (948-554 011). Adjoining the tourist office is the impressive 12th century Palace of the Kings of Navarre *Palacio de los Reyes de Navarra* now a museum and art gallery. Opposite are the impressive flight of steps to the Church of San Pedro de la Rúa with its beautiful 12th century cloister, two sides of which are missing, evidence of its troubled past. It was here that the Kings of Navarre took their oaths and is worth a visit despite the noise of traffic on the busy N-111 immediately to the rear. Open before evening mass and guided tours are also available – check with the tourist office. On the other side of the river Ega (for ease of orientation take the main road bridge out of St. Martin's square) we find the bustling main square *Plaza de los Fueros* filled with cafés and the austere church of San Juan Bautista taking up the eastern side. A further 200m along the c/Mayor you come to the more intimate Plaza de Santiago with its ancient fountain. A variety of inexpensive restaurants, bars and hotels are located in the surrounding streets. The area to the north of the river was called Lizarra (Basque for ash tree) and was the original village built on the slopes of the hill of San Millán where today we find the modern Basilica of the Virgin of le Puy. Quick to realise the enormous potential of the pilgrim road to Santiago Sancho Ramírez created a separate Borough in 1090 for French pilgrim settlers on the other side of the river and referred to it as L'Izarra (Basque for star) which became *Estella* (Spanish for star) with all its connections with the Milky Way *Via Lactea* otherwise

Steps to Iglesia San Pedro

known as the 'Way of the Stars' to Compostela. This marks the beginning of stage IV of the Codex Calixtinus.

As in other areas along the Way, artisans were encouraged to return and bring their skills with them. It was this inflow of stonemasons and artists that created the beautiful buildings, monuments and bridges, hospitals and cathedrals that we still admire and use today. However, the ever-present human characteristics of jealousy and greed also created disharmony, open warfare and mindless massacres. The unification of the different boroughs into one town in 1266 did not end the hostilities. The flowering Jewish colony was expelled in the 14th century and the destruction of the castle adjoining San Pedro also destroyed two sides of its exquisite Romanesque cloister. Even up to the last century, Estella was one of the strongholds of the Carlists in the conflict over the successor to King Ferdinand, no doubt contributing to the town's royalist reputation. Today, the fiery Navarrese blood is cooled in the Court of Justice *Juzgado*, which now occupies the original town hall immediately to the left of the steps to the church of San Pedro in Plaza San Martín.

REFLECTIONS:

❏ **To attain knowledge, add things every day.**
   To attain wisdom, remove things every day. *Lao-tzu*

MAP 06 *681.7 km (423.6 miles) to Santiago de Compostela*

ESTELLA – LOS ARCOS (Navarra)

▬▬▬	Path / Track	--- ---	18.1 ---	*86%*
▬▬▬	Quiet Road	--- ---	2.7 ---	*13%*
▬▬▬	Main Road	--- ---	0.3 ---	*1%*
Total km	**Total distance**		**21.1 km** (13.1 miles)	

Adjusted for climb 22.9 km (accrued ascent 370m = 1.8 km)
Alto ▲ High Point: Albergue Monjardín 650m (2,132 feet)

The Practical Path: As in yesterday's stage, the majority of this scenic route (86%) is on delightful natural paths. The first section is through native Holm oak and pine trees as we wend our way up to Monjardín. There are magnificent views southwards over the alternative route, which passes above Luquín. The two routes join for the last stretch into Los Arcos taking us through remote vineyards and open country but with little shade and few water fonts. Take food and water for the isolated day ahead, particularly for the alternative route. **Intermediate accommodation** (distance from albergue [1] in Estella): Hotel Irache (5 km) – Monjardín (9.6 km). None on the alternative route.

❏ **The Mystical Path:** Will you find the fish that circle the stone fountain, symbol of the hidden Christian life swimming in its waters? The fish are located at the centre of these ancient cloisters. How long will they remain? How long will we? This monastic community was founded here as early as 958 and it became one of the first monasteries to receive pilgrims on their way to venerate the recently discovered tomb of San Tiago. It later earned the status of the first university in Navarre. For over a millennium it was a respected seat of learning and hospitality. Today it is uninhabited, abandoned by the monks that gave it life for over a thousand years. Perhaps the ferns that gave these majestic buildings their name will yet reclaim them.

❏ **Personal Reflections:** *"... Everywhere there are fountains. Some contain refreshing drinking water to hydrate the body; others wine to fortify it. I now find myself being offered a different water to quench a different thirst. In a display of loving kindness, offered without any expectation of anything in return, I am showered with generosity. I leave this oasis of service with the gift of a little booklet entitled* Living Water *and based on the Gospel of Saint John. Tears well up in me as I open the book and find a handwritten message from Anton. "I give this book for you to find Jesus Christ. God help you!" I reflect on my purpose for this journey and smile at the exclamation mark. God help me indeed! ..."*

río Odrón

Ⓐ 3.0 Albergue *Muni.[70]*

(Pop. 1,300 – Alt. 450m)
LOS ARCOS

Ⓐ La Fuente ☎ 948-640 797
Ⓕ

A-12

N-111

Portillo de las Cabras

Fuente del pozo de Baurín
◄ 5.7 Puente

Puesta del Sol
S   O

Salida del Sol
E

río Caudiel

Cugullo (ruinas) ancien hospital de peregrinos

Cruce 3.7 →   ◄ 2.8 Cruce

Castillo Alt. 890m

(Pop. 150 – Alt. 670m)
VILLAMAYOR de MONJARDÍN
Asoc.[25]

Luquín 3.7 → Ⓕ
Urbiola
N-111

Ⓕ Ⓐ 1.5 Albergue
Ⓐ *S.Cruz Par.[22]*
← *Fuente de los Moros*

◄ 3.1 Azqueta

Puente 3.0 →

Montejurra

Ⓗ 1.6 Hotel Irache

río Ega

② ①
Opción 3.4 →

Monasterio Irache
Fuente de Vino
AYEGUI
Ⓐ

ESTELLA
(Pop. 13,000 – Alt. 430m)

Albergue [1] 0.0
Muni.[105]
Ⓐ

Leaving the albergue continue up calle Rúa into Plaza San Martin **[F]** past the tourist office **[0.2 km]** and out through the medieval city gate *Puerta de Castilla* and cross over the busy junction of the N-111 **[0.3 km]** (albergue [4] right). Veer right> past the Avia petrol station and continue up through the modern suburb of Ayegui passing **[F]** *el Piojo* **[1.0 km]** (with sports hall and albergue [5] up to the left). Continue s/o up Calle del Camino de Santiago and Calle Mayor to turn down sharp <left **[0.6 km].** *(For an **alternative** route direct to Hotel Irache continue straight on past children's play area to the Hotel visible straight ahead (1.6 km) where the waymarked route rejoins from the left.)* Turn <left downhill and cross over the N-111 **[0.3 km]** and up the dirt track opposite to rear of the Bodegas Irache with its famous **wine fountain** *Fuente del Vino* **[0.4 km]**

where pilgrims can fortify themselves for the journey ahead at the generosity of the Bodegas. Continue to tree-fringed square **[F]** and the entrance to the ancient Benedictine **Monasterio de Irache [0.1 km]** (left) which has long been connected with Roncesvalles and the camino. A community of monks served pilgrims here since the 10th century but were forced to vacate in 1985 due to a lack of novitiates. Now serving as a somewhat austere museum it can be viewed from 09.30

Irache – Wine Fountain

Wed-Fri and 08.30 Sat & Sun. If it is closed you can still view the impressive Romanesque door to the 12th century Benedictine Church of San Pedro, around to the left. The Bodegas Irache has a **wine museum** opposite. Continue along dirt track for **[0.5 km]** to a fork in the path with wooden signpost.

3.4 km Irache Opción [?]

Alternative scenic route via LUQUÍN (+ 1.4 km). Entire is on natural pathways but facilities en route are limited so bring provisions. Veer up left under A-12 and up through delightful woodland to high pasture and fields of lavender. This ancient route follows the *road less travelled* away from the bustle of the main camino and skirts the lower slopes of the mystical *Monte Jurra* (1045m) to:

3.0 km **Puente** wooden bridge across mountain stream (dry). Shortly afterwards the route breaks through the tree line to reveal the conical peak of Monjardín to the north. The track continues through the ridge ahead where a magnificent view south over Luquin opens up. This is the high point of the route at 720m. We now start the gentle descent into:

Monjardín from Luquin route

3.7 km **Luquin** typical hill village with winding streets radiating out from the Basilica and the parish Church of San Martin. The latter has an interesting and finely carved portico and adjoins the main square with seating and **[F]**. Community café/bar San Isidro (often closed). Wind your way down through the village and out onto an open path crossing over the N-111 (close to the village of Urbiola where the Knights of St. John maintained a medieval pilgrim hospice) continue under the A-12 to:

2.2 km **Cruce** Here we rejoin the main waymarked route from Monjardín.

For **recommended route** via Monjardín veer right> at Option point (wooden signpost) down and over the N-111 to:

1.6 km **Hotel Irache.** Take the road between the hotel and camping complex under the new bypass and out onto a pathway through peaceful Holm oak and pine forest to:

3.1 km **Azqueta** quiet village now bypassed by the new N-111 with the parish Church of San Pedro. At the far end of the village veer off right> down past farm buildings and then steeply up towards Villamayor. Just before entering the village we pass the 13th century Fountain of the Moors *Fuente de Los Moros* with its splendid double arch of distinctly Mozarabic influence, to:

Fuente de los Moros

1.5 km **Villamayor de Monjardín** lying at an elevation of 650m with splendid views of the surrounding countryside and dominated by the tower of the 12th century San Andrés Church. The conical peak of Monjardín with the ruins of St. Stephen's Castle *Castillo de San Esteban* forms a distinctive backdrop to the village. Opposite the church is a new parish hostel •**Albergue** [1] *Santa Cruz* open all year with 28 spaces in bunk beds and mattresses. Shared meal (no kitchen). Further up at the top end of the village is the original •**Albergue** [2] *Hogar Monjardín* (948-537 136) confraternity hostel run by a Dutch ecumenical group and open from April to October. Prominently situated overlooking the main square with 20 beds in 4 rooms and good facilities in this refurbished village house (no kitchen but shared meals with grace are offered at basic cost). Village Bar with pilgrim menu. *[Next Albergue: Los Arcos – 11.5 km].* The route now follows the access road down past the Monjardín Bodega to turn off right> onto a lovely pathway down through vineyards and woodland where the alternative route joins via the A-12 underpass.

Monjardin & Albergue [2] *(above)*
Albergue [1] Santa Cruz *(below)*

2.8 km **Cruce** at this point we join pilgrims coming from Luquin and continue along remote farm tracks for a glorious 8.7 km of uninhabited countryside of mixed farmland and vineyards interspersed with olive trees, but with little shade. We pass the site of the ancient pilgrim hospital *Cugullo* and Fountain of the Well *Fuente del pozo de Baurín* (not drinkable) by the adjoining río Caudiel (dry) but with pleasant shade from the pine trees. Finally we take a gentle climb up through the Pass of the Goats *Portillo de las Cabras* before our descent into:

8.7 km **Los Arcos** we enter the town (with 3 pilgrim hostels) on its sleepy northern side and make our way down the old c/Mayor passing: •**Albergue** [1] *de la Fuente (casa de Austria)* private hostel on travesia del Estanco adjacent to c/Mayor (María Ruiz 948-640 797). Open all year with 48 places in several dormitories individual rooms also available with all facilities and small patio.

Continue on to the splendid 12th century Church of St. Mary of the Arches *Iglesia de Santa María de los Arcos.* The church was embellished in 16th, 17th and 18th centuries and in addition to the original Romanesque has Gothic, Baroque and Classical elements without affecting the overall harmony. The bell-tower and peaceful cloisters are particularly noteworthy and the sumptuous interior has a fine statue of Santiago Peregrino. The balcony choir stalls also have a relief of both St. James *Maior* and *Menor*. Pilgrim mass each evening.

Santiago Maior (left) and Menor (right)

Leaving the church to the left, continue out through the only original town gate still extant *Portal de Castilla* and cross the road *and* river to turn right> by the pilgrim fountain *Fuente de Peregrinos* to: •**Albergue [2]** *Isaac Santiago* the original municipal hostel administered by a Flemish confraternity and accessed off c/Río Odrón (behind the modern civic centre and library) with 70 beds in a main dormitory + 4 other rooms and all facilities including an outside patio. Close by in c/El Hortal is •**Albergue [3]** *Casa Alberdi* private hostel (María Concepción Alberdi 948-640 764)

entered via converted garage which also serves as a lounge area. Open all year with 22 beds in 5 rooms and basic facilities. **Alternative accommodation:** Pensión •**Mavi** (948-640 081) on c/ del Medio 7 (separate to bar/ restaurant Mavi at the central crossroads opposite Hotel and bar •**Mónaco** H**(948-640 000) on Plaza del Coso. •**Hostal Suetxe** (948-441 175) in a refurbished building on c/Karramendabia (opposite side of N-111) and further out on c/La Serna (on the road to Zarragoza) •**Ezequiel** Hs (948-640 296). There are several shops and bars including the popular basement restaurant below the Gargantúa bar opposite the church and useful grocery *alimentacón* adjoining (see town plan).

LOS ARCOS is a compact crossroads town (population 1,300) straddling the N-111 and connecting Estella with Logroño with regular bus service to both. It was and remains a classical pilgrim halt and has Roman origins. The eastern gate (no longer visible) into the old walled city was called Gate of the Shells *Portal de la Concha* which also provided access to the Jewish quarter in the town. A *Turismo* sometimes opens in either the town hall or library. Wander around the narrow streets and simply soak up the peace of this historic town.

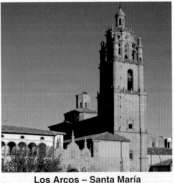

Los Arcos – Santa María

LOS ARCOS
(Pop. 1,300 – Alt. 450m)

REFLECTIONS:

❏ **Your daily life is your temple and your religion.** *Kahlil Gibran*

MAP 07 *660.6 km (410.5 miles) to Santiago de Compostela*

LOS ARCOS (Navarra) **– LOGROÑO** (La Rioja)

▬▬▬	Path / Track	--- --- 21.5 ---	77%
▬▬▬	Quiet Road	--- --- 4.4 ---	16%
▬▬▬	Main Road	--- --- 2.2 ---	7%
Total km	**Total distance**	**28.1 km** (17.5 miles)	

Adjusted for climb 29.6 Km (accrued ascent 300m = 1.5 km)
Alto ▲ High Point: Ermita de N. Sra. del Poyo 570m (1,870 feet)

The Practical Path: A wonderful 77% of this stage is on natural paths and dirt tracks through open arable farmland. Shade is limited to a few isolated pockets of pine and drinking fonts are few, so fill up the water bottle and wear your hat. This is a long stage and there are some short but very steep sections into the rio Linares (Torres del Río) and Cornava river valleys so be particularly mindful when negotiating these steep paths. Just before entering Logroño we pass into the great wine-producing region of La Rioja. **Intermediate accommodation** (distances from albergue [3] Isaac Santiago): Sansol (7.0 km) – Torres del Río (8.0 km) – Viana (18.6 km). **Note:** If you don't want to stay in a busy city hostel or want more time to visit Logroño, consider staying in Viana where there are now 2 albergues (see details). This would allow a longer stopover at Logroño the following day (9.5 km from Viana centre) to spend more time exploring this interesting city (it may be possible to leave your backpack in the hostel although it doesn't officially open till after noon) or visit the city briefly on your way through to the next intermediate hostel at Navarette (12.4 km) for a total of 21.2 km for this alternative day.

❏ **The Mystical Path:** Will you visit this holy temple reputedly built by the same Order of Knights that created the magnificent church at Eunate? Will you sense the similarity of form and look up and see the eight-sided star that forms this simple structure, symbol of the sacred and full of grace and mystery? The beautiful 13th century figure of Christ crucified hangs above the altar. If our life is a reflection of our temple, to whom have we dedicated it and what have we placed upon its altar?

❏ **Personal Reflections:** *"... The deepening lines on her aging face cannot hide her welcoming smile. Her name means happiness and she has welcomed pilgrims for decades giving her blessing and stamping credenciales. Some see her unofficial presence an intrusion, preferring to hurry by to avoid interaction. I sit beside her and observe myself judging them as they are judging her. A whole Order was condemned to die by those fearing a loss of control and wanting an exclusive right to bless. We crucified God's Son for the same crime. I realise in this moment that no one needs permission to offer love. We all have the right to bestow blessings – perhaps it is our primary duty..."*

N-111

Turismo ☎ 941-291 260 ⓘ ◻ Ⓐ ◀ 3.8 **Albergue** Asoc.[88]

(Pop.145,000 – Alt.380m)

LOGROÑO

Puente de Piedra

LA RIOJA

Cantabria

AP-68 E-804

Camping La Playa

Pantano de las Cañas

2.5 **Cruce**

NAVARRE

Arroyo. Labraza

N-232

río Ebro

Capilla 3.2 N-111
N.S de Las Cuevas

Arroyo Valdearas

Andrés Muñoz **Muni.**[54] ◻ Ⓐ ◻◻

Santa María **Par.**[16]

VIANA
(Pop. 3,500)

◻ Ⓐ 4.9 **Iglesia Santa María**

Rio Cornava

Cornava (ruinas)

3.1 **Rio Cornava**

Barranco Mataburos

W
Sunset

S

▲ 570m

Bargota

2.6 **N.S.del Poyo**

Sunrise

E

río Linares

N

TORRES del RIO

Casa Mariela **Priv.***[54]**Albergue** 1.0

Santo Sepulchro

Ⓐ

3.8 **Albergue** Priv.[14] Arcadi

SANSOL

Busto

N-111

3.2 **rio San Pedro**

Capilla San Blas ◀ †

río Odrón

Ⓐ ◀ 0.0 **Albergue** Muni.[70]

LOS ARCOS
(Pop. 1,300 – Alt.450m) †

From the main albergue in Los Arcos turn up past the cemetery (the inscription over its portal translates; *'you are what I once was, and will be what I am now'*). Flexing our physical and spiritual muscles we stride out along a wide earth track leaving the 13th century Capilla de San Blas and the main N-111 (left). We continue along a delightful track through arable farmland to:

3.2 km **Rio de San Pedro** cross this small stream with Sansol directly ahead on the horizon and join the quiet country road into:

3.8 km **Sansol** café at entrance. To visit the church or pilgrim hostel turn up right> Iglesia de San Zoilo *(a Christian martyr who gives his name to this sleepy little village and also to the monastery in Carrión de los Condes).* •**Albergue** *Arcadi* (618-197 520) with 14 bunk beds. From here the way crosses the N-111 down a very steep ravine [!] to a stone bridge across the Río Linares **[F]** left and up steeply, passing the welcoming café / restaurant *Casa Lili* (left) up into:

1.0 km **Torres del Río Plaza** •**Albergue [1]** *Casa Mariela* (948-648 251) network hostel 54 places with all facilities and restaurant. •**Albergue [2]** *Casa Mari* (948-648 018) private hostel tucked away behind the parish church at the top of town in c/Casas Nuevas, 13. Open all year with 21 places in 4 rooms and good facilities including patio with terrace overlooking the surrounding countryside. The former albergue *Via Láctea* remains closed but continues as bar *la Pata & Oca*. Grocery store adjacent to casa Mariela.

Torres del Río – Casa Mariela

TORRES DEL RÍO: Quintessential pilgrim village perhaps best known for its exquisite 12th century church *Iglesia de Santo Sepulcro* linked with the Knights Templar and based on the octagonal church of the Holy Sepulchre in Jerusalem. The lofty cupola, with its cross-ribbed vault forming an 8 sided star, is particularly notable and emblematic of the Knights. The simple interior has a 13th century crucifix and, like the church in Eunate, fine acoustics if you feel inclined to offer a song of prayer! If the church is closed ask for the custodian *guardián* who lives adjacent (usually open mornings and evenings depending on season.)

Torres del Río – Santo Sepulchro

Continue up through the village past the cemetery and out on a dirt track that undulates across the open countryside avoiding the N-111 which snakes its way around hairpin bends to your right. Join the main road briefly to pass:

2.6 km **Ermita de Nuestra Señora del Poyo** Precariously situated on the road at its high point (*poyo* means raised platform or podium) from here we have a good view west over the flat plains with Viana and Logroño in the distance. We now cross the N-111 over a secondary road that leads to the village of Bargota (right). From here the path drops steeply down into a steep ravine [!] to cross the river Cornava (often dry).

| 3.1 km | **Rio Cornava** and past the ruins of an ancient settlement. From here we wind our way up again and to the N-111 onto a path straight to Viana now clearly visible ahead. Cross back over the N-111 through the suburbs and climb steeply up into the medieval heart of Viana town;

| 4.9 km | **Viana Iglesia de Santa María** 13th century church with fine recessed doorway in front of which is the tomb of the notorious Cesare Borgia who was killed nearby *(initially buried in the church but when his mausoleum was vandalised he was re-interred outside.)* The interior has an early statue of St. James. The parish has recently converted an adjoining building to a pilgrim hostel •**Albergue** [1] *Santa Maria* with 16 places and a shared meal with grace. Access is from the main square *Plaza de los Fueros* with its central fountain and collection of cafes and bars. The town hall has a fine carved façade with colonnades and houses the Turismo (948-446 302). Continue down the main street past the 15th pilgrim hospital at #18 (now casa de Cultura) to the far end and turn sharp <left by the impressive ruins of San Pedro to the main hostel (400m from Santa María):

Portico Santa María *(above)*
Albergue [1] Paroquial *(below)*

•**Albergue** [2] *Andrés Muñoz* municipal hostel (948-645 037 / 530) on c/San Pedro located in a quiet part of the old town with wonderful garden terrace overlooking Logroño in the distance. Open all year (you may need to phone ahead in the winter) with 54 beds in several open sections in tiers of three! – all facilities including a magnificent lounge-dining hall and a fine terrace overlooking the route to Logroño. Originally a monastery, it was acquired and transformed into a pilgrim hostel by one of the great *amigos* of the way, Andrés Muñoz.

Albergue [2] Municipal

Other accommodation •**Casa Armendáriz** P**(948-645 078) in c/Navarro Villoslada, 19. •**San Pedro** P**(948-446 221) or, at the top end of the market (and the town – opposite the ruins of San Pedro) is the beautifully restored palace •**Palacio de Pujadas** H***(948-646 464) which also runs the popular cafetaria Portillo (directly on the camino). Beds also available at Casa Rueda, #46 just off the camino as you leave town (948-645 149). There is a wide selection of shops bars and restaurants. *[Next accommodation: Logroño – 9.5 km]*

Palacio de Pujadas & Café

VIANA is a lively town with a resident population of 3,500. The camino passes through its historical centre which is little changed since medieval pilgrims plodded through its ancient streets – its architectural heritage still largely intact. Back in the 15th century Viana was a major pilgrim halt with no less than 4 *hospitales de peregrinos* and it was during this period that Cesare Borgia became linked to the town. *[Illegitimate son of Rodrigo Borgia, who was elected Pope Alexander VI in the pivotal year of 1492, Cesare was appointed commander of the Papal armies and patronised both Leonardo de Vinci, who acted as his military architect, and Machiavelli who, no doubt, helped form some of his political ideology. When Pope Alexander VI died, his successor promptly banished Cesare to Spain where he was killed defending Viana in the siege of 1507. Colourful to the end, it has been suggested that Borgia's strong countenance may have been used by artists of the period, such as Leonardo, to model the popular image of Christ Jesus.]* Owing to its border location the town has always been something of a hot spot and its defensive walls are well preserved on its western side (as you leave).

To stay or not to stay, that is a question – whatever you decide, stay long enough to reflect on the ruins of the Church of St. Peter *San Pedro* and to soak up the atmosphere of this abandoned church and the terraced gardens that lead from it. Leave the town through the medieval stone arch *Portal San Felices* and drop down to the suburbs below following the path around the back of houses and over waste ground and abandoned factory buildings to cross over the N-111 onto a quiet road to:

3.2 km **Ermita de la Trinidad de Cuevas [F]** peaceful picnic spot with grove of trees and a small tributary of the Ebro. Site of an earlier pilgrim hospice of the Trinitarian Order of nuns. Continue to fork in the track where a new variant (recommended) continues s/o <left to make a wide curve towards the lakes (original road route right). The extensive lakes *Lagunas de Las Cañas* are now visible ahead with the Cantabrian Hills behind. *The low-lying meadows in this area where notorious for the witches' covens that gathered here in the 16th century.* Bird observatory (left). Watch carefully for the camino waymarks (other local walks around the lakes are also marked) and make your way back to cross the busy N-111 [!] by paper factory over stream to pass from Navarra into the famous wine growing region of La Rioja:

3.0 km **Cruce / La Rioja** Here the autonomous region of La Rioja begins at the new city bypass adjoining an industrial complex and *Papelaria Ebro*. Make your way under the new ring road towards the Cantabrian hill *Cerro de Cantabria*, its flat outline clearly visible ahead. We follow a new earth-coloured asphalt track, a 'gift' from the local government and climb gently up the northern flank of the hill and past the site of the prehistoric city of Cantabria – excavations of its Roman (and earlier) ruins are still in progress. Just where we begin to drop down again prepare to part with a few cents for good luck and in memory of Felisa, another legendary gatekeeper of the camino whose niece, also called Felisa, is now in charge of this welcoming border post where you can get your credencial stamped while you have some refreshments. Continue to the stone bridge *Puente de Piedra* across the wide waters of the Ebro into the city of Logroño. The bridge, rebuilt in 1880, replaces the earlier medieval pilgrim bridge attributed to St. John Of the Nettles *San Juan de Ortega*. Once over the bridge turn right> across dangerous junction [!] into the cobbled c/ Ruavieja (the original 'old' road) past the 12th century Church of Santa Maria del Palacio with its graceful octagonal tower, which is situated next to:

3.8 km Logroño •Albergue [1] municipal
hostel /La Riojan association (941-260 234)
c/Ruaviejo, 32 well situated for sightseeing
in the old quarter. 90 spaces on 3 floors (in
cubicles of 4 in large dormitories) with all
facilities and outside patio. •Albergue[2]
puerta del Revellín welcoming new private
hostel (629-170 447) in the modern Plaza
Martínez Flamarique, 4 (adjoining cafe El
Albero) 700m east of puente piedra. 40 beds
in 1 room. **Other central accommodation:**
Hotel F&G, puente piedra (941-008 900).

Logrono –Albergue [1]

Near the cathedral are: •**La Numantina** Hs
(941-251 411) Sagasta, 4. •**Niza** Hs (941-206 044) on c/Capitan Gallarga, 13
also •**La Bilbaina** P (941-254 226) at No. 10. Close by is the newly refurbished
•**Marqués de Vallejo** H***(941-248 333) c/Marqués de Vallejo, 8. Near the exit
of the old town is •**Portales** H***(941-291 145) and further out in the modern
suburbs are a variety of modern hotels including •**Murrieta** H*** (941-224
150). **Conde de Haro** H*** (941-208 500).

LOGROÑO is a lively university city (population 130,000) capital of La Rioja
and a pleasant blend of medieval and modern. 500m south of the albergue is a
helpful Turismo (941-291 260) located in the main square *Paseo de Espolón* on
the side of the c/del General Vara de Rey. If you plan to break your journey in
Logroño the office can provide details of excursions in the area (see Clavijo).
The city is also capital of the famous wine-growing region of La Rioja and the
festival of San Mateo heralds in the harvest in a week-long frenzy of celebration
at the end of September.

There are a multitude of bars, restaurants
and shops centred around the pedestrian
main street c/ de Portales and the 14th
century Gothic Catedral Santa María
de la Redonda (built on an earlier round
Romanesque structure). Its impressive
twin towers *Las Gemelas* (the twins) were
a later addition and it adjoins the Plaza del
Mercado lined with shops and cafés – try
the delightful Café Moderno on c/Matínez

Logrono – Café Moderno

Zaporta which opens (relatively) early for pilgrims trying to get back to the
hostel before it closes its doors. Off the west end of c/de Portales is the neo-
colonial edifice of the main Post Office *Correos de Telégraphos* adjoining the
18th century Palacio del Espartero (museum) off which is c/Laurel, famous for
its tapas bars. At the east end of c/de Portales close to the junction with the busy
c/Muro de Cervantes is Plaza Amós Salvador and the Iglesia San Bartolomé
with its exquisitely carved 13th century porch. Adjoining the albergue is the 12th
century Santa María del Palacio built on the site of an earlier palace with its
impressive cloisters and slender tower (known locally as the needle). For other
monuments along the Ruaviejo, see *leaving the albergue (next stage)*.

Detour: Clavijo is only 16 km south of Logroño. The sombre ruins of its castle
stand sentinel over the fields where legend has it Santiago first appeared on his
white charger to turn the tide of this historic battle in favour of the Spaniards
over the occupying Moors in 844. It is, however, approached through a rather
disappointing and untidy village landscape (enquire at Turismo for details).

LA RIOJA One of the smallest and yet more diverse of the autonomous regions of Spain and justifiably renowned for its superlative wines. However, it is not only its grapes that will tempt you, for here you will meet a friendly people who have been welcoming pilgrims since medieval times. Indeed, kings and noblemen were promoting the camino through La Rioja as early as the 11th century as a means of exporting its famous wine and wares throughout Europe (and a way of attracting artists and stonemasons to build the great cathedrals, monasteries and monuments along the route). Sandwiched between the mountains of Navarra and the flat plains of the meseta of Castilla y León, La Rioja is geographically split between High Rioja *Rioja Alta* to the northwest (the main wine growing region) and the lower *Rioja Baja* where market gardening is more prominent. The famous battle of Clavijo marks a turning point in the turbulent history of the provinces. With the defeat of the Moors came a great boost to Christianity and by extension, the Camino de Santiago. Logroño has good road and rail connections to all parts of Spain.

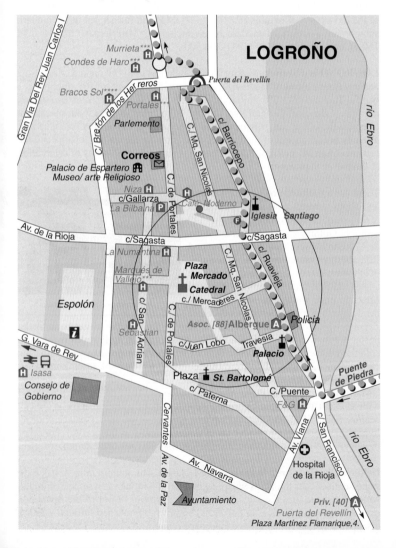

REFLECTIONS:

_____
_____
_____
_____
_____
_____
_____
_____
_____
_____
_____
_____
_____
_____
_____
_____
_____
_____
_____
_____
_____
_____
_____
_____
_____
_____
_____
_____
_____
_____
_____
_____
_____
_____
_____
_____

❏ **We are speeding up our lives and working harder,
in a futile attempt to slow down and enjoy it.** *Paul Hawken*

MAP 08 *635.5 km (394.9 miles) to Santiago de Compostela*

LOGROÑO – NÁJERA (La Rioja)

▬▬▬	Path / Track	--- ---	18.5	---	*63%*
▬▬▬	Quiet Road	--- ---	1.7	---	*6%*
▬▬▬	Main Road	--- ---	<u>9.2</u>	---	*31%*
Total km	**Total distance**		**29.4 km** (18.3 miles)		

Adjusted for climb 30.9 km (accrued ascent 300m = 1.5 km)
Alto ▲ High Point: Path at Poyo Roldán 600m (1,968 feet)

The Practical Path: One third of this stage is alongside the busy main roads that lead out of Logroño and into Navarette and Nájera. With constant road improvements, waymarking may be disturbed, so stay fully focused or you might lose your way – or your body. If nerves become frayed, you can always take refuge in the beautifully renovated intermediate albergues in Navarette or Ventosa. The natural pathways now turn to the rich red clay soil of La Rioja – beautiful in the sun and a nightmare in the wet as it clings to footwear like a leech! **Intermediate accommodation** (with distances from Logroño albergue): Navarette (12.4 km) and Ventosa (20.0 km).

❏ **The Mystical Path:** Hundreds of pilgrims have taken time to make a cross and place it in this godforsaken place. The cross is a symbol of that greater mystery that lies beyond the suffering of this world – are you inclined to add yours? Will you stop awhile to admire the beautiful stone portal, gateway to another journey that awaits us? Will you ponder the adjoining monument to a modern pilgrim who goes this way? Will you notice the roar of traffic and heed its urgency or will you 'get the hurry off you' and take a more leisurely pace? Will you take the direct route or venture to Ventosa? The choice, as always, is yours.

❏ **Personal Reflections:** *"... I found him hanging up some pilgrim's washing. His smile said welcome; his refuge was a veritable haven of peace. He suggested I stop and stay the night – we could share part of our journey over a meal together. Kas had urged me to meet him but I declined his invitation and now hurried onward anxious to reach the destination I had set myself. However, the next hostel was full and the hotel had no vacancy. I hurried on. It was getting late and I was already tired. The next village was two hours away ..."*

Leaving the albergue at Logroño follow the brass scallop shells inlaid into the sympathetically restored c/Rúaviejo which becomes the c/Barriocepo by the time it reaches the handsome pilgrim fountain *Fuente de los Peregrinos* decorated with Jacobean motifs. It adjoins a modernised square with mosaics

NÁJERA inset

Museo † Santa María la Real
C/S.Miguel
Pz.Navarra
España A Sancho[10]
Pz.Cruz
C/Mayor C/Carmen
Albergue [90]
río Nájerilla
San Fernando Pz.San
Francisco a Rioja
NÁJERA
C/Cepa Madre de Dios
Hispano Santa Elena
C/de Yuso

Muni.[90]
Albergue 3.3 → † Sta.María A Turismo ☎ 941-360 041

---NÁJERA---
(Pop.7,000 – Alt.490m)
río Nájerilla

Puente 6.1

río Yalde
Alesón Alto de San Antón Huércanos
▲ Alto 610m
N-120 Poyo de Roldán

(Pop.150 – Alt.650m)
VENTOSA
Albergue 5.9 A †
San Saturnino **Priv.***[50]

Sotés

Arco S. Juan →
Cementario 1.7 →
El Cántaro **Priv.**[16] A
Bilbao 〉
A-68
Haro 〉
NAVARETTE A **3.6 Albergue**
(Pop.2,200 – Alt.560m) Muni.[40] N-232

San Juan de Acre —
(ruinas)

▲ 540m
2.9 Alto Grajera

Plantano de
La Grajera
N-120
Plantano 3.8 F

Sunset
W
S N
E
Sunrise

A-68 túnel
Cruce 2.1

río Ebro

Cathedral †
(Pop.145,000 – Alt.380m) A **0.0 Albergue** Asoc.[90]
LOGROÑO

representing the pilgrimage in a board game *Juego del Oca* and up ahead is the impressive façade of the 16th century Iglesia de Santiago el Real (right) with a fine statue of Santiago Matamoros high up above the south door. The present building occupies the site of an earlier 9th century church erected to celebrate the defeat of the Moors at Clavijo. The interior also has several images of St. James. Continuing on through the narrow cobbled streets of the Old Town

Logrono – Iglesia Santiago

Casco Antiguo until it opens up into the paved Parliament Square *Plaza del Parlamento* with the impressive facade of the Parlamento de la Rioja whose building has been used for activities as diverse as a Carmelite convent and a tobacco factory!

We now leave the medieval quarter through the original pilgrim's gate *Puerta del Camino* [**0.5 km**] alternatively called Muralla del Revellín or Puerta Carlos V, the latter being a reference to the splendid armorial shields that adorn it. [!] Take a moment to collect your bearings – the next 3 km are through the frenzied suburbs of Logroño. With awareness, you will make it to the peaceful lake-shore café of La Grajera with relative ease – but stay focused! Yellow arrows will accompany you but they have to compete with the distracting symbols of commercialism, and are less obvious. The main route out is straight down the busy Marqués de Murrieta (signposted Burgos N-120) and over the railway line into Av. Burgos for [**1.6 km**] until you reach:

2.1 km **Cruce** Nissan Garage [!] Turn <left into c/Portillejo and make your way along the linear park and take the underpass [**1.6 km**]. The next section is through open parkland along a newly paved track with concrete benches, somewhat hard underfoot (and buttocks) but at least separated from the motorway bypass. This leads to a grove of pine trees visible ahead and after [**2.2 km**] we reach:

3.8 km **Plantano de la Grajera [F]** turn right> along the reservoir wall, through pine forest and over a footbridge up to the café and picnic area with good views of the lake. Be careful of the waymarking here, the route leads you around the lake shore along gravel pathways onto an asphalt track up towards the woodland on the horizon to:

2.9 km **Alto de la Grajera** providing a good view back over the route and Logroño. Now at the top of the rise the track runs alongside the highway where hundreds of crosses have been made out of strips of bark from the adjoining sawmill and placed on the wire fence that separates us from the busy city bypass: a timely reminder, perhaps, of the sacred nature of our journey and the tenuous boundary that separates us from a secular perspective. We now join the hard shoulder of the N-232 [!] and follow it until it veers off to our right and we continue along the N-120 towards Navarette before crossing over [!] onto earth track through fields and vineyards crossing over the autopista A-68 where, on the far side, we come to the ruins of the medieval monastery of the Order of San Juan de Acre founded in the 12th century to look after pilgrims on the way. The splendidly carved entrance porch has been re-sited as the gate to the cemetery that we will pass on the far side of town. Continue up the steep stone steps and over the bypass and into Navarette:

| 3.6 km | **Navarrete•Albergue[1]***municipal* hostel (Inmaculada 941-440 776) centrally located in the old town adjoining bar Los Arcos in c/San Juan. Open March-October (check possible availability in winter) with 40 beds in 4 rooms on 3 levels. All facilities including a washing machine *lavadora and* dryer *secadora* which makes up for the lack of any outside drying area. **•Albergue [2]** *El Cántaro* private hostel (941-441 180) adjoins the busy main road in a modern town house c/Herrerías, 16. Open all year with 16 beds (*[Next albergue: Ventosa – 7.6 km]*). Other accommodation: **•La Carioca**

Navarrete – Albergue [1] Municipal

Hs (941-440 805/006) c/Prudencio Muñoz, 1 on the main road or the more up market (quieter and centrally situated) **•Villa de Navarette** H* (941-440 318) on c/La Cruz opposite the church square.

NAVARETTE Another historic camino town where effort (with a few notable exceptions) has been made to maintain the original period houses with handsomely carved family crests and armorial shields. The imposing 16th century Church of the Assumption occupies a commanding position overlooking the top square **[F]** and below it is a Turismo (941-440 005 summer only). Bar Los Arcos provides simple food and at the other end of the medieval arcade is the tapas bar Deportivo with tables on the square. At the lower end of the town, on the main road, is a busy square with a number of other cafés and restaurant.

Leaving albergue [1] pass along the arcaded cobbled street up to the church square into the c/de Santiago and the c/San Roque down to join the main road at:

| 1.7 km | **Cementerio** with the splendidly carved 13th century entrance gateway (relocated here from the ruins of the hospice of San Juan de Acre on the eastern outskirts). One of the capitals depicts the battle between Roldán and Ferragut (see *Poyo Roldán* which we pass later.)

Continue past the cemetery where the camino now runs parallel to the main road along a track of bright red Riojan earth through vineyards, over the Río de la Fuente and minor road to Sotés, passing by the wine cooperative Vitivinicola. The route now lurches (somewhat confusingly) back to the main road before climbing back up towards the village of Ventosa atop a rise. Waymarks now offer the opportunity to bypass the village or visit it and the albergue (immediately the other side of the church above). To enter Ventosa turn <left and immediately right> up into the quiet village square with shop and bar and right> again to:

| 5.9 km | **Ventosa •Albergue** *San Saturnino* network* hostel (941-441 899) located just below the church. Open all year with 50 beds in 6 rooms and all facilities with pleasant dining area where a shared meal is often available. This is a sensitively restored and well-maintained hostel. *[Next Albergue: Nájera 9.4 km]*.

Albergue with church above

To continue, proceed back around (or over) the hill and pick up the waymarked path through peaceful countryside to the track that winds its way up through an isolated pass between two small hills where you will find a multitude of little stone mounds erected by individuals pausing to soak up the mystery of this mythical place. On our left is *Alto de San Antón* site of an early pilgrim hospital established by the Antonine Order *Ruinas de Convento de San Antón* (no longer discernible) while on the right is Roldan's Mound *Poyo de Roldán. (Here we are led to believe Roldán slew the Muslim giant Ferragut with a well-aimed rock. Roland liberated the town (where Ferragut ruled) and freed the captive Christian knights of Charlemagne's army. This legend, reminiscent of David and Goliath, retains its powerful impact along the camino.]* The magical surroundings are somewhat tarnished by overzealous waymarkers! Continue through the narrow pass (the high point of this stage at 610m) and head down towards Nájera, crossing a minor road to:

6.1 km **Puente** pilgrim footbridge over the river Yalde. Continue around the side of the gravel works along a track through vineyard to a large factory at the outskirts of Nájera where you cross the main road through a residential area that leads onto the busy main street. Pass the Guardia Civil and the Convento de Santa Elena and follow the main road as it narrows and descends towards the Río Nájerilla. Cross over the modern bridge (that replaced the medieval bridge erected by San Juan de Ortega) turning <left to take the riverside road to:

3.3 km **Nájera** •**Albergue** [1] *municipal* hostel in modern industrial style building off Plaza del Mercado adjoining the river. Open all year with 92 beds on one floor. All facilities but somewhat crowded (it has replaced the much loved former hostel in the old Franciscan monastery on Plaza de Santa María la Real which is undergoing restoration). •**Albergue** [2] *Sancho III* private hostel (941-361 138) on corner of c/San Marcial, 6 close to the monastery of

Nájera – Albergue [1]

Santa María, adjacent to restaurant La Juderia. Open from Easter to end of October with 10 beds in 1 room and pilgrim menú in restaurant. *[Next albergue: Azofra – 5.8].* **Other accommodation** in the old town is limited to •**Fonda el Moro** c/Martires, 21 (941-360 052) or the up-market •**Ciudad de Nájera** Hs² (941-360 660) calleja San Miguel, 14 (backing on to the cliffs) or •**Duques de Nájera** H² (941-410 421) on el Carmén, 7. On the other side of the river: •**Hispano** Hs (941-362 957) paseo San Julián, 12 or •**San Fernando** H² (941-363 700) also in paseo San Julián adjoining the river.

NÁJERA: Another historic town, capital of the Kingdom of Navarre in the 11th and 12th centuries, with strong connections with the Camino de Santiago, marking the beginning of stage V of the Codex Calixtinus. Pride of place is the Monasterio Santa María de la Real with its magnificent Royal Pantheon housing the burial place of many of the illustrious kings, Queens and knights of Navarre. Of singular beauty is the tomb of Doña Blanca de Castile y Navarre (1156). The Pantheon is part of this fine church, as is the cave, which gave rise to it. *[The church was built at this spot following the legend that the son of Sancho the Great, Don García, followed his hunting falcon into this cave and came upon a statue of the Virgin Mary.]* The church also has interesting choir stalls bearing pilgrim motifs carved into the seat rests. The splendid Knights Cloister is accessed through the Museum.

Nájera has a population of 7,000 and we enter through the modern eastern quarter with the old town sandwiched between the river Najerila and high rock face that acts as a dramatic backdrop. The narrow c/Mayor with a wide selection of shops, bars and cafés leads to the myriad side streets including Plaza San Miguel where at Nº 10 we find the *Turismo* (941-360 041). At the far end of town (close to the albergue) are the Plazas de España and Navarra with a variety of bars and restaurants serving pilgrim menus.

Detour: San Millán de la Cogolla and the monasteries of Suso and Yuso. This World heritage site represents one of the earliest known monastic communities in Europe dating back to the 6th century and is also credited with being the birthplace of the Spanish language. *(See next section under Azofra for full description of this and the Cistercian abbey at Cañas).* It can be walked (a very full day) from Nájera to San Millán (18 km on LR 205) and back via Cañas to Azofra (14 km on LR 206) but is more realistically visited as part of a tour or shared taxi from Nájera or by staying overnight at San Millán but accommodation is limited so book beforehand (see next section for details or enquire at the tourist office).

REFLECTIONS:

_____
_____
_____
_____
_____
_____
_____
_____
_____
_____
_____
_____
_____
_____
_____
_____

❑ **Yesterday is history, tomorrow a mystery and today a gift – that is why it is called the present.**

MAP 09 *603.1 km (374.8 miles) to Santiago de Compostela*

NÁJERA – SANTO DOMINGO de la CALZADA (La Rioja)

Path / Track	--- ---	17.4	---	*83%*
Quiet Road	--- ---	2.4	---	*11%*
Main Road	--- ---	1.2	---	*6%*

Total km Total distance　　　　**21.0 km** (13.0 miles)

Adjusted for climb　22.5 km (accrued ascent 300m = 1.5 km)

Alto ▲ High Point: Cirueña 745m (2,444 feet)

The Practical Path: The majority of this stage (83%) is on wonderful wide country tracks passing through remote and gently undulating farmland with only the last stretch into Santo Domingo alongside the main road. Beyond Azofra the camino crosses a secondary road (to Alesanco) where waymarks offer you the opportunity to join the busy N-120 (right) to 'save' you 1.5 km of delightful countryside. There is little shade and few drinking fonts on this stage so put on the hat and fill up the bottle as you pass Azofra and Cirueña (both have *fuentes*). **Intermediate accommodation**: Azofra 5.8 km – Cirueña 15.1 km.

❑ **The Mystical Path:** Will you pause to admire the medieval stone column that marks an ancient border? What does it mark and symbolise to you? Where is the border between your ancient Homeland and the world you now inhabit? Will you rest awhile in the leafy shade of the cool glade beyond to ponder such mysteries? How many pilgrims in the past has this venerable grove sheltered from the noonday sun and how many will it shelter in the future? Will you accept its sombre gift in the passing moment, a present from the acorn past?

❑ **Personal Reflections:** *"… I entered the cool interior and realised I was the only person present. I had the urge to leave but at that moment the bells stopped ringing and the nuns began to file in. I knelt in silence and then lifted my head at the sound of approaching footsteps. I looked up into eyes that beamed such love and acceptance that I momentarily lost any sense of ego-self as I followed her to the choir stall. Tears began to stream down my face as the nuns started their heavenly chanting… The unconditional love with which I was embraced overwhelmed me as my head began to spin and I collapsed onto the pew. The nun in front turned and quietly laid her hand on mine. She produced a tissue from the sleeve of her habit and bent down and whispered gently, 'breathe.' I write these notes in the quiet of the convent, and am struck by the realisation that she could not have known where I was from and yet spoke the only word in English that was needed. In that moment she, or rather that which she represented, quite literally inspired me. I am utterly unable to convey the gratitude I feel …"*

SANTO DOMINGO DE CALZADA
(Pop.5,600–Alt.640m)

río Oja

Haro >

5.9 Albergue [1]
Asoc.[80] Casa del Santo

Conv.[34]
Abadía Cisterciense

N-120

San Francisco

Parador

Miguel

c/ San Juan Carlos · Av. Juan Carlos · Paseo de Espolón

Turismo
i **Correos**

C/Castro

Parador
c/del Pinar · Salas · c/Isidoro

Plaza Santo
Catedral

Plaza Mayor

Plaza Alameda

**Autobus
Taxi**

c/ San Roque

Casa del Santo

c/ de las · Monjas

Abadía

El Corregidor

Santa Teresita

Av. Calatorra

**SANTO DOMINGO
DE LA CALZADA**

Virgen de Guadalupe
Cirueña 9.3 *Priv.*

Ciriñuéla
Priv.[12]

▲ Alto
745m

*Rioja Alta
Golf Club*

**Monasterio
San Millán**
(Azofra–16 km)

Cañas
(Azofra–6 km)

**Abadía
Cisterciense**

Alesanco

I ← picota XVI (columna justicia)

fuente de los romeros

5.8 Albergue *Muni.[60]*

La Fuente Priv.[12]

AZOFRA
(Pop.300)

río Tuerto

O

*Puesta
del Sol*

S

N ►

Z O N A

N A T U R A L

N-120

*Salida
del Sol*

E

Muni.[90] Albergue 0.0 ►

NÁJERA
(Pop.7,000 – Alt.490m)

Leaving the albergue at Nájera make your way through the Plaza de Navarre past the Church of Santa María Real and continue up the street passing the pelota court (left) and enter the delightful *zona natural* climbing steeply up between pine trees on a wide red earth track to the high point **[1.0 km]** (460m). The track continues for another **[2.9 km]** until it joins a quiet asphalt road for the remaining **[1.9 km]** into the village of:

Azofra – Albergue [1] Municipal

| 5.8 km | Azofra •**Albergue** [1] purpose built municipal hostel (941-379 049) in c/ Las Parras, 200m (right) from the central fountain. Open all year with 60 places in rooms with just 2 beds. Its extensive facilities includes a patio rest area. •**Albergue** [2] *La Fuente* private hostel centrally situated adjoining the fountain. Closed in recent years but indications that it may reopen. •**Albergue** [3] original parish hostel (María Tobia 941-379 057) adjoining the Church of Our Lady of the Angels *Nuestra Señora de los Angeles* often opens for pilgrim mass - statue of Santiago Peregrino. The church is situated at the top of the street, above the central fountain. 26 beds and small patio by the entrance that gets the last of the evening sun. The lean-to structure was renovated many years ago by a German Confraternity (Herbert Simón). The cool, atmospheric surroundings compensates for the basic facilities. Exclusive hotel Real Casona de las Amas (941 416 103) on c/Mayor, 5 rooms from €130. *(Next albergue: Cirueña – 9.3 km).*

AZOFRA A tranquil village with a population of barely 500 that owes its continuing existence to the camino. As you leave the village a small park **[F]** (left) is dedicated to the patroness of La Rioja *Virgen de Valvanera* and on the other side of the road (50m off route) the ruins of the medieval pilgrim's fountain *Fuente de los Romeros* adjoining a lay-by with a modern monument. There are 2 inconspicuous shops (adjacent to the albergues) and several bars that compete to provide the pilgrim with sustenance. There were several pilgrim *hospitals* here in medieval times. Azofra is also the easiest place to start a detour of the 'monasteries route' *ruta de los monasterios* and the birthplace of the Spanish language *la cuna del Castellano* in Yuso.

Detour [1] Cañas 6 km south along a quiet country road. The village is home to the splendid Cistercian abbey of Santa María *Abadía Cisterciense de Cañas* founded in 1170 for the order of nuns that still occupy it (closed Mondays). It is unusual among religious buildings for the natural light *luz* that pours into it through the original alabaster windows that reach up to the vaulted roof. Off the adjoining

Cañas – Sarcophagus

garden courtyard is a small museum housing the early 13th century sarcophagus of Doña Urraca López de Haro founder of the abbey and, reputedly, one of the finest sarcophagi in Spain. The abbey is also celebrated for the visit of Saint Francis of Assisi who allegedly stayed here while journeying to Santiago. Cañás is the birthplace of Santo Domingo de Silos (not to be confused with Santo Domingo de Calzada) who restored the famous monastery that now bears his name and the home of Gregorian chant in Spain (see Burgos detours).

Options: from here you can either: (a) return back to Azofra and continue along the camino or (b) take the country road out of Cañas to Cirueña and rejoin the camino there or (c) continue to:

Detour [2] San Millán Yuso and Suso Monasteries 10 km south of Cañas (16 from Azofra). Declared a world heritage site by UNESCO in 1997 as testimony to its unique contribution to Christian monasticism from the 6th century and as birthplace of the Spanish language, one of the most widely spoken in the world today. It was here in the 10th century that the native Spanish language, Castilian *Castellano*, was first written down by an anonymous monk. Two centuries later it was further embellished in the verse of the poet monk Gonzalo Berceo.

Suso (the smaller and higher of the two monasteries) is set on the hillside in this gloriously peaceful valley located just beyond the village of Berceo. It has Visigothic, Mozárabe and Romanesque characteristics while Yuso, built from 11th century onwards, is mainly Baroque and houses some fine artefacts including the famous library. Realistically you will really need an extra day to explore this area. Part of the monastery at Yuso is now a luxury hotel •Hostería del Monasterio de San Millán H**** (941-373 277) single from €90. Former pilgrim accommodation in the monastery is no longer available but •**Hostal La Calera** Hs (941-373 268) has rooms from €40 and several other possibilities available in Badarán 5 km •**Pensión Alaska** (941-367 005) is at the cheaper end. Return via Cañas (see options).

From Azofra continue over the junction by the village park **[F]** and bear off <left onto a track passing the medieval marker *la picota*. From here several paths wind their way through the fertile fields (avoid the ones that take you back to the N-120) and follow the waymarks directing you up towards the new golf complex on the rise in front *Rioja Alta Golf Club*. Pass the grove of Holm oak into the village of:

9.3 km **Cirueña** café/bar Jacobeo (50m left as you enter) •**Albergue** *Virgen de Guadalupe* opened in 2009. Continue right to **Option [?]** as you leave the village there is an option to go direct to Ciriñuela clearly visible ahead (right) a detour of ½ kilometre to •**Albergue** hostel with basic facilities summer only. To continue on the camino veer <left down the road and <left onto farm track that undulates over the surrounding fields until you reach the outskirts of St. Dominic of the roadway *Santo Domingo de la Calzada*. Here we pass behind industrial buildings before reaching the busy N-120, which we now follow until crossing over into the old town. If you lose the waymarks in the busy streets ahead follow the signpost for the *Parador* up the c/Mayor to:

5.9 km **Santo Domingo de la Calzada** •**Albergue [1]** *Casa del Santo* operated by the Spanish Confraternity (941-343 390) who also publishes the pilgrim magazine *El Peregrino* from here. Centrally situated in the old quarter on c/Mayor, 42. Open all year with 83 beds (4 rooms upstairs + overflow in ground floor dormitory to the rear). All facilities including delightful shaded garden with chicken coop where the cocks and hens are kept for their pivotal part in the cathedral myth (See below). •**Albergue [2]** *Abadía Cisterciense* delightfully cool and peaceful hostel run by Cistercian nuns (941-340 570) on c/Mayor, 29 (left) as you enter the old quarter (opposite rear entrance of Hotel El Corregidor) at junction of the Street of the Nuns and the High Street *calle de las Monjas and calle Mayor*. Open May – September with 34 beds in 6 rooms and all facilities with a large atmospheric diningroom and peaceful shaded terrace. All pilgrims (both genders) are very welcome. Vespers *Vísperas* at 18.30. *(Next albergue: Grañon – 7.0 km).*

Other accommodation •**Hospedería Santa Teresita** Hs** (941-340 700) modern hostel also run by the Cistercian nuns c/Pinar, 2 (to the rear of albergue [2]). •**Río** P (941-340 277) c/Etchegoyen, 2. **Pensión** •**Albert** P (941-340 827) c/ Beato Hermosilla, 20. •**El Peregrino** P (941-342 128) Av. de Calahorra (behind the town hall). •**Miguel** P (941-343 252) c/Juan Carlos I, 23 on far side of paseo in modern part of town. In the higher price bracket are: •**El Corregidor** H*** (941-340 827) c/Mayor, 20 or for 4 star luxury in the original pilgrim hospital on Plaza del Santo (opposite the cathedral) •**Parador** H**** (941-340 300) or try the latest edition to the Parador chain •**Parador de Santo Domingo Bernardo de Fresneda** H*** (915–166 666) located at the far end of town beside the pilgrim monument in the recently refurbished 16th century Convento de San Francisco.

SANTO DOMINGO de la CALZADA: The winding streets of this ancient town evoke a sense of history that is intimately linked with the camino. It owes its inspiration to *Saint Dominic of the Road*, so called because he effectively dedicated his life to improving the physical route for pilgrims and was responsible for building many of the roads and bridges that we pass along. This was in the 11th century, so they have been rebuilt several times since then but his spirit is as alive today as are the cock and hen in the cathedral coop. A giant among men he was born in humble surroundings in Villamayor del Río (see next stage) and, allegedly, turned away from the monastery at San Millán because of his illiteracy. The loss to the intelligentsia has been the gain of pilgrims for the past millennia. He built a pilgrim hospital, now the Parador and a church which has evolved

Santo Domingo

into the Cathedral both are situated in the historic town square *Plaza del Santo* and, like many other religious structures, renovated over many centuries and therefore combining different architectural styles. The original church was consecrated in the 12th century, although the independent tower was not added until the 18th century. The dark interior houses the tomb of Santo Domingo, the chapel of La Magdalena and a fine altarpiece. One of the more unlikely exhibits is a chicken coop at the rear of the church containing 2 live fowl.

[The chicken coop relates back to the story of the Miracle of the Cock and Hen. Embellished over the years it has become one of the more endearing legends along the Way of St. James. Legend has it that a pilgrim couple and their son stopped at an inn here on their way to Santiago. The pretty innkeeper's daughter had her eye on the handsome lad, but the devout young fellow thwarted her advances. Incensed by his refusal she hid a silver goblet in his backpack and reported him for stealing it. The innocent lad was caught and condemned to

hang. Some accounts suggest the parents continued on their way, oblivious of the fate of their son and on their return from Santiago they found him still hanging on the gallows but miraculously still alive thanks to the intervention of Santo Domingo. They rushed to the sheriff's house and found him just about to tuck into dinner. Upon hearing the news, he retorted that their son was no more alive than the cock and hen he was about to eat, whereupon the fowl stood up on the dish and crowed loudly. The miracle was not lost on the sheriff who rushed back to the gallows and cut down the poor lad, who was given a full pardon. We are left to speculate on the fate of the foxy maiden.] Indeed so many miracles were ascribed to the intervention of Santo Domingo that the town that came to carry his name was also referred to as the *Compostela of Rioja*.

A museum is attached to the cathedral and on the opposite side of the square is the original pilgrim hospital, now the luxury Parador that still retains its medieval splendour. The town has a wide variety of restaurants, bars and shops along both the c/Mayor and the busy Paseo and the narrow interconnecting streets all serving the inflow of tourists, pilgrims and the local population of 6,000. The town and its network of medieval streets has been declared a site of historic interest. The helpful tourist office *Turismo* (941-341 230) is just past the cathedral at c/Mayor, 70. The town's main fiesta, in honour of the saint, takes place during the first 2 weeks in May.

REFLECTIONS:

❐ **When you meet anyone, remember it is a holy encounter.**
   And as you see them you will see yourself. *A Course In Miracles*

MAP 10 *582.1 km (361.7 miles) to Santiago de Compostela*

SANTO DOMINGO de la CALZADA – BELORADO
(La Rioja)   (Castilla y León)

▬▬▬	Path / Track	--- ---	10.4	---	*44%*
▬▬▬	Quiet Road	--- ---	2.3	---	*10%*
▬▬▬	Main Road	--- ---	<u>11.2</u>	---	*46%*
Total km	**Total distance**		**23.9 km** (14.9 miles)		

Adjusted for climb 25.4 km (accrued ascent 300m = 1.5 km)
Alto ▲ High Point: above Vilamayor del Río 810m (2,657 feet)

The Practical Path: It is a strange tribute to the Saint who did so much to assist the pilgrim that today we are forced by new road works to travel closer to the dangerous N-120 more than at any other stage of our journey so far. Waymarking is also not obvious and if you are not careful you might end up walking on the main road all the way to Belorado! Be prepared for half today's walk to be parralel the busy main road with little shelter and water, apart from the villages you pass through. **Intermediate accommodation** (distances from Santo Domingo albergue [1]): Grañón (7.0 km) – Carrasquedo (8.1 km) 1.1 km *off* route – Redecilla (11.0 km) Castildelgado (12.8 km) – Viloria de la Rioja (15.0 km) – Villamayor del Río (18.7 km) 300m *off* route.

❐ **The Mystical Path:** There is much to reflect on as you walk the road of the Saint. Denied access to the seat of knowledge, yet endowed with wisdom. Which do you seek? Which will provide you with real meaning? The burial place is on all the maps but will you discover the place of birth? Will you stay awhile and soak up the light of this peaceful place and drink the cool water from the same well that perhaps nurtured the infant child? – not as obvious as the tap in the square, but more refreshing. The only monument to this extraordinary Saint is a ruined house protecting the peace of this place from the tour buses. This is truly an elevated place providing refreshment for the soul and space to contemplate our own renewal.

❐ **Personal Reflections:** *"… I resisted his advances and resented his intrusion. He could see I was limping badly and persisted in his offer to help. My resistance finally crumpled and he removed my boot and sock with tenderness. My foot was an awful mess – it had gone way beyond what any reasonable person would have asked of it. He fetched a basin of warm water and gently washed away the blood. The broken skin was easily dressed and the remaining blisters drained. Afterwards he took my torn boot to the nearby cobbler to have it stitched. He had healed my foot and mended my boot but the real healing was happening inside of me. How many times had I adversely judged my fellow travellers when each one is a Christ in disguise …"*

BELORADO
(Pop. 2,000 – Alt. 770m)

Plaza
A 1.0 Albergue [3]
Par.[46] Santa Maria

A 4.5 Albergue [1]
Priv.[110] A Santiago*

Alto 880m

▲ Alto 820m
Fabrica
● km 64

VILAMAYOR del RÍO
Restaurant León
F 3.4 Fuente

la aldea encantada
C Quintanilla del Monte

Priv.[36]*
San Luis de Francia

Villamayor

Fresneña

Cuna de Sto. Domingo
VILORIA de la RIOJA
Albergue 2.2 A
Acacio y Orietta Priv.[12]*

N-120

CASTILLA y LEÓN

Arroyo Relachigo

H El Chocaltero
1.8 Castildelgado

REDECILLA del CAMINO
Albergue 4.0 A
Muni.[50]

LA RIOJA

GRAÑÓN
A 2.7 Albergue *Par.[40]*
San Juan Bautista

Carrasquedo 1.1 A
Albergue Juvenil [40]

Corporales

Cruz de los Valientes †

4.3 <Camino

Herramélluri - Leiva - Tormantos >

N-120

SANTO DOMINGO DE CALZADA
(Pop.5,600 – Alt.640m)

A 0.0 Albergue
Casa Santo Asoc.[90]

río Oja

Inset map (Belorado town)

Av. de Burgos
urgos
Ojarrre
H Belorado
c/Extramuros

Cuatro Cantones
c/Hipólito
A 5 [60]
S.Francisco

N-120

Jacobeo

[22] *El Caminante

i Plaza Mayor
A 4
A 3
Santa Maria [46]
Corro [40]
A 2
c/Corro
C

c/ Mayor
Verdeanco

A 1 A Santiago*[110]

Compass

O
Puesta del Sol
N
S
E
Salida del Sol

Leaving albergue [1] at Santo Domingo we pass the cathedral and head out along c/Mayor and pick up the main road (signposted Burgos) to the small *ermita* on the bridge over the río Oja. *(Before the arrival of bridge-building Dominic, medieval pilgrims had to veer off right here along the river towards Leiva to follow the Río Tirón into Belorado. There is still an alternative route to Belorado via Herramélluri, Leiva (Peregrina) and Tormantos to the North. This is approximately 3 km longer, mostly by road and is little used.)* Cross the Saint's Bridge *Puente del Santo* along track (right) before crossing over the main road and continuing along a gravel path on the far side. A remote cross (left) *La Cruz de los Valientes* so called because of the combat between two locals, one from Santo Domingo and the other from Grañon, over disputed ownership of some nearby land. *[In medieval times, it was sometimes the custom to submit such matters to the Divine Judge on the basis that He would protect the innocent party – the guy from Grañón was favoured in this instance.]* Beyond the road junction (right) veer off <left onto track (avoid continuing along the main road):

4.3 km <**Camino** veer <left and then right> along farm tracks with cerro del Mirabel and Grañón visible on the horizon.

2.7 km **Grañón •Albergue** parish hostel located in the upper floors of the annex to the adjoining Church of Saint John the Baptist. Open all year with 40+ mattresses on the attic floor and one small bedroom and reserved only for pilgrims who have travelled from further back than Santo Domingo. The atmospheric lounge dovetails as a dining area with small but adequate kitchenette from which a shared meal is often prepared. Basic hostel much treasured by pilgrims for the hospitality offered, the cool interior and tranquil setting, accessed directly off the village plaza with its shaded garden.

Grañón – Parish Albergue

GRAÑÓN VILLAGE: This walled town was inspired by the camino and had 2 monasteries and a pilgrim hospice. Today, we find a quiet village that remains typically Jacobean. Iglesia de San Juan Bautista has a fine high altarpiece, recently restored and a pilgrim mass is offered by the welcoming priest. If the albergue is full or you want to extend your stay in this peaceful oasis you can:

Detour to the pretty Basilica of Nuestra Señora de Carrasquedo, the patroness of Grañon village, situated amidst a grove of trees on the outskirts of the town (1.1 km) on the road to Corporales along a delightful tree-lined pathway. You can stay in the youth hostel, a venerable period building adjoining the basilica •**Albergue** *de Carrasquedo* (941-746 000) accommodation available on basis of dinner (21:00) bed and breakfast (09:00) (phone in advance to check availability).

From Grañon turn <left out of the village and continue on track turning right> to cross stream and then <left up to a monstrous modern signboard heralding the fact that you have left modest La Rioja behind and stepped into the autonomous region of Castilla y León (province of Burgos) a fact that the authorities seem keen to remind you of as frequently as they can from their ivory towers in León.

CASTILLA Y LEÓN The largest autonomous region in Spain with an area of 95,000 km² (11 times the size of the region of Madrid) but a population of only 2.5 million (less than half that of Madrid). You will spend over 50% of your time travelling through 3 of its 9 separate provinces BURGOS, PALENCIA and LEÓN. It contains the incomparable *meseta* the predominately flat table or plateau region that makes up a third of the Iberian peninsular and lies between 1,000 and 3,000 metres above sea level and follows the line of the Duero river basin. Cereal crops *cerales* hold sway here, mainly wheat but with oats on the poorer land and some sheep and goats grazing on the hillier parts. It is a sparsely populated arid region, primarily flat but with gently rolling hills. However, the seemingly endless horizons are broken up with delightful villages seemingly unaffected by the speed of modern life.

Distant mountains break up the horizon. We start off walking through the Montes de Oca with the Sierra de la Demanda to our left (south) and the Cordillera Cantábrica to our right (north) with the occasional view of the snow covered Picos de Europa behind them – the highest peak is Peña Vieja 2,613m (8,500 feet). We then pass through the Montes de León which supports one of the enduring symbols of the *camino francés* the Iron Cross *Cruz de Ferro* at the high point of our route 1,505m (4,937 feet). Beyond this is the western arm of the Cordillera Cantábrica, which forms the boundary between Castilla y León and Galicia, which we enter through the Puerto de Pedrifita do Cebreiro at 1,110m (3,640 feet) but that is over 400 km away!

You will find many pamphlets and books along the way (some in English) that will detail the rich history of this vast region. Suffice to say that the ancient kingdom of Castile is well named for its many castles, which sought to protect and promote the kingdom. This promotion was nowhere more conspicuous than along the *Camino de Santiago*. It is well to recall that, up until the time the Saint's tomb was discovered, Spain was largely under the influence of the Moors. Fernando I established Castile in 1035 and the 1090's saw the legendary figure of El Cid turning the tide against the Moors from his base in Burgos. 200 years after its foundation Castile was united with León under Fernando III *El Santo*. It was an uneasy union and even today you will see many defaced signboards that bear the joint arms of the former separate jurisdictions, a separation that some would clearly like to see re-imposed. The general and medical emergency *emergencias* number for the area is 112.

Cross the N-120 into Redecilla del Camino with rest area **[F]** and *Turismo* (947-588 080 summer only). Proceed into the main street to the church dedicated to Our Lady of the Street *Nuestra Señora de la Calle* which has a beautiful 12th century baptismal font and is located directly opposite the pilgrim hostel.

4.0 km **Redecilla del Camino** •**Albergue** municipal hostel (947-588 078) c/ Mayor built on the site of the medieval hospital of San Lázaro, now a busy bar. Open all year with 50 spaces in 4 rooms and all facilities. Passing between the church and the albergue continue up the c/Mayor before crossing the N-120 onto track which runs parallel to the road into:

1.8 km **Castildelgado** 16th century Church of San Pedro that has fared better than the adjoining ruins of the house of the Counts of Berberana and the pilgrim hospice founded by Alfonso VII that the village once supported. Hospitality is now limited to •**El Chocalatero** Hs (947-588 063) on the main road. The camino goes through the back of the village to pick up the track again parallel to main road for **[1.0 km]** before turning off <left onto country road for **[1.2 km]** into:

2.2 km **Viloria de la Rioja** •**Albergue*** network hostel* (Acacio & Orietta 947-582 220 / 679-941 123) just below the church on a tranquil square in the centre of this delightful village, open all year with 12 spaces and outside terrace with all facilities including communal dinner. Acacio is a key figure in the Asociacion Jacobea *paso a paso* and instigated the network association *red de albergues* that has done so much to improve pilgrim facilities along the camino. Paulo Coelho

Viloria de la Rioja – Albergue

is a supporter and godfather *padrino* to this hostel. This peaceful village was the birthplace *cuna* of Saint Dominic, but the Romanesque baptismal font that witnessed his Christening has been removed and, inconceivably, the adjacent house where he was born was demolished – a blessing perhaps, as tourist coaches bypass this historic idyll. Perhaps you will pause awhile by the shaded rest area **[F]** (there is a fresh spring just behind the church) and give thanks for the famous illiterate son of this quaint village who did so much to help pilgrims along the Way. Proceed out of the village by quiet country road for **[1.3 km]** to rejoin a track alongside the N-120 for another **[2.1 km]** slog into:

3.4 km **Villamayor del Río [F]** •**Albergue*** *San Luis de Francia* network hostel* (Maria Carmen & Roberto 947-562 022) 300m off route, on the far side of N-120 (sign clearly visible from the main road). Open all year with 52 places in 9 rooms recently refurbished and dinner and breakfast also available. At the end of road, in Quintanilla del Monte, is the enchanting casa rural •**la Encantada** where Ana de la Cruz offers a warm pilgrim welcome (947-580 484). Restaurant León on the main road also has a shop selling up-market products from the region including quality wines, air-dried sausages *embutidos*, blood sausage *morcillas* and *chorizo*. The camino continues parallel to **N-120 for [5.5 km]** all the way into Belorado. Just before entering the town cross the N-120 [!] by picnic area and follow wide track into Belorado passing:

4.5 km **Belorado** •**Albergue*** **[1]** *A Santiago* network* hostel on the back road into town (1 km from Belorado centre) 110 beds (947-562 164). Facilities include café/restaurant & small swimming pool but pilgrims generally prefer the welcome found in the town centre. Continue along the back road into town passing Casa Rural Verdeancho and •**Albergue [2]** *El Corro* (670-691 173) private hostel on corner of c/Mayor and El Corro, with 40 bed spaces in various rooms. Open all year with good range of facilities and adjoining the church:

1.0 km **Belorado** •**Albergue [3]** *Santa María* the original parish hostel (947-580 085) adjoining the church of Santa María in a quiet oasis 500m north of the main square. Open all year (hospitaleros in summer) with 24 places in a refurbished building adjoining the church. The welcoming ambience and tranquil setting softens the minimalist furnishings. Behind the albergue are cliffs with ancient (and modern) cave dwellings and a path up to the castle ruins. •**Albergue*** **[4]** *El Caminante* (947-580 231) network* hostel opposite the church with 22 places + individual rooms and meals available. Open April – October. At the other end of town we find the popular •**Albergue [5]** *Cuatro Cantones* (696-427 707) private hostel in renovated building just off the main square in c/Hipólito Lopez Bernal, 10. Open all year with 60 places in 2 main dormitories and excellent facilities with outside patio area and small swimming pool in summer. *[Next albergue – Tosantos 5.0 km].*

Other accommodation several casa rurales. •**Casa Verdeancho** (659-484 584) c/El Corro. •**Casa Waslala** (947-580 726) c/Mayor, 57. Pensions include •**Ojarre** P (947-580 223) c/Santiago, 16 and •**Toni** P (947-580 525) c/Redecilla del Campo, 7 (by the *Correos*). •**Hotel Jacobeo** on the busy main road near the centre and further out •**Belorado** H*(947-580 684) Av. Generalismo, 30.

BELORADO: has a delightful 'down at heal' ambience where the population of 2,000 conduct their affairs at a leisurely pace. *Turismo* (947-580 226) located in the town hall on the spacious plaza Mayor that has an interesting medieval arcade and is lined with shops, bars and restaurants. Belorado is another historic town along the Way created in the steep valley of the río Tirón. The 16th century Church of Santa María has a fine altarpiece with images of *Santiago Matamoros y Peregrino* and is built up against the limestone cliffs. The ancient cave dwellings, once home to hermits, are still visible behind the Church (as well as an interesting modern conversion!). San Capraiso was one of the hermits that sought refuge here, but inspired by the fearlessness of a young martyr, he gave himself to also be martyred for his faith and subsequently became patron saint of the pilgrim route to Rome *Via Francigena*. The castle ruins also point to the town's defensive past straddling the old border of Castile and it has Roman origins. The hermitage of Our Lady of Bethlehem *Nuestra Señora de Belén* is on the eastern outskirts and is all that remains of the pilgrim hospital that used to adjoin it and as we leave town on the western side we pass the Convento de Santa Clara. The two other churches, in the centre of the town, are dedicated to San Nicolás and San Pedro.

REFLECTIONS:

❏ **Man cannot stand a meaningless life.** *Carl Jung*

MAP 11 *558.2 km (346.9 miles) to Santiago de Compostela*

BELORADO – SAN JUAN de ORTEGA

	Path / Track	--- ---	21.1	---	88%
	Quiet Road	--- ---	1.0	---	4%
	Main Road	--- ---	2.0	---	8%
Total km	**Total distance**		**24.1 km**		**(15.0 miles)**

Adjusted for climb 26.6 km (accrued ascent 500m = 2.5 km)
Alto ▲ High Point: Montes de Oca (above Valdefuente) 1,050m (3,444 feet)

The Practical Path: Today is one of much variation in terrain and unlike yesterday a glorious 88% on paths and earthen tracks. From the suburbs of Belorado the path continues parallel to the N-120 along level open countryside but with some shade provided by hedgerow and woodland. Half way along this stage, at *Villafranca Montes de Oca*, the path climbs through these 'mountains' (high point at just over 1,000m) with its cover of oak and then pine before dropping down to the remote pilgrim village of St. John of the Nettle *San Juan de Ortega* a disciple of Santo Domingo. Here, far from the distractions and speed of the modern world we find a slower pace and time, perhaps, to contemplate the inner journey. **Intermediate Accommodation** (distances from Belorado albergue [1]): Tosantos (5.0 km) – Villambistia (6.8 km) Epinosa del Camino (8.4 km) – Villafranca de Oca (11.9 km)

❏ **The Mystical Path:** Here at the start of the 21st century our path takes us past the ruins of this ancient monastery whose roots extend back to the 9th. The rough masonry is softened by the horseshoe entrance, a symbol of its Mozarabic past. Where were we when the first stone was laid in this ancient memorial to God? Where will we be when the last stone falls to the ground and is lost to physical sight and memory? Will we have served our purpose for this incarnation? 'It takes so many thousand years to wake, but will we wake for pity's sake.'

❏ **Personal Reflections:** *"… Finally, I was able to pay my dues. The last time I stayed here I had been indignant at its shabby interior and as retribution I had left without offering a contribution towards its upkeep. I never considered why the mop had been left there. I presumed it was for someone else to do the cleaning. How many times have I passed a mop and bucket with the expectation that someone else would clean up after me? Is this the pilgrim way? Before enlightenment: chop wood, carry water, clean floor. After enlightenment: chop wood, carry water, clean floor. In the trivia of life one finds the meaning of Life. That I will awaken is not in doubt, but when, oh when? …"*

A ← 6.5 Albergue *Par.[60]*
■ **ST. JUAN de ORTEGA**
(Pop. 20 – Alt. 950m)

† *Ermita Valdefuente*
F ← 2.0 **Fuente** *Valdefuentes/Carnero*

Puerto Pedraja
1,095m

▲ *Alto 1,100m*

arroyo Peroja

(m) ← 2.3 **Monumento** *a los Caídos*

Ermita Virgen de Oca †

Pozo F
San Indalecio Martír

F ← 1.4 **Fuente** *de Mojapán*

río Oca

† *San Antón* **Priv.[12]**
■ **VILLAFRANCA MONTES DE OCA**
Muni.[38] **Albergue [1]** 3.5 → A H *El Pajaro*   *(Pop. 200 – Alt. 950m)*

río Oca

San Felices (ruinas)

EPINOSA del CAMINO
A ← 1.6 **Albergue** *Priv.[10]* **La Campana**

VILLAMBISTIA
Piedra del Mar **Par.*[30]** **Albergue** 1.8 F A

TOSANTOS
San Francisco de Asís **Par.[20] Albergue** 5.0 → A ■

† *Ermita Virgen de la Peña*

F

San Miguel de Podroso

W *Sunset*
S
N
E *Sunrise*

río Tirón

■ *Santa María*
BELORADO
(Pop. 2,000 – Alt. 770m)
† A ← 0.0 **Albergue [3]**
■ *Par.[40] Santa María*

Leaving albergue [3] at Belorado enter the **Plaza Mayor** and cross it diagonally past café (right) turning <left into the narrow c/Hipolito Lopez Bernal past albergue Cuarto Cantones (right). The camino winds its way through the suburbs for **[1.0 km]** out onto the N-12. Continue for another **[1.0 km]** past the hotel Belorado and across the wooden footbridge over the **río Tirón** (adjoining one originally built by Santo Domingo) and turn off <left just beyond the petrol station (signposted San Miguel de Pedroso) and immediately right> onto a path that continues parallel to the main road for **[3.0 km]** past a picnic spot by a stream **[F]** to:

5.0 km Tosantos popular •Albergue *San Francisco de Asís* (947-580 085) parish hostel in a renovated building opposite the church on the main road. Open from April – October with 30+ places on mattresses on floor in 3 rooms. The basic facilities are enhanced by the warm welcome and there is a pleasant garden area in front. A communal meal with prayers is offered. Bar *El Castaño* is located on the main road. **Detour:** 1 km away on the opposite side of the main road is the unusual hermitage of Our Lady of the Rock *Ermita de la Virgen de la Peña* built into the side of the cliffs and dating from the 12th century. It is usually locked and so the mystery of what lies within remains hidden. You can, however, see its white facade from the camino as you leave Tosantos. Continue to the back of Tosantos along a farm track to:

1.8 km Villambistia new •Albergue *San Roque* (947-582 147) private albergue (see photo) open summer period with 27 places and all facilities in the centre of this small hamlet with Ermita de San Roque and **[F]**. Cross over the stream and continue for **[1.6 km]** crossing N-120 into:

1.6 km Espinosa del Camino •Albergue *La Campana* (José Mir 678-479 361) open during the summer period with 10 places in 2 rooms. Limited facilities but meals are provided. Pass along the short main street of this sleepy hamlet onto an earth track up a short rise at the top of which Villafranca becomes visible. Continue down the other side passing the 9th century ruins of Monasterio de San Felices de Oca with its distinctive Mozarabic horseshoe arch. Count Diego Porcelos, founder of Burgos, is buried below these ruins – we pass his statue on the way into the city. The track now takes a wide sweep to avoid the main road that we have to join for a dangerous [!] 900m slog to cross the río Oca and enter:

3.5 km Villafranca de Montes de Oca •Albergue **[1]** municipal hostel (see photo) with welcoming hospitaleros (947-582 124) on the busy N-120 adjoining the farmacia and part of the community health centre and school building. Open all year with 36 places in 2 dormitories (rear room quieter) with basic facilities and large courtyard to the rear. •Albergue **[2]** *San Antón Abad* new hostel open in 2009 to the rear of the exclusive hotel (of

Villafranca – Albergue [1]

which it is part). The owner has travelled the camino on several occasions and this hostel fulfils his wish to 'give something back'. 12 bed spaces with all modern facilities. **Other accommodation:** •**Hotel San Antón Abad** luxury hotel. •**Hostal El Pajaro** (947-582 029) situated above the bar on the noisy main road, popular with both truckers and pilgrims (opens early for breakfast). On the opposite corner of the main road is the modest entrance to a

Villafranca – Albergue [2]

pilgrim friendly shop with good range of products.

VILLAFRANCA de MONTES de OCA: The untidy approach, with its truck stop for vehicles using the Puerto de la Pedraja, belies the historic roots of this town that welcomed pilgrims as early as the 9th century. This is one of several *Villafrancas* along the way that became home to Franks arriving as pilgrims and returning as artisans thus giving these towns their familiar appellation. The Spanish translation for goose is *oca* giving a romantic notion of wild geese whereas the name may actually derive from an earlier settlement *Auca*.

The village is located at the foot of the *Montes de Oca*, formerly a wild unpopulated area and notorious for the bandits that roamed its slopes preying on pilgrims. The bandits in turn would doubtless pray for protection from the Saint himself in the safety of the Church of Santiago (rebuilt several times and housing an unusual shell baptismal font and several images of the Saint) or perhaps find shelter and succour from the pilgrim Hospice of Saint Anthony the Abbot *Hospital de San Antonio Abad* which has recently been restored. This handsome building was sometimes referred to as the Queen's Hospice, as witnessed by the royal coat of arms that adorn the entrance gate. Today, the town straddles the noisy N-120 which cuts its way through the Pedraja pass and runs broadly parallel to the camino until the latter strikes off to the remote village of San Juan de Ortega. **Detour:** Just outside the village on the main N-120 there is a cul-de-sac to the left to the remote Chapel of Our Lady of Oca. A local pilgrimage *romería* is made here on 11th June each year, the feast day of San Indalecio, to commemorate his martyrdom. To the rear of the chapel is a well of pure water named in his memory, *Pozo de San Indalecio*. Return to Villafranca to continue and add 2 hours for this detour, which is not recommended unless you plan to stay in Villafranca.

Opposite the albergue **[F]** turn up right> off the main road passing the Church of Santiago (left), hospital de San Antonio Abad (right) and climb steeply up into beautiful oak woods to refresh ourselves at:

1.4 km **Fuente de Mojapán [F]** *Moisten Bread Fountain* (one assumes the early pilgrims did just that) and rest area. From here we have the shade offered by oak woods and later on the pine forests that accompany us all the way to San Juan de Ortega. We continue climbing for **[2.3 km]** until reaching:

2.3 km **Monumento de los Caidos** (1,020m) A stark monument to the fallen during the Spanish Civil War. From here we descend steeply to a footbridge over the Peroja stream *arroyo Peroja* before climbing up the other side and dropping down again to:

2.0 km **Ermita de la Valdefuentes [F]** adjacent to the main road, this tiny chapel and its cool spring water offer refreshment before the final isolated passage through the pine forest and heather covered moorland. Here we climb to the highest point of today's route at 1,050m before descending gently to:

San Juan de Ortega

6.5 km San Juan de Ortega •**Albergue** historic parish hostel (947-560 438) and one of the classic pilgrim halts for the medieval and modern *peregrino* alike. Open all year with 58 places in 3 spacious (draughty) rooms and basic facilities with access to fine 16th century courtyard patio. Another traditional gateway on the camino and its peaceful setting and ancient buildings provide a monastic atmosphere and soften the lack of services and spartan maintenance. The parish priest José María became famous for his bread and garlic soup offered to pilgrims – he died in 2008. *[Next albergue: Agés – 3.6 km].* The adjoining Bar Marcela is a popular halt and serves a wholesome pilgrim dinner.

SAN JUAN was a disciple of Santo Domingo and like his mentor became known for his great works to serve the pilgrim to Santiago. He built bridges, hospitals, churches and hostels throughout this region. Here, in this wild and isolated place (*Ortiga* is Spanish for nettle) fraught with danger and difficulty for the medieval pilgrim, he founded an Augustinian monastery in 1150. The chapel is dedicated to **San Nicolás de Barri**, who allegedly saved San Juan from drowning on his way back from pilgrimage to the Holy Land and is constructed in such a way that at each equinox the rays of the setting sun strike the Virgin Mary in the scene of the annunciation. A representation of this biennial miracle of celestial light, which is linked to San Juan's miraculous powers in restoring fertility, is portrayed in the adjoining photograph. The barren Queen Isabel of Castile *la Católica* came here in 1477 and later conceived a child and in consequence greatly embellished the church. In the crypt there is a beautiful Romanesque sepulchre with fine tracery stonework bearing an effigy of the Saint. San Juan, however,

Scene of the Annunciation

is buried in the monastery church in a simpler stone sarcophagus depicting scenes from his life; a more down to earth resting place for this most practical of saints.

REFLECTIONS:

_____
_____
_____
_____
_____
_____
_____
_____
_____
_____
_____
_____
_____
_____
_____
_____
_____
_____
_____
_____
_____
_____
_____
_____
_____
_____
_____

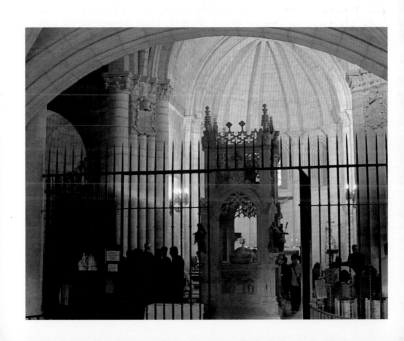

❏ **I don't know what your destiny will be, but one thing I do know; the only ones among you who will be truly happy are those who have sought and found how to serve.** *Albert Schweitzer*

MAP 12 *534.1 km (331.9 miles) to Santiago de Compostela*

SAN JUAN de ORTEGA – BURGOS

	Path / Track	--- ---	15.4	---	*60%*
	Quiet Road	--- ---	3.4	---	*13%*
	Main Roads	--- ---	<u>6.8</u>	---	*27%*
Total km	**Total distance**		**25.6 km** (15.9 miles)		

Adjusted for climb 26.6 km (accrued ascent 200m = 1.0 km)
Alto ▲ High Point: Sierra Atapuerca (viewpoint) 1,080m (3,543 feet)

The Practical Path: Today we start off along a delightful path through oak and pine woods that drop down to the peaceful valley of the río Vena before ascending the lonely Sierra Atapuerca. From here we descend again to Obaneja village. This makes up 70% of today's stage but prepare for the hard slog into Burgos – after the quiet of the route from San Juan de Ortega city life can come as something of a shock. The situation has improved since the long awaited new pilgrim hostel opened its doors in 2008 – right next to the cathedral in the centre (the former hostel at El Parral was 1.7 km further out and is now closed). However one consequence of this is the likely pressure on the limited accommodation at Hornillos and San Bol (next stage) and the next popular destination at Hontanas is 31.3 km from Burgos centre. You might consider staying for an extra day and go on one of the several excursions to places of interest in the area (see under detours). **Intermediate accommodation:** Agés (3.6 km) – Atapuerca (6.2 km) – Olmos de Atapuerca *alternative route* (9.2 km) – Cardeñuela Riopico (10.9 km) Vilafría *alternative route* (16.9 km).

❏ **The Mystical Path:** On each side of the Montes de Oca we find two ancient monasteries each one the final resting place of a noble personage from this area. One inherited his title the other earned it through service to God. Why is one in ruins while the other remains intact to offer shelter? Why does the spirit of *St John of the Nettles* live on to feed the souls of the hungry? How hungry are you and has your soul found nourishment here?

❏ **Personal Reflections:** *"… I met them in the Park. Their welcome was ecstatic even though Ramón was in much pain and was making arrangements to go home. The hospital had diagnosed a stress fracture. He had simply gone too far too fast. His disappointment and sense of failure was palpable. Above all he didn't want to leave the friends he had made along the way. We all have to leave the camino at some stage, but our friendships don't have to end. He looked reassured as I took my leave. I can still see his tears and his hand waving as I passed out of sight – but not out of mind Ramón; not out of mind …"*

Solar el Cid

Catedral

Castillo

A 3.3 Albergue *Muni.*[76]

< Santo
Domingo
(60 km)

N-1

A-1

Cruce 4.5 ⊕ 4.2 Cruce

N-623

Santander >

BURGOS
(Pop. 170,000 – Alt. 860m)

Villayuda

Cartuja de Miraflores

2.6 Hotel *Buenos Aires*

Fuente 3.5
CASTAÑARES

VILLAFRÍA

N-120

rio Arlanzón

① ② 1.0 Opción

ORBANEJA
Café 2.4 ⊕ 3.5 Café

CARDEÑUELA
Muni.[16] Albergue 1.5 **A**

① ②

Mina

fuente romano →
Villaval

1.0 Opción
Alto 1,050m

Zalduendo

Cruceiro 2.2 †

arqueológico (Yacimiento)

A 2.4 Albergue *Muni.*[32]

OLMOS

N-1 A-1

ATAPUERCA
① ②

C A La Hutte *Priv.*[20]

Bilbao >

el fin del rey

A 2.6 Albergue [1] *Peregrino Priv.**[48]

Parque Arqueológico (Yacimiento)

3.San Rafael *Muni.*[36]
2.El Pajar *Priv.**[38]
1.Caracol *Priv.**[38]

Puente Canto

A 3.6 Albergue [1]

AGÉS

Santovenia

rio Vena

N-120

ST. JUAN DE ORTEGA † **A** 0.0 Albergue *Par.*[58]
(Pop. 20 – Alt. 950m)

O
Puesta
del Sol

S
N

E

Salida
del Sol

Steel yourself for the long hike through the industrial and residential suburbs to the Cathedral and albergue in the city centre along one of the busy access roads – 7.8 km via the N-120 from Castañares (**recommended**) or 7.5 km via the alternative N-1 from Vilafría. Try working with the energy of the traffic rather than fighting against it (see solution in the introduction). Pilgrims who are not prepared for this entry often have a hard time or end up resorting to public transport. Due to the insatiable demands of a modern economy many of the original paths into the city have been obliterated by the bulldozer. We can usefully take this time to reflect on areas of our own life where we have allowed these materialistic forces to bulldoze our own inner pathway out of *seeming* existence. Burgos is perhaps a perfect reflection of our 'developed' world. It is easy to blame the faceless government and developer but they only build to feed our desire for a more convenient lifestyle. How many cars are parked in our home and are we prepared to reduce or eliminate that number or look to car sharing? How did we arrive to the starting point of the camino? Are we ready to embrace a life of voluntary simplicity, not because we have to but because we want to? "*Only when the last tree has died and the last river been poisoned and the last fish has been caught will we realise that we cannot eat money.*" Wisdom attributed to the First Nation Cree.

Leaving the albergue continue over the road (left brings you to Santovenia and the N-120) onto a path that climbs through pine and scrubland levelling out onto open hill pasture. There are a number of tall wooden crosses on this stage that can be a helpful guide, especially in the early morning mist that is frequently experienced at these relatively high altitudes of around 1,000m. The camino here is little changed from what the medieval pilgrim experienced right down to the stone surfaced road into the tiny village of:

3.6 km Agés **[F]** •Albergue [1] *Casa Caracol* private hostel (947-430 413) on c/la Iglesia at the entrance, open all year with 10 beds in several rooms. •Albergue [2] *El Pajar* (the hay loft) private hostel (Maria Isabel 947-430 388 & Josefa Picón 699-273 856) c/Paralela del Medio, 12. Open from March – November with 38 beds in variety of rooms with all facilities including meals. •Albergue [3] *San Rafael* the adjoining municipal hostel (661-263 289) open all year with 36 beds in one large room. No kitchen but meals available in the bar-restaurant. [*Next albergue: Atapuerca – 2.6 km*].

Agés – Albergue [1] Caracol

Albergues [2] *(left)* **and [3]** *(right)*

The humble parish church of Santa Eulalia rose to fame when the mortal remains of the Navarrese King Don García were interred here after he was slain by his brother, Fernando I of Castile, in the battle of Atapuerca in 1054. A stark stone memorial marks the lonely spot between here and Atapuerca (to the left, *off* the road – not the replica on the main road). Don García's final resting place, you may recall, is back in the Royal Pantheon in the church of Santa María de Real in Nájera.

Beyond the village is the simple medieval stone bridge built by San Juan de Ortega. It stands idly over the río Vena that flows into the majestic río Arlanzón in Burgos. You will pass over its waters again as you enter the medieval city through the Arco San Juan. The peaceful surroundings at the bridge of song *Puente Canto* are a far cry from those in the Plaza San Lesmes in Burgos. Listen to the sound of the trickling brook here and listen again to the self-same waters as they flow under the bridge in front of St. John's Arch. What sounds do you hear and which nourishes you more?

| **2.6 km** | **Atapuerca** •Albergue* [1] *El Peregrino* network* hostel (Rocío García 661-580 882) centro turístico on the main road at the entrance to the village. Open all year with 36 places in 6 rooms and all facilities including a large garden terrace. •**Albergue** [2] *La Hutte* private hostel (Jacqueline & Fernando 947-430 320) 300m off the camino (right) located on open ground just below the parish church clearly visible on the rise above. Open all year with 20 beds in one dormitory. All facilities but if you want more space and luxury try the adjoining casa rural •**Papasol** which is also managed by the owners. Several restaurants (•**Palomar** opposite albergue [1]) also has rooms. Bar on the square on the main road.

Albergue [1] El Pergrino (above)
Albergue [2] La Hutte (below)

Homo Antecessor: It's official – this is where our ancestors came from! The prehistoric caves of Atapuerca were declared a UNESCO World Heritage site in 2000 on account of their source as the earliest human remains ever discovered in Europe dating back over 900,000 years and providing an exceptional record of the way of life of the first human communities. The site is 3 km off route (left) and was discovered while cutting a rail link to the nearby mines. The archeological dig is ongoing and the latest, unconfirmed analysis, is of human activity going back over 1,000,000 years ago and, oh yes, it is also confirmed that our ancestors were cannibals. A more accessible information centre has been built just outside the village 500m (right). This includes a mock-up of an early settlement, which feels disappointingly artificial. Continue through the village – bar and **[F]** (right) where we have an option:

Option: Alternative route **[2]** to Olmos de Atapuerca with municipal hostel •**Albergue** (947-430 444) located in a traditional village house opposite the parish church in c/La Iglesia. Open From Easter – November with 32 places (18 in bunk beds and 14 on mattresses). All facilities provided with a quiet garden to rear. This is a pleasant 2.4 km detour along a quiet country road with a direct route out of Olmos de Atapuerca to the Alto Cruceiro (2.6 km). To rejoin the camino turn up through the village onto track that winds its way up the sierra Atapuerca, through Holm oak and scrubland – round trip 5.0 km.

For **main route [1]** veer <left across games pitch and turn <left up into the Sierra Atapuerca. Shaded picnic site (right). The gradual climb becomes a steeper rocky path towards the summit and is rewarded with splendid views.

| **2.2 km** | **Cruceiro / Punto de Vista**. This is the high point at 1,070m. To the

west is our first sight of the city of Burgos (unless it is shrouded in the early morning mist that frequents this high sierra). Down below us to the left are the villages we will pass through to reach Burgos. Along the stony ridge to the right (north) are the ugly scars of an open cast mine and TV mast. We now descend until we reach a fork in the path:

1.0 km Opción [?] For **alternative route [2]** veer right> at the option point and down the track that meanders delightfully through cereal crops fields and just before the autopista ahead a track veers off <left **[3.0 km]** towards the village for a to pass the parish church of San Millán Abad **[0.5 km]** into:

3.5 km **Orbaneja** where the recommended route joins from the left.

For **recommended route [1]** turn down <left at option point through the ancient hamlet of Villalval **[0.5 km]** still watched over by its disintegrating parish church and straddling the narrow valley road that seeks to connect it to the modern world beyond. At the far end of the village we find an ancient Roman well, looking none the worse for its 2 millennia of service. Adjoining it is a picnic area and modern tap **[F]** (left). We follow the road that curves gently around the valley floor for another **[1.0 km]** into:

1.5 km Cardeñuela del Río Pico
•**Albergue** *municipal* hostel (947-430 911) situated above, and behind, the town hall (see photo right). Key with town hall or in the lively bar La Parada just beyond. Open all year with 16 beds in 1 room with basic facilities (no kitchen).

We continue by road **[2.2 km]** (ignoring road to Quintanilla on the left) into:

2.4 km **Orbaneja** where the alternative route joins from the right.

N.B. This is the last opportunity to fill your water flasks and obtain a snack before heading into the suburbs of Burgos – food at Anna's cabina-bar is likely to taste twice as good as anything you will find in the suburbs at half the cost! Proceed over the A-1 autopista and just beyond the bridge by new development **[0.9 km]**:

1.0 km Opción [?] Here we are faced with another choice.

For the **alternative road route [2]** proceed straight on along the secondary road and over the railway line. To your right is the bell tower of the parish church presiding over what remains of the old town of Villafría that was granted to the monastery of San Pedro de Cardeña in the 10th century. Veering left cross over the main road [!] to the garish sign for the Hotel Buenos Aires, into:

2.6 km **Villafría** with several hotels and restaurants •**Buenos Aires** HR** (947-483 770) – •**Las Vegas** HR** (947-484 453) – •**Iruñako** HsR (947-484 126). Villafría is a modern industrial suburb of Burgos with a bus service into the centre of Burgos. Continue along the N-1 past the industrial complexes of Gamonal into c/Vitoria where the city high-rise starts. You pass the impressive 13th century church dedicated to N.S. La Real y Antigua de Gamonal (left), in front of which is a handsome stone cross with an image of St. James as a pilgrim and pass the junction with c/ Santiago Apóstol (left) to join your fellow pilgrims, who have come via Castañares, at:

4.2 km **Cruce** Glorieta de Logroño (Junction of c/Vitoria with Av. de la Constitución Española at the Guardia Civil (opposite the prominent Telefonica building).

For **recommended route [1]** at the new development (former military barracks) just over the A-1 we turn sharp <left down onto a farm track that runs alongside airfield (right) traversing crop fields that yield to wasteland at the outskirts of:

3.5 km **Castañares** Fountain (dry) a sleepy outer suburb of the city that seems to reluctantly straddle the N-120. Opposite the fountain (on the other side of the main road) is a small square with welcoming café El Descanso. **Note:** As in all cities that we pass through you will have to stay very focused amid the bedlam of city traffic and the numerous streets you cross over. This is particularly true in Burgos where there is no clearly defined *camino* as in most other cities. The Cathedral and albergue lie in a due westerly direction so note the position of the sun as you enter and use it as a compass to help orientate yourself through the city. You have several options at this point but try and avoid the option by default (the one where you get lost and blunder your way to the cathedral or the albergue!) A regular bus service direct into the city centre leaves from here throughout the day and provides a tempting option to avoid the traffic.

At the **[F]** turn right> to follow the *camino oficial* that soon joins a path along the N-120 and we find ourselves in the roar of city traffic as we head through the extensive industrial area *Poligroño Villayuda* crossing río Pico **[1.3 km]** and at junction of c/del Alcade Martin Cobos **[0.5 km]** we cross the N-120 (now called Carretera de Logroño) turning right> into c/Mayor in Villayuda. This becomes a pathway that leads under the railway **[1.4 km]** and over Av. del Arlanzón into c/de Villafranca turning right> into c/Real and <left when we reach the major thoroughfare of Av. de la Constitución Española for the remaining **[1.3 km]** to:

4.5 km **Cruce** – pause at the major roundabout *Glorieta de Logroño* to get your bearings. This is a major junction of c/Vitoria (where the alternative route via Villafría joins) with Av. de la Constitución Española at the Guardia Civil HQ and Militar Academia (opposite the prominent Telefonica building).
An alternative route here is to head straight to the city centre along c/Vitoria to the next roundabout *glorieta – Plaza del Rey* and [1] turn left and then right over the river for albergue *Emaus* (check availability first) or [2] continue straight on again (this is still the lengthy c/Vitoria) into the Paseo Espolón and the Arco Santa María leading to the cathedral and albergue (right) – see city plan.

For the **recommended** and historic camino route cross over c/Vitoria towards the large military complex and *Museo Militar* set in parkland (right) and up the tree-lined c/San Roque crossing over just before the new shopping centre *Via de la Plata* **[0.4 km]** to veer <left into c/Farmaceutica-Obdulio Fernandez and right> into the busy Av. Cantabria **[1.0 km]**. Wait for gap in traffic and cross over **[0.1 km]** into c/de las Calzadas which brings us directly into Plaza San Lesmes **[0.7 km]** formerly plaza San Juan with the lovely ruins of the Antiguo Monasterio de San Juan Evangelista (left as we enter) part of which building is the Museo Marceliano with the Iglesia de San Lesmes (right). San Lesmes is patron saint of Burgos and in his earlier days was a French abbot called Adelhelm who was persuaded to stay in Burgos by the wife of Afonso VI. In the centre of the square looking up towards the cathedral from atop his steed is a statue of the founder of the city, Diego Porcelos, whose burial site we passed at the Monasterio de San Felices de Oca. We now cross over the río Vena (whose calm waters we heard back in Agés) over the well-trodden medieval bridge and under the 13th century Arco de San Juan and into the medieval city itself.

Continue into c/San Juan *[you can turn left into the busy c/Santander to visit the House of the Cord Casa del Cordón, 150m left with its outstanding 15th century facade, Columbus was royally received here on his return from the Americas]* or continue straight over to the hotel Norte y Londres opposite which is Plaza Alonso Martínez with main tourist office (right). Continue into the c/Avellanos that joins into to c/San Gil veering <left into c/Fernán Gonzalez up the cobblestones to no. 28:

3.3 km Hostel •Albergue [1] *La Casa del Cubo - Lerma* new municipal hostel (947-460 922) opened in August 2008 in a beautifully restored 16th century building adjacent to the cathedral and administered by the Burgos pilgrim association (who managed the former hostel El Parral which accommodated over 17,000 pilgrims in 2007). Open all year with 76 places and all facilities but less bed spaces than formerly so likely to fill up quickly. Also close by is •**Albergue** [2] *Divina Pastora* (947-207 952) association hostel on c/Laín Calvo, 10 above the chapel of La Capilla de la Divina Pastora. Open all year with only 18 beds in 1 room. No kitchen but its central location is convenient to all facilities and the adjoining chapel offers respite from the bustle of the city and pilgrim mass at 20:00. Popular hostel that tries to admit pilgrims in need so often *completo*.

Albergue [1] Casa del Cubo *(above)*
Albergue [2] Divina Pastora *(below)*

On the far side of the river in the southern suburbs the former Emaús hostel has transferred itself into •**Casa Parroquial** at c/San Pedro Cardeña adjoining the Jesuit college. 20 places with shared meal following the tradition of Emmaus with Christian prayer and blessing. Other possibilities in the busy summer period are: •**Burgos Youth Hostel** *albergue juvenil Gil de Siloé* (947-220 277) on Av. de Cantabria with 110 beds and hostel Monasterio Benedictinas de San José (947-205 373 / 241 000) who maintain a hostel for religious groups on c/Emperador (directly on the camino) and may also accommodate individual pilgrims. It is also possible that the old albergue •El Parral and the adjacent sports halls may be pressed into service during busy periods – check at the new albergue.

Other accommodation: there are several tourist kiosks around the city and the main *Turismo* is on Plaza Alonso,7 (947-203 125) with a list of accommodation in every price bracket. Burgos is always busy, so find accommodation before setting out to explore. The following selection is shown on the town plan, sequentially from the entrance. •**Puerta de Burgos** H**** (947-241 000) c/Vitoria, 69. – •**Carrales** HsR** (947-205 916) Puente Gasset, 4. – •**Acacia** HsR** (947-205 134) c/Bernabé Pérez Ortiz, 1. – •**Lar** Hs** (947-209 655) c/Cardenal Benlloch, 1. – •**Manjón** HsR** (947-208 689) c/Gran Teatro, 1. – •**García** HsR* (947-205 553) c/Santander, 1. – •**Hidalgo** HsR* (947-203 481) c/Almirante Bonifaz, 14.

On the camino itself are: •**El Jacobeo** Hr* (947-260 102) c/San Juan, 24. – •**Joma** Hs (947-203 350) c/San Juan, 26. – •**Norte y Londres** Hr (947-264 125) Plaza Alonso, 10. – •**Palacio de los Blasones** H**** (947-257 680) Fernán Gonzaléz, 10. – •**Mesón del Cid II** H**** (947-208 715) Fernán Gonzaléz, 62 – and at the top end of the city and price bracket •**Abba Burgos** H**** (947-001 100) Fernán Gonzaléz, 72-76 (it takes in the whole edifice of the former Seminario above the *Solar El Cid*). On the far side of the river are: •**Conde de Miranda** HR**(947-265 267) c/Miranda, 4 adjoining the bus station. – The modest •**Temiño** HsR* (947-208 035) c/Concepción, 14 located just behind – the 4 star •**NH Palacio de la Merced** (947-479 900) which overlooks the river from c/Merced.

Burgos cathedral – 13th century Catedral de Santa María among the most beautiful of Spain's many cathedrals and one of its largest (after the Giralda at Sevilla). Essentially Gothic, it nevertheless combines many different styles, having been embellished by the great master builders and architects down through the centuries. Soak in its magnificent edifice and inspirational spires and the bustle of the medieval streets that surround the cathedral – designated a World Heritage Site. Whatever condition you are in, it is worthy of a visit to the interior. You are unlikely to find much peace in its crowded aisles but you will find a wealth of art treasures and artefacts to satisfy the most jaded of palates.

The west door, off Santa María square, is the most striking but we enter by the equally evocative south door. Admission (office below south door) is by ticket only which seems to have eliminated the notorious pseudo 'guides' and includes a floor plan and pamphlet (in English) and access to the left luggage lockers *consigna*. Open throughout the day in high season (otherwise closed for lunch 13.30 – 16.00). Amongst the many outstanding chapels (there are 21) are St. Thecla and St. James (off Plaza Santa María) and St. John & St. James behind the high altar with a statue of St. James the Moor-slayer *Santiago Matamoros*. The north door (closed) has the lovely Renaissance Golden Staircase *Escalera Dorada* designed by Diego de Siloe, while at the transept crossing, directly underneath the huge star lantern at the heart of the cathedral, lie El Cid and his wife Jimena. The 14th century Gothic cloisters have an array of sculptures.

If you want to find somewhere cool and quiet try the Church of San Nicolás with its magnificent altarpiece, situated directly on the camino immediately above the cathedral (at the top of the steps). Its austere 15th century façade and the steep climb up from the cathedral square *plaza Santa María* acts as a deterrent to the crowds of tourists milling around the cathedral and so preserves the relative peace to be found here. Alternatively head out to the river through the impressive Arco de Santa María the medieval entrance dating back to the 14th century to the Puente de Santa María which joins the linear park that runs along the banks of the río Arlazón. Rest awhile under the shade of the trees or take a well-earned drink in one of the cafés that line the river bank.

BURGOS CITY: While warning of the vagaries of city life (stories abound of theft and overcharging) we must also emphasise the beauty of many of the city's buildings and their artefacts. Burgos is a veritable architectural jewel and full of monuments worthy of exploration and appreciation. The city marks the beginning of stage VI of the Codex Calixtinus. Sometimes referred to as the Gothic capital of Spain, it was also the seat of Franco's Government until 1938, an indication of its nationalist and establishment leanings. A burgeoning population approaching 200,000 seems unable to shake off its austere religious and political image. It is, after all, named after its heavy defensive town towers (burgos) and was home to the warlord El Cid. The week either side of 29th June is the city's main festival of San Pedro y Pablo. Accommodation at this time is doubly difficult to secure at twice the price.

Count Rodrigo Díaz de Vivar the champion *campeador* was better known as *El Cid* a Muslim title of respect, and remains the great legendary son of Burgos. He was born here in 1040 and the camino passes the site of his house by Arco de San Martín. On the death of Ferdinand I the kingdom was divided between the monarchs 5 children. The eldest son, Sancho, felt he should have inherited the lot and so set about recovering it from his siblings and the Moors – enter El Cid who was appointed his commander-in-chief of the armed forces. All was going well for El Cid until Sancho was killed trying to recover the town of Zamora from his sister Urraca. Now enters Sancho's surviving brother Alfonso VI who both despised and feared El Cid and alternately exiled him (twice) and in between married him off to his niece Jimena. El Cid died in Valencia in 1099 having recovered the city from the Moors. His body, and that of his trusty horse *Babieca*, were eventually re-interred in the monastery of San Pedro de Cardena and then El Cid and his wife were re-re-interred in the cathedral!

On your way out the following day, suitably refreshed, you might be more inclined to explore the fascinating monastery **Monasterio de Las Huelgas Reales** and the adjacent **Hospital del Rey** (now part of the university) both of which are within a few minutes walk off the camino near Parque El Parral in the westerly suburbs and well worth a visit. Las Huelgas was founded in 1187 by Alfonso VIII who, along with several other royal personages, was crowned and subsequently buried there. Founded as a Cistercian convent, primarily for aristocratic novitiates, it has a lovely cloister and is now a museum. Amongst its many fine treasures is the statue of St. James with a moving arm that was used by the Order of the Knights of Santiago to bestow knighthoods. Hospital del Rey was one of the largest and best-endowed pilgrim hospitals along the camino. The Pilgrim's Gate *Puerta de Romeros* is a Plasteresque jewel and now forms one of the entrances to the university. Other more distant detours might be considered (check with tourist office): **Detour [1]** Cartuja de Miraflores 4 km. **[2]** Beyond [1] Monasterio San Pedro de Cardeña (9 km from Burgos). **[3]** Santo Domingo de Silos (62 km south) site of the world renowned Gregorian chanting monks.

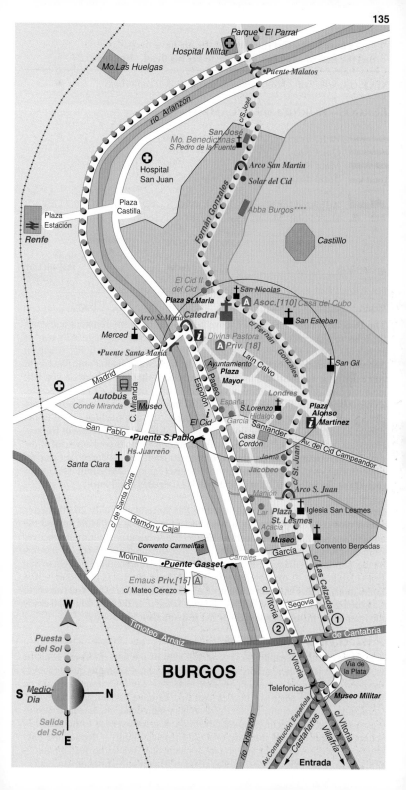

BURGOS

❒ **Foxes have holes and the birds of the air have nests,**
But the Son of Man has no place to lay his head. *Matthew 8.24*

MAP: 13 *508.5 km (316.0 miles) to Santiago de Compostela*

BURGOS – HORNILLOS del CAMINO

	Path / Track	--- ---	12.8	---	*64%*
	Quiet Road	--- ---	4.0	---	*20%*
	Main Road	--- ---	3.2	---	*16%*
Total km	**Total distance**		**20.0 km** (12.4 miles)		

Adjusted for climb 20.7 km (accrued ascent 150m = 0.7 km)
Alto ▲ High Point: Meseta above Fuente de Praotorre at 950m (3,117 feet)

The Practical Path: Today we leave behind the built environment and enter the relative wilderness of the sublime **Meseta**. Over half this stage is by way of earth track (64%) across the peace and quiet of the endless crop fields; wheat on the better ground and barley and oats on the higher and poorer soil. We might come across a shepherd and his flock or the occasional fox, otherwise you will have the birds to keep you company. There is little or no shade on the meseta, so protect yourself from the sun. Hornillos has limited facilities but these are already improving in response to the closure of the intermediate hostel in the parque El Parral following the opening of the new hostel in the centre of Burgos. Hornillos provides a welcome respite from the conspicuous consumerism of the city. **Intermediate accommodation** (distances from new albergue *La Casa del Cubo* in Burgos): N-120 on outskirts of Burgos (2.2 km) – Villalbilla de Burgos (6.7 km) – Tarjados (10.2 km) – Rabé de las Calzadas (12.2 km).

Options: If you plan to stay at Hornillos; this stage is now only 20 kilometres which provides an opportunity to visit the monastery at Las Huelgas and the ancient pilgrim hospital *hospital de Rey* on the way out... and time to recover from the busy-ness of Burgos in the peaceful surroundings of one of the few medieval pilgrim villages still surviving. Many pilgrims continue straight to San Bol (+5.8 km) or to the popular pilgrim village of Hontanas (+5.0 km – 30.8 km in total). In this latter case you need to leave Burgos early but you can get to Castrojeriz early the following day and take some time there to relax and enjoy the interesting historical sites, cafes and restaurants it has to offer.

❒ **The Mystical Path:** The forces of materialism are nowhere more evident than in city life. A wealthy professional, a man of the law, informed Jesus he would follow him wherever he went – prompting Christ's famous quote (above) recorded in Matthew's gospel. Another man then came to Jesus and said he would follow him wherever he went but first he must go and bury his father. Christ replied 'Follow me and let the dead bury their dead.' As we leave Burgos we pass a former pilgrim hospital converted at great expense to house a law school and the opulent monastery of Las Huelgas built to shelter the elite daughters of the aristocracy and as a royal pantheon to house the dead monarchs of Castilla. Who will we follow today, God or Mammon? Christ or Ahriman?

(Pop. 100 – Alt. 820m)
HORNILLOS del CAMINO
†*Iglesia Santa María*
Ⓐ ◄4.4 **Albergue** *Muni.*[32]
Ⓒ *de sol*

río Hornazuela

Cuesta de Matamulos

N-120

Alto Meseta 950m ▲

Pedras Sagrado

Ⓕ ◄3.4 **Fuente de Praotorre**
✗

M E S E T A

río Arlanzón

Ermita
Libéranos Dómine **Priv.**[25] Ⓐ **Priv.**[18] *Santa Mariña y Santiago*
RABÉ de las CALZADOS Ⓐ ◄2.0 **Albergue** [1]

río Urbel

Muni.[12] **Albergue** 3.5► Ⓐ

†
TARJADOS
(Pop. 700 – Alt. 830m)

León >
A-231

N-620a
N-120

Albergue *Muni.*[18] ◄ Ⓐ 5.3 **Opción**
VILLALBILLA *Halt Apeadero*

A-231

N-120

río Arlanzón

Ermita de Santo Amaro → † Ⓗ *Abadía*
Ⓗ *Puerta Romeros*
Azofra Ⓗ
Hospital del Rey
Universitario
El Parral
parque
Mo. Huelgas 🏛

◄1.4 **Puente de Malatos**

Arco S.Martin

Arco S.María
Catedral
†††ıııı†
Ⓐ ◄0.0 **Albergue**
BURGOS
(Pop. 170,000 – Alt. 860m)

O
Puesta del Sol
S ———●—— N
Salida del Sol
E

❏ **Personal Reflections:** *"... The Aries full moon slowly breaks the eastern horizon, an enormous orb of reflected silver light. It is awesome against the pale blue of the early evening sky. I am alone lost in the deep peace of the empty meseta. But I don't feel lost or lonely. I take out the small phial I have been carrying since leaving Findhorn. A gift of love from the sacred mountain of Kailash offered to the world and poured into the deep rich soil of the camino. The words of the Great Invocation linger in the cooling air before rippling out into the universe. Two deer break cover in the stillness. I was not alone after all ..."*

From the albergue continue along the cobbled c/Fernán González past the cathedral and church of San Nicolás (right) and the luxury Hotel Abba Burgos to the twin obelisks of the Solar el Cid **[0.5 km]** which provide a simple monument to this notorious soldier of fortune and pugnacious son of Burgos who lived in a house on this spot with splendid view over the city. Just beyond we leave the medieval city through what remains of its fortified walls and the *Arco de San Martín*. We now head across the road and down into c/Emperador to the Jacobean church of San Pedro de la Fuente **[0.2 km]** (left) and •hostal Monasterio de San José. Turn <left into c/Benedictinas de San José into Paseo de la Isla to cross the río Arlanzón over the 'Bridge of Maladies' **[0.7 km].**

| 1.4 km | **Puente de Malatos / Opción:** The waymarked route continues through the parkland *El Parral* ahead. As this is a relatively short stage this is a good opportunity to visit the Royal Monastery *Monasterio de las Huelgas Reales.*

Detour: Monasterio de las Huelgas Reales 600 metres. Take the road alongside the park Paseo de los Comendadores and turn <left [400m] into c/ de Bernardino Obregón to the monastery straight ahead [200m]. Allow at least an hour to look around its copious buildings. The Chapel of St. James *Capilla de Santiago* contains the unusual statue of the saint with a moving arm. The *Sala Capitular* contains the royal standard *pendón* used in the battle of Las Navas de Tolosa (you may have seen the heavy chains, another trophy from this battle, back in Roncesvalles). Soak up the atmosphere in the spacious Romanesque cloisters with their elegant twin columns, reminiscent of the cloisters at San Pedro de la Rúa in Estella (coincidentally this suburb of Burgos was also called San Pedro). There is also the museum of medieval fabrics *Museo de Telas Medievales.*

For the waymarked route continue through parque El Parral (former pilgrim refuge left) and out the gate at the far end to the tiny chapel opposite **[0.8km]** dedicated to the pilgrim saint *San Amaro de peregrino* named after a humble pilgrim from France who, on his return from Santiago, settled here and dedicated his life to the welfare of other pilgrims leaving a legacy of healing miracles. From here we can also admire another piece of pilgrim history – the beautiful Kings Gate *Puerta del Rey* (60m left) on Pilgrim street *calle de los Romeros*. The magnificent 12th century King's Hospital *Hospital del Rey* was formerly a pilgrims hospital and is now the law faculty of Burgos university. From San Amaro turn right> and join the N-620 and N-120 (to Palencia and Carrión respectively) by •**Hotel Puerta Romeros** H**(947-460 012) on the corner and turn <left along main road with handsome pilgrim statue (see photo) and continue past the •**Hotel Abadía** (947-040 404) and the modern university campus and leave the main road by

Pilgrim monument

car park right **[0.8 km]** and follow the minor road for **[0.7 km]** onto a track with poplar plantation and state prison on far side of the río Arlanzón. Continue to railway halt and level crossing **[3.0 km]** option **[?]**.

5.3 km Villalbilla / Opción:

To stay at the pilgrim hostel in Villalbilla detour <left and make your way up to the centre of this small town (a suburb of Burgos) to the community centre (stone porch and post box *buzón*) in Sagrado Corazón [0.4 km] the hostel is directly behind it – not well marked but it is a small town so keep asking! •**Albergue** *municipal* hostel (947-291 210) open all year with 18 places (8 beds + 10 *colchones*) in 2 rooms and basic facilities (no

Villalbilla – Albergue

kitchen) in modern building, not generally well maintained. Summer overflow is provided in sports hall. The town itself lies sandwiched between the rail line and the N-120. •**Hostal San Roque** (947-291 229) is located on main road (noisy). *[Next albergue: Tarjados – 3.5 km]*.

From the option point continue along earth track past workshop (dogs) and cross over the río Arlanzón (for the last time) via *puente del Arzobispo* which replaced a much earlier wooden construction known as Bridge of the Plank *puente La Tabla*. We now join the N-120 and pass under the motorway to pick up a path on the far side that follows the main road past handsome *Rollo* (left) into the village of Tardajos with 2 bars and a shop on the main road. •**Bar Ruiz** has rooms. Keep straight on (where the main road veers off to the right) into c/Mediodía and continue past the town square (panadería up side street) and on the outskirts in a modern terraced house on your left (not well signposted but with scallop shell above door) we find:

3.5 km Tardajos •**Albergue** *municipal* hostel (Maria Victoria Galindo 947-451 189) in modern semi-detached building. Open all year (key with town hall in winter) with 12 beds. No kitchen or lounge but there is a small garden. Continue on quiet asphalt road over río Urbel (formerly a marshy area, hence the suffix of the next town Rabé *causeway*) up into the village clearly visible ahead:

Tarjados Albergue

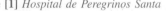

2.0 km Rabé de las Calzadas •**Albergue** [1] *Hospital de Peregrinos Santa Marina y Santiago* private hostel (Michèle & Félix 607-971 919) centrally located on Plaza Francisco Ribera, 6. Open April – November with 58 places (38 beds + 20 mattresses). On the opposite side of the square is: •**Albergue** [2] *Libéranos Dómine* private hostel with 25 places in a somewhat run-down building in the centre of town opposite albergue [1]. Popular with pilgrims in 2008 despite its basic facilities but plans for refurbishment in 2009. Run by José M[a]

Rabé Albergue [1]

& Tinín (brother owns Bar La Peña at the lower end of town and has a key (629-920 501). Fill up your water flask at the drinking fountain **[F]** (scallop shell motif) in the centre of this ancient camino village with its 13th century Iglesia de Santa Mariña and pass by the tiny Ermita de Nuestra Señora de Monasterio and cemetery on the outskirts before heading up onto the incomparable *meseta* and take a rest at:

3.4 km **Fuente de Praotorre** isolated picnic spot whose fountain may be dry and the young trees still struggling to provide shade. The camino continues up through the peaceful landscape temple with its sacred stones *piedras santos* and cereal fields stretching to the horizon to the high point on the meseta before descending steeply down the aptly named Mule-Killer Slope *Cuesta Matamulas!* Cross a quiet road that runs alongside the río Hormazuela into:

4.4 km **Hornillos del Camino** •**Albergue** *municipal* hostel (Ana 947-471 220) located 50m off the camino (right) by the Gothic Church of San Román in the Plaza de la Iglesia in attractive renovated building. Open all year with 32 beds in 3 rooms and all facilities with good kitchen and patio area (overflow space may be available on *colchones* in either the large sports hall to the rear or in the town hall). Other accommodation: •**Casa Rural** *de sol a sol* (Samuel Palacín Alcalde 649-876 091) 7 rooms at the entrance to the village opposite shop. When full they can arrange for pilgrims to be transported to casa rural el Molino (947-560 302) in the adjoining village.

The church occupies the dominant position in this delightful medieval village and adjoins the picturesque Hen Fountain *Fuente del Gallo*. Hornillos del Camino is a classic pilgrim village and important medieval halt on the way to Santiago, little changed over the past centuries and a good place in which to soak up some of the ancient atmosphere of the way. The name Hornillos possibly derives from kiln or oven *horno* with the diminutive *illos* suggesting a small stove. All along the meseta we find this suffix – *illos* appended to place names. It has been suggested that this might have arisen due to a sense of the relative impermanence of man when experienced against the seemingly endless horizon under the vast vault of the meseta sky. We can likewise use this idea to contemplate the relative insignificance of the physical body when compared with the eternal nature of our spiritual identity. Apart from such musings there is little to occupy the pilgrim here other than the priceless peace that pervades this village. A small shop and bar further up the main street offers the possibility of a meal. Chill out and try doing nothing *nada* – and experience being-ness. Note: the closure of the intermediary albergue at El Parral in Burgos is likely to stretch the village resources so expect changes and some increased activity.

Hornillos Albergue (above)
Casa Rural *de sol a sol* (below)

REFLECTIONS:

❑ **The holiest of all the spots on earth is where an ancient hatred has become a present love**… *A Course In Miracles*

MAP: 14 *488.5 km (303.5 miles) to Santiago de Compostela*

HORNILLOS DEL CAMINO – CASTROJERIZ

▬▬	Path / Track	--- ---	14.8 ---	70%
▬▬	Quiet Road	--- ---	6.4 ---	30%
▬▬	Main Road	--- ---	0.0	
Total km	**Total distance**		**21.2 km** (13.2 miles)	

▲ **Adjusted for climb** 22.4 km (accrued ascent 250m = 1.2 km)
Alto ▲ High Point: The Meseta above Hontanas at 950m (3,117 feet)

The Practical Path: Today we again travel the lonely meseta with the sounds of nature the only likely intrusion on the peace that pervades it. There is little or no shade and so again we need to take care with the sun and carry plenty of water. **Intermediate accommodation:** Sanbol (5.8 km) – Hontanas (10.8 km) – San Antón (16.5 km).

❑ **The Mystical Path:** … *Forget not that a shadow held between your brother and yourself obscures the face of Christ and the memory of God. Around you angels hover lovingly, to keep away all darkened thoughts, and keep the light where it has entered in. Your footprints lighten up the world, for where you walk forgiveness gladly goes with you.* Will we walk today with a forgiving heart or hold on to old hurts that keep us feeling separated from our fellow pilgrims, destroying our sense of peace? Will you find the sacred symbol of healing used by knights and monks, ancient and modern? Will you place your hand in the niche that offered bread to passing strangers and will you break bread with a stranger today? Will we compound the problem or become part of the solution?

❑ **Personal Reflections:** *"… She asked me if she could stitch my torn shirt and began to sew. I had not met her before and yet she seemed familiar. Santiago and his jovial friend showed me how to make a real Spanish tortilla. We ate together with great merriment despite our fatigue and difficulty with language. Such deep respect and joy amongst strangers who were not strangers. Our laughter sent great vortexes of loving energy out into the world. If only we would live our lives with this open heartedness – what changes might we bring about to our war-torn world …"*

Leaving the albergue follow the main street *c/Real* which is part of the original camino and fork right at the far end past the stand of poplars and start the gentle climb back up onto the meseta. The track levels out and continues in a westerly direction until we begin the gentle descent to the arroyo San Bol where the isolated refuge is clearly visible (left).

Inset map: CASTROJERIZ

Iglesia S. Juan

El Refugio **Asoc.** ③ A

H

Mesón

S. Esteban

A ④ *Muni.*

Plaza
Mayor

H *Posada*

Concello

Museo

H

Puerta del Monte

H

*Palacio
(ruinas)*

H *La Taberna*

*Castillo
(ruinas)*

Casa Nova
Priv. ② A

† *Museo
S.Domingo*

*Monasterio
(ruinas)*

ⵏ *La Cachava*

Priv. ① A

Camping

< *Sta. Clara ½ km*

El Manzano H

† *Colegiata de La
Virgen del Manzano*

CASTROJERIZ

A ◄ 4.7 **Asoc.**[28] *El Refugio*
Albergue ③

*Castillo
(ruinas)*

½ km †
*Convento
de Sta. Clara*

*Convento
(ruinas)* **San Antón**
Arco de San Antón
Albergue 5.7 ► A
Priv.[12]

*San Miguel
(ruinas)*

Muni. El Nuevo [20] *El Viejo* [14] *La Escuela* [21]
Albergue 5.0 ► A
*Priv.**[30] *El Puntido*
HONTANAS A
C

*Castellanos
de Castro*

Alto 950m

Villandiego

Iglesias

San Bol
Muni.[20]**Albergue** 5.8 ► A
río San Bol

*Puesta
del Sol*

O

S

N

*Salida
del Sol*

E

M E S E T A

HORNILLOS del CAMINO
(Pop. 100 – Alt. 820m)
A ◄ 0.0 **Albergue** *Muni.*[32]
C

5.8 km **Arroyo San Bol** Cross over the stream and continue straight on or turn left to visit San Bol 200m •**Albergue** *municipal* hostel (947-161 053 or Alvaro García 617-165 327) adjoining the river. Open May – October with 20 places (12 beds and 8 mattresses) in one common room. The basic facilities spill out onto a delightful picnic spot shaded by a grove of poplar trees. The waters from the well are said to have healing properties and to cure aching feet; the peace of this isolated spot can heal more than feet. The nearest village is Iglesias approximately 4 km further off the camino along a dirt road. At one time a monastery dedicated to San Boal (or San Baudito) of the Antonine order and connected with St Antón (see later) served this area and gave it its name. Climb up again out of the narrow Sanbol valley back onto the meseta. Pass over a minor road (linking Iglesias and Olmillos de Sasamón) and spectacularly the meseta suddenly falls away to reveal:

5.0 km **Hontanas** another classic pilgrim village tucked down in a fold in the meseta. Situated off a minor road into Castrojeriz and largely undiscovered except by pilgrims. The solid 14th century church of the Assumption (see photo) dominates the tiny village square and contributes to an air of quiet reverence that pervades this little Jacobean haven of the fountains *Fontanas* from which the name derives and a fine example **[F]** spills out its refreshingly cool waters in the shade of the church.

•**Albergue***[1] *El Puntido* network* hostel (Toñi &Maria Carmen 947-378 597) centrally located opposite the church in c/La Iglesia, 6. Open from Easter to mid October with 30 beds in 3 rooms (private rooms also available). All facilities and popular bar and mesón. The municipal hostels are all well maintained by a team of ladies from the village on c/Real, 26 at the bottom end of the village. •**Albergue** [1] *San Juan El Nuevo* municipal hostel (947-377 021) Open all year with 20 beds in 2 rooms with excellent facilities but no outside patio although pilgrims spill out along the road. The lounge is built over the original medieval foundations (visible through the glazed floor) and the hostel won an architectural award for its imaginative reconstruction. When this hostel is full the other municipal albergues are opened as follows: •**Albergue** [2] *El Viejo* located in the Town Hall with 14 beds in 2 rooms with showers and toilets and use of kitchen in [1] above. •**Albergue** [3] *La Escuela* 21 beds in one dormitory in the old schoolhouse with showers and

Albergue [1] *Puntido* (above)
Albergue [2] *St Juan* (below)

toilets and use of kitchen in [1] above. Alternative accommodation includes: Opposite El Puntido •**Fuente Estrella** Hs* (947-377 261) with more up-market rooms. For a decidedly down-market experience try •**Victorino's** at the top of town (as you enter) which offers very basic accommodation and a pilgrim meal eaten at a communal table. Victorino is one of the colourful characters along the camino and can drink a litre of wine from a porrón (jug with spout) without drawing breath, and frequently does, so the menu is somewhat variable. A log fire adds to the convivial atmosphere if the night is cold but beware of amorous advances if you're on your own. There is a small shop close to the church. *[Next albergue: Castrojeriz – 10.4 km]*.

Continue through the village past the municipal swimming pool with bar-café (open high summer only) and cross over the minor road shaded with trees (an alternative is to walk the quiet country road and avail of the shade). The waymarked path continues roughly parallel to the road passing the ruins of an old mill and the long abandoned village of San Miguel to rejoin the road just before:

5.7 km San Antón •**Albergue** private hostel (607-922 127) situated amongst the splendid Gothic ruins of the ancient convent. Open only May-September with 12 places and all basic facilities where a communal meal may be offered. Pass St. Anthony's archway *Arco de San Antón* with recessed alcoves where bread was left for pilgrims of old – the tradition continues with pilgrims leaving messages here. This was the ancient monastery and hospice of the Antonine Order founded in France in the 11th century and

San Antón – Albergue *(left)*

connected to the work of the hermit Saint Anthony of Egypt *San Antón Abad* patron saint of animals and usually depicted with a pig at his feet. The Order's sacred symbol was the 'T' shaped cross known as the Tau – nineteenth letter of the Greek alphabet and symbolising divine protection against evil and sickness. Increasingly referred to and worn as the Pilgrim Cross *Cruz del Peregrino*. The Order was known for its ability to cure the medieval scourge known as St Anthony's fire (a fungal skin disease often turning gangrenous leading to death) essentially by using the power of the Tau (Love) in its healing practise.

As we leave these magnificent ruins behind Castrojeriz the Convento de Santa Clara *Clarisas* opens up to our left (½ km) founded in the 14th century where you can buy one of Tau crosses made by the nuns out of wood (open most days, closed through lunch) – or buy one in Castrojeriz which now opens to view in front of us – its welcoming hostels still 4.5 km away by road. The prominent castle (also in ruins) stands sentinel over the town and surrounding countryside. At the entrance to the town is the collegiate Church of Our Lady of the Apple *Nuestra Señora del Manzano*. Its spacious interior is cool after the road and the delightful rose window sheds light on some interesting treasures, including a fine statue of St. James in full pilgrim regalia festooned with scallop shells and a fine statue of Our Lady. The church has recently been renovated and part is now open as a museum. The town is laid out in one long straggling line between the road and the hill and is 2 kilometres from start to finish – interim distances between albergues is provided (in metres).

At the start of the village opposite the church is the welcoming Bar and Hostal El Manzano. 300 metres further along c/Virgin del Manzano is private hostel •**Albergue [1]** *Camino de Santiago* (300m) part of the camping site and also a casa rural (Robert Luis 658-966 743 or 947-377 255). Open March to November with 40 beds (private bungalow rooms also available) the extensive facilities include large terrace area with a backdrop of trees, a shop, bar and restaurant. Continue along the upper street into c/Real Oriente with a selection of 'up market' casa rurales and rural hotels. The parish church and museum of St. Dominic *Iglesia y museo de Santo Domingo* (right) has displays of ancient tapestries. •**Albergue [2]** *Casa Nostra* (600 metres) private hostel (Juan José Martínez Pardo) in traditional town house on c/Real Oriente 54, with a cool interior and outside patio. Open all year with 20 places. Continue on up to a small square with the option to continue straight on to the Plaza Mayor (300 metres) directly to municipal albergue [3] (400 metres) or <left *down* the steps and immediately right> for the recommended route to the next small square beside the Mesón de Castrojeriz and into c/Cordon with several bars and cafés and the original albergue in the centre:

Albergue [2] Casa Nostra

4.7 km **Castrojeriz Centro** (300 metres) •**Albergue [3]** *El Refugio Tradicional San Juan* (Resti 947-377 400) centrally located on c/Cordón – part of the camino. An atmospheric local association hostel run by hospitalero *Resti* one of the caminos enduring characters. Open all year with 28 beds in 2 dormitories no kitchen but a spacious garden. From here you can take a right hand turn (not waymarked) up into the Plaza Mayor (200 metres) •**Albergue [4]** *San Esteban* in a commanding position overlooking the Plaza Mayor at the top end of town. Municipal hostel (947-377 001) on upper floor of restored civic building that is also the *Casa Cultura*. Open from May – October with 25 beds (+ 20 mattresses) in one large open dormitory. Good showers and toilets but no other facilities. Pilgrims not staying in this municipal albergue usually bypass the Plaza Mayor (see town map) a delightful square with several cafés and shops. Both routes join at the 16th century Iglesia de San Juan largely Gothic but with a Renaissance baptismal font

Albergue [4] San Esteban

attributed to the 15th century master sculptor and architect Diego de Siloé whose outstanding work we have already come across in Burgos, his city of birth. There is also a fine cloister and the entire has recently been renovated and now acts as a museum and art gallery.

Other accommodation (sequentially from the entrance): **Bar-Hostal El Manzano** H*on c/Colegiata (620-782 768) (opposite the church). – •**La Cachava** H**(947-378 547) c/Real, 93. – •**La Taberna** P (620-782 768) c/Real de Oriente, 34. – •**Casa de los Holandeses** CR (947-377 608) c/Real de Oriente, 58 – •**Puerta del Monte** Hs**(947-378 647) – •**La Posada** H***(947-378 610) c/Landelino Tardajos, 3. – •**Mesón Castrojeriz** Hs**(947-377 400) c/Cordón, 1. *[Next albergue: Puente Itero – 9.1 km].*

CASTROJERIZ: Delightfully sleepy town with a resident population of around 1,000 who seem to be permanently occupied with siesta except during the garlic festival *fiesta del Ajo* in July which adds a bit of seasoning to life. It had a more active past evident in its ruined castles and monasteries. An historic fortified town *castrum* with Roman and Visigothic remains, it was the scene of much fighting between Moor and Christian (fine statue of Santiago Matamoros in the *Manzano* church museum). Castrojeriz rose to prominence during the *reconquista* and as a major stopping place on the medieval camino with no less than 8 pilgrim hospitals. If you have the energy, a walk to the hilltop castle *castillo* (established in the 9th century) will be rewarded with fine views over the town and countryside – otherwise a short walk to the sites already referred to will give you a flavour of this historic town. Alternatively, just hang out with a cool beer in one of the bars of this typically pilgrim town – or join the locals and take a siesta.

REFLECTIONS:

❏ If you follow your bliss, you put yourself on a kind of track, that has been there all the while, waiting for you, and the life you ought to be living is the one you are living. *Joseph Campbell*

MAP 15 *467.3 km (290.4 miles) to Santiago de Compostela*

CASTROJERIZ (Burgos) – FRÓMISTA (Palencia)

▬▬▬	Path / Track	--- ---	21.9	--- 86%
▬▬▬	Quiet Road	--- ---	2.3	--- 9%
▬▬▬	Main Road	--- ---	1.3	--- 5%
Total km	**Total distance**		**25.5 km** (15.8 miles)	

Adjusted for climb 26.7 km (accrued ascent 250m = 1.2 km)

Alto ▲ High Point: Alto de Mostelares at 900m (2,952 feet)

The Practical Path: A glance at the map of today's stage might give you a false impression. Look carefully and you will see that while the camino appears in a web of asphalt roads it seldom connects with them. A glorious 21.9 km (86%) is on earthen tracks. Be prepared for the strenuous climb out of Castrojeriz onto the meseta. The view back over the valley floor, coupled with the knowledge that what goes up must come down should be enough to revive any flagging spirit. Apart from the trees that line the río Pisuerga and the Canal de Castilla there is little shade and few water fonts, so take precautions. **Intermediate accommodation** (distances from albergue [3] in Castrojeriz): Puente de Itero (9.1 km) – Itero del Castillo (10.6 km) *off* route. – Itero de la Vega (11.0 km) – Boadilla (19.1 km).

❏ **The Mystical Path:** The track we start off on today was laid two thousand years ago. Tomorrow's track is the first stretch of the soulless modern *senda* with its ugly concrete bollards that flies over the Frómista bypass and was built only a few years back. How many pilgrims have walked the old Roman road and how many will walk the modern senda? How many followed their bliss? How many have paid equal respect to the inner and outer path? Which path are we on? Is our life in tune with our purpose? What is our purpose? Life without an inner direction is fruitless and only leads down a cul-de-sac called despair with only disillusionment and death at the end. Bliss is found another way – along the inner pathways of soul.

❏ **Personal Reflections:** *"… I have seldom witnessed such dedication to a path of service – the whole family's unwavering hospitality to pilgrims on their way to Santiago. Every action is performed with such care and precision and made to feel right, not just look right. I am reminded how much my own life has been squandered in posturing. The pretence that comes from making something look right on the surface, while ignoring the underlying lack of integrity and the feeling of discontent that follows. Tamed man addicted to the approval of family and friends masking the wild man desperate for the freedom that comes with authentic living while painting a larger canvas. Eduardo's mother is an artist in more ways than one …"*

a Carrión

N-611

N-611

< Palencia

S.Martín XII
A 1.3 Albergue *Muni.*[56]
H
S.Pedro XV
H A Estrella del Camino
N-611a

mesón Bodega A

FRÓMISTA
(Pop. 1,000 - Alt. 790m)
S.Maria del Castillo
(Leyenda del Camino)

3.3 Canal *esclusa*

1.8 Canal de Castilla

Santa María XV
columna justicia XV
En El Camino
Priv.[56] **Albergue** 5.4 A
Escuela Muni.[12] A
Putzu Priv.[16] A

BOADILLA del CAMINO
F
Canal de Castilla

T I E R R A de C A M P O S

2.7 Canal de Pisuerga

Canal Pisuerga

Bodegas

1.9 Albergue *Muni.*[20]

ITERO de la VEGA
A Priv.[20]

P A L E N C I A
Puente Itero
Muni.[16]
A 1.5 **Albergue**

río Pisuerga
Itero del Castillo

Albergue 1.3 A
St. Nicolás Asoc. [12]

B U R G O S

F 4.3 **Fuente del Piojo**

▲ Alto 900m
3.5 **Alto Mostelares**

Puesta
del Sol
O

S

N

Salida
del Sol
E

(Pop. 1,000 – Alt. 810m)
■ St.Juan
CASTROJERIZ
A 0.0 **Albergue** *Central*

río Odrilla

Leaving albergue [4] in the centre of Castrojeriz pass by the church of San Juan, and cross over the main road to join the old Roman road over the río Odrilla (its waters flow into the río Pisuerga which we cross later). The slopes of Mostelares lie ahead as we start the climb to:

| 3.5 km | **Alto de Mostelares** where a monument marks the occasion but the real masterpiece is the landscape temple that surrounds us. A small rest area, with local flora information, has been created to help us get our breath back. Continue along the high meseta dropping down again to:

| 4.3 km | **Fuente del Piojo** a modern picnic area with some shade and cool spring water. We now join the minor road to:

| 1.3 km | **Ermita de San Nicolás** •**Albergue**
directly on the camino just before the bridge. This popular hostel is open only from June-September with 12 places. No electricity, phone or other mod-cons (excepting a shower and toilet in an extension to the rear) but a shared dinner and breakfast is part of the menu. The 13th century buildings were restored by an Italian Confraternity who retain candlelight as the source of illumination which adds to the healing atmosphere of this veritable haven. Space is strictly limited so count your blessings if a bed or mattress is available. The original pilgrim hospice was founded in the 12th century and later a Cistercian monastery was added.

Detour: Itero del Castillo 1.5 km along the road to the right (before crossing the river). You can just make out the tower of the church on the horizon. Its name refers to its strategic position on this historic border point on the banks of the río Pisuerga. •**Albergue** basic municipal hostel (947-377 357) located in the town hall on Plaza Ayuntamiento. Open all year with 12 places (6 beds + 6 colchones) and limited facilities (no kitchen). Return via the asphalt road.

Puente de Itero a fine Romanesque structure whose eleven arches carry us over the río Pisuerga and into the Provincia de Palencia. The river provided the natural historical boundary between the kingdoms of Castilla and León. *[Several place names around here start with Itero a derivation of Hito meaning landmark or boundary stone].*

Provincia de PALENCIA Land of Fields *Tierra de Campos*. An extensive agricultural area well served with rivers and canals that irrigate its rich soils. Here we also see the cultivation mainly of wheat with some vegetable and wine production. It is a flat region lying between the rivers Pisuerga and Cea at Sahagún. There are few trees to offer shade from the relentless sun that dries the deep red earthen walls of many of the adobe villages you will pass through. The absence of wood and stone made earth the natural building material – initially air-dried bricks and eventually kilns speeding up the process and stability but still lacking long-term durability. There is also increasing evidence of wine cellars *bodegas* whose Hobbit-like structures, built into the sides of hillocks, appear all over the countryside to store the local wine in the relative cool of their subterranean stores.

A shaded track follows the river past the 13th century Ermita de la Piedad (with rest area and a statue of St. James inside) to:

1.9 km Itero de la Vega •**Albergue** [1] *municipal* hostel (979-151 826) opposite the 16th century parish church of St. Peter in Plaza Iglesia. Open all year with 20 places and limited facilities, no kitchen but rear patio area. •**Albergue** [2] *La Posada* private hostel (979-151 781) on c/Santa Ana. Open all year with 18 beds (4 rooms) and no kitchen but meals available in the restaurants and with an outside terrace and bar. Also •**Hostal Fitero** (979-151 822) at the entrance providing

Albergue [1] Municipal

various private rooms (the family also run the Hostal Santiago with pilgrim accommodation in Carrion). *[Next albergue: Boadilla – 8.1 km].* The town is liberally embellished with yellow arrows which, paradoxically, adds confusion rather than clarity to direction finding. For the albergue, head for the church or swing right for Plaza Mayor with its attractive fountain of prancing ponies watched over by a handsome Gothic rollo. It's a small village but supports a bar and shop catering for locals and pilgrims alike.

Leave the town by the asphalt road and continue straight over the T-junction onto a wide farm track. A village with the name Bodegas is over to our left with an extensive wind farm on the ridge beyond. Continue to:

2.7 km Canal Pisuerga. This whole area has been opened up to intensive farming as the result of the building of a series of canals in the late 18th century. The farm track continues all the way up a gentle incline and then down to a shaded river stretch with unusual wheel pump **[F]** (left) in:

5.4 km Boadilla del Camino the original population of over 2,000 that served its several pilgrim hospitals has now fallen to less than 200 – a characteristic of many rural communities along the way. But the re-awakening of the camino is beginning to turn the tide. The school has been turned into a pilgrim hostel and the schoolmaster returns at weekends to help his family run the new albergue and casa rural in the village centre! The 16th century parish Church of Santa María contains an exceptional 14th century stone baptismal font and there is an equally fine medieval jurisdictional column *Rollo* in the square complete with scallop shell motifs. Bar Dory has patio-seating area out the back and shop to the rear, neither of which is evident from the outside.

•**Albergue** [1] *municipal* hostel (Victoria Santos 979-810 776) in the former school building on c/Escuelas. Open all year with 12 beds in 1 room and basic facilities (no kitchen). The run-down children's playground provides space for relaxation. •**Albergue***[2] *En El Camino* network* hostel (979-810 284) centrally located beside the church and jurisdictional cross *Rollo* with Jacobean motifs. Open March – October with 48 beds (2 dormitories) in converted barn also individual rooms in the main house *Casa Rural.* Excellent facilities including extensive landscaped grounds with small swimming pool. Typical Castilian menu prepared by artist Begoña whose paintings adorn the walls. The whole family work tirelessly to offer the pilgrim a wonderful welcome. (Note: a third albergue in large agricultural

Albergue [2] En El Camino

building at the entrance to the village has subsequently closed). *[Next albergue: Frómista – 6.4 km].* Continue out the village onto another farm track through the *Tierra de Campos* to:

| 1.8 km | **Canal de Castilla** that flows all the way into Frómista along a peaceful tree-lined path. While the modern Canal Pisuerga was designed exclusively for irrigation purposes, this 18th century canal provided transportation of the cultivated crops as well as power to turn the corn mills. With the advent of motorways its use is now restricted to irrigation and leisure. There is a plan to restore the canal system with all its original 50 locks.

| 3.3 km | **Frómista Canal** lock gates *esclusa* which we cross on the uppermost of a flight of locks (disused), that stretch out below us, and continue down to the main road to pass under the rail line up to the main crossroads *Turismo* (979-810 180 summer only) in Paseo Central which we cross over veering right and then left into the Plaza de San Martín:

| 1.3 km | **Frómista** •Albergue [1] municipal hostel just beyond the hotel. Open all year with 56 beds in 6 rooms. Modern facilities (lacking only a kitchen) and open patio. •Albergue [2] *Infanta de Castilla* new private hostel (979-888 048) converted railway building at the station with adjoining restaurant Mesón Bodega. •Albergue [3] *Estrella del Camino* new private hostel (979-810 053) 34 beds and sheltered patio. Other accommodation: Adjoining

Frómista – Albergue

albergue [3] (same family) •**Camino de Santiago** H (979-810 282). Adjoining albergue [1] •**San Martín** HR* (979-810 000) and •**Marisa** P (979-810 023) while just beyond the albergue in C/Magistal Aguado, are casas rurales: •**Antonio y Marcelino** CR and •**Serviarias** CR (979-810 055). *[Next albergue: Población – 3.8 km].*There are several bars and cafes but for an authentic Castillian meal in an historic pilgrim hospital try Hostería Los Palmeros, opposite the Church of San Pedro on Plaza San Telmo. The square is presided over by San Telmo, patron saint of sailors, who was born here in the 12th century and who died along the *camino Portugués* and is buried in Tui.

FRÓMISTA is best known (and visited) for the beautiful 11th century Iglesia de San Martín (consecrated in 1066) and reputedly one of the finest examples of pure Romanesque in Spain. The church has exquisite proportions and is built with a lovely mellow stone with over 300 external corbels each carved with a different human, animal or mystical motif. It was de-consecrated, painstakingly restored and declared a national monument all in the same breath. Endless coach parties have turned it into a must-see tourist site and it appears to have lost something vital in the process. At the other end of town is the 15th century Gothic Church of San Pedro that has a more prayerful atmosphere and a small museum of religious artwork that is installed there along with a statue of St. James.

Iglesia de San Martín

The importance of Frómista to the camino is evident in the fact that there were several pilgrim hospitals here in medieval times such as the Hostería Los Palmeros. *Palmeros* is a reference to pilgrims to the Holy Land whose symbol was a palm leaf as distinct from the scallop shell representing the pilgrim to Santiago. Frómista is derived from the Latin word for cereal *frumentum* this area having provided copious supplies of wheat to the burgeoning Roman Empire and is also perhaps the reason why we find the unusual reference to pilgrims heading east to Jerusalem via Rome rather than west to Santiago. This marks the beginning of stage VII of the Codex Calixtinus.

REFLECTIONS:

❏ **So I began to have an idea of my life… as the gradual discovery and growth of a purpose that I did not know.** *Joanna Field*

MAP: 16 *441.8 km (274.5 miles) to Santiago de Compostela*

FRÓMISTA – CARRIÓN DE LOS CONDES

▬▬▬	Path / Senda*	--- ---	16.5	--- 84%
▬▬▬	Quiet Road	--- ---	3.2	--- 16%
▬▬▬	Main Road	--- ---	0.0	
Total km	**Total distance**		**19.7 km** (12.2 miles)	

▲▲ **Adjusted for climb** **19.9 km** (accrued ascent 50m = 0.2 km)
Alto ▲ High Point: Carrión 830m (2,725 feet)

The Practical Path: Yesterday over 80% of our journey was on natural paths. Today we have our first taste of the soulless *senda* sometimes referred to as *pilgrim autopistas* that run alongside the main roads. We have entered Palencia, which along with its neighbouring province of León, has engaged in a modernisation programme built, perhaps, on the back of too much wealth and too little forethought. In today's stage we can increase the natural paths by leaving out the senda from Poblacíon to Villalcázar de Sirga and taking the scenic path via Villovieco. This alternative follows a tree lined riverside path which offers both shade and peace. Try and find time to visit the monumental Templar church in Villalcázar. **Intermediate accommodation**: Población de Campos 3.8 km – Vilarmentero 9.6 km – Villalcázar de Sirga 14.3 km.

❏ **The Mystical Path:** Each step takes us nearer our destination, but where are we headed for? Today we will walk around 21 km approximating to 21,000 steps and we can choose to make each step a prayer for peace as we walk through the 21st century. Humanity is coming of age and we hold the key to a new era. The choice is ours as to which way we turn it, but we have only two real choices. We can add to the problems humanity currently faces or become part of the solution. Know that the choice we make will imbue the next millennia with either love or fear. May each step we take be blessed as we awaken to the purpose of life.

❏ **Personal Reflections:** *"… I sit on the balcony and look out to the soft evening colours changing from delicate blue to pink and now turning to a deepening red. It is strange how we universally experience the sun sinking whereas in reality the light is fixed and the earth and I are merely turning away from it into the shadow. The Inquisition offered Galileo the opportunity to recant on his challenge to the orthodox view or face a painful death. The possibility that the earth was not the centre of the universe was simply too threatening to the established authority. As I, too, begin to challenge the consensus reality around me, I ask for the courage to stay open to truth as it is revealed in each changing moment and not to seek the protection afforded by the popularly held perspective. My purpose becomes clearer with each passing day …"*

Leaving the albergue return to the crossroads (popular bar with outside tables) and head out along the P-980 signposted Carrión de Los Condes over the Frómista bypass **N-611** and onto the pilgrim gravel track *senda*. On the outskirts of Población **[3.3 km]** is the 13th century Romanesque St. Michael's hermitage in a shaded glade on the opposite side of road. Turn right> down the concrete path to the cemetery *Paseo del Cementerio* for **[0.5 km]** to:

3.8 km Población de Campos •Albergue as you enter the village, municipal hostel (979-810 271) converted from a former school building with 18 beds in 2 rooms. All facilities (basic) surrounded by tranquil playground. *[Next albergue: Villalmentero – 5.8 km]*. Población is a small town with several bars, restaurant and shop in main street (not obvious) and casa rural •**Paso Camino Santiago** CR (979-882 012) on c/Francesas. The parish church is dedicated to Mary Magdalene. Continue down the *c/Francesas* past the diminutive 13th century Ermita de la Virgen del Socorro (left) to the stone bridge over the río Ucieza.

0.4 km Puente / Opción [?]

For **alternative route [2]** via riverside path do *not* cross the bridge but pick up the less obvious waymarks (with the tree-lined río Ucieza – left) into:

3.4 km Villovieco parish Church of St. Mary with Santiago artefacts. Leave the village by the bridge and turn immediately right> along the other tree-lined bank to join the quiet country road (P-981 from Arconada) at:

4.9 km Ermita de la Virgen del Río Hermitage of Our Lady of the River housing an image of Santiago. Turn <left, passing the Hermitage of Cristo de la Salud and continue along road into:

1.8 km Villalcázar de Sirga where the main route joins from the left.

For the main route via senda continue over the bridge onto gravel path into:

3.3 km Revenga de Campos small village with church of San Lorenzo and bar; pick up the *senda* again as you exit (picnic halt and **[F]** right) straight into:

2.1 km Villarmentero de Campos •Albergue *Amanecer* (dawn or daybreak) private hostel with 18 beds and individual cabins to the rear and bar run by Jesús. Church of San Martín de Tours on opposite side of road, adjacent to the pilgrim friendly CR •**Casona de Doña Petra** (979-065 978) which also offers dinner. Continue through the town **[F]** (right) onto the *senda* straight into:

4.3 km Villalcázar de Sirga where the alternative route joins from the right. •Albergue *Casa de Peregrinos* basic municipal hostel (979-888 041) access off the shaded Plaza de Peregrino as you enter the town (see photo) with 20 places in 2 rooms (If closed, enquire in bar for key). Limited facilities in this traditional pilgrim hostel overlooking the main square and church of Santa María la Blanca to the rear.

Other accommodation: •**Albergue** *Casa Aurea* (979-888 163) casa rural and restaurant with private rooms but also has dormitory for pilgrims. •**Infanta Doña Leonor** HsR* (927-888 015) as you enter which also operates •**Las Cántigas** Casa Vidal CR (927-888 151) on c/Cantarranas *[Next albergue: Carrión de los Condes – 5.8 km].*

VILLALCÁZAR DE SIRGA (VILLASIRGA – town of the canal towpath) is well known for its hospitality having welcomed pilgrims here since the 12th century when it became a commandery of the Knights Templar. There is a popular bar opposite the church and traditional restaurant El Mesón also on the main square in a well preserved medieval building. The town is home to the magnificent church of St. Mary the White *Santa María la Blanca* built by the Templars in the 13th century it houses the tombs of nobles and royalty and has been declared a national monument. The porch with its sculptured south door is particularly noteworthy as

is the rose window. If visiting churches along the way is not your 'thing' make an exception for this one: open 10:00–13:00 and 16:00–20:00 and have a look in the side aisle (opposite the entrance) and light up the retablo (coin operated) which has a splendid panel depicting the life of St. James; his meeting with Jesus, his subsequent ministry, martyrdom and transference to Galicia. In a side chapel is the statue of Santa María La Blanca, to whom is ascribed many miracles. The tombs of Infante Don Felipe (son of Fernando III and brother of Alfonso X the wise *el Sabio*) and Felipe's wife Doña Leonor are also housed here.

On leaving the town make your way back down to the main road and pick up the raised gravel *senda* that runs parallel to it all the way to the outskirts of Carrión de los Condes **[5.2 km]** where we veer <left onto side road for **[0.2 km]** to:

•**Albergue [1]** *Monasterio de Santa Clara* (979-880 134) prominently located (left) at the entrance to the town. Convent hostel run by the *Madres Clarisas* and open all year with 30 beds in 5 rooms (individual rooms also available). All facilities are accessed from a delightful courtyard that also gives access to the *Ermita de La Piedad.* St. Francis of Assisi allegedly stayed in its 13th century buildings.

The parish hostel in the **centre of town is [0.4 km]** further on – continue up to the main road and cross over by Turismo (979-880 932 summer only) site of the Puerta de Santa María that provided the entrance to the old walled city and the 12th century Romanesque church of St. Mary of the Way *Santa María del Camino*. Unusual buttresses form the main entrance which depicts the miracle wrought by the Church's namesake, when the notorious annual 'tribute of the 100 maidens, *doncellas'* imposed by the Moors on the Christian population was finally broken. Turn right> immediately after the church into square (market every Thursday) and:

5.8 km Carrión de los Condes •Albergue
[2] *Santa María* parish hostel (979-880 768
/ 072) centrally located behind the church
in c/Clérigo Pastor (off plaza Santa María.
Open all year (pilgrims may be housed
in the adjacent old albergue in the winter
months) with 60 places in 2 rooms (main
dormitory with 42 beds). No kitchen but
facilities include *lavadora* and *secadora*
and a welcome from the parish priest.
•**Albergue [3]** *Santiago* private hostal (979-
881 052) with main access from Plaza de los
Regentes 8 (adjoining plaza Santa María) and
dormitory for pilgrims as well as individual
rooms. •**Albergue [4]** *Espíritu Santo*
monastery hostal run by the brothers Hijas
de la Caridad (979-881 052) on c/San Juan
4, near the health centre (behind Pescaderia
Amaya on main road). Open all year with
70 places. No kitchen but otherwise good
facilities. If accommodation is full in the
summer – try the youth hostel with 150 beds
(979-881 063). *[Next albergue: Calzadilla
de la Cueza – 17.5 km]*

Albergue [2] Santa María *(above)*
Albergue [4] Espíritu Santo *(below)*

Other Accommodation: Opposite the church is •**La Corte** Hs* (979-880 138)
c/Santa María, 34. •**La Abuela Me** CR adjoining café Yadira on main road
(Plaza Conde Garay). •**El Resbalon** P*(979-880 433) c/Fernan Gomez, 19
above the restaurant of the same name. •**Santiago** HsR*(979-881 052) Plaza
de los Regentes. •**Alba** HsR*(979-880 874) Esteban Colantes,2. On the other
side of the river •**Casa Tía Paula** (979-880 331) c/Obispo Santo Vizoso and if
you're looking for luxury close by is •**Real Monasterio San Zoilo** H***(979-
880 050). The town has a wide selection of shops, bars and restaurants.

San Zoilo with its splendid 16th century Renaissance cloisters is now a national
monument and has been restored as a private hotel similar to a Parador. Here
you can rest your weary limbs and stroll at leisure around the cloisters and
'meet' the Counts of Carrión whose murdered remains are laid to rest more
permanently in its hallowed halls.

CARRIÓN DE LOS CONDES occupied a strategic position in this volatile
border area and at the height of its influence had a population in excess of 10,000;
now reduced to some 2,500. This interesting town retains a medieval atmosphere
within its meandering side streets and was home to no less than 14 pilgrim
hospitals. It was effectively the capital of much of the *tierra de campos* area

and ruled by the Leónese Beni-Gómez family, the
Counts of Carrión, several of whom met a premature
death at the hands of the equally pugnacious
El Cid, after they reputedly, and very unwisely,
mistreated his daughters. These intrigues and
disputes were not limited to this medieval period.
The Church of Santiago was destroyed during the
War of Independence (1809) but thankfully leaving
the magnificent facade and frieze intact (Christ in
majesty) as a national monument.

"If we could read the secret history of our enemies, we should find in each person's life – sorrow and suffering enough to disarm all hostility." Longfellow

REFLECTIONS:

_____
_____
_____
_____
_____
_____
_____
_____
_____
_____
_____
_____
_____
_____
_____
_____
_____
_____
_____
_____
_____
_____
_____
_____
_____
_____
_____

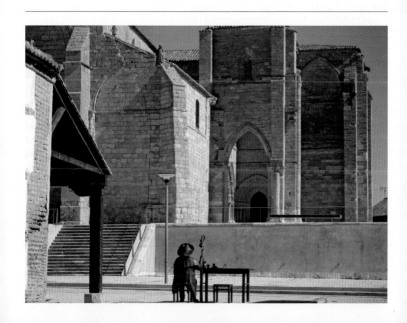

❑ **An eye for an eye only ends up leaving the whole world blind.**

Mahatma Gandhi

MAP 17 *422.1 km (262.3 miles) to Santiago de Compostela*

CARRIÓN de los CONDES – TERRADILLOS de los TEMPLARIOS

▬▬▬	Path / Track --- ---	18.3	---	68%
▬▬▬	Quiet Road --- ---	6.0	---	22%
▬▬▬	Main Road --- ---	2.5	---	10%
Total km	**Total distance**	**26.8 km** (16.6 miles)		

Adjusted for climb 27.3 km (accrued ascent 100m = 0.5 km)

Alto ▲ High Point: Picnic area above Ledigos 900m (2,950 feet)

The Practical Path: We pass through a flat and somewhat featureless landscape with little or no shade. 68% is on natural paths, some of which forms the old paved Roman road known as the *Via Aquitana* that connected Rome with Astorga. The few drinking fonts between the villages are often dry so make sure your water flasks are full and you either have breakfast before you leave or bring something to eat with you as there are no facilities on the first stretch to Calzadilla, a distance of 17.5 km. **Intermediate accommodation** (distances from central albergue [2] in Carrión): Calzadilla de la Cueza 17.5 km – Ledigos 23.7 km.

❑ **The Mystical Path:** Today we leave a fortified town that has witnessed countless battles, conquests, re-conquests, shameful violations, betrayals and revenge killings. We pass the murdered relics of the Counts of Carrión and the martyred San Zoilo. But what of our own sense of justified retribution and how often have we wished someone ill? When did we last send healing thoughts of love and peace to our supposed enemy? Mahatma means Great Soul and it takes one to incarnate in a Hindu body to re-interpret the Christian scriptural teaching (above) to remind us of the futility of revenge. Will we find the courage today to open our heart and offer love instead of fear whenever we feel attacked?

❑ **Personal reflections:** *"... I only saw him after I had collapsed onto the rickety metal chair. He just sat there looking at me with those intense black eyes framed by jet black curls of hair that fell down over his shoulders. Spread across his face was a half smile that disappeared into the thick beard. I think he had intended to scare me. He reminded me of a picture I once saw of Rasputin ... I returned from the village, thankful that he was nowhere to be seen. My sense of relief quickly faded when I opened the door to the bunkroom. Behind it stood his evil looking staff, festooned with black feathers and other symbols of his craft. It was strange how I felt him before I actually saw him ..."*

Leaving the albergue continue down the c/Santa María through the old town with its myriad shopping streets and squares past the Church of Santiago into the c/Pina Blanco and over the substantial bridge to the poplar-lined path at the far end and:

(Pop. 100 – Alt. 885m)
TERRADILLOS de TEMPLARIOS ✝
← *Los Templarios Priv. [56]*
Jacques de Molay Priv[50]* **Albergue** 2.8 →

Población de Arroyo

Cruce 5.6 →
✝ Santiago
Albergue ← 5.2
El Palomar Priv.[42]
④ **LEDIGOS**
río Cueza
A-231
① ② ③ *Santa Maria de las Tiendas*
Opción 0.9 →
H ✝ **CALDADILLA de la CUEZA**
A ← 7.0 **Albergue** *Camino Real Priv*[100]*
N-120
Casa Romana
Quintanilla de la Cueza

Bustillo del Páramo de Carrión

Cruce 4.5 →

Fuente del Hospitalejo
F
Villotilla

Calzada Romana 4.8 →
Vía Trajana
Abadía de Benevívere (ruinas)

Calzada de los Molinos

O
Puesta del Sol
N
S
Salida del Sol
E

N-120
A-231
río Carrión
San Zoilo 1.2 → H
río Carrión

CARRIÓN de los CONDES
(Pop. 2,400 – Alt. 840m)
✝ A ← 0.0 **Albergue** *Par.[54]*

< Palencia

1.2 km **San Zoilo** formerly a magnificent monastery and now a splendid hotel and museum. Just beyond San Zoilo we join the new Carrión by-pass intersection. Make your way [!] to the other side and pick up the quiet country road passing the Red Cross building (right) and just before crossing the second of 2 small streams we find the ruins of the once illustrious 12th century Franciscan Abbey *Abadía Santa María de Benevívere* known for its 'good living' *bene vivere* **[4.0 km]** (right). Shortly afterwards the asphalt road turns sharply northwards (to Villotilla) and we continue straight on for **[0.8 km]** to:

4.8 km **Calzada Romana** *Via Aquitana* otherwise known as the *Calzada de los Peregrinos*. There are no obvious signs, other than the straight and level nature of the route (a full 12 km), to indicate we have joined another fine stretch of the Roman road *Via Romana* still intact after 2,000 years of use. What is even more remarkable on this section is the fact that it goes through an area of bogland devoid of any stone for its construction. It is estimated that a hundred thousand tons of rock was needed just for the substrata and to raise the surface above the winter flood levels and every ton had to be transported from elsewhere. No wonder Roman villas and other remains have been found in the area (most notably at Quintanilla de la Cueza 5 km South of Calzadilla de la Cueza on the N-120). We pass the *Fuente del Hospitalejo* **[1.8 km]** located in a small poplar grove (right) and cross an ancient drove road *cañada* linking this area to the south of the Iberian peninsular via the camino de Madrid which joins the camino Francés in Sahagún. Continue for **[2.7 km]** crossing one of several small streams *arroyos* to:

4.5 km **Cruce** we cross the road to Bustillo del Páramo de Carrión and the río Seco for the remaining stretch of **[7.0 km]** straight into:

7.0 km **Calzadilla de la Cueza** •Albergue*
[1] *Camino Real* (979-883 163) network* hostel located on the left on entering the village. Open all year with 100 Beds on 2 floors in an industrial style building. No kitchen but *lavadora + secadora* and extensive outside patio and small swimming pool with tables. When the hostel is full the old (original) municipal hostel on the main street is pressed into service and provides another 24 places but facilities are basic (no hot water). *[Next albergue: Ledigos – 6.3 km].* Other accommodation is provided in •**Hostal Camino Real** (979-883 187) further into town and well waymarked which also has a popular bar and restaurant (the owner César Acero, a seasoned pilgrim, also runs the albergue). Calzadilla is a typical camino village with a central street that forms the way itself. The parish Church of San Martín has an altarpiece installed when the nearby *monasterio de Santa María de las Tiendas* was de-consecrated. Leaving the village continue over the bridge and the N-120 where a map has been carved into a stone block showing 4 optional routes:

0.9 km **Opción [?]** If you don't plan to stay in Ledigos you can save having to cross the main road by taking the river path which is the route recommended in this guide. The minor variations include:

[1] Recommended river route (*del rio Cueza*)
[2] A track parallel to the road into Ledigos (*zona boscosa*)
[3] The road route (*sendra otra*)
[4] A short detour off route [1] past a dovecot (*al palomar*)

For the alternative route [3] keep on the main road; for route [2] stay on the track running parallel to the road, past the dilapidated monastery of St. Mary of the Stores (left), a far cry from its illustrious past as the Hospice of the Great Knight, a reference to its 12th century existence as a grand hospice administered by the Knights of St. James. The path now takes us gently up to the top of a rise with views across the rolling countryside. We drop down to the road (river route left) and cross the road to access:

| 5.2 km | **Ledigos** •Albergue *El Palomar*
(Ana Pérez 979-883 614) private hostel on c/Ronda de Abajo at lower end of the village as you enter. Open all year with 52 beds in 7 rooms (including 5 twin) and all facilities with large courtyard. There is a small shop and bar in the village and the 13th century parish church of Santiago has several images of the saint. *[Next albergue: Terradillos de los Templarios – 3.0 km].* We return to the main road that we cross again to join the recommended route [0.7 km].

For the recommended route *del río Cueza* veer <left along track into woodland and along the river bank all the way to:

| 5.6 km | **Cruce** here we cross the minor road (to Población de Arroyo) and continue on a track parallel to the main road crossing the río Cueza before veering <left into:

| 2.8 km | **Terradillos de los Templarios** •Albergue*[1] *Jacques de Molay* (Marisa Pérez 979-883 679) the original network* hostel in the centre of this small village. Open all year with 35 beds in 6 rooms. No kitchen but the resident family follow in the traditions of the Templars by offering wholesome home cooking (dinner and breakfast) other facilities include *lavadora + secadora* and there is a small private garden with public picnic area opposite. •Albergue

Albergue [1] Jacques de Molay

[2] *Los Templarios* (667-252 279) a splendid new private hostel augments the original and is open all year with 56 beds in various rooms and with excellent modern facilities including laundry room. No kitchen but also provides all meals in its dining room at pilgrim prices. *[Next albergue: San Nicolás del Real Camino – 5.9 km].*

After the relative luxury of Carrión here in Terradillos de los Templarios we experience the simplicity of this humble village, thankfully bypassed by the N-120 and the modern world. Formerly a stronghold of the Knights Templar nothing, on a physical level, remains of this noble Order but its spirit lives on in the place name and that of the stream *arroyo de Templarios* that separates it from the next village which, like Villalcázar de Sirga, also had historical links with the Templars. Jacques de Molay was the last Grand master of the Order. The simple red brick parish church is dedicated to San Pedro and houses an unusual 13th century crucifix. Terradillos de los Templarios is the halfway point between St. Jean de Pied de Port and Santiago de Compostela. There are now 395.3 kilometres to our destination, *St. James of the Field of the Stars.*

❒ Something opens our wings. Something makes boredom and hurt disappear. Someone fills the cup in front of us. We taste only sacredness. *Rumi*

MAP 18 *395.3 km (245.6 miles) to Santiago de Compostela*

TERRADILLOS de los TEMPLARIOS *(Palencia)* **via SAHAGÚN** *(León)*
to: [1] HERMANILLOS de la CALZADA – [2] El BURGO RANERO

▬▬▬	Path / Track	--- ---	20.1	--- 75%
▬▬▬	Quiet Road	--- ---	3.8	--- 14%
▬▬▬	Main Road	--- ---	3.0	--- 11%
Total km	**Total distance**		**26.9 km** (16.7 miles)	

Adjusted for climb 26.9 km (effectively a level walk)
Alto ▲ High Point: Terradillos de los Templarios 880m (2,890 feet)

The Practical Path: The majority of pilgrims stop in Sahagún, a town full of artistic treasures and monuments. If you stop the night the next logical step is to El Burgo Ranero (a further 17.8 km) – both towns have a wide choice of accommodation. The alternative is to visit Sahagún and possibly stop for lunch on your way through to Hermanillos de Calzada. The first section (to the option point) is by path parallel to the N-120. Option **[1]** *via romana* almost the entire is by earth tracks across remote bush country. Ensure that you have water, especially for this last part of the journey from Calzada de Coto. The path is level but with little shade and only one water font just before Calzadilla. Option **[2]** *real camino frances* the most popular route by road and gravel path *senda* that starts alongside the autopista. **Intermediate accommodation:** [1] San Nicolás (5.8 km) – Sahagún (13.1 km) – Calzada del Coto (18.2 km) *in addition for route [2] Bercianos 10.3 km from Sahagún.*

❒ The Mystical Path: Yesterday we sought to forgive another and to see past any apparent attack – to the cry for help that it disguised. Perhaps when we look past error we will witness our own innocence. Will you look for the mundane or the divine in your fellow traveller? What will fill your cup today? Will you drink the pure waters that flow from the scallop shell at the pilgrim fountain and taste only sacredess?

❒ Personal Reflections: *"… The evening light was painting the countryside pure pink. I stopped to rest awhile and to absorb the warmth of the colours. It was not until I slaked my thirst from the pilgrim fountain that I noticed him. He stood 100 metres from me and yet I could see every facet of his wrinkled face. He wore a smile of such unconditional love that I became enraptured by the embrace. Surrounded by his flock of quietly grazing sheep, this shepherd held the focal point of a biblical picture of such sublime proportions and colours, that I was momentarily transported to an overwhelming sense of pure bliss… While leaning on his crook, he raised his hand slowly to greet and bless me. Tears rolled down my cheeks in a flood of joy. No words passed between us and none are able to convey the sense of total love and acceptance I felt from this*

EL BURGO RANERO

Graneras

[A] [7.5] Albergue *Muni.[28]* D. Laffi
[A] *Priv.[30]* El Nogal

CALZADILLA de los
Albergue [2.1] → [A] **HERMANILLOS**
Muni.[22] [C] *Casa el Cura*
Via Trajana

Fuente [4.3] → [F] *Fuente del Peregrino*

BERCIANOS del
REAL CAMINO
Albergue [5.7] → [A]
Par.[48]

Virgen del Perales †
A-231

N-120

real camino francés ② ① *via romana* [2.3] Puente

Opción [3.6] **CALZADA de COTO**
[A] ← [0.5] Albergue *Muni.[24]*

río Cea
C-111

Puente [1.0]

< San Pedro LE-941
de las Dueñas
SAHAGÚN [A] ← [2.8] Albergue *Muni.[100]*

< *Camino de Madrid* >
< *Grajal de Campos C-111*
río Valderaduey
Opción [4.5] → *Virgen del Puente*

río Sequillo

LEÓN

Laganares Priv.*[22] Albergue [2.5] → [A] *N-120*
SAN NICOLÁS
del REAL CAMINO

PALENCIA

Iglesia S.Tomás [3.3] [F]
MORATINOS *A-231*

río Templarios

(Pop. 100 – Alt. 885m) [F] [A]
TERRADILLOS de losTEMPLARIOS
Jacques de Molay Priv.*[50] Albergue [0.0] → [A]

*stranger who yet seemed so familiar. My heart began to ache with the unfamiliar
intensity of this greeting. My hands spontaneously went to my longing heart.
Namasté, I whispered, 'When the God in me greets the God in you, in that, we
are One'..."*

Leaving the albergue proceed out of the village by dust road (parallel to the N-
120) and continue over the arroyo Templarios and a quiet road (to Villada) onto
track again with a line of poplar trees providing some shade into:

| 3.3 km | **Moratinos** small village with brick built parish church dedicated to
St. Thomas and large shaded porch with benches **[F]**. Continue down the main
street *calzada Francesa* identifying it with the camino and continue to:

| 2.5 km | **San Nicolás del Real Camino**
•**Albergue** *Laganares* private hostel (629-
181 536 *Marisa* 979-188 142) adjoining
the church in the village square *Plaza
Mayor*. Open April – October with 20
beds in 4 separate rooms. All facilities
(except a kitchen) in this delightful hostel,
which has a friendly bar and restaurant.
Newly refurbished using the traditional
local mud and straw method.

This is another peaceful village linked to the Templar Order. The parish church
Iglesia de San Nicolás Obispo is built of the familiar clay brick of the area. Its
humble exterior serves as a pelota court and disguises a fine Baroque altarpiece.
At the far end of the village is a shaded picnic spot and water font **[F]**. Leave
the village (the last in Palencia) and continue on track to Alto del Carrasco.
Waymarks do not hold well on the bare earth but we are heading due west
parallel the N-120 that we join to enter:

PROVINCIA DE LEÓN: The largest, wealthiest and most populous province
we pass through (population 2.5 million) offering the pilgrim the most varied
terrain on the camino. We start off with a continuation of the now familiar *Tierra
de Campos* with its flat and well-irrigated agricultural land. The adobe walls of
the villages, bright red in the intense Leónese sun, rise up to greet us out of
the flat plains. Then we enter the busy and sophisticated style of the capital of
León itself. Artisans, museums, restaurants, hotels and shops all compete for
your attention. León is famous for its pork products – cured hams, chorizos and
morcilla or try the local cheese and quince jelly *queso con membrillo*.

Then we enter the *Maragatería* and the *montes de León*. Here, between Astorga
and Molinaseca, we experience the remnants of Maragato culture in the
distinctive dress and cuisine of this mountainous region. The cakes and pastries
mantecadas are worth sampling and the hills provide game and trout from the
streams. The obscure origins of the Maragatos may date back to the 7th century
when King Mauregato and became isolated in this remote area during the Arab
invasions. Today the isolationism continues in the abandoned villages of the
mountains, such as Foncebadón. Beyond Ponferrada we enter the magic of the
Bierzo, its gently rolling hills host to a multitude of small vineyards. In the
spring, you can see the white of the cherry blossom, in the autumn the bright red
of its fruit and, in between, every shade of green. Eat of its sun ripened fruits and
drink of its wines and the friendliness of its people.

4.5 km Rio Valderaduey – Option [?]: An alternative route along the main road brings us directly into Sahagún. For the recommended route turn right> along the river for **[0.4 km]** to the tranquil (except on April 25th when a local pilgrimage *romería* takes place here) hermitage of Our Lady of the Bridge *Ermita Virgen del Puente*, an unpretentious brick built sanctuary with 12th century Romanesque foundations but the

Virgen del Puente

original pilgrim hospice has long gone. The tiny Mudéjar-style chapel occupies a cool and shady poplar grove adjoining the river.

Continue up towards Sahagún along the grass path (the edges of which are blackened by effluent from the town) and under the N-120 bypass towards the grain silos and over the town access road passing the modern 3 star hotel •**Puerto de Sahagún** and, just beyond it •**Albergue***[1] *Viatoris* popular new network* hostel (987-780 975) on Travesía del Arco. Open all year with 80 bed spaces

Albergue [1] *Viatoris*

(70 in bunks in main dormitory and remainder in private rooms). Excellent facilities and breakfast is available in reception area. The centre of town is now only ½ a kilometre away past the bull ring and over the railway bridge (station left) and turning right> to:

2.8 km Centro •**Albergue** [2] *Cluny* municipal hostel (Jandri 987-782 117) Open all year with 85 places (64 in bunk beds in cubicles remainder on mattresses). Located on the upper floor of the iglesia de la Trinidad with tourist office and exhibition space on the ground floor – easily identified by the pilgrim statue at the church entrance.

Albergue [2] *Cluny (above)*
Albergue [3] *Benedictinas (below)*

At the other end of town (on the way out) •**Albergue** [3] *Hospedería las Madres Benedictinas* part of the convento de Santa Cruz. Open during the summer season with 20 beds in 5 small rooms kept spotlessly clean by the voluntary hospitalera from the Madrid association. Limited facilities include a small kitchenette and use of a delightful courtyard and an air of tranquillity. *[Next albergue: Calzada del Coto – 5.1 km].*

Other accommodation: Sahagún offers a wide choice of hotels and pensions in variety of price brackets. The **Turismo** (987-782 117) has current list and prices. •**Asturiana** P (987-780 073) Plaza de Lemses Franco, 2. •**Don Pacho** Hs* (987-780 775) Av, Constitución, 86. •**El Ruedo** Hs* (987-780 075) Plaza Mayor, 1. •**Escarcha** Hs** (987-781 856) c/Regina Franco, 12. •**La Cordoniz** Hs** (987-780 276) opposite the albergue. •**Alfonso VI** Hs** (987-781 144) c/Nicolás and in the top price bracket (adjacent to *Viatoris*) the new •**Puerta de Sahagún** H**** (987-781 880).

SAHAGÚN: In medieval times Sahagún was a seat of great ecclesiastical power, largely courtesy of the influence of Alfonso VI who, along with his various wives, is buried in the Benedictine convento de Santa Cruz. Owing to the lack of stone for building purposes many of the grand edifices were constructed with brick and, accordingly, many have disappeared. Little remains of the famous abbey of San Benito which was founded in the 10th century and rose to become one of the most important Benedictine monasteries in Spain. Charlemagne was also linked with the town, which from these earliest times has given shelter to the pilgrims on their way to Santiago de Compostela, so we follow illustrious footsteps. Monasteries, churches and pilgrim hospices abounded. The foundations of the town however extend much further back to its Roman past. It was here that Saint Facundo was martyred which gave rise to a monastery bearing his name as early as the 9th century. Despite Arab invasions and counter attacks that destroyed the monastery on several occasions, it was ultimately the loss of interest in things religious that finally reduced it to the rubble that now lies to the west of the town. However, the martyr lives on in the name Sahagún itself, a derivation of Sanctum Facundum, and lies buried in the church of St. John along with fellow martyr Primitivo.

Despite decaying edifices you will not be at the loss of religious buildings and art to admire. If you follow the *yellow* route shown on the town map in this guide (the waymarked route is indicated in *grey*) you will pass the following: Baroque Church of San Juan (just past the albergue) with a sculpture of the town's patron saint *San Facundo*. Continuing down the c/del Arco you come to Plaza San Lorenzo and its outstanding 13th century Iglesia de San Lorenzo a fine example of the brick Mudejar style and whose prominent tower is a good landmark. From here it is a short walk to the Plaza Mayor where you can refresh yourself in its array of cafés and bars and admire its handsome Town Hall *Ayuntamiento*.

Exit via c/Flora Florez (the narrow street behind the bandstand) and turn sharp right> down c/San Benito into Plaza Lesmes Franco and turn <left to Plaza de San Tirso where the distinctive tower of Iglesia de San Tirso leads to the first church, built in the 12th century, to use brick and credited with starting the craze for the Mudejar style in the area. Adjoining is Parque San Benito and the ruins of the monastery of that name which became one of the most powerful in Spain leading, inevitably, to its downfall. We now have an opportunity to walk under its impressive arch *Arco de San Benito* which adjoins the Convento de Santa Clara and its interesting *museo* which houses the beautiful statue of the Virgin dressed as a pilgrim which originally adorned the church of the *Monasterio de la Peregrina* whose crumbling brick walls and Moorish arches are situated on the outskirts of town (past the Escolar Fray Bernardino c/San Francisco on the rise ahead.)

Arco San Benito

Note [1]: If you want to view the interior of *all* the above sites you will need to stay the night. Otherwise, allow extra time to walk around them and don't leave Sahagún at such a late hour that you end up, unintentionally, in the very basic albergue at Calzada del Coto (or Bercianos on the alternative route). **[2]:** If you are continuing on the **recommended route** (less travelled) to Calzadilla de los Hermanillos it is advisable to have a midday meal in Sahagún and perhaps to buy supplies for the journey ahead; an evening meal and something for the

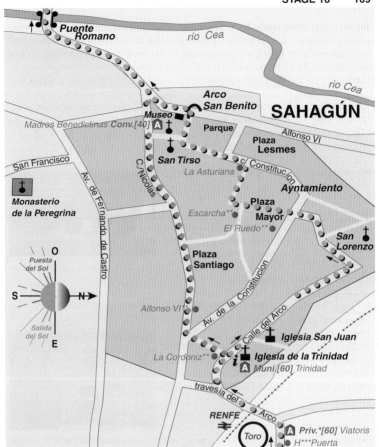

following day to Mansilla de las Mulas (as Calzadilla and Calzada del Coto have only limited facilities). **[3]:** Not particularly recommended (unless you have specific interest) are 2 detours on the camino from Madrid that joins here in Sahagún. **Detour [a]** Further afield (5 km south of Sahagún on the LE-941) is another gem of a national monument, the Romanesque monastery of **San Pedro de las Dueñas** where the Benedictine Mothers operate another hospedería (check tourist office for details) adjacent to the 12th century church with its impressive crucifix. **Detour [b]** 8 km south on the C-611 are the sweeping walls of the monumental castle and palace at **Grajal de Campos** birthplace of legendary knights and scene of epic battles.

Just past the Arco Benito and the MM Benedictinas museum we join the main waymarked route into c/Antonio Nicolas down to:

1.0 km **Puente Canto** (1 km from the albergue / turismo) to this historic stone bridge (originally Roman but reconstructed in the 11th and 16th centuries) its five strong arches have stood the test of time and the powerful waters of the river Cea. Continue along the side of the main road (the N-120 is now realigned as part of the new bypass). This stretch offers some shade from the poplar grove otherwise known as *The copse of Charlemagne's lances* where legend has it that the lances of his troops turned into saplings after they had been planted in the earth here; an ominous sign to the forthcoming battle with the Moors which was to litter the area with corpses. Continue out past the *Camping Pedro Ponce* and municipal sports grounds to:

3.6 km Option [?] junction with N-120 and N-601. **For recommended route [1]** The original Roman road *Via Aquitana* also known as the pilgrims road *Calzada de los Peregrinos* and sometimes also referred to as *Via Trajana* – proceed over the motorway into Calzada de Coto.

For alternative route [2] the Royal French Way *Real Camino Francés* (via Bercianos to El Burgo Ranero) stay on this (left) side of the bridge. Note the alternative route is by modern *senda* running parallel to the autopista. The first feature you come to is the simple brick 12th century hermitage of Our Lady of the Pears *Ermita de Nuestra de Perales*. The *senda* continues to an asphalt road that takes you into:

5.7 km **Bercianos del Real Camino** •**Albergue** parish hostel (987-784 008) on c/Santa Rita (top end left) open all year with 45 places (20 beds + 25 mattresses) in several rooms with basic facilities including a kitchen and dining area and a tranquil meditation room. – there is a small inconspicuous shop 100m. Other accommodation: •**Rivero** HsR* (987-744 287) on c/Mayor, 12 which also has a restaurant. *[Next albergue El Burgo Raneros – 7.5 km].* Pick up the *senda* again on the western edge of the village that continues under the autopista where you pick up the asphalt road into:

7.5 km **El Burgo Raneros** •**Albergue [1]** *Domenico Laffi* municipal hostel (987-330 023) dedicated to the 17th century Italian pilgrim and located at the edge of the town (head for the water-tower). Open all year with 28 beds in 4 rooms. Excellent facilities and attractive purpose built hostel in the idiom of the area using mud and straw in its construction. Close by on the other side of the street is a new •**Albergue [2]** *El Nogal* private

Albergue [1] *Domenico Laffi*

hostel with 30 places in several rooms with all basic facilities – open all year. Further on is another new •**Albergue [3]** *La Laguna* private hostel (987-330 094) part of the casa rural *Piedras Blancas*. Open all year with 20 places in bunk beds and all facilities + private rooms in the B&B. Other accommodation: •**Fonda Lozano** (987-330 060) or •**Hostal el Peregrino** (987-330 069) with 14 rooms, also several bars, restaurants and shop centred around the Plaza Mayor. Town of the Frogs *ranas* provides one possible clue to its name – they can certainly be heard in the evenings cavorting in the local pond. *[Next albergue: Reliegos – 13.0 km. or 19.1 km to the albergue in Mansilla de las Mulas – See next stage for details.]*

Recommended route [1] The original pilgrim road *Calzada de los Peregrinos* is a continuation of the Roman road *calzada Trajana*. Cross over the bridge (A-231) into:

| 0.5 km | Calzada del Coto •Albergue *San Roque* municipal hostel (987-781 233), prominently located at the entrance to the town beside the pelota court. Open all year with 24 beds in 2 rooms and basic facilities (no kitchen) situated in the town parkland and children's play area. The town has minimal facilities with small shop, bar and restaurant. *[Next albergue: Calzada de Hermanillos – 8.7 kilometres].*

Continue through the town via c/Mayor, past the parish church of San Esteban and out onto the *Via Romana* on the western outskirts of the town **[0.5 km]** where you pick up the earth track. Waymarks are few but you head straight out for the railway bridge on the horizon **[1.8 km]** and cross over railway:

| 2.3 km | **Puente** take the ridge over the railway and continue on the earth track that winds its way though scrubland in the area of the remote farm *Dehesa de Valdelocajos*. Here there is nothing to disturb the wilderness except the occasional shepherd grazing his flock and a few sporadic metal camino signposts with their inane cartoon character. Even the game hunters appear to have taken offence at these signs, as evidenced by the lead shot that has been fired at them! We pass a remote country lodge with dogs (right) to arrive at a shallow valley with the village of Hermanillos in the distance:

| 4.3 km | **Pilgrim fountain [F]** *Fuente del Peregrino* in a shaded rest area in a poplar grove by an old riverbed. Continue for the final leg into:

| 2.1 km | Calzada de los Hermanillos •**Albergue** municipal hostel (987-330 023) on the left at we enter the village. Open all year with 16 beds in 2 rooms (+6 *colchones*) with cubicles of 4 bunks and all basic facilities. No patio area but the village provides a quiet haven to rest in. Other accommodation: •**Casa El Cura** CR (987-337 502) on c/La Carratera, 13 on the northern outskirts (right of the camino) 18 places in variety of rooms with dinner, bed & breakfast package for pilgrims. *[Next albergue: Religos Mansilla de las Mulas – 28.0 km, or albergue at El Burgo Raneros on opposite side of rail tracks on alternative route [2] 8.0 km].*

Albergue *(Above)*
Casa El Cura *(Below)*

In days long gone by the monks *Little Brothers of the Road* welcomed pilgrims here but the hospitality is still felt here especially in *Comedor Via Trajana* adjacent to the albergue that caters for hungry pilgrims. A small inconspicuous shop (behind the Pelota court and only open late afternoon for a short period) and 2 smoky bars make up the other facilities. The parish church is dedicated to St. Bartholomew where there is an impressive statue of him overpowering the devil.

❏ **Silence is golden.**

MAP 19 *368.4 km (228.9 miles) to Santiago de Compostela*

HERMANILLOS DE LA CALZADA – MANSILLA DE LAS MULAS

▬▬▬	Path / Track	--- ---	19.3 ---	79%
▬▬▬	Quiet Road	--- ---	4.4 ---	18%
▬▬▬	Main Road	--- ---	0.8 ---	3%
Total km	**Total distance**		**24.5 km** (15.2 miles)	

Adjusted for climb   24.7 km (accrued ascent 50m = 0.2 km)
Alto ▲   (Effectively a level walk along the *Via Romana*).

CALZADILLA *870m*

The Practical Path: On the recommended route, once we have left the access road to Hermanillos, we will encounter no asphalt roads, no sendas, no town, no village, no farmyard, no houses, no water fonts and few trees and therefore little shade. Classified as the most perfect extant stretch of Roman road left in Spain today (see later). We follow in the footsteps of Emperor Augustus himself but he will have travelled with a retinue of servants not available to a humble pilgrim – so make sure your flasks are full and that you bring some food to fortify you along this ancient way. Enjoy the silence. **Intermediate accommodation:** El Burgo Ranero 8.0 km (4.5 km *off* route) – Reliegos 17.4 km ½ km *off* route.

❏ **The Mystical Path:** Only the weeds and wild flowers have changed in the two millennia since this path was laid. While Roman artefacts lie behind glass cages in dislocated museums in the cities, here you walk on the original Roman road itself. The muted silence of the museums, broken by the giggles of tour parties, are nothing to match the original stone in its original setting and the golden silence of the wide prairie. Here the call of the occasional bird of prey only seems to emphasise the silence and adds to the tranquillity. The hum of the bee busily extracting pollen from the wild flowers brings a sense of unhurried calm that pervades this place. The bee transforms the pollen to golden nectar. Will the alchemist in you extract the purest gold from this day?

❏ **Personal Reflections:** *"... In my exhaustion I missed the hostel on the way into the village. Seemingly out of nowhere a group of children appeared and started to dance around me shouting and waving. They evidently did not know of my need for quiet at the end of a long day. What an unreasonable expectation of mine. A few minutes later I saw their enthusiasm in a different light, as a means to gain access to the albergue in order to empty out the donation box, which they did with alacrity. Why did I assume it would go straight into their pockets and not straight to the hospitalero or parish priest? I am still so quick to judge and condemn others. Perhaps it is a reflection of my own dishonesty. But it takes only an instant to change an unloving thought to a loving one – What, then, is this process? Is it just intention? Can it be that I simply see what I choose to see? What did the shepherd see in me? What did Christ see in the thief crucified alongside him? ..."*

Albergue **6.1** ► **A** ◄ **1.7** Albergue *Muni.[70]*

(Pop. 1,800 – Alt. 800m)
**MANSILLA
de las MULAS**

A-231

Campolar

N-601

H

◄ **5.9** Cruce

rio Esla

Canal

RELIEGOS
Albergue **3.5** ► **A** ◄ **1.8** Alto / Opción
D.Gaifferos Muni.[60]

N-625

Bodegas

Puente **9.5** ► ◄ **2.8** Puente *arroyo Santa María*

Arroyo Valdearcos

Villamarco

5.7 Cruce

W

Sunset

N

② ①

S

Sunrise

E

3.2 Puente

**EL BURGO
RANERO**

A *Priv. [20+] La Laguna*

H **A** ◄ **0.0** Albergue
Piedras Blancas **A** *Muni.[28] Domenico Laffi*
El Nogal **Priv.[30]**

3.4 Cruce

Canal

A-231

**CALZADILLA
de los HERMANILLOS**
(Pop. 200 – Alt. 820m)

Casa El Cura [16]

C

Muni. [22] **Albergue** **0.0** ► **A**

🔲 *Via Trajana*

Alternative route [2] El Burgo Ranero – Mansilla de las Mulas via Reliegos 19.1 km (11.9 miles). The entire section is by modern *senda* running alongside an asphalt road parallel to the motorway. The monotony somewhat relieved by several small streams, mostly dry in summer and the maturing shelter belt of trees that line the path. From El Burgo Ranero continue down the main street and onto the *senda* crossing the road to Villarmarco and proceeding to:

9.5 km **Cruce** here we cross the rail line picking up the *senda* again, passing a series of *bodegas* built untidily into the sides of the surrounding hillocks. The ruins of the fortress church of San Antonio Abad are visible above as we enter:

3.5 km **Reliegos** •**Albergue** *D.Gaiferos* municipal hostel (987-314 103) located in a former school building on c/Escuela. Open all year with 70 places (50 beds + 20 colchones) in 2 separate dormitories and all facilities with extensive dining-lounge area but lacking any outside space. Shortly after leaving the village
pick up the *senda* again to cross the main road on the outskirts of Mansilla de las Mulas passing over canal to enter the town through the medieval gate at the **Puerta Castillo** (only the walls remaining) up c/Santa María and into **Plaza del Pozo** where the recommended route (from Hermanillos) joins from the right. Continue straight on, into c/del Puente and:

6.1 km **Mansilla de las Mulas** •**Albergue** (see recommended route for details).

Recommended route [1]: The original Roman road *Via Aquitana* or the pilgrims road *Calzada de los Peregrinos* and sometimes referred to as *Via Trajana* – Leave the albergue and proceed down the main street and out onto a vast flat plateau of wheat and other cereal crops to cross over irrigation canal **[1.2 km]** and continue for **[2.2 km]** to:

3.4 km **Cruce** T-junction (the left fork goes directly to El Burgo Ranero on the alternative route 3.2 km) but we now leave the asphalt and continue straight onto the *Calzada Romana* for a glorious 15.7 km of uninterrupted natural pathways. This stretch of Roman road is largely intact despite the intervening 20 centuries. It is part of the *Via Aquitana* the east/west highway built to link the gold mines of Gallaecia to Rome via Astorga *Asturica Augusta* and used by Ceasar Augustus in his campaigns against the Cantabrians. It was subsequently used by the armies of Islam and Christianity including Charlemagne in their battles for supremacy over the Iberian peninsular. After the re-conquest it became known as the Pilgrim Road *Calzada de los Peregrinos* and countless millions of pilgrims have walked this self-same path that is known and loved today as the Camino de Santiago. Of course this is not the only stretch left for us to walk but it is the most complete and spectacular section. It is also referred to as the *Via Trajana* this latter being the spur that connected the route to Bordeaux.

On our right (northern) horizon are the Cordillera Cantábrica (an extension of the Pyrenees) and just visible behind (on a clear day) are the Picos de Europa with the highest peak at 2,648m (8,687 feet). El Burgo Raneros rail halt is on our left with the town some distance beyond it.

3.2 km **Puente** bridge over the meandering *arroyo Solana* with a small plantation of pine struggling to establish itself in the bleak landscape. The path now takes a wide curve towards the railway line:

5.7 km Cruce *Paso de Villarmarco* remote railway halt with level crossing to the village of Villarmarco just visible on the horizon. Stay this side of the tracks and continue over several small riverbeds to:

2.8 km Puente *arroyo Valle de Santa María* we now encounter a more pronounced river valley with a grove of poplars (left) offering shade if a rest or picnic is needed. A new concrete bridge has removed the need for pilgrims to ford this river and the path now climbs gently through scrubland to the high point of this day's stage:

1.8 km Cruce / Opción (Alto 920m): We now have the option to [1] continue straight past the radio mast and join the alternative route in Reliegos which is now only ½ kilometre and which has several bars and an albergue (see alternative route for onward route details) or [2] turn right> and start the long descent into the río Esla valley towards Mansilla de las Mulas just visible on the horizon. The latter path continues for another **[3.3 km]** through cultivated fields to merge with an asphalt road for **[1.6 km]** until we reach:

5.9 km N-625 Cruce now back to 'civilisation' we turn <left onto the main road past the modern **hotel Bahillo [0.6 km]** down under the bypass onto Paseo del Esla and through the only remaining medieval city gate still in existence **Arco de Santa María [0.7 km]** and straight on up c/de la Concepción passing the exclusive Alberguería del Camino (left) before turning right> in **Plaza del Pozo** into c/del Puente and on our (left) **[0.4 km]**:

1.7 km Mansilla de las Mulas •Albergue municipal hostel (987-310 138/368) c/del Puente, 5 – where the charming *Laura* and a team of volunteers has been welcoming pilgrims for many years. Open all year with 70 places (50 beds + 20 mattresses). The hostel is actually several buildings that stretch back to the main street and accommodation is being expanded to take the large numbers accessing this popular hostel. All facilities are provided including a central patio. *[Next albergue: Vilarente – 5.6 km].*

Alternative accommodation: adjoining the albergue (front) •**La Delicias** Hs* (987-310 075) c/Los Mesones, 22 with popular restaurant (pilgrim menu). •**San Martín** Hs* (987–310 094) Av. Picos de Europa, 32. • **El Gallo** Hs** (987-310 359) c/Cistierna, 17. For refined luxury try •**Alberguería del Camino** Hs** (987-311 193) c/Concepción, 12.

MANSILLA DE LAS MULAS: An important pilgrim halt today, no less than in its illustrious medieval past, which sheltered pilgrims in 3 separate pilgrim *hospitales* (long disappeared). This was and remains the meeting place for the two converging routes, the *Real Camino Francés* which enters the old quarter via the south gate *Puerta de Santiago* (only the wall remains) and the *Calzada de los Peregrinos* which enters via the east gate *Arco de Santa María*. The name of this interesting old town is derived from *Mano en Silla* (hand on the saddle) that also defines the town's coat of arms. The addition of *de las mulas* (of the mules) most likely refers to the town's earlier prominence as a livestock market. Whatever about its agricultural roots, the medieval wall still protects the town from the encroachment of modernity.

The *Turismo* (987-310 138 summer only) c/los Mesones, 16 (the busy main street) can provide a map of the town and also a street plan of León showing the major sites to visit there tomorrow. The town has a range of shops and a variety of bars and restaurants (most offering a pilgrim menu). Take time to wander the meandering streets and admire the architectural layout and buildings around Plazas del Grano and Leña or just watch the trout jumping for the evening fly as the sun sets over the río Esla... or join them and take a swim from the sandy shore accessed by a footbridge towards *el camping* (see town plan).

Several detours are available from here (only advised if you have special interest) as follows: **Detour [1]** Over the bridge (first turning left 1.1 km) takes you through Mansilla Mayor and on to Vilaverde de Sandoval and the 12th century Romanesque *Monastery of Santa María de Sandoval*, an important Cistercian monastery in its day but now de-consecrated – 8 km round trip (or continue on to León). **Detour [2]** Over the bridge (first turning right 1.4 km) takes you via Vilafalé to the 10th century *Monastery of San Miguel de Escalada* designated a national monument on account of its exceptional Mozarabic architecture – 25 km round trip (share a taxi?).

San Miguel de Escalada

Forward planning for León: You have been on remote paths over the past few days so prepare for the walk into León tomorrow along the busy N-601 and the bustle and noise of this major city with its store of artistic treasures. You may recall the tiresome access into Burgos along the busy roads into that city. Whatever your prior experiences and respecting your intention for this pilgrimage, there is the possibility to avoid the busy (and dangerous) main road into León by taking the regular bus service from Mansilla direct to the city centre. Both the route into León alongside the N-601 and out along N-120 is very wearisome. If you take this bus option spare a prayer for your fellow pilgrims on foot who you will see trudging their way along the main roads. The bus depot is ½ km on the outskirts of Mansilla on the Valladolid road. Several bus companies vie for this lucrative route and leave every half hour or so from about 07:00. This way you could explore the city at leisure, stay overnight and bus it to La Virgen del Camino early again the following morning. Refreshed from your break you could pick up the recommended route via Villar de Mazarife and make it to Hospital de Órbigo (29.1 km) a pleasant town with 3 good albergues and several restaurants. 60% of this route (from La Virgen del Camino to Hospital de Órbigo) is by natural path over quiet open countryside known as *el Páramo* and the remainder is along quiet country lanes (no main roads). The following day would facilitate an easy morning walk to Astorga (16.6 km) and allow ample time to explore that interesting city.

The vast majority of pilgrims will have committed to travel the whole route by foot, which is highly commendable but others have different time constraints. If the idea of taking public transport seems like heresy it might be useful to ask yourself – why not? You could more than make up the distance by walking to Finisterre! The ego and its obsessive behavioural patterns can be just as limiting as a *laissez faire* attitude and indifference. What is your motivation for this journey, the intention you set out with? How does your decision to walk rather than take the bus serve that purpose? Do you judge others who take the bus as inadequate pilgrims in some way? Can we know all the circumstances surrounding individual decisions to judge the actions and motivations of others? Let us walk today with love in our hearts – making every step a prayer for peace and acceptance.

MANSILLA de las MULLAS

Arco de San Agustín

Plaza Picara Justina

río Esla

C/ San Agustín

† *Convento*

Plaza Convento

C. de la Noria

Centro Salud ✚

Las Delicias

León →

Ayntamiento

C/ los Mesones

i

H Plaza S. Nicolás

Estación de Autobuses

A Muni.[70]

← Marcelo

Plaza del Pozo

C/ del Puente

Santa María †

Plaza del Grano

C/ Santa María

Albergueria H

San Martín ■ Casa de Cultura

Plaza de la Leña

Puerta Castillo

H Los Faroles

H San Martín

Arco de   Santa María

N-601

Camping

REFLECTIONS:

When we judge others we don't condemn them – we condemn ourselves.

❏ **Why should I be gloomy when I can be glad? Here inside of me is a force that makes its own weather, winning through thickest clouds to the shining sun.** '*J.B.' His Life and Works*

MAP 20 *343.9 km (213.7 miles) to Santiago de Compostela*

MANSILLA DE LAS MULAS – LEÓN

	Path / Track	--- ---	10.2	---	55%
	Quiet Road	--- ---	3.7	---	20%
	Main Road	--- ---	<u>4.7</u>	---	25%
Total km	**Total distance**		**18.6 km** (11.6 miles)		

Adjusted for climb   19.1 km (accrued ascent 100m = 0.5 km)

Alto   High Point: Arcahueja (Alto del Portillo) 890m (2,920 feet)

Alto del Portillo
900m - **Valdelafuente** - ▲ 900m - - - - - -
MANSILLA   **Vilarente**   ○   **LEÓN**
■ 800m   820m
| | Río Porma | | |
00 km   5 km   10 km   15 km

The Practical Path: Apart from a brief respite along a dedicated pilgrim track around Arcahueja this stage is mostly road or *senda* that runs parallel to the busy N-601. It seems as if the city fathers have more pressing matters on their hands than to consider the needs of the walking pilgrim. Tourism and industrial activity, with their requirement for rapid transport, are decidedly *número uno*. A walking pilgrim requires nothing more than a simple path and respect for the ancient camino and both are in short supply around León. Take great care crossing the main road in Valdelafuente (alto del Portillo), a notoriously dangerous stretch with presently no option but to brave the fast moving traffic! From this point on you need to stay very focused so as not to miss the waymarks amongst the busy-ness of the city centre and decide now where you intend heading: albergue [2] in the southern suburbs – albergue [1] in the old city– an alternative hotel – the cathedral and adjacent tourist office? **Intermediate accommodation:** Villarente (5.6 km) – Arahueja (10.4 km).

❏ **The Mystical Path:** What route does your heart follow today? Never mind about the outer path, what awareness is there of the inner journey – is it flat or mountainous? Never mind about the outer weather, are you aware of the inner conditions – is there sunshine or cloud? The outer is fixed, only the inner can be changed at will. "*It is not what life does to you that is important – but what you do with what life does to you that really matters.*"

❏ **Personal Reflections:** "*... The rain was heavy and persistent, drenching my papers every time I tried to take notes. I followed the sign by the consultorio and shortly afterwards realised the only way forward was across a deep trench. Too lazy to return and not realising the depth of the ditch I slithered down the steep bank and found myself waist deep in cold, grey water. I started to curse out loud, the offending expletives borne away on an unusually stiff wind. Old regretting patterns started to emerge and by grace, not will, I came to the sudden realisation that I created my own weather. I started to smile, cleansing my dark thoughts in the ripples of laughter that bubbled up from somewhere deep inside ...*"

La Virgen del Camino

Trobajo del Camino

Parador

Plaza S.Marcos

✝ **S.Isodoro**

Plaza S.Marcelo

ℹ ✝ **Catedral**

✝ Iglesia Mercado
✝ Santa María del Camino

Ⓐ 1.6 **Albergue**
Benedictinas Conv.[120]

c/Barahona

(Pop. 130,000 – Alt. 840m)
LEÓN

N-120

N-630

N-630

Plaza San Francisco

✝ **Plaza Santa Anna**

Av. Europa

Plaza de Toros

Av. Ladreda

3.5 **Cruce/Opción**

Albergue 1.8 → Ⓐ
Muni.[70]

AP-71

río Torío

Pasarela

PUENTE CASTRO

Hospital ✚

Alto del Portillo

Cruce Vilgilante

< Benavente

río Bernesga

VALDELAFUENTE

Valdefresno

N-601 3.3

Camino Real Ⓗ

Ⓐ *Priv.[12] Bar La Torre*
ARCAHUEJA

✚ 4.5 **Fuente**

Canal de Porma

San Felisimo

N-601

O
Puesta del Sol

Cruce Repsol

S

Salida del Sol E

Ⓐ *Priv.*[64] San Pelayo*

VILLARENTE
Puente 1.6 → Ⓐ *Priv.[20]*

Casa Blanca Ⓗ

río Porma

4.1 **Villarmoros**

Villaverde de Sandoval ■

Mansilla Mayor

Lancia (ruinas)

San Miguel de Escalada (16 km) >

río Esla

MANSILLA de las MULAS
(Pop. 1,800 – Alt. 800m)

Ⓐ ← 0.0 **Albergue** *Muni.[80]*

Leaving the albergue at Mansilla proceed out over the río Esla and onto the *senda* that runs parallel to the main road passing the turn-off for Mansilla Mayor-Sandoval (left) **[1.1 km]** and Vilafalé-San Miguel (right) **[0.3 km]**. Next we pass an Agip petrol station behind which is the ancient hill fortress and settlement of Lancia (a short 1 km detour) where the indigenous Asturians, despite their heroic defence of their native lands, met their demise at the hands of the Roman legions. Artefacts have also been recovered here from the Neolithic period and excavations are ongoing. Continue for another **[2.7 km]** passing over the río Moro into:

4.1 km **Villarmoros de Mansilla** formerly *Villamoros del Camino Francés* with its Iglesia de San Esteban. Continue on the pilgrim track passing the down-at-heel fonda •**Casa Blanca** to the medieval bridge where we have to compete with the road traffic [!] to cross over the río Porma on the Giant bridge *puente Ingente* so called on account of its 20-arch span into:

1.6 km **Villarente** shaded rest area down by the river. The first building (left) was a medieval pilgrim hospital which operated a donkey 'ambulance' service into León while (right) we pass •**Albergue** [1] *Residencia El Delfín Verde* (Inés 987-312 065) with private pilgrim hostel set back off the main road but readily visible with 30 places in several small rooms with basic facilities. 50 metres further on *off* the main road (right) at the end of c/El Romero beside a grove of trees is the popular new •**Albergue***[2] *San Pelayo* (Julio García 987-312 677 / 650-918 281) network* hostel open all year with 64 places and with excellent facilities, meals also available. Continue through this modern satellite town of León past the health centre *Centro de Salud Consultario* and turn off right> **[1.5 km]** onto the dedicated pilgrim track (opposite the Repsol filling station) and continue for **[3.0 km]** over the canal del Porma climbing up the gravel path passing a rest area with water font **[F]** (often dry) to the top of the rise in:

Albergue [2] *San Pelayo*

4.5 km **Arcahueja** This is the last chance to take a rest in the relative quiet before we hit the city traffic. 300 metres off route (left) is the welcoming bar and •**Albergue** *La Torre* (987-205 896) private pilgrim hostel open all year with 12 beds in 3 rooms. No kitchen but meals available in the bar. Continue along track through Valdefresno **[F]** and turn <left at the asphalt road that is the start of an industrial park and up to the main road at:

3.3 km **N-601 Valdelafuente** various bars and showrooms spread along this busy section of the N-601, one of the main arterial roads into León. We skirt up briefly around a fence at Alto del Portillo before dropping down to cross the crazy stretch of dual carriageway [!]. Every year I pray fervently as I cross over the central reservation and pray again the far side for the central government to provide an over or under pedestrian pass – in the meantime wait for a break in that traffic flow … once on the far side don't forget to offer thanks! Proceed down the narrow margin at the side of the dual carriageway to cross a high level pedestrian bridge over the bypass by Hospital Santa Isabel veering <left off the main street in Puente Castro whose modern buildings disguise the fact that this was an influential Jewish district in the 12th century and site of a former Roman settlement. Continue via the footbridge *pasarela* **[2.4 km]** over the río Torio with pilgrim information kiosk *Turismo* (summer only). We now make our way up to the wide main road to busy roundabout *glorieta* **[1.0 km]** and:

3.5 km **Cruce / Opción.** If you plan to stay the night in León and want to stay in one of the hostels this is decision point (also a pilgrim information point). For the alternative route to albergue [2] (not recommended) turn left into Av. de Fernandez Ladreda. Continue down it towards the bullring *Plaza de Toros* turning left into c/Monseñor Turrado, passing the Guardia Civil headquarters into c/Campos Góticos and:

City Suburbs •**Albergue** [2] *Ciudad de León* (987-081 832) municipal hostel located 1.8 km west *off* the camino (see city plan). Open all year with 64 beds in rooms of 8. All modern facilities including TV! so if you want to watch the latest soap or have the convenience of a microwave oven – look no further. The León youth hostel is also part of this unattractive modern building (formerly the *Colegio de Huérfanos Ferrovias*) so

Albergue [2] *Ciudad de León*

additional accommodation might be available if the pilgrim hostel is full.

For the **recommended route** along the historic camino into the old city and the central albergue [1] proceed over the major roundabout (pedestrian crossing) into Av. Miguel Castaño that merges with Av. Del Europa which we also cross to bring us into St. Anne's Square *Plaza de Santa Ana* where a fountain and small shaded park provides an opportunity to calm any frayed nerves and take stock; we're nearly there but "many a slip t'wixt…" Take the street to the left of Iglesia de Santa Ana (painted a warm yellow) into c/Barahona and through Money Gate *Puerta Moneda* one of the original gateways to the medieval city (note the vast city walls as you pass) and just *before* reaching Iglesia N. S. del Mercado (with its lions guarding the entrance) turn right> into c/Escurial to:

1.6 km **Centro** •**Albergue** [1] *Santa. María de Carbajalas* (monasterio de las Benedictinas) (680-649 289) conveniently situated in the old city in a quiet square. Open all year with 180 beds in several dormitories and good basic facilities but no kitchen (the area has ample restaurants). Meticulously run by the Benedictine nuns who have created a haven of peace and serenity (excepting when the adjacent school is open) in this otherwise busy city area. Few pilgrims attend the sung Vespers (19:00) or the pilgrim benediction

Albergue [1] *Santa María*

(21:30) in the convent chapel which can provide a powerful sense of the sacred and reminder of the true nature of all our journeying. If you stay in this albergue you may be further blessed with a cup of tea or coffee to set you on your way in the morning! *[Next albergue: Mazarife – 22.1 km].*

Before turning in for the night you might visit the adjacent and atmospheric *Barrio Húmedo* (wet quarter, as in drink – on account of the variety of bars that abound here!) which is centred around the beautiful and intimate squares of Plaza Martín that leads into Plaza Mayor with the original 17th century Baroque Town hall (only 500 metres from the albergue) or simply lose yourself in the maze of narrow streets that connect them. But beware the carriage home doesn't turn into a pumpkin at 22:00 – *not* midnight!). Or simply admire the cobbled squares *Plaza del Grano y Santa María del Camino* watched over by the cherubs who play in the central neoclassical fountain symbolising the two rivers that embrace this magical city. Also in this square we find the 10th century Church of Our Lady of the Market *Iglesia Nuestra Señora del Mercado* (with the lions). Here you can see a statue of the Virgin, Patroness of León (some say of the camino itself). Indeed the church was formerly called Iglesia Virgen del Camino until that honour was bestowed on the sanctuary on the western suburbs, which, along with the route through the city and the main sites, are described in the next stage.

Helpful **Turismo** (987-237 082) opposite the cathedral in Plaza Regla has list of options. **Other accommodation:** In the old quarter in the vicinity of the cathedral and those directly on the waymarked camino are marked on the city plan) include: •**La Posada Regia** Hr*** (987-213 173) c/Regidores, 9. •**París** H*** (987-238 600) c/Ancha, 18. •**Guzmán el Bueno** HsR* (987-236 412) c/López Castrillón, 6. •**Hospedería Fernando I** Hr*** (987-213 173) •**San Martín** HsR*(987-875 187) plaza Torres de Omaña, 1. •**Boccalino** Hs**(987-223 060) plaza S. Isodoro, 9.

Options in the modern quarter between Plaza Francisco (Correos) and Plaza San Marcos include: •**Reina** Hr* (987-205 212) c/Puerta de la Reina, 2. •**Alvarez** HsR* (987-072 520) c/Burgo Nuevo, 3. •**Padre Isla** HsR* (987-228 097) Av.Padre Isla, 8 and opposite (with 3 stars and 3 times the price) is •**Alfonso V** H*** (987-220 900) Av.Padre Isla, 1. Further on (just off the avenue) is •**Padre Isla** HsR* (987-092 298) on c/Joaquín Costa, 2. •**Londres** H* (987-222 274) Av. Roma, 1. •**Don Suero** HsR** (987-230 600) Av. Suero de Quiñones, 15 – and for incomparable 5 star luxury in the original pilgrim hospital try •**San Marcos** H***** (987-237 300) on Plaza San Marcos. Pick as you please or as your pocket dictates. Restaurants and bars abound to suit all tastes.

LEÓN CITY: at one time León was a Roman military garrison and base for its VIIth Legion, hence the name – León, derived from *Legion*. Later it became the capital of the old kingdoms of Asturias and León. It was conquered and re-conquered by Visigoth, Moor and finally Christian forces. Ancient and modern now straddle the banks of the río Barnesega and, within the hectic nature of any modern city it is a meeting that seems somehow effortless. The city, like the river, flows naturally along its tributaries, absorbing all in its welcoming embrace. Here every period and style is seamlessly accommodated: from Roman remains which now support the medieval walls to the exquisite Romanesque Royal Basilica of St. Isodoro *Real Basílica de San Isodoro*, the Gothic splendour of León Cathedral *Pulchra Leonina*, the magnificent intricacy of Renaissance *San Marcos* with its Plasteresque façade, the controversial austerity of the neo-Gothic in Gaudi's *Casa de Botines*, to the glass and steel edifices of today's modern architects.

This resident population of 140,000 plays host to many tourists and pilgrims who pour through the city. You could spend days here and not see the half of it especially if you arrive during any one of the festivals that seem to take place throughout the year but particular highlights include: *San Juan and San Pedro* from the 21st – 30th June which sees giant displays and running of the bulls during the day and concerts and fireworks at night. *San Froilán* runs from the 5th – 12th of October with more parades and a local pilgrimage *romería* to the Virgin of the Way *Virgin del Camino*. If you are just passing through – then the camino itself (marked rather too discreetly with tasteful brass scallop shells embedded in the pavement) will bring you around the prime sites in the medieval quarter. These historic sites are described in detail in the next stage.

Town Hall *(left)* **& Casa Botines** *(right)*

Cathedral at night *(above)*

Río Bernesga & Snow covered peaks
Cloisters – San Marcos Parador

Santiago over the Parador Entrance
San Marcos Square

REFLECTIONS:

❏ **Solitude shows us what we should be – society shows us what we are.**

Lord Cecil

MAP 21 *325.3 km (202.1 miles) to Santiago de Compostela*

LEÓN – VILLAR de MAZARIFE

	Path / Track	--- ---	12.5	---	54%
	Quiet Roads	--- ---	1.6	---	7%
	Main Roads	--- ---	9.0	---	39%
Total km	**Total distance**		**23.1 km** (14.4 miles)		

Adjusted for climb 24.3 km (accrued ascent 250m = 1.2 km)
Alto ▲ High Point: La Virgen del Camino 910m (2,985 feet)

The Practical Path: The route described below follows the waymarked circuit past the cathedral and out of the city via San Marcos but you need to have pencil sharp eyes to see the discreet shells in the pavement that compete with the many distractions in the busy streets. Once you leave Virgen del Camino, on the **recommended route**, there are few facilities along this relatively isolated stretch, so take a break in this outer suburb and stock up with fruit or snacks for the latter part of this stage. **Intermediate accommodation** (distances from albergue [1]): Virgen del Camino (8.7 km).

❏ **The Mystical Path:** To what small band of pilgrim friends do we owe the gratitude for discovering an alternative way to the intrusive main road? In one stroke it has changed a frenetic experience into another, more peaceful, world, '*Never doubt that a small group of thoughtful people can change the world, indeed it's the only thing that ever has.*' And what of the ultimate peace, that passes all understanding? Where will that be found? What needs to change in us to discover what was never lost, only hidden behind some imagined veil?

❏ **Personal Reflections:** "*... The cafe was crowded but our small group comprised six different nationalities all huddled in heated debate into city life versus the countryside. For me, the city has too many distractions, too much sensual and intellectual stimulation. I become isolated from my Self amongst the shops and factories, the museums and churches. The glamour of the sense-perceptible world hides the reality of the super-sensible. It is in the solitude of the camino that I seem to reach some altered state and find a deep peace. It is easier, for me, to see the Christ in the lone shepherd than in the shop assistant. Each mirrors a different aspect of my-self; in one I find peaceful serenity, the other pretentious servility masking a bored indifference.*

Leaving the albergue in Plaza de Santa María pick up the c/de la Rua and turn <left into the delightful Plaza de San Marcelo presided over by the splendid *Ayuntamiento* and the 12th century Iglesia San Marcelo. Here we have a good view of Gaudi's architectural masterpiece, the neo-Gothic palace *Casa de Botines*. This structure marks an historical and artistic turning point – it is one of the first monumental buildings constructed with private funds as a secular, middle class statement. Heretofore, buildings of this magnitude were funded by religious institutions or the aristocracy. While built on the back of a new

VILLAR de ✝ MAZARIFE
(Pop. 400)
Tio Pepe **Priv.[28]** Ⓐ 🏠
Jesús **Priv.[40]** Ⓐ

VILLADANGOS DEL PÁRAMO

Ⓐ 7.4 *Albergue Muni.[85]*

4.1 Albergue
San Antonio Priv.[50]

Estación

Chozas de Abajo 5.6

Chozas de Arriba

Robledo de la Valdoncina

1.5 San Miguel

Aldea de la Valdoncina

4.8 Valverde

Oncina 2.3
de la Valdoncina

① ③   ②

FRESNO del CAMINO
Opción 2.2
❓

río Oncina

N-120

A-66

A-66

❓

3.9 Cruce/Opción

Conv.[40] Ⓐ
Central Ⓗ

LA VIRGEN DEL CAMINO
(Pop. 3,300 – Alt. 910m)

A-71

Industrial

Cruceiro (ruinas) ✝

2.9 Cruce
Bodegas

N-120

N-630

✝ *Capela Santiago*

TRABAJO DEL CAMINO

Albergue Ⓙ

2.1 Puente

río Bernesga

San Marcos
✝ *San Isodoro*

Albergue 0.0 Ⓐ
Conv.[120]

(Pop. 130,000 – Alt. 840m)

✝ *Catedral*   **LEÓN**

N-630

S   W

Sunset

Sunrise

E

wave of industrial endeavour Gaudí still follows a medieval expression with the slender towers and the image of St. George slaying the dragon above the main door. Adjoining it (right) is the equally magnificent 16th century *Palacio de los Guzmanes* now the council offices and worth popping in to have a look at the marvellous inner courtyard. We now pass up shopping mecca c/Ancha to:

Catedral [0.8 km] taking up the whole east side of Plaza Regal, opposite the Turismo where you can obtain more detailed information (in English) on the cathedral and other sites. Enter the late 13th century Gothic Cathedral via the west door with the Virgin *Nuestra Señora la Blanca* adorning the central column (photo opposite) and *Santiago Peregrino* to the right – now well worn by the hands of devout pilgrims. The cathedral is renowned for its magnificent 125 stained glass windows set high in the walls that shed such a lightness of touch to the interior. H. V. Morton described it as, "… a conservatory that instead of keeping out the light, as most Spanish churches do, actually invites it in, showering this mosaic of colour all over it to become the gayest church in Spain.' He goes on to remind us, "one of the chief functions of the medieval church was to instruct the illiterate and to give them pictures they could understand, to show them the story of the Gospels and the legends

of the Saints – the novels of the medieval world. What more glorious picture book could there be than this church, whose illustrations are illuminated by God's own light." One consequence of this lightness is that the structural integrity of the building has been compromised and part of the nave caved-in during the 19th century following an earlier collapse in the 17th century! The cloisters off the north side and the cathedral museum *Catedral Museo* are also worth a visit.

Next make your way back down the side of the tourist office to the tiny plaza Torres de Omaña where myriad narrow medieval streets branch out in all directions, head down c/Fernandez Regueral (Hostal San Martín left) into Plaza San Isidoro, and:

San Isidoro [0.5 km] the fountain in the square was built to commemorate the VIIth Roman Legion. Here, bedded into the Roman foundations and the medieval city wall, is this wonderful 11th century Basilica Church. The remains of San Isidoro were brought here from Sevilla to be buried in Christian Spain as the south was still under Moorish influence at that time. Admire the Door of Forgiveness

Puerta del Perdón (right) through which medieval pilgrims, too ill to travel on to Santiago, could still receive the same indulgences. The exquisite sculptural work is from the hands of Maestro Estaban who also created the justly famous Puerta de las Platerías in Santiago cathedral.

Take time to visit the fascinating *Museo* that provides access to the cloisters *claustros* and the royal burial vaults *Pantheón Real*. The Pantheón is the only part of the original 11th century building remaining and the final resting place of no less than 11 Kings, 12 Queens and 23 Princes. Look at the beautiful frescoes, still vivid 800 years after they were first painted, and because of which it has been called Spain's *Romanesque Sistine Chapel*. If you now need fresh air and refreshment try the cafés opposite the entrance in c/El Cid that also has a delightful small park – or continue into c/Sacramento and turn left at the rear of the basilica and cross directly over the busy Av. de Ramón y Cajal into c/Renueva, crossing Av. del Padre Isla into Av. de Suero de Quiñones to:

Plaza San Marcos [0.8 km] take time to admire the Renaissance craftsmanship that built and adorned the stunning Plateresque edifice of this ancient monastery dedicated to St. Mark. Originally a more modest pilgrim hospital built by Doña Sancha in the 12th century it became the headquarters of the Knights of the Order of Santiago which was formed to protect the pilgrim way. Later still it was acquired and further embellished by King Ferdinand. The façade is a storybook in itself with many pilgrim motifs including the sword of Santiago entwined with the lion of San Marcos. A profusion of scallop shells cover the pediment of the church (and museum) entrance. Less evident are the interesting copper medallions all along the front (just behind the dwarf hedge) with scenes from the pilgrim cities and towns we have passed through. You may also notice a modest pilgrim sitting at the base of the stone cross, admiring the stately surroundings while resting his weary feet.

Take a peek inside the magnificent courtyard of the Parador (its cloistered galleries a museum in themselves) or perhaps treat yourself to a night in these sumptuous surroundings. You will find many fellow pilgrims checking out in the morning! Visit the Museo next door and admire the tantalising 11ᵗʰ century ivory crucifix *Cristo de Carrizo* (many of the artefacts are in the process of being moved to another location). All reminders of the influence and the gifts of the Way of St. James on León which, in times past, had no less than 17 such pilgrim *hospitales*. Take your leave of the central city and San Marcos Square, over:

2.1 km **Puente de río Bernesga** 16ᵗʰ century stone bridge over the river Bernesga. We now make our way through the busy suburbs of León until we reach the open countryside of the páramo. The first 2.9 km are on or beside the N-120 (signposted Astorga) before branching off right uphill through an industrial area to rejoin the main road in La Virgen del Camino.

Continue into Av. Quevedo, past the Parque de Quevedo **[0.2 km]** (right) named after the great 17ᵗʰ century Spanish poet whose writings so challenged the nobility that he was incarcerated in San Marcos during its spell as a prison! Join the main Astorga road until we reach a pilgrim cross and pedestrian bridge **[1.3 km]** where we have a brief respite from the N-120 as we take an elevated walkway over the railway line and rejoin the main road again in the area known as Trobajo del Camino. This area has many links with the original camino as evidenced by the small chapel dedicated to St. James *Ermita Santiago* (right) with Santiago statue – just beyond which the waymarked route takes us a short detour (left) into Plaza Sira San Pedro back up to the main road. **[1.4 km]** to:

2.9 km **Cruce** cross main road and take the first turn right> up steeply (**3t** sign). [!] Many pilgrims, their heads bent low against the incline, miss this turning and keep on along the busy N-120. We now pass a collection of bodegas to the crest of the hill with stone pedestal (left) base of another former pilgrim cross no doubt pillaged, like the one in San Marcos square, to adorn some more 'important' setting. Its ruined state is a strangely powerful reminder that we are on the historic camino. Hopefully, sufficiently out of sight of the city fathers, it will long remain in its dilapidated state and we will be saved some modern concrete replacement. A good point from which to look back over the sprawling expanse of León below, before proceeding along the c/Camino de la Cruz for **[3.2 km]** through the industrial area of Virgen to join the N-120 in:

3.9 km **La Virgen del Camino** Iglesia San Froilán. Last of the suburban sprawl of León and an opportunity to take some refreshment at the cafetería y pastelería El Peregrino which also operates the •**San Froilán** Hs (987-302 019) just off the main road opposite the ultra modern sanctuary of the Virgen built in 1961 on the site of the shrine where a shepherd, in the early 16ᵗʰ century, saw visions of the Virgin who told him a church would be built in this spot.

The place became a pilgrimage in its own right on account of the miracles performed here. The huge bronze statues of the 12 Apostles stand above the west door with St. James looking out towards Santiago and the Virgin floating above them all. Cross over [!] the N-120 to camino information board showing the alternative routes available.

Accommodation in the area includes: •**Soto** Hs (987-802 925). •**Villa Paloma** H** •**Central** Hs (987-302 041) and behind the latter, in peaceful gardens at the edge of town is the new •**Albergue** *D.Antonino y Dña. Cinia* municipal hostel (615-217 335) previously part of the seminary and open from May to October with 40 places. Spotlessly clean with excellent modern facilities including washing and drying machines in each of its separate ladies and gents washrooms.

Proceed down to the point where the routes diverge [?] **[0.2 km]** marked by unsightly and unseemly paint sprawled across the asphalt road as Mazarife competes with Villadangos for your soul and wallet): Recommended country route [1] via Mazarife or alternative road route [2] to Villadangos del Páramo:

Alternative route [2] via Valverde to Villadangos del Páramo – a total distance of 22.7 km (9.0 km from León to this point and a further 13.7 km). The opening of the new autopista has actually reduced the traffic along this stretch of the N-120.

At the hand-painted sign (Mazarife left) keep straight on up the asphalt road which leads onto a track that takes a wide sweep left to pass under the autopista **[2.8 km]** to pick up a path that runs parallel to the N-120 for **[2.3 km]** into:

4.8 km **Valverde de la Virgen** it formerly had the suffix *del Camino* that it seems to have dropped along with any connection to the pilgrim. Continue straight through the town alongside the main road all the way into:

1.5 km **San Miguel del Camino**. The camino now continues on a path adjoining the main road all the way into Villadangos passing the hotel •**Avenida III** Hr** (987-390 311) and petrol station for a long stretch before crossing the road to:

7.4 km **Villadangos del Páramo** •**Albergue** *municipal* hostel (987-390 003) on main road as you enter the town. Open all year with 80 beds in 2 main rooms with additional floor space available in this converted former schoolhouse. All facilities and set back slightly from the main road by a lawn.

Other accommodation: •**Alto Paramo** Hs** (987-390 311). •**Libertad** Hs** (987-390 123) several shops, bars and restaurant. Visit the Iglesia de Santiago with its statue of Santiago Matamoros above the main altar that, unusually, shows him leaping out towards us (rather than in profile). This old town of Roman origins sits uneasily astride the main road. In the past it supported a pilgrim hospital and legend has it that in the numerologically significant year of 1111 a battle was waged here between the forces of Doña Urraca of León and those of her former spouse Alfonso of Aragón.

Recommended route [1] via Mazarife here we veer <left away from the N-120 on a gravel track to cross the new A-66 and A-71 intersection which we skirt around to follow a quiet road to:

2.2 km **Fresno del Camino** Iglesia San Andrés. Here another alternative **route [3]** veers right under the enormous viaduct to follow the line of the railway before rejoining the alternative route [2] in Villadangos. To take this route head out in the direction of La Aldea de la Valdoncina **[F] [3.0 km]** and on to Robledo de la Valdoncina **[3.5 km]** whose original church was connected to the Order of Santiago but you wouldn't think so to look at its modern replacement. We continue parallel to the rail line to bypass Estación de Villadangos **[7.0 km]** and into the village of Villadangos on the N-120 **[1.5 km]** a total alternative distance (from the option point) of 15.0 km.

For recommended route [1] continue through the village and into the wooded Fresno valley to:

2.3 km **Oncina de la Valdocina** pretty village *bonito pueblocito* with fountain **[F]** and parish church of San Bartolomé. Take the wayside path (signposted Chozas) up out of the valley onto the glorious open countryside of the *páramo*. The rich red earth provides nourishment for crops and wild flowers in equal proportion. This wonderful natural path continues for **[5.2 km]** until you join the asphalt road for **[0.4 km]** into:

5.6 km **Chozas de Abajo** another pretty village with a bar and shop in Plaza San Martin. Continue for another peaceful **[4.0 km]** of natural paths to pick up the **[0.1 km]** of asphalt road into:

4.1 km **Villar de Mazarife** •Albergue **[1]** *San Antonio de Pádua* (987-390 192) private hostel at entrance to the village in modern bungalow. Open all year with 40 beds in one dormitory. All facilities and what it lacks in character it makes up for in modern utilities.

Albergue [1] *Antonio de Pádua*

•**Albergue [2]** *El Refugio de Jesús* (987-390 697) private hostel in c/Corujo (left at artist studio). Open all year with 30 beds in 9 small rooms. What it lacks in modern facilities and maintenance it makes up for in character! Built around a courtyard with a peaceful dilapidated atmosphere.

•**Albergue [3]** *Tio Pepe* private hostel on c/ Teso de la Iglesia, 2 (adjacent to the church) in the centre of the village. Open all year with 20 beds and all facilities and also providing meals and a bar.

Albergue [2] *Jesús (above)*
Albergue [3] *Tio Pepe (below)*

Mesón Rosy anxious to pick up some of the new pilgrim business has commissioned half the town to be painted with yellow arrows leading to her hostelry on the outskirts! *[Next albergue: Hospital del Órbigo – 14.4 km]*

VILAR DE MAZARIFE is a decidedly pilgrim friendly village where even the fruit shop is called *Frutas de Camino de Santiago* and the church is also dedicated to St. James with several images of the saint inside. Several bars and restaurants, a gift shop, museum and art gallery make up some of the facilities of this peaceful hamlet with a population of barely 500. The local artist *Monseñor* a neo-Romanesque painter *Pintor Románico* specialises in religious works of art. Pepe Giner who runs albergue San Antonio de Padua is dedicated to the pilgrim way and a physiotherapist to boot which might come in handy.

REFLECTIONS:

_____
_____
_____
_____
_____
_____
_____
_____
_____
_____
_____
_____
_____
_____
_____
_____
_____
_____
_____
_____
_____
_____
_____
_____
_____
_____
_____
_____
_____
_____
_____
_____

❏ To dry one's eyes and laugh at a fall,
And, baffled, get up and begin again. *Robert Browning*

MAP 22 *302.2 km (187.8 miles) to Santiago de Compostela)*

VILLAR DE MAZARIFE – ASTORGA

▬▬▬	Path / Track	--- ---	18.8	--- 62%
▬▬▬	Quiet Road	--- ---	11.3	--- 38%
▬▬▬	Main Road	--- ---	0.0	
Total km	**Total distance**		**30.1 km** (18.7 miles)	

◣◤ Adjusted for climb 31.3 km (accrued ascent 250m = 1.2 km)
Alto ▲ High Point: Cruceiro Santo Toribio 905m (2,970 feet)

The Practical Path: The majority of this stage is relatively solitary so bring food and water with you (there are few villages on the way) however there are attractive sections with trees and other shade in which to rest out of the sun. The first part to Hospital de Órbigo (13.6 km) is relatively flat and easily covered. If you are planning to continue to Astorga (16.3 km) the total distance is 29.9 km so leave early and allow some time to savour Órbigo (you could lunch here, it's around halfway). Note that the last section beyond Órbigo has some (gentle) hills. **Intermediate accommodation:** Hospital de Órbigo (13.8 km) – Santibáñez (18.9 km) – San Justo (26.8 km). *(See also **alternative route [2]** by the N-120 from Villadangos del Páramo).*

❏ **The Mystical Path:** What of your own inner battles, the jousting tournaments of the soul? How easily do you fall and how quickly do you get up again? Many knights, even an exiled bishop, fell to the earth on this very spot and rose again, dusted themselves down, and began afresh. True greatness is not in ever falling, but in picking ourselves up every time we do.

❏ **Personal Reflections:** *"... I sit in the shade of a grove of orange trees and sketch a stork patiently waiting by the lake to pluck a fish from its cool waters. I wonder why I don't take more time to observe and draw the beauty of life around me. I am so often caught up in my mental world of worries and responsibilities that I miss the wonder of the present moment. More tears begin to flow as I write this. Are they tears of sadness at lost opportunities or of gratitude at the peace that surrounds and holds me in its tranquil embrace?"*

Leaving the albergue in Villar de Mazarife head down through the town, over the secondary road (linking Villadangos on the alternative route with Santa María del Páramo) and out on the quiet country lane through the open *páramo* that goes directly to crossroads:

5.7 km **Cruce** cross straight over onto earthen track with the village of La Milla del Páramo (right) to the **Canal del Páramo** with pleasant shaded picnic and rest area. Proceed along the peaceful pathway to pick up the asphalt road to the bridge over the railway line in:

Asoc.[150]
Albergue 3.3 Ⓐ

ASTORGA
(Pop. 12,000 – Alt. 900m)

N-120

N-VI

N-VI

A-71

A-6

Ⓗ

1.4 **San Justo** *de la Vega*

Río Tuerto

Cruceiro 0.9 †

6.5 **Cruceiro**
de Santo Toribio

Cruce 9.0

< *Ruta de la Plata* >

② ①

† Ⓐ 2.6 **Albergue** *Par.[60]*
SANTIBANEZ de VALDEIGLESIA

2.1 **Villares de Órbigo**

Opción 0.9

HOSPITAL DE ÓRBIGO
Ⓐ *Asoc.*[40] San Miguel
Ⓗ Ⓐ *Par.[70]*
Ⓐ *Muni.[32] El Camping*

Puente 3.7   3.1 **Puente**

Río Órbigo

4.1 **Canal**

Canal

Puesta
del Sol

O

VILLAVANTE
Puente 3.9

Salida
del Sol

S

N

E

SAN MARTÍN
del CAMINO

Ⓐ 4.4 **Albergue**
Muni.[60]

Ⓐ

Milla
del Páramo

< Bustillo
del Páramo

Cruce 5.7

Ana Priv.[40]

①

②

VILLADANGOS *del PÁRAMO*

Muni.[80]

Ⓐ 0.0 **Alb.**

(Pop. 400 – Alt. 880m)
VILAR de MAZARIFE

N-120

Iglesia Santiago †

Ⓐ 0.0 **Albergue** *San Antonio Priv.[50]*

A-71

3.9 km **Villavante** small village with limited facilities a bar and the 17th century parish Church of the Candles *Iglesia de las Candelas*. Take the bridge over the railway turning <left onto a track alongside it till we cross the arroyo Huergas with a view (right) up along the tree-lined banks to one of the several old mill buildings in this area. We turn right> when we reach the asphalt road over the autovia **[2.5 km]** to cross the N-120 [!] onto track where the alternative routes join at an ornate brick water tower **[0.8 km]** we now make our way together onto a cobbled path for the remaining **[0.4 km]** into the village of Puente de Órbigo (on *this* side of the river) with the parish church of Santa María (right). The significance of this village diminished in the 12th century when the Knights Hospitaller of St. John built a hospital on the far side. We are now at:

3.7 km **Puente de Órbigo** one of the longest and oldest medieval bridges in Spain dating from the 13th century and built over an earlier Roman bridge which formed one of the great historical landmarks on the camino. Its myriad arches carry you across the Río Órbigo via the passage of honour *Paso Honroso* so called because of the famous jousting tournament that took place here in the Holy Year 1434. A noble knight from León with the handsome name of Don Suero de Quiñones, scorned by a beautiful lady, threw down the gauntlet to any knight who dared to pass as he undertook to defend the bridge (and presumably his honour) against all comers. Knights from all over Europe took up the challenge. Don Suero successfully defended the bridge for a month until the required 300 lances had been broken. Together with his trusted comrades he then proceeded to Santiago to offer thanks for his freedom from the bonds of love and for his honour, now restored.

> Honour has come back, as a king, to earth
> And paid his subjects with a royal wage;
> And Nobleness walks in our ways again;
> And we have come into our heritage.
>
> *Rupert Brooke*

Apart from its link to such chivalrous acts, which may have been an inspiration for Cervantes *Don Quixote*, it also witnessed the battle in 452 when the Visigoths slaughtered the Swabians and subsequently provided the scene of confrontation between Christian forces under Alfonso III and the Moors. More productively it has facilitated trade since Roman times including the passage of livestock as part of the cattle trail *camino de la cañada* not to mention sweaty pilgrims like you and I! Pass over the bridge to the equally delightful village which, on the far side, becomes Hospital de Órbigo and a Knights Commandery of the ancient Order of St. John *Caballeros Hospitalarios de San Juan* who maintained a pilgrim hospital here with the parish church *Iglesia de San Juan Bautista* (right) **[0.4 km]** with just **[0.1 km]** to: **Hospital de Órbigo** and •**Albergue** [1] *Santa María* parish hostel (987-388 444) on the main street c/Alvarez Vega, 32. Open March-October with 70 beds in 3 rooms. All basic facilities in this historic building renovated by a German Confraternity yet retaining its antiquated character and central courtyard which provides pilgrims with a convivial place to congregate.

Albergue [1] *Santa María*

•**Albergue** [2] *San Miguel* network hostel (609-420 931) opposite the parish hostel and open all year with 80 places and excellent facilities in a refurbished building that also retains its period features and has a tranquil atmosphere. (see photo opposite).

A short detour from the bridge is •**Albergue** [3] *El Camping* municipal hostel (987-388 206) situated deep within the woodland park 0.8 km from the bridge beyond the campsite. Open all year with 38 beds in 6 small rooms and all basic facilities in this peaceful but somewhat isolated setting accessed past the camping site back at the bridge.

Other accommodation: •**El Caminero** (Jesus & Mayka Abad 987-389 020) a popular upmarket B&B on c/Sierra Pambley 56 just off (left) of the main street. Dinner bed and breakfast rate available in this finely restored 17th century town house. •**Don Suero de Quiñones** Hs** (987-388 238) great position on the bridge (you can't miss its gaudy neon sign) but you pay for its position! •**Paso Honroso** Hr** (987-361 010) and far other side of the bridge is •**Fonda Isidro**. Also other hotels on the main road and around the town centre are several bars and restaurants: *La Pista* by the bridge is cheap or for something more upmarket try the refurbished *Hosteleria Moran Salvadores* adjacent albergue [1].

Alternative route via N-120 from Villadangos del Páramo

Leave albergue and turn up right through the old town and onto a tree-lined path that comes out on to the N-120 at a camping site. A path runs parallel to the N-120 for most of the way into:

| 4.4 km | **San Martin del Camino** •**Albergue** [1] *Ana* (987-378 653) new private hostel (left) on the main road with 48 beds in 2 dormitories to the rear + private rooms all facilities including garden rest area and diningroom serving meals throughout the day.

Albergue [1] *Ana (above)*
Albergue [2] *Municipal (below)*

•**Albergue** [2] under (literally) the water-tower at the other end of town (right). Municipal hostel (Rosario 987-377 086) open all year with 60 beds in converted schoolhouse. All facilities and shaded garden area also on the main road. Continue through the town and immediately past the Canal del Páramo turn off right> onto a shaded path lined with poplars that essentially runs parallel to the main road to:

| 4.1 km | **Canal Presa de Cerrajera** the village of Puente de Órbigo now appears on the horizon. After **[1.9 km]** watch out for the waymarks that will bring you diagonally across a track to join up with the recommended route [1] for the remaining **[1.2 km]** into:

| 3.1 km | **Puente de Órbigo** (see recommended route for details).

From the bridge continue straight on past the church and albergues in c/Álvarez Vega to:

`0.9 km` **Opción [?]** For **recommended route [1]** fork right> at the last house (with artesian well) and continue on a track into:

`2.1 km` **Villares de Órbigo** with parish church dedicated to St. James with an image of *Santiago Matamoros*. We now enter onto a pleasant pathway that climbs gently passing rest area with **[F]** to join an asphalt road down across a small stream into:

`2.6 km` SantibañezdeValdeiglesia•Albergue
parish hostel (Sara 987-377 698) just beyond
the Centro Social. Open Easter-September
with 60 beds in several rooms and all facilities,
including orchard to the rear. Its bleak facade
hides a delightful tranquil interior. The church
of the Holy Trinity *Iglesia de la Trinidad* has
images of San Roque peregrino and Santiago
Matamoros. *[Next accommodation: Hotel San
Justo – 7.9 km]*.

Continue *up* out of the village onto one of the most serene and naturally beautiful paths of the camino. For a glorious 7.2 km the track winds its way through orchards, woodland with holm oak and citrus trees down to pass a small isolated lake before climbing out of this gentle valley through scrubland into arable fields past a farm building (dogs) where shortly afterwards we come to the prominent:

`6.5 km` **Cruceiro Santo Toribio** stone cross commemorating the 5th century Bishop Toribio of Astorga who supposedly fell to his knees here in a final farewell having been banished from the town. It is Astorga's Mount Joy *Monte Gozo* and from here we have a wonderful view northwest, down over a wide fertile valley to Astorga Cathedral with its twin towers in the distance (see photo under *Reflections*). Behind the city stand the Montes de León that we will cross in the days ahead and bring us to the highest part of the whole journey at 1,515m (4,970 feet). Over to the left (southwest) lie the connecting Sierra del Teleno crowned by El Teleno a mountain sacred to the Roman god Mars at 2,185m (7,170 feet) while due north stands Peña Ubiña at 2,417m (7,930 feet) marking the eastern flank of the Cordilera Cantábrica. When you have taken in the scale of it all, focus carefully on the ground immediately ahead as the path now drops steeply to pick up the asphalt road into:

`1.4 km` **San Justo de la Vegas** here the alternative road route joins as we enter the town, an expanding residential satellite of Astorga with bars and restaurants including •**Hostal Juli** HsR* (987-617 632) on the main street.

Alternative route via N-120: at the option point by the last house in Hospital de Órbigo – continue straight onto track which veers left to the N-120 **[2.0 km]** from here the route is on or immediately parallel to the main road which undulates up and down the rolling countryside before turning off right> at the top of a rise alto **[7.0 km]**:

`9.0 km` **Cruce** onto a track that runs along the top of a ridge to:

`0.9 km` **Crucero Santo Toribio** recommended route [1] joins from the right.

From San Justo de la Vega we continue out over the bridge and the *río Tuerto* **[0.6 km]** and turn off right> **[0.1 km]** to take a pleasant track that runs along the lush river valley past the side of a large factory crossing the Roman footbridge *Puente de la Moldería* **[1.6 km]** up to the main road and over railway tracks veering <left under the walls of the town to spiral steeply up through the *Puerta del Sol* **[1.0 km]** into:

| 3.3 km | Astorga Plaza San Francisco with
•**Albergue** [1] *Siervas de María* (987-616 034) new municipal hostel administered by the local pilgrim association on the left side of the square. Open all year with 150 places in dormitories + some smaller individual rooms all with excellent modern facilities (this hostel has replaced the previous barracks at the other end of town which has now become part of the adjoining police department.) The fate of the other municipal hostel diagonally opposite is also uncertain but continues to provide additional accommodation. •**Albergue** [2] the original municipal hostel on the corner of the square and c/Matias Rodriguez adjoining the town park *Jardín de Sinagoga* with 36 beds and basic facilities.

Albergue [1] *Servias de María*

Another popular network hostel is situated at the other end of town close to the cathedral. •**Albergue***[3] *St Javier* (987-618 532) network* hostel associated with the Via de Plata which joins in Astorga. Conveniently located close to the cathedral in c/Portería, 6.

Albergue [3] *St. Javier*

Open all year with 110 beds (4 rooms + attic) and all facilities with extensive dining and lounge areas and small open yard. This is a lovely conversion of one of the historic buildings in the old quarter close to the main sites in the town including hotel Gaudí with which it also seems to be connected.

Other accommodation: •**La Peseta** Hsr** (987-617 275) Plaza San Bartolomé with award winning Maragatería restaurant (and no TV!). •**Pensión García** (987-616 046) c/Bajada Postigo. •**Astvr Plaza** H*** (987-618 900) Plaza Mayor. •**Casa de Tepa** H*** (987-603 299) historic building on Santiago,2. •**Gaudi** Hr*** (987-615 654) opposite the Gaudí palace and cathedral. Several other (noisier and cheaper) hostales and pensiones further out of town on the main road include: •**Gallego** Hsr** (987-615 450) Av. Ponferrada and •**Coruña** (987-615 009). There are a variety of restaurants, bars and cafés – try some of the local cuisine *cocido maragato* which starts with a hearty meat stew, usually pork *and* black pudding (blood sausage) with beans and cabbage followed by vegetables and finished off with a bowl of broth! Or simply try some of the local pastries and biscuits *mantecadas*.

Turismo (987-618 222) Glorieta Eduardo Castro, 5 is near the cathedral but the museums tend to carry a town plan (showing the pilgrim route *Ruta Peregrino* and Roman route *Ruta Romana)* and provide basic information. If you are just passing through the town and want to visit the main sites *or* plan to stay in one of the hotels *or* for the most direct route to albergue [3] take the following 'tour' which takes in the main sites (see town plan) starting where we entered at the southern entrance *Puerta del Sol*.

[1] Plaza San Francisco with pilgrim hostels and lovely public gardens (fine views over the mountains), the Church of St. Francis of Assisi *Convento de San Francisco* (St. Francis allegedly came here on his pilgrimage to Santiago in 1212) and the adjoining Roman foundations (under a glass covering).

[2] Plaza Bartolomé where we find the *Iglesia San Bartolomé* and the *Ergástula* a Roman construction used down the ages as access tunnel, slave enclave, gaol and now a museum that also provides a short video (in Spanish) of life in Astorga during its Roman period.

[3] Plaza Mayor *España* and the graceful 17th century Baroque facade of the *Ayuntamiento* that houses one of the flags from the battle of Clavijo. Take a break in the square so that you can watch its ornate clock strike the hour as two mechanical figures (a man and a woman dressed in Maragato costume) strike the central bell. Before leaving this end of town there are a number of other Roman sites of interest. To the rear of the municipal library *biblioteca municipal*, situated off Synagogue Garden, are substantial remains of the original Roman walls and drains *murallas y cloachas Romanas* and the Roman baths *termas Romanos*.

[4] Plaza Santocildes identified by the handsome lion monument *monumento a los Sitios* in memory of the siege of Astorga during the Peninsular War. Continue out the far side of the square and on the left is c/Jose María where we find the *Museo del Chocolate*. Astorga was a main centre for the production of chocolate and the curator is a friend of the way and has been president of the local association.

[5] Plaza Obispo Alcolea here we another of the original entrances to the walled city – the King's Gate *Puerta de Rey* no longer visible but to one side of which we can admire the façade of the Casa Granell. We now head towards the jewels in Astorga's crown:

[6] Plaza Catedral where the sensational Gaudí building known as the Bishop's Palace *Palacio Episcopal* greets us, its neo-Gothic turrets soaring heavenwards. It houses no bishops but the splendid museum of the Ways *Museo de los Caminos* with historical notes and artefacts on the many Roman roads that converged on this city and provided the main trade, military and pilgrim routes through northern Spain. Don't miss the section on the *Caminos de Santiago* and the original Iron Cross *Cruz de Ferro* that once stood atop Monte Irago. Also in this area is the cell which housed the city's hookers *Celda de las Emparedadas*, the Turismo and the Iglesia de Santa Marta behind which is the splendid 15th century Gothic Cathedral standing majestically over the square, a wonderful blend of Romanesque, Gothic and later styles of architecture and a Renaissance altarpiece with a Romanesque statue of the Virgen de la Majestad after whom the cathedral is dedicated. Behind the cathedral are the Puerta Romana and a well-preserved stretch of the original Roman walls that acts as an open-air museum in its own right.

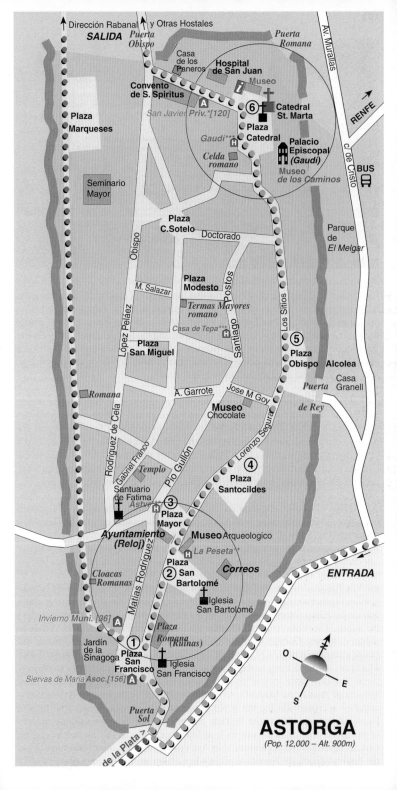

ASTORGA

(Pop. 12,000 – Alt. 900m)

Try and make time to visit the adjoining diocesan museum *Museo de Catedral* (a joint ticket will provide access to this and the Palacio Episcopal). This museum has a magnificent 15th century painting of the burial of St. James entitled 'The bridge of Life and Queen Lupa' *El puente de la Vida y la Reina Lupa* it shows the bulls pulling the sarcophagus of St. James and the bridge caving in by divine intervention, thus preventing the Roman soldiers from seizing the Apostle's disciples and their sacred cargo. There are many other depictions of pilgrimage and sacred art and artefacts sensitively displayed.

Adjoining the cathedral museum is the ancient Hospital de San Juan in which St. Francis reputedly stayed on his way to Santiago and further on the extensive monastery buildings of the Holy Spirit *Convento de Sancti Spiritus.* If you are heading on towards Rabanal turn right> and make your way out through Bishop's Gate *Puerta Obispo* into c/San Pedro and over the busy N-VI Madrid to La Coruña road. Alternatively, if you are staying the night then head towards your preferred hostel or the bars and restaurants around the many lively *plazas*.

ASTORGA *Asturica Augusta* an attractive city (more akin to a lively market town) set atop a steep ridge with a wide range of shops and general facilities and an interesting array of historic buildings all tightly packed within its medieval walls. Originally a powerful Asturian community it became an equally important Roman city on account of its prominent position at the junction of several major routes. This is where the French Way *Camino Francés* (part of the Via Trajana linking this area with Bordeaux) and the Roman Road *Calzada Romana* (otherwise known as the Via Aquitana) joined the Roman Silver route *Vía de La Plata* (otherwise known as the *Camino Mozarabe*) from Sevilla and the south. This convergence of routes gave rise to over 20 pilgrim hospitals in medieval times. George Borrow, visiting Astorga in 1840, wrote 'Almost the entire commerce of nearly one-half of Spain passes through the hands of The Maragato whose fidelity to their trust is such that no one accustomed to employ them would hesitate to confide to them the transport of a ton of treasure from the sea of Biscay to Madrid'. As if this wasn't enough activity Astorga also acted as a crossroads for the royal drove roads *Cañadas Reales* that herded livestock up and down the Iberian peninsular. This European-wide system of nomadic grazing is known as transhumance and can still be witnessed on various caminos and is celebrated in Astorga (along with many other towns) in the festival *Fiesta de Transhumancia* when sheep are driven through the town.

Next we enter the *Maragatería* and the *montes de León*. Here, between Astorga and Molinaseca, we experience the remnants of Maragato culture in the distinctive dress and cuisine of this mountainous region. The cakes and pastries *mantecadas* are worth sampling and the hills provide game and trout from the streams. The obscure origins of the Maragatos may date back to the 7th century when King Mauregato and the Visigoths became isolated in this remote area during the Arab invasions. Today the isolationism continues in the abandoned villages of the mountains, such as Foncebadón.

Astorga is also sometimes referred to as the 'capital' of the Maragatería but the Maragatos themselves defy classification. Some suggest they are descended from the Berber tribes who came to Spain as part of the Moorish invasion in the 8th century becoming 'misplaced' in this remote mountainous region. Others link them to the Visigoths and their king Mauregato. Most agree they were muleteers and their number has dwindled to 4,000 spread around 40 villages in the area. Martin Martinez, president of the Maragato Cultural Society, in a recent Telegraph interview stated simply, 'We are trying to recuperate some of our traditions before it is too late. By celebrating our traditional games and weddings in our way we hope to keep it alive.' It is the same story we will hear in the Bierzo and Galicia. The mystery of the Maragatos may never be penetrated but we can experience the hospitality found amongst the villages that line the path ahead.

REFLECTIONS:

❏ **Distrust yourself and sleep before you fight.**
T'is not too late tomorrow to be brave. *John Armstrong*

MAP: 23 *272.1 km (169.1 miles) to Santiago de Compostela*

ASTORGA – RABANAL DEL CAMINO

▬▬▬	Path / Track	--- ---	11.9 ---	56%
▬▬▬	Quiet Road	--- ---	9.5 ---	44%
▬▬▬	Main Road	--- ---	0.0	
Total km	**Total distance**		**21.4 km** (13.3 miles)	

▲ Adjusted for climb   23.4 km (accrued ascent 400m = 2.0 km)
Alto ▲ High Point: Rabanal del Camino 1,150m (3,770 feet)

The Practical Path: Today we head towards the mountains and tomorrow we climb to the highest point of the entire route. Rabanal can feed you, but it won't clothe you for the mountain weather, which can be unpredictable at the best of times. Astorga is the last opportunity to kit-out before the ascent. However, there are several small villages on today's stretch where you can buy food and refreshments, many bearing the suffix *somoza* from the Latin *sub montia* or *under the mountain*. This should be a relatively gentle day and the promise of a good nights rest in Rabanal to prepare you for the climb the following day. **Intermediate accommodation** (from albergue [1] on Plaza San Francisco): Murias de Rechivaldo (5.3 km) – Castrillo Polvazares (7.3 km *off* route) – Santa Catalina (9.4 km) – El Ganso (14.3 km).

❏ **The Mystical Path:** Where are the mountains of the soul? How high do you need to climb to reach the top and what will you find there? How well are you equipped and what do you need to take and, perhaps more importantly, leave behind? Rest awhile and pause for reflection before attempting to meet the guardian of the threshold. Tomorrow is time enough to climb towards another peak in your journey. What gift will you deposit at the top so that you can continue on, unburdened by the dross in your life?

❏ **Personal Reflections:** "*... The wind howled against the window as I warmed myself by the log fire. It was the constant squeaking of the bookcase that eventually roused me to quieten it and an old and faded document fell out from behind. It appeared to have been hidden and was entitled* The Third Secret of Fatima – The Collapse of the Roman Catholic Church. *The more I read, the deeper I became aware of the awesome impact that this document, true or false, would have on the future of the Church. Recent press revelations of scandals reaching at the very heart of the hierarchy made its predictions utterly clear. The irrational fear I felt was compounded when I read that the person who had professed to having seen the original letter had died in mysterious circumstances. I hid the document back where I found it, pondering on both the risk of collapse and the opportunities for renewal that the fulfilment of such a prophesy would entail...*"

N.S.Pilar *Priv.*[74]   Hostería el Refugio
RABANAL del CAMINO Sta. María
(Pop. 50 – Alt. 1,160m) *Muni.*[40] 3.2 **Albergue** *Gaucelmo Asoc.*[46]

El Tessin Priv.[34] Rabanal
Viejo

Ermita del Bendito Cristo→

(roble peregrino) →

Puente de Pañote 3.9 La Fucarona
(Minas Romanas)

Santa Colomba
de Somoza

Albergue 4.9 **EL GANSO**
Muni.[16] Gabino *Priv.*[28]

río Jerga

río Turienzo

Muni.[38] **Albergue** 2.0 → **SANTA CATALINA de SOMOZA**
San Blas *Priv.*[20] → *Priv.*[22] El Caminante

2.8 **Cruce**

Cruce 2.1 → Cuca la Vaina
2.0 **Castrillo
de Polvazares**

A-6

N-120

Albergue 2.2 → Casa Flor
Las Águedas *Asoc.**[40] *Muni.*[18]
**MURIAS de
RECHIVALDO** Puente

3.1 **Autopista**

Ecce Homo

Valdeviejas

A-6

St. Javier*

Catedral

(Pop. 12,000 – Alt. 900m)

ASTORGA

Albergue[1] 0.0
Siervas de María *Asoc.*[150]

río Tuerto

O
*Puesta
del Sol*
N
S
*Salida
del Sol*
E

Leaving albergue [1] in Plaza San Francisco follow the waymarks towards the cathedral **[0.8 km]** and turn <left opposite the west door and out through the Puerta Obispo into Barrio de Rectiva thence c/San Pedro and past the modern church of the same name across the N-VI (Madrid – A Coruña) at busy crossroads (modern shops and cafés) signposted to Santa Colomba de Somoza straight ahead.

Note: We have noted how Astorga was a major crossroads since Roman times and the connecting point for the route from Sevilla and the south usually referred to as the Silver Route *Via de la Plata* although scholars suggest 'plata' is a corruption of the Arabic word for wide *not* silver. Semantics aside, we travel the next few days over mountain terrain that produced gold, silver and other valuable ores from the mines between here and Ponferrada (Las Médulas). Here also medieval pilgrims would have to choose between the shorter but steeper route through Rabanal and Puerto Irago (1,505m) or the more circuitous but less steep Puerto Manzanal (1,225m) which today is where the N-VI and A-6 autopista and rail line cut through the Montes de León to connect Ponferrada and Astorga. The medieval writer König von Vach stated, "I advise that you avoid Rabanal at all costs." Today we can ignore such advice as Rabanal has since earned the reputation as one of the most authentic and welcoming villages along the entire camino so we can continue confidently but cautiously (several pilgrims have been killed on these very roads in recent years and a cross on our right marks one such spot) for the next **[2.3 km]** past the Residencia San Francisco and the tiny medieval hermitage (restored) *Ecce Homo* the only remnant of a former pilgrim hospice, bypassing the suburb of Valdeviejas (right) to:

3.1 km **Autopista flyover** we now enter onto a dedicated pilgrim track parallel to the secondary road to cross over the río Jerga and pick up a grass track <left into:

2.2 km **Murias de Rechivaldo •Albergue*** **[1]** *las Águedas* network* hostel (987-616 765) the last building on the right as we leave the town. Open all year with 60 beds in 3 rooms and all facilities including a small grocery store and centred around a delightful courtyard in this traditional village house.

Albergue [1] *Las Águedas*

•Albergue [2] municipal hostel (Vicente Alonso 987-691150) located on the main road adjoining a picnic site. Open all year with 22 places and all basic facilities in a former school building. Opposite we have the Mesón Casa Flor (987-603 148) offering *cocido Maragato* and B&B. *[Next albergue: Santa Catalina – 5.7 km].*

Murias de Rechivaldo is a typical Maragato village with interesting rustic parish Church of St. Stephen and several bars, restaurant, shop and **[F]** on the camino. **Option [?]** you can

Albergue [2] *Municipal*

proceed directly to Santa Catalina via the new *senda* (4.3 km) the recommended route [1] or via the local road to the classic Maragato village of Castrillo de Polvazares (declared a national monument) and thence via path to join the main route (5.7 km).

For this alternative route [2] pick up the minor road by albergue [2] and turn <left (LE-142 to Santa Columba) straight to the village visible ahead:

2.0 km **Castrillo de Polvazares** the classic Maragato village with its cobbled main street lined with traditional stone buildings with tourist accommodation, bars and restaurants. Painstakingly rebuilt by local artesans it lacks the authentic ambience found in the crumbling villages spread along the camino itself. At least the tourist buses are kept at the entrance car park. The village is brought to life by the novelist Concha Espina who depicted life in

Castrillo de Polvazares

Castrillo in her novel The Maragato Sphinx *La Esfinge Maragata* available only in Spanish. If you want to stay the night there are several guesthouses pampering to tourists or the central •**Hostería Cuca La Vaina** (987-691 034). Proceed the **[0.7 km]** through the village veering left at the central cross to pick up the (poorly) waymarked camino across a small stream (tributary of the río Jerga) and start the **[1.9 km]** climb up to rejoin the asphalt road above you:

2.8 km **Cruce** to join the recommended route for the remaining **[1.1 km]** into Santa Catalina.

For the **recommended route** via a wide earth track, continue past the pilgrim fountain **[F]** with café (left) and albergue (right) onto the track that runs in a straight line alongside the overhead power cables to:

2.1 km **Cruce** cross the minor road (Castrillo de Polvazares right) and pick up the pilgrim track that runs parallel to the old asphalt road to enter:

2.0 km **Santa Catalina** •**Albergue** [1] *El Caminante* private hostel (987-691 098) c/Real, 2 (left) as you enter the village with private rooms, café/bar and patio. Just past it is •**Albergue** [2] *Hospedería San Blas* c/Real, 11 (Rubén Merino 987-691 411) private hostel open all year with 24 places in variety of rooms. Facilities include café/bar serving meals. Further down the main street, just past bar Camino Real, through an opening (left) in the stone wall we find •**Albergue** [3] *municipal* the original municipal pilgrim hostel (987-691 819) open all year with 38 beds and basic facilities (no kitchen) but pleasant building in quiet location, now generally bypassed by the commercial opportunities on c/Real itself. *[Next albergue: El Ganso – 4.6 km].*

Albergue [3] *Municipal*

Santa Catalina is another village typical of the region in both its layout and population now reduced to a mere 50 persons – in bygone days it supported a pilgrim hospital. The parish church houses a relic of San Blas after whom the church and albergue are named. Continue through the village and back out onto the minor road and a track parallel that escorts us into:

4.9 km **El Ganso** a hauntingly crumbling village, evoking a sense of loss or, perhaps, a reminder of a less hurried time. In the 12th century it boasted a monastery and a pilgrim hospital and is now enlivened somewhat by the Cowboy

Bar (with side entrance to Bar la Barraca) and the latest hostel •**Albergue [1]** *Gabino* (660-912 823) new private hostel on c/Real with all facilities. Open all year with 30 places in 2 rooms. 300m *off* route is •**Albergue [2]** *municipal* hostel (Carolina 987-691 088) part of the village health centre and converted from the village school and located on the left (southern) outskirts at the end of c/las Eras beside [F]. Open all year with 16 beds and basic facilities only but clean and what it lacks in creature comforts it makes up for in the splendid view across the wide valley to the peaks of Monte El Teleno, often capped with snow. *[Next albergue: Rabanal – 6.9 km].*

El Ganso is the first of several semi-abandoned Maragato villages that we pass through in the relatively solitary mountains. However, amidst the collapsing thatch cottages are some signs of new life, such as the Cowboy Bar adding to the incongruity of the modern *sendas* by which you arrive and leave this enchanting piece of history. There is a Parish church dedicated to St. James with a statue of Santiago Peregrino and the Capilla de Cristo de los Peregrinos. If the opportunity arises to meet the locals, don't pass it by!

From here all the way to the top at the Cruz de Ferro true 'Friends of the Way' have recently forged tracks either side of the LE-142. This road is heavily undulating with many blind spots so take care and do take every opportunity to use the natural pathways on either side. Here again we find many pilgrims, heads bent to the incline, staying on the narrow asphalt road – several accidents have been reported in recent years so don't let fatigue rob you of focus. Ignore signs to Rabanal Viejo and the Gold route *Ruta de Oro* (unless you want to visit the *site* of the original Roman gold mines 1.5 km up on your right, the *Minas de La Fucarona*). Continue straight on through this tranquil valley to:

3.9 km **Puente de Pañote** a modest bridge carries you over the arroyo Rabanal de Viejo a good place to refresh ourselves in its cool mountain waters before continuing the steeper ascent through mixed native woodland, holm oak *encina*, oak *roble* and pine *pino* past the specimen 'pilgrim oak' which now has a bench seat so you can rest in the shade of its branches (the leafy season is very short up at this altitude). Just before entering Rabanal we pass the 18th century *Ermita del Bendito Cristo de la Vera Cruz* (left) and veer right> off the road into c/Real the typical paved main street of Rabanal del Camino [**2.8 km**] and •**Albergue [1]** *El Tesin* (Ángela & Damián 650-952 721) private hostel in newly converted traditional stone house (left) as we enter. 24 beds in dormitory + individual rooms, café/bar and shop. Continue up the steep c/Real for [**0.4 km**] passing the 18th century Capilla de San José (right) with entrance porch enabling viewing of the ornate retablo with image of Santiago Peregrino and up past small shop into the main village square:

3.2 km **Rabanal del Camino** and the 12th century Romanesque Iglesia de la Santa María occupying the tiny central square and on the left •**Albergue [2]** *Gaucelmo* (987-691 901) administered by the London based Confraternity of St. James and the Bierzo association. Open April – October with 46 beds in 2 rooms + converted barn with all facilities including a small library, courtyard and orchard area. Sensitively restored (1991) and exceptionally well maintained. Breakfast is provided.

Albergue [2] *Gaucelmo*

•**Albergue** [3] *N.S del Pilar* private hostel (Isabel Rodríguez 987-691 890) located down on the main road in plaza Gerónimo Morán Alonso (look for prominent heraldic shield above entrance). Open all year with 68 beds in large dormitory area, all facilities including lively bar with tables around an attractive central courtyard. Adjacent, also fronting the main road •**Albergue** [4] *municipal* hostel (987-691 272). Open May-October with 42 places (including mattresses) and a picnic BBQ area adjoining the road. *[Next albergue: Manjarín 10.0 km].*

Other accommodation directly on the camino are: •**Hostería el Refugio** Hs* (987-691 274) centrally located adjoining the church with popular bar and restaurant (pilgrim menu) and the more exclusive •**La Posada Gaspar** (987-691 079) located at the top end of the village in a renovated 17th century former pilgrim hospital. •**San Salvador** (see below).

Rabanal del Camino continues a centuries old tradition of caring for the pilgrims before they take the steep path up and over Monte Irago. This was the IXth stage of Aymeric Picaud's classic itinerary and the Knights Templar are thought to have had a presence here as early as the 12th century ensuring the safe passage of pilgrims over this remote mountain terrain – the 12th century Church of Santa María was probably built by them. Today an order of monks originating from Germany have recently taken up residence in a building on the square and the church, now restored, is once again resounding to the sound of Gregorian chant at evening Vespers (19.00) and compline (21:30) with pilgrim blessing offered by the Benedictine missionary monks of monastery of San Salvador del Monte Irago established here in 2001 and affiliated to the Abbey church of St. Ottilien based in Austria. Apart from spiritual sustenance the delightful monks also run a small shop in the square and have residential accommodation for a minimum 2 nights retreat (987-691 277).

REFLECTIONS:

❐ **On all the peaks lies peace.** *Goethe*

MAP: 24 *250.7 km (155.8 miles) to Santiago de Compostela*

RABANAL DEL CAMINO – MOLINASECA

	Path / Track	--- ---	13.6	---	51%
	Quiet Road	--- ---	12.5	---	47%
	Main Road	--- ---	0.4	---	2%
Total km	**Total distance**		**26.5 km** (16.4 miles)		

Adjusted for climb   29.5 km (accrued ascent 600m = 3.0 km)

Alto ▲ High Point: La Cruz de Ferro 1,505m (4,940 feet)

The Practical Path: Today we head up through the pass of Irago to the highest point of our whole journey. While the ascent is steep in places and will require your determination and physical exertion remember that far more injuries (sprains, strains and breaks) are experienced going *down*hill. Many pilgrims stick to the asphalt road which has many blind spots and is therefore dangerous. Use the new track that runs roughly parallel to the road effectively making the majority of this stage a safer natural pathway. When pausing to rest or meditate, remember that body sweat will turn cold quickly at this altitude as soon as physical exertion stops – so find a sheltered spot out of the mountain breeze and dress warmly. There are several drinking fonts [**F**] along the way and the mountain villages are coming to life again supporting pilgrims with hostels and cafés but it is sensible to take some snacks and we need to fill our water bottles before leaving Rabanal. **Intermediate accommodation:** Foncebadón (5.8 km) – Manjarín (10.0 km) – El Acebo (17.0 km) – Riego de Ambros (20.8 km).

❐ **The Mystical Path:** For many, today is a peak experience. How allusive to the rational mind is that peace that passes all understanding. What does an altered state mean to you? Words cannot convey the experience of a unified perspective, beyond the duality offered by the physical eyes. How long yet will we allow the sense-perceptible world to limit our perception and keep us imprisoned in our separate state? Will we allow our Self soar to new heights today and sense the super-sensible, beyond space, beyond time?

❐ **Personal Reflections:** *"... How my spirit soars in high places, connecting me to that place within me that touches God. My perspective shifts and I get an expanded sense of Self. This giant chestnut supports my back as I write these notes, shading me from the afternoon sun. I feel peaceful in its giant embrace and welcomed through the connection from previous visits and blessed by its unyielding yet undemanding presence. Strong yet silent but for the gentle rustle the your leaves ..."*

← Las Médulas (23 km)

→ **Ponferrada**

Albergue 1.2 → A
Muni.[85]

A Santa Marina **Priv.***[84]

MOLINASECA
(Pop. 800 – Alt. 610m)

C *Casa El Reloj*

H *Casa El Palacio*
S.Nicolás ← 4.5 **Puente**

■ *Angustias*

río Maruelo

Peñalba de Santiago →

Albergue 3.8 → A   **RIEGO de AMBRÓS**
Muni.[50]
C *Casa Riego de Ambros*

San Cristobal

Epinosa de Compludo

Par.[24]
ACEBO
A
A ← *Mesón* **Priv.**[24]
Herrería ■   A ← 4.7 **Albergue** *Muni.[10]*
F

O
Puesta del Sol
N

▲ *Punto Alto*
(1,515 m)

S

Salida del Sol

E

río Maruelo

← 2.3 **Cruz** *(Militar)*

F
A ← 2.2 **Albergue** *Priv.[30]*
MANJARIN

Ermita
Puerta Irago   2.0 **La Cruz** de Ferro
(1,505 m) ▲

← *Monte Teleno*

FONCEBADÓN   A ← *Domus Dei* **Par.[22]**
Albergue 5.8 → A ← *El Convento* **Priv.***[20]
Monte Irago **Priv.***[35]

RABANAL del CAMINO
(Pop. 50 – Alt. 1,160m)   A ← 0.0 **Albergue** *Gaucelmo* **Asoc.[46]**

Leaving albergue [2] in Rabanal proceed up through the village onto a rough track at the far end that crisscrosses the asphalt road and with spectacular views across the río Turienzo valley towards Monte El Teleno all the way up until we reach a camino signboard and turn off <left into:

5.8 km Foncebadón •**Albergue*** [1] *Monte Irago* (Marta & Felipe 695-452 950) new network* hostel in renovated stone house (left) open all year with 35 places and good facilities. •**Albergue** [2] *Convento de Foncebadon* (658-974 818) new private hostel in renovated building with 21 places including private rooms + bar and restaurant. •**Albergue** [3] *Domus Dei* parish hostel part of the recently renovated church in the village centre. Open April-September with 28 beds and all basic facilities and a calm and prayerful atmosphere.

Albergue [1] *Monte Irago*

This semi-abandoned village is now stirring back to life with the reawakening of the camino. It was home of the 12th century hermit Gaucelmo who built a church and simple pilgrim hospital here. A stark wooden cross adds a haunting beauty to this isolated mountain hamlet. During the last few years several of the abandoned houses have been undergoing renovation together with its 'main' street including La Taberna de Gaia with its adjoining *palloza* located below hostal Convento.

Albergue [3] *Domus Dei*

We continue out the top end of the village onto a muddy track (mountain springs) to rejoin the road and make our way up through the mountain gorse and heather to *the doorway through the mountain* and its memorable cross that opens up to guide us, as it has for countless millions of other pilgrims over many centuries.

2.0 km **Puerto Irago / Cruz de Ferro** such a humble monument to mark such a noble gateway. This majestic spot stands 1,504m (4,934) above sea level and a simple iron cross stands atop its weathered pole that has become one of the abiding symbols of the pilgrim way of St. James. Pause awhile to reconnect with the purpose of your journey before adding your stone or other token of love and blessing to the great pile that witnesses to our collective journeying. A modern stone chapel *Ermita de Santiago* built to commemorate an earlier Holy Year, remains locked but a grander chapel surrounds us that will remain forever open and welcoming. A track continues parallel to the road to:

2.2 km **Manjarín** •Albergue private hostel open all year with 35 places (mattresses) and basic facilities which includes an outside toilet and water from a well on the other side of road. The simple facilities are being organically developed along ecological lines with a solar panel providing (some) hot water while an open fire provides the smoky space heater. A simple communal meal is offered for those staying the night in this mountain sanctuary. *[Next albergue: Acebo – 7.0 km].* This is another 'abandoned' village brought vividly to life by the modern knight *hospitalero Tomás* who now gives the village an official resident population of 1 and has renovated one of the abandoned houses (a pilgrim's hospital existed here as early as the 12th century linking it to the Knights Templar). You may have arrived in time for the ancient Temple ritual of blessing the new day and all pilgrims on the path. Perhaps Gregorian chant (from a well-worn tape out of the Cluny sanctuary of Taizé) will call you to stop or maybe the inviting aroma of coffee is your cue to visit this little mountain refuge. The atmospheric surroundings are enhanced by a virtually constant mountain mist. Continue by road below the communication mast and military base that watches over our every step. A threatening image to some and to others an encouraging sign of habitation and potential support in the lonely mountains.

2.3 km **Cruce Militar** continue past the turn off to this mountain top observation post to another high point on the path at 1,515m. (4,970) *[or you can have a peak experience by taking the wide track straight on (right) to climb to the cairn at 1,535m (5,036 feet!) and soak in the panorama, weather permitting and continue down the track to join the waymarked route below].* The sprawling suburbs of Ponferrada are still an insignificant blot on the landscape ahead towards the western horizon. The path now descends sharply [!]. Don't miss the path through a narrow gorge right> (it relieves some of the road work and a hairpin bend) shortly afterwards you cross the road and descend (very sharply) [!] to the fuente de la trucha **[F]** before entering:

4.7 km **Acebo** •Albergue **[1]** *Elisardo Panizo* basic municipal hostel the first building (right) as we enter this typical mountain village. Open in the summer only with 10 beds in one room. A shower and a toilet make up the limited facilities – key with albergue **[2]**. •Albergue **[2]** *Mesón El Acebo* (Gumesindo Flórez 987-695 074) private hostel at c/Real, 16 (left). Open all year with 24 beds in 3 rooms and good facilities (no kitchen) but bar with pilgrim menu and open terrace to the rear. When full they open the former private hostel of local character José *Taberna de José* at c/Real, 19 at the lower end of the village (right) with 14 places in 3 rooms and basic facilities. A new parish hostel opened its doors in 2008 •Albergue **[3]** *Parroquia San Miguel* adjacent to the parish church in a renovated stone building with 24 beds in one dormitory and with excellent modern facilities. *[Next albergue: Riego de Ambrós– 3.6 km].*

Albergue [3] *San Miguel*

Acebo is another typical mountain village of the region with one principal street running down the middle and an open surface drain as a token gesture to channel the rain that frequently overflows it. The parish Church of San Miguel has a statue of Santiago Peregrino and is located at the far end (left). Other accommodation includes: •**Casa Rural** La Rosa del Agua (616-849738) CR – •**La Trucha** CR (987-695 548) – •**La Casa del Monte Irago** CR (639-721

242). In plaza Pena by the church is a small shop *Tienda Casa Josefina* and a good picnic spot. On the way out of the village you pass a modern sculpture of a bicycle outside the village cemetery **[0.5 km]** memorial to another pilgrim killed on the roads here and the opportunity for several detours by quiet country roads (signposted but not waymarked).

Detour [1] Herrería immediately beyond the cemetery is a turn off for the medieval iron foundry of Herrería **[2.0 km]** 'hidden' in the steep valley floor. One of the oldest forges still in use with a millrace providing power to its heavy machinery. A delightful and peaceful tree-lined glade alongside the river brings you to this historic site. Note: The 4 km round trip is equivalent to twice that on account of the very steep descent and ascent – only contemplate it if you plan staying in El Acebo or the next village. **Detour [2] Compludo [3.5 km]** (2 km beyond Herrería) is the birthplace of monasticism in this region with the founding of a monastery here in the 7th century by San Fructuoso. This is a strenuous 7 km round trip by quiet road from El Acebo. This was one of the routes followed by pilgrims to the Valley of Silence and was protected by the Knights Templars and the Monastery of Compludo (no longer evident). There are a number of casa rurales in Espinoso de Compludo •Las Cuatro Estaciones CR (987-970 092) from €50 single. The beautiful valley of silence *Valle del Silencio* and Peñalba de Santiago is a further 19 km beyond Compludo *uphill* by asphalt road. You need to be fit and in need of space and silence to contemplate this detour to the hilltop monastic settlement founded by San Genadio in the 10th century on these white crags *peñalba*, which are often covered in snow. Only the church with its Mozarabic double horseshoe arch remains (a national monument) but the lasting legacy is the mountain scenery and silence now under threat by tourist parties coming from Ponferrada 27 km away and the easiest access route by taxi or bus.

Continue along asphalt road veering off <left **[1.8 km]** onto a path that winds down for **[1.5 km]** into:

3.8 km Riego de Ambrós •Albergue private hostel (Pedro Gabella Fernandez 987-695 190) just below the chapel of San Sebastián (right) as we enter this pretty village. Open all year with 24 beds in cubicles of 4 (+25 mattresses). Good facilities including small patio in this bright and spacious building.

Albergue *Riego de Ambrós*

This is another attractive mountain village with the traditional overhanging balconies. Due to the relative proximity of Ponferrada and a distinctly warmer climate at this lower altitude, almost all the previously abandoned houses have been renovated for residential use (including, unfortunately, the former bar in the delightful village centre). However, a friendly bar and restaurant with pilgrim menu can be found on the main road up right from the centre of the village opposite the parish Church of Santa María Magdalena which has a beautiful early 18th century altarpiece. *Restaurante Ruta de Santiago* (987-418 151) 200m *off* the camino. Also back on the main road is •**Pension Casa Riego de Ambros** (987-695 188).

Make your way down the main street veering left in the centre (restaurant straight on) and veer off right down a steep rock defile [!] (very slippery when wet) onto a beautiful path past a magical grove of giant sweet chestnut trees *castañas* some of which have recently been torched.

> Up the airy mountain,
> Down the rushy glen,
> We daren't go a hunting,
> For fear of little men.
> *William Allingham*

We now make our way up and over the road to continue down this breathtakingly beautiful valley to rejoin the road just above Molinaseca, passing the *Iglesia de las Angustias* built up against the steep cliffs to cross:

4.5 km **Puente de Peregrinos** handsome medieval bridge carries us over the río Meruelo into the delightful and historical village of Molinaseca. The 17th century Church of San Nicolás (with statue of San Roque) stands atop a rise to the left while the original camino continues along c/Real. The house at the junction of c/Torre is reputedly that of Doña Urraca, later Queen of Castilla y León, which provides some idea of the exclusivity attached to this genteel area that today provides a range of bars and restaurants to suit all tastes and pockets. Accommodation in this tranquil quarter includes: •**El Palacio** HsR** (987-453 094) by the bridge and •**La Posada de Muriel** H** (987-453 201) on Plaza del Cristo (Michelin recommended). Several *casa rurales* around c/Real including •**Paquita** CR (987-453 037) and •**El Reloj** CR (987-453 124) by the road. Continue along the c/Real to join the road for the short remaining distance to:

Albergue [1] *Santa Marina*

1.2 km **Molinaseca** •**Albergue*** [1] *Santa Marina* (Cris 653-375 727) new private network* hostel with 56 places in spacious dormitories and excellent modern facilities with dinner and breakfast available and an outside terrace. •**Albergue** [2] *San Roque* municipal hostel (Alfredo Alvarez Pérez 987-453 180) on the main road as you leave the historic town. Open all year with 30 beds + 50 mattresses and tents in the summer and all facilities with adjoining field for camping. Imaginative conversion of the former chapel of San Roque and while directly on the main road, passing traffic is minimal. *[Next albergue: Ponferrada – 6.9 km].*

Albergue [2] *San Roque*

❏ **The only successful manifestation is one that brings about a change or growth in consciousness; that is, it has manifested God.**

A Pilgrim in Aquarius *David Spangler*

MAP: 25 *224.2 km (139.3 miles) to Santiago de Compostela*

MOLINASECA – VILLAFRANCA DEL BIERZO (via PONFERRADA)

▬▬▬	Path / Track	--- ---	15.4	--- 50%
▬▬▬	Quiet Road	--- ---	11.6	--- 38%
▬▬▬	Main Road	--- ---	3.7	--- 12%
Total km	**Total distance**		**30.7 km** (19.1 miles)	

Adjusted for climb 31.7 km (accrued ascent 200m = 1.0 km)
Alto ▲ High Point: Alto Villafranca (albergue) c. 550m (1,805 feet)

The Practical Path: There are several options to avoid the worst of the busy road network around Ponferrada. And while this stage involves some road walking as we pass through the city, there are many cafés and bars to refresh us along the way. Remember also that waymarks through the city and its suburbs have to compete with the consumer culture and its advertising signs so extra vigilance is required. And we also have the beautiful *Bierzo* to look forward to with its sheltered micro-climate and vineyards. **Intermediate Accommodation**: Ponferrada (7.0 km) – Cacabelos (23.9 km).

In order to make sense of the road layout into and out of Ponferrada, this stage has been shown from Molinaseca to Villafranca. If you decide to stay in Ponferrada there is much to do and see and several interesting detours that you can take from there. Alternatively, you can visit the main sites (all of which are directly along the camino) and still make your way relatively easily to the albergue in Cacabelos (23.9 km) or with greater effort to Villafranca del Bierzo (30.7 km) by evening. But in this latter case, you must leave Molinaseca early in the morning.

❏ **The Mystical Path:** Out of the ruins of the Templar Castle and the fire that consumed its inhabitants, arises the phoenix, that ageless symbol of change and growth that reveals the Divine behind the manifested form. Behind the symbols is the reality of the Love that informs them. Will we allow the flames to burn up our old outworn beliefs and allow the new to reveal itself? Are we ready for a leap of faith, ready to withdraw our investment in the limited consensual reality and bank instead on Reality unlimited?

❏ **Personal Reflections:** *"… Somewhere I passed an old man pushing a wheelbarrow. His toothless smile touched me so deeply that I had a momentary impression that he was my father: a representation of The Father. Tears well up again and I am left speechless … my reality is shifting … why is it that I cannot recall the last few hours? This altered perception and emotional surge*

VILLAFRANCA del BIERZO
(Pop. 4,000 – Alt. 530m)
●Plaza Mayor

Albergue [2.9] → A ← [3.2] Albergue *Muni.[72]*

A-6

Cruce [1.8]

F ← [1.5] **Valtuille** *de Arriba*

Valtuille de Abajo

Castro Ventosa

PIEROS ← [2.1] **Opción**

San Clemente

río Cúa

Monasterio de Carracedo †

A ← [1.5] **Albergue** *Muni.[70]*

CACABELOS   H

H

F ← [3.4] **Fuente**

N-120

▲ O
Puesta del Sol
S
Salida del Sol
E
N

Puente [1.6]

F

Co-op de Vinos   **CAMPONARAYA**

← [1.9] **Cruce**

N-VI

F ← [2.7] **Fuentes Nuevas**

† ← [2.2] **Columbrianos (ermita)**

CL-631

río Sil

Av. De Portugal

Av. De Galicia

Túnel

† ← [2.7] **Compostilla (Iglesia)**

PONFERRADA
(Pop. 62,000 – Alt. 540m)

Santa María Vizbayo †

H

H H

Puente [2.5]
Mascarón

[1.7] **Pons Ferrada**

A *Conv.[180] San Nicolás de Flüe*

Campo [1.5] → F *Romano*

Villar de los Barrios

Embalse de Bárcena

A-6

Opción [2.2]

río Boeza

Albergue [0.0] → A
Muni.[85]

(Pop. 800 – Alt. 610m)
MOLINASECA

is overwhelming me. My heart feels so open my chest is aching. I seem to break in and out of conscious awareness, one instant of complete clarity, the next only haziness. I resolve in this moment to continue my pilgrimage in total silence. I don't know for how long; I know only that something is seeking to reveal itself that can only be heard in the quiet. Amidst these uncontrollable tears I write this simple message to hang around my neck. I trust others will understand what I can't articulate and barely comprehend myself. I don't even know if it makes sense in Spanish, 'Saludos. Yo peregrino a pie, caminante en silencio. Paz.'

Leaving the albergue in Molinaseca continue down the main road (or just beyond the tennis court turn off right> to pick up a track parallel with the road that winds its way alongside fruit orchards before picking up the road again) to top of a rise with Ponferrada visible ahead:

2.2 km **Opción [?]** another *Monte Gozo* with towers of the basilica, occupying the high point in the old town, now visible in the middle distance.

The alternative route into Ponferrada is 1.2 km shorter (2.0 km shorter if you are making directly for the new albergue off Av. del Castillo). Veer right staying on the main road down to Puente río Boeza **[1.0 km]** formerly this entry into Ponferrada was known as the Passage of the Boat *Paso de la Barca* as there was no bridge and the deep river could only be crossed with the help of the ferryman. After **[0.4 km]** veer left off the main road opposite factories onto a path past swimming pool complex through waste ground to cross railway line **[1.3 km]** veering left for **[0.1 km]** to:

2.8 km •**Albergue** *San Nicolás de Flüe* (Miguel Ángel & Rafael Canseco 987-413 381) parish hostel situated in the grounds of the convento del Carmen on c/de la Loma (off Av. del Castillo). Open all year with 200 beds in small rooms of 4 + overflow space and all modern facilities in this purpose built hostel with extensive sheltered patio and garden area. *[Next albergue: Cacabelos – 17.5 km].* To continue to the Templar Castle and the camino

Albergue – *San Nicolás de Flüe*

turn left on Av. del Castillo and shortly after veer right at a tourist information board into c/Peregrinos and then c/Temple to rejoin the recommended route at:

0.8 km **Castillo de los Templarios.** Alternatively, go straight over the Av. del Castillo into c/Esteban de la Puente and into the main square *Plaza Ayuntamiento* where most of the shops and restaurants are situated and the relocated Tourist office (see town plan and recommended route for other accommodation).

For the **recommended** route veer <left onto wide track-road for **[1.5 km]** into:

1.5 km **Campo** historic village with well preserved buildings emblazoned with coats of arms. An interesting Roman water cistern *Fuente Romano* is still functioning and worth the 200m detour (to the right as you enter the village) and the 17th century Church of St. Blase in a grove of olive trees. Continue down the c/La Francesa past the city rubbish dump into Los Barríos, a modern suburb of the city to:

2.5 km **Puente Mascarón / Opción** **[?]** **[a]** If you intend staying the night in Ponferrada at the new albergue then keep straight on over the river bridge (río Boeza) then over the railway (Santiago-León) and up onto the busy Av. del Castillo [0.4 km] were the hostel is now visible over to the right [0.3 km]. **[b] Detour [1]** (see other detours below) Iglesia de Santa María de Vizbayo, designated ' a national asset of cultural interest'. Just before the bridge turn up left on the camino de Otero. The road snakes its way uphill for 2 km to this delightful 11th century Romanesque church with a fine view back over the city from its wooded site.

Note: the following (waymarked) route takes us through the old medieval city and past the main historic sites: It is 1.7 km in length and the time you take to do it depends on how long you spend at each site and whether you are continuing on to Villafranca today.

Veer <left over the medieval bridge (see town map) and follow the waymarked route up the camino Bajo de San Andres under the railway bridge passing c/ Camino Jacobeo (which passes the site of the old albergue which closed in 1998 to make way for road works and the new hotel El Castillo) turn right> into c/del Hospital past the Renaissance Hospital de la Reina and into the old city and turn <left at the far end opposite the 17th century Baroque Church Iglesia San Andrés (with its statue *Cristo del Castillo* linking it to the Templars) to arrive directly at the entrance of the **Templar castle** *Castillo de los Templarios*. The magnificent

12th century castle has been declared a national monument and recently reopened after extensive renovations so we are again able to explore its interior and revel in its romantic past. Ponferrada came under the protectorate of the Templar Order by decree of King Fernando II in 1178. Their official presence here was short lived as the Order was outlawed in 1312 and disbanded by a Church fearful of their increasing power and esoteric tradition.

The new town is on the other (western) side of the río Sil, visible from the castle entrance. Several cafés opposite the castle serve pilgrim menus (and breakfast if you have come from Molinaseca) and adjoining the castle walls is a tourist office (987-424 236) c/Gil y Carrasco, 4 – behind which is the office of the Friends of the Camino in El Bierzo.

•**Albergue** the new hostel is situated 800m back through the town (see alternative route for details of the albergue and the map for directions). **Other Accommodation:** In the old city centre is limited and includes the new •**Hotel El Castillo** H*** (987-456 227) by the castle in Av. El Castillo and the recently refurbished •**Hotel Los Templarios** H** (987-411 484) c/Flores Osorío, 3 opposite the museum (left just before the clock tower). The old town has a range of inexpensive restaurants; the café in the plaza Encina, La Fortaleza (opposite the castle) and La Fonda (first floor) on Plaza Mayor are regular pilgrim haunts. The tourist office has a list of the many alternative hotels and guesthouses in the modern part of the town which include: near the railway station •**Hostal Santa Cruz** Hsr* (987-428 351) c/Marcelo Macías,4 and on Av. Galicia, 85 Hostal Conde de Lemos Hs* (987-411 091) for upmarket luxury •**Hotel Temple** H**** (987-410 058) on Av. Portugal.

PONFERRADA a modern metropolis with a population of 60,000 and capital of El Bierzo with its unique micro climate that produces the respected Bierzo wines worth sampling along with the thick pork sausages *botillo* locally marinated and served with boiled potatoes and vegetables *cachelos*. Most of the historic sites are neatly condensed into the old medieval city that occupies the high ground around the castle. The camino winds its way past these sites and so they can be explored on the way through between *Puente Mascarón* (entry) and Iron Bridge *Pons Ferrata* (exit). This latter bridge gives the city its name and is the reason for the sprawling modern suburbs that support a strong industrial base built on the back of the coal and iron reserves that have been mined in this area from medieval times. The original bridge was reinforced with iron as far back as the 11th century. There are a number of earlier Roman and Mozarabic sites in the area that include:

Detour [1] Iglesia de Santa María de Vizbayo (described above from Puente Mascarón). It is one of the oldest churches in the area and has a splendid view over the city from its quiet hillside site. **Detour [2] Iglesia de Santo Tomás de las Ollas** in the northern suburbs (2 km north of the Plaza Mayor, past the Parque del Planto) we find this magnificent Mozarabic 10th century church with its distinctive horseshoe arches. The original pilgrim road into the city used to go by here. It is little visited by pilgrims but well worth the trip if you are staying in Ponferrada for the night. Further afield – by bus or share a taxi are: **Detour [3] Santiago de Peñalba** another 10th century Mozarabic Church located in its magnificent mountain hideaway in the Valley of Silence *Valle del Silencio* 25 km out of Ponferrada (referred to under Acebo detours) and usually visited along with **Detour [4] Las Médulas** – the Roman gold mines on the slopes of the Montes Aquilianos 23 km away off the road to Peñalba.

From the Templar Castle we can head back towards the new pilgrim hostel (see city map) or continue up the c/Gil y Carrasco (Fitzroy's outdoor clothing and equipment left) into the attractive Plaza Virgen de la Encina with popular café (right) and the 16th century Basílica de la Encina. In bygone days this whole region was covered with evergreen holm oak *encina* and in one such tree a vision of the Virgen appeared elevating this church to Basilica status and the Virgin to patroness of the Bierzo region. Take the c/del Reloj and just before the handsome clock tower that gives the street its name is the Museo del Bierzo (right) and worth a visit just for the beautifully restored building that houses the interesting artefacts inside. Continue under the 16th century arch of La Torre del Reloj into the Plaza Mayor with and tourist office and its impressive town hall *Ayuntamiento*. This covers the main highlights of the old city.

If you plan to go on to Villafranca del Bierzo then you won't have time for any further exploring and should proceed <left down the winding steps (beside the modern kiosk) turning <left again into c/Calzada and cross the río Sil at:

1.7 km **Pons Ferrada** (1.7 km from our entry into the city at Puente Mascarón) into Av. de la Puebla. Note: don't take old waymarks that point straight on towards the bus station and bring you through busy and confusing modern streets. Instead turn immediately right> to the recommended route via the delightful linear *Parque de la Concordia* that runs beside the río Sil passing by (not over) Puente de Hierro **[0.6 km]** before turning up <left by football pitch **[0.6 km]** to join roundabout with central statue on the modern Av. de la Libertad. Here at the outskirts of the city we continue for **[1.5 km]** past the coal slag-heaps and derelict power station turning <left into the neatly ordered suburb of Compostilla. The route here is well waymarked with concrete bollards that direct us through an archway to:

PONFERRADA
(Pop. 62,000 – Alt. 540m)

2.7 km Compostilla *Iglesia Santa María* with decorative murals around the covered portico and memorial to Santiago Peregrino. Turn right> down the side of the sports club passing a pilgrim cross and another mural on the gable end of a small chapel **[0.4 km]** onto a track and under pylons to skirt the end of the suburbs at c/Cubo de Finisterre. The camino now heads out through a tunnel under the ring road **[0.8 km]** past vineyards to the Iglesia de Columbrianos **[0.5 km]** with delightful views from its arcaded rear porch over Ponferrada with its backdrop of mountains to Cruce **[0.3]** crossing the busy main road **[!]** into the village of Columbrianos itself, a busy suburb of Ponferrada with several bars and restaurants, veer <left at the far end by:

2.2 km Columbrianos *Ermita San Blas y San Roque* this small chapel with its colourful pilgrim mural is the site of the original pilgrim hospices. Follow sign to Felix Castro S. A. onto minor road through market gardens all the way to:

Columbrianos – *San Blas*

2.7 km Fuentes Nuevas tiny chapel ermita del Divino Cristo with pilgrim fountain **[F]**. If you need something stronger there is a handy café opposite. Proceed down the main street of this delightfully sleepy village all the way to:

1.9 km Cruce / **Camponaraya** a straggling industrial suburb with the busy N-VI running through it (the waymarks impressed in the pavement slabs) passing a small garden with shade and fountain **[F]** which adjoins the modern parish Church of San Ildefonso. •**Albergue** a municipal hostel opens in the summer with 6 places – basic facilities only and no kitchen (check availability at the church or town hall). Proceed over the río Naraya to the far end of town continue straight on (left) to pass the wine cooperative *Cooperativa Viñas del Bierzo* (do *not* continue past the Petronor station) and pass a shaded rest area and **[F]** and just beyond it we come to a bridge over the autopista.

1.6 km Puente A-6 we now pick up a lovely wide earth track through vineyards down into the peaceful Magaz valley over the arroyo Magaz and continue through woodland to cross over the N-VI **[2.7 km]** and continue for **[0.7 km]** down a wide track to **[F]**:

3.4 km Fuente Cacabelos pilgrim rest area and drinking font **[F]** just before we enter the town. Note that the albergue is the far side of Cacabelos (1.5 km away). We enter the village from the quiet eastern end via the c/de los Peregrinos with the stone edifice of the wine store Prado del Tope built close to the site of the former pilgrim hospital in Plaza San Lázaro which now offers us •**Hotel Moncloa** H** (987-546 101). Continue past a variety of bars and restaurants to the 16th century church of **Santa María** (its original 10th century apse still in place) inside it safeguards a Baroque statue of the Virgin. Detour 100m (left) to the attractive tree-lined *Plaza Mayor* with colonnaded houses and cafés and Turismo (987-546 011).

CACABELOS with a population of 5,000 was an important medieval pilgrim halt with 5 hospices founded for the care of pilgrims on the way. Today you will find a like number of hotels and pensions to care for you. The town has an archaeological museum displaying artefacts found at the nearby Roman settlements and a wine museum celebrating the increasingly popular wine from the area and the history of its production. The albergue is still 1.0 km further on. **Other accommodation** in the central area on c/Santa Maria include hostales: •**Santa María** Hs** (987-549 588) and •**La Gallega** Hs* (987-549 355) with cyber café and also pensión •**El Molino** (987-546 829).

There are several detours to sites of historical interest in the area: **Detour [1]** 10th century Monasterio de San Salvador de Carrecedo which later became Abbé de Santa María la Real. Located 3 kilometres south (left) of the route (6 kilometres round trip) in a beautiful and very peaceful landscape. Interesting monastic complex with royal palace including the exquisite Queen's balcony and museum on monastic life. **Detour [2]** to Castro Ventosa-Bergidum Flavium birthplace of El Bierzo with pre-Roman and Roman settlements. Situated on an elevated site 1 km south (left) of the camino, easily accessed from Pieros.

Continue past the church to join the N-VI to cross the bridge over the río Cua past the ancient olive press and weir to:

1.5 km Las Angustias at the far end of Cacabelos on the right (*not* the Residencia El Camino left) •**Albergue** municipal hostel (Manoli 617-909 991 / 987-546 011) on Plaza del Santuario. Open April–October with 70 beds in chalet style rooms with 2 beds in each

Albergue Municipal

arranged in a semi circle around the church. All facilities and shaded open area around the church. The 18th century Capilla de Las Angustia occupies the site of an earlier chapel and pilgrim hospice. *[Next albergue: Villafranca – 7.5 km].*

We continue along a busy stretch of main road N-VI up past simple wooden cross (left). The hill behind was the site of the Asturian city of Castrum Bergidum, which was later conquered and occupied by the Romans. Continue past the small village of Pieros **[1.7 km]** with 11th century parish church and **[F]**. After **[0.4 km]** towards the top of the hill we reach:

2.1 km Opción [?]

For the alternative road route keep straight on passing arroyo Valtuilles and the turn off for Valtuille de Arriba and just beyond that, mesón Venta del Jubileo. Stay on the N-VI and watch out for the arrows that will take you off the main road to a pleasant track (right):

1.8 km **Cruce** we now turn right up onto a track that winds its way up through vineyards to rejoin the recommended route [2.5 km] just before entering Villafranca del Bierzo [0.5 km].

2.9 km **Villafranca del Bierzo** •Albergue

For the **recommended** old road *c/Viejo* turn right> onto a short stretch of asphalt and veer off <left onto a wide gravel track that winds its way through vineyards onto a shaded lane down to the delightful sleepy hamlet of:

1.5 km **Villatuilla Arriba [F]** we continue past the c/Camino de Santiago that suggests that medieval pilgrims may also have come this way. Today, perhaps unfazed by the constant flow of pilgrims along the more established routes, the villagers appear to have retained their deep respect for the Way of Santiago and its travellers. Make your way through the village (do not take the asphalt road on your left that brings you back onto the main road) continue over the stream at the far end into the Plaza del Fondo del Lugar and pick up a farm track. Proceed up (and down) through the rolling hills covered with vineyards (towards a whitewashed house between two pines on the horizon) before beginning our final descent down to:

3.2 km **Villafranca del Bierzo** •Albergue[1] *municipal* hostel (987-542 680) situated below the path (first building right as you enter) overlooking the town. Open April-November with 73 places (62 in bunks + 11 mattresses) in 4 separate rooms + attic area (very hot in summer) and all facilities in this purpose built modern hostel. Just beyond the municipal hostel we come to the beautiful 12th century Romanesque Church of Santiago with its north entrance Door of Forgiveness *Puerta del Perdón*. Medieval pilgrims unable

Albergue [1] *Municipal*

to continue to Santiago received absolution here the same as they would in Santiago. On this account Villafranca was sometimes referred to as the 'other' Santiago. Certainly in these contemporary times an 'alternative' physical and spiritual healing may still be available to the modern pilgrim for immediately adjoining the church is the legendary:

•**Albergue*** [2] *Ave Fenix* network* hostel (987-540 229). Open all year with 77 beds + overflow space on mattresses. Facilities include solar heated showers (may run cold later in the day) and no kitchen but bar and dining room offering a communal pilgrim supper followed, perhaps, by a mystical *Queimada*. There is a pleasant patio area overlooking the town. An additional service offered by the family is to take backpacks

Albergue [2] *Ave Fenix*

mochilas up to O'Cebreiro to await your arrival at the albergue there and hands-on healing may also be available by donation. (These services are available whether staying at this hostel or not). The Ave Fenix rises, literally, from the ashes. The previous hostel was destroyed by fire, although many will recall with affection the interim tented encampment, a veritable haven of hospitality and healing offered by Jesús Jato and his family. Recent reports have not been so favourable but the pilgrim accepts with equanimity the changing standards he finds along the way. However the truth behind the philosophy of Jesús does not change. It appears in a faded copy of a newspaper article that hangs on the wall. The simple message is worth repeating and needs no translation but a lifetime of learning to assimilate its profundity: *"El Camino es tiempo de meditación interior, no itinerario turístico."*

•**Albergue** [3] *de la Piedra* new welcoming private hostel (Unai 666-655 052 & Livia 987-540 260) on c/Espíritu Santo, 14 (one of the last houses as you leave the town) open all year with 38 places including dormitory and private rooms and all facilities including healing massage. Villafranca is a popular tourist venue as well as a pilgrim halt, so there is a wide range of **alternative accommodation**. At the top end of the town and price bracket is •**Parador*** (987-540 175) Av. Calvo Sotelo (just beyond the Castillo de Marqueses) also

Albergue [3] *de la Piedra*

•**La Puerta del Perdón** CR (987-540 614) Plaz Prim 4. – •**San Francisco** H*(987-540 465) also central on Plaza Mayor. •**Hospedería Convento de San Nicolás el Real** (987-540 483) is located just beyond the main square in an austere monastic building offering 100 beds (individual rooms also available) and a restaurant serving simple pilgrim meals. •**La Llave** CR (Manuel Baquero 987-542 739) c/del Agua 37. Near the exit are: •**Casa Mendez** Hs* (987-542 408) c/Espiritu Santo 1. •**Venecia** P (987-540 468) on main N-VI. •**El Cruce** Hs* (987-542 469) c/San Salvador 37, and •**Hostel Burbia** Hs** Fuente Cubero, 13 overlooking the river Burbia. •**Las Doñas del Portazgo** (987-542 742) at the corner of c/del Agua and the bridge over the river Burbia – luxury boutique hotel on the camino with pilgrim discount (formerly toll house). N.B: wherever you stay make sure you get a good nights sleep to fortify yourself for the strenuous but stupendous hike the next day. Tomorrow brings you up and over the pass into O'Cebreiro and Galicia.

VILLAFRANCA DEL BIERZO with a population of 5,000 has a full range of restaurants and shops including *La Casita del Espejo* on c/del Agua which offers gifts for the pilgrim including Reiki massage and Tarot with Paula. A helpful Turismo (987-540 028) on Av. Bernardo Díez Olebar is located beyond the main square and overlooking the park. This delightful town began to develop in this idyllic spot along the *camino francés* in the 11th century. A tour of the main historic sites includes: **[1]** 12th century **Church of Santiago** a Romanesque jewel with its fine *Puerta de Perdón* and handsome statue of St. James in full pilgrim regalia inside. **[2]** 15th century **Castillo Palacio de los Marqueses** (just below the albergues) with its distinctive turrets, several of which were destroyed during the Peninsular War of 1808 and, further down into town is: **[3] Plaza Mayor** with its Ayuntamiento and café tables spilling out onto the square. Up to the right along c/San Geronimo we come to **[4] Monasterio de San Francisco** founded at the request of Doña Urraca in the 13th century (some say by Saint Francis himself). *[Note: if you continue past this church a footpath will bring you back to the albergues on the opposite side of the valley.]* Beyond Plaza Mayor we arrive at the austere 17th century **Iglesia San Nicolás [5]** (see above for accommodation details) further on is **[6] Turismo** and adjacent **[7] Convento Divina Pastora** (formerly one of the 5 pilgrim hospices that attended the large numbers of medieval pilgrims that passed this way). A walk through the open gardens **[8] Jardin Municipal** *Alameda* will bring us to **[9] Iglesia Colegiata** formerly the Iglesia Nuestra Señora de Cluniaco (the monks from Cluny were amongst the first arrivals from France). We can end this circular route by continuing out and up towards O'Cebreiro or return to the albergues via the medieval Water street **c/Agua** with its noble houses bearing their armorial shields. The famous Spanish novelist Gil y Carrasco was born here and we also pass **[10] Convento de San José** founded in the 17th century by the canon of Santiago Cathedral and finally into c/Rua Nueva to **[11] Convento de la Anunciada** where the Marqueses from the Palacio, where we started this tour, are buried.

❏ **This is the way of peace; overcome evil with good, falsehood with truth and hatred with love.** *Peace Pilgrim*

MAP 26 *193.5 km (120.2 miles) to Santiago de Compostela*

VILLAFRANCA DEL BIERZO – O'CEBREIRO
Recommended route [1] via Pradela.

▬▬▬	Path / Track	--- ---	15.3	--- 51%
▬▬▬	Quiet Road	--- ---	12.6	--- 42%
▬▬▬	Main Road	--- ---	2.2	--- 7%
Total km	**Total distance**		**30.1 km** (18.7 miles)	

◣◤ Adjusted for climb 36.1 km (accrued ascent 1,200m = 6.0 km)
Alto ▲ High Point: O Cebreiro 1,310m (4,297 feet)

The Practical Path: A strenuous day's walking bringing us up and into Galicia. We have 3 options on leaving Villafranca and the choice will be determined by: [a] prevailing weather conditions [b] personal level of fitness and, [c] the kind of experience you want to create. All routes are likely to prove demanding. This stage represents one of the steepest of the whole pilgrimage but the climb is rewarded with stunning views along the Valcarce valley that will keep spirits high. The least taxing option is the noisy N-VI stretch and while the completion of the A-6 motorway has greatly reduced traffic using it, there are several dangerous bends, so stay alert. **Intermediate accommodation** on recommended route 1 *(distances from albergue [1]):* Trabadelo (11.7 km) – Portela Valcarce (15.3 km) – Ambasmestas (16.9 km) – Vega de Valcarce (18.3 km) – Ruitelán (20.5 km) Herrerías (21.8 km) – La Faba (24.9 km) – Laguna (27.4 km). Note: first hostel on alternative route [2] is Pereje (5.5 km) and first available hostel on alternative route [3] is Herrerías (26.1 km). The valley is steep sided (Val carce *Latin; Vallis Carceras* = narrow valley) and heavily wooded with mostly pine and chestnut, so all options provide shade. There are shops, bars, hotels and pilgrim hostels all along the valley floor in the villages we pass through, but make sure you have water and some snacks for the Pradela route before leaving Villafranca and full provisions for the remote Dragonte route.

❏ **The Mystical Path:** We cannot give peace unless we first create peace in our own hearts and minds. By giving Love we extend Love and thereby reverse the laws of this world for Love increases the more we give it away. How much can we find to give away today? When we are able to respond lovingly to all our interactions we send an expansion of loving energy into our fear-filled world.

❏ **Personal Journal:** "… *Sleeping out under the stars has deepened my experience but today my physical and spiritual muscles ache and my heart feels*

Xunta [80] **Albergue** 0.3 A
O'CEBREIRO C H 2.4 **Santa María**
(Pop. 50 – Alt. 1,330m) *Aurillac*

Albergue 2.5 A **LAGUNA de CASTILLA**

GALICIA

Asoc.[35] **Albergue** 3.1 A **LA FABA**

CASTILLA Y LEÓN

O
Puesta del Sol

S
Salida del Sol
E

HERRERÍAS
Albergue 4.8 A 1.3 **Albergue** *Miriam Priv.[20]*
800m

1.400m rio
RUITELÁN
A 2.2 **Albergue** *Pequeño Potala Priv.*[34]*

1.000m cruce
Alto 1.005m
1.600m cruce A 3.0 **Albergue** *Muni. [64]*
Saracín **VEGA de VALCARCE**
Vilasinde 4.1 A *do Brasil Priv.*[84]*
2.300m
Celia

AMBASMESTAS
700m rio A *Das Animas Priv.[30]*
LA PORTELA de VALCARCE
1.100m ^cruce A 3.6 **Albergue** *El Peregrino Priv.[50]*
H *Valcarce*

San Fiz de Seo 4.7 900m *Cantina*
900m rio
2.600m cantera *Quarry Cantera*

Alto 1.055m **TRABADELO**
300m cruce> **Albergue** 4.8 A 4.3 **Albergue** *Muni.[30]*
Vilar 2.7 400m fuente *Crispeta Priv.[34]* A
de Corales 800m iglesia

ruinas *Pradela*
1.500m rio> *bar 'A Focara'*

700m fuente 3.0 **Moral de Valcarce**
700m <cruce 935m

1.600m cruce> *Alto 1.050m* 3.1 **Alto**/*Peña Roldan*
Quarry Cantera *La Corona*
Dragonte 5.8 **PEREJE**
Albergue 4.5
Muni.[30] 3.3 **Vista**/*altars*

③ ② ①

Corullón 1.0 **Opción** / **Puente de río Burbia**
Albergue 0.0 A **VILLAFRANCA del BIERZO**
(Pop. 4,000 – Alt. 530m)

heavy. I don't understand what is happening to me but I will continue to walk in silence and trust that everything will reveal itself in time; 'when the student is ready the Teacher will appear.' The weariness I felt was intensified by a busload of raucous pilgrims. They might have been touring for charity but there was nothing charitable about the way in which they swamped the path and when I finally arrived soaked and exhausted they had completely surrounded the bar. It was an age before I could get the proprietor to read my note requesting a room and so I unwittingly chose to extend anger instead of love. They were my teachers and I failed the lesson that peace starts within myself. If I am dependent on the behaviour of others for my sense of serenity, I will never become free ..."

---

[1] Ruta Pradela [30.1 km] (adjusted for climb 36.1 km – total ascent 1,200m). This recommended route is very beautiful and makes the most of the early morning sun which doesn't penetrate into the lower Valcarce valley until later in the day. The steep climb up (400m) is rewarded with wonderful views back over Villafranca, but you will need to allow an extra hour or two for this longer route and the ascent and steep descent it involves.

[2] Ruta Carretera [28.7 km] (adjusted for climb 32.7 km – total ascent 800m). The road route is the shortest with several villages providing shops and bars along the way. However, it is dangerous where you have to cross the N-VI so stay focussed and walk inside the crash barriers wherever provided. The new autopista has reduced traffic on the N-VI but it is still unsightly and noisy.

[3] Camino Dragonte [34.4 km] (adjusted for climb 44.1 km /ascent – 1,950m). *Note: Plan to stay at Herrerias 26.1 km (32.5 adjusted).* To avoid the main road completely you need to take this route, the longest and most arduous and, accordingly, the most beautiful and spectacular. You need to be fit and take food and water with you as the way is remote with only one bar (often closed), although there are several water fonts. Waymarking is poor so you need a good sense of direction and reserve energy to retrace your steps should you get lost. The extensive woodland offers protection from rain or sun but mountain weather is unpredictable at any time of year so stick to the other routes if in any doubt.

Leaving albergue [1] in Villafranca del Bierzo make your way down the c/ Aqua (c/Ribadeo) and at the far end turn <left (by hotel Las Doñas) up the steps by pilgrim statue and:

1.0 km **Opción / Puente del río Burbia** cross over the bridge, just above its confluence with the río Valcarce (Hostel Burbia upriver right) to the first option point only 50m [!] *not* well indicated. If you intend to take the recommended Pradela route you *must* leave the asphalt road here up the steep cobbled street right> [!] past the new peluquería Ana. *Alternative road route [2] via the main N-VI is described after Trabadelo. Alternative detour route [3] via Dragonte is described after Herrerías.*

For **recommended route [1] Camino de Pradela** turn up right> into c/Pradela and, if the warning signs for fitness worry you, remember that if you have made it this far you should encounter no undue problems. Indeed, the lower route along the main N-VI may carry greater risk of injury and, depending on the time of day and year, the sun will not penetrate the valley floor in the morning.

It appears that many pilgrims use the road route because they are unaware of a choice or miss the narrow turning up into Pradela. Continue up the steep incline that shortly gives way to an earthen path that skirts smallholdings and vineyards on our left and pine forest above until we reach a rock outcrop – here a large boulder protrudes onto the path and acts as a 1 km marker from the bridge (2 km from the albergue). The path now climbs less steeply and levels out as we make our way along a ridge to:

3.3 km Vista / *altars* wonderful viewpoint back over Villafranca and Valcarce that has inspired the creation of personal 'altars' to the journey. Continue above the tree line to the high point at:

3.1 km Alto / *Peña Roldan* (track to radio mast right) we now enter a delightful stretch through chestnut woods (sign to bar 'A Focara' 500m is just over 1 km into Pradela from here). Several woodland paths converge in this area but continue straight ahead to emerge onto an asphalt road (to Pradela) and cross over onto path that winds down steeply [!] into: on a new pilgrim track (cutting out the gentler but longer road bends) to rejoin the main road at:

4.3 km Trabadelo [F] with several bars and albergues (see below). Pilgrims who have come via road route [2] (described below) join here.

Alternative road route [2] via N-VI this snakes its way up alongside the main road and follows the river valley. It has been realigned many times and the traffic is now much reduced on account of the new autopista. It has also been improved with the addition of crash barriers that now separate pilgrims from the traffic but care is still needed when crossing over. At Puente del río Burbia (option point 1.0 km from albergue [1]) keep straight on (ignoring Pradela waymarks on your right) and continue for 150m to 2nd option point by Casa Mendez *(turn left over 2nd bridge for Dragonte route [3] (see later)* for road route turn right at hotel and continue along the río Valcarce on the old N-VI all the way into:

4.5 km Pereje •Albergue municipal hostel (987-542 670). Open all year with 30 beds in 2 rooms and all facilities + outside terrace. Other accommodation •**Las Corinas** (987-540 138). The original main street is called *Camino Santiago* witnessing to its pilgrim focus in earlier times. Indeed the administration of Pereje was the cause of a long dispute between the establishments at O'Cebreiro and Villafranca taking both the monarchy and papacy to resolve it in favour of O'Cebreiro who had built a pilgrim hospice there. This seems to mirror the struggle between the culture of the lowlands and the highlands and between León and Galicia. Although you do not officially enter Galicia until just below O'Cebreiro, the atmosphere, topography and weather all seem to change in this valley. Rejoin the N-VI into:

4.8 km Trabadelo •Albergue [1] *Crispeta* (620-329 386) private hostel opened in 2008 with 20 places in dormitory + 7 private rooms. All facilities + outside terrace. •Albergue [2] municipal hostel (987-566 447). Open all year with 32 beds and every facility + outside terrace. Both on c/Camino de Santiago. Other accommodation: •**Nova Ruta** Hs & restaurant (987-566 431). •**Casa Ramón** CR (665-610 028). •**Pilar Frade** CR. From as early as the 9th century the church was under the possession of the cathedral in Santiago. An uneasy peace existed here with other centres of administration and the castle of Auctares and the hills above Trabadelo were a base for outlaws to exact their own 'tolls' on innocent pilgrims. Out the far side of the village join the pilgrims who had taken the Pradela route.

The path continues parallel (above) the main N-VI rejoining it briefly several times before reaching the outskirts of Portela •**Hostal Valcarce** Hs (987-543 180) and restaurante on main road (primarily a truckers-stop before braving the mountain doorway into Galicia *Puerto de Pedrafita*.) We cross road into:

3.6 km La Portela de Valcarce •**Albergue** *El Peregrino* private hostel (Gervasio & Sonia Fernandez 987-543 197) prominent position, open all year with 50 beds including individual rooms in modern building. Facilities include bar and restaurant with pilgrim menu + outside terrace. Continue through Portela before turning off for Ambasmestas (signposted Vega de Valcarce). At this point we finally leave the N-VI *[we now have 4 days walking ahead before we have to join the national network again, the N-547 at Palas de Rei.]* Continue into the traditional village of Ambasmestas **[1.4]**. For the hostel turn left in the village centre and cross over the river and on the left is •**Albergue** *Das Animas* private hostel (Yazmina Pérez 619-048 626) on c/Campo Bajo. Open Easter-November with 30 places (20 beds + 10 mattresses) all facilities (kitchenette with microwave only) and terrace overlooking the river. Ambasmestas is where the río Balboa joins the río Valcarce to give the area its name (aguas mestas) its rural idyll somewhat spoilt by the A-6 flyover that serves as its backdrop, continue along the valley floor for a further **[0.6 km]** to •**Albergue*** *Do Brasil* network* hostel (987-543 045) a modern building set back from the road on the outskirts of Vega de Valcarce. Open all year with 36 beds in one dormitory + mattresses. All facilities and shared meals available. Continue for **[1.0 km]** around the next corner to:

Albergue – *Do Brasil*

3.0 km Vega de Valcarce •**Albergue** *municipal* hostel (María Rodríguez Fernández 987-543 248) turn right on entering the village up c/Pandelo (below the A-6 flyover) off Plaza municipal. Open all year with 64 beds + mattresses and all facilities. Pleasant village built around the río Valcarce and offering a variety of shops, bars and restaurants, marred somewhat by the proximity of the A-6 above. Shortly after leaving the village the menacing outline of the 14th century *Castillo de Sarracín* opens up on the ridge to our left. The town was founded by in the 9th century by Count Sarraceno from Astorga (not some Muslim overlord). Continue by quiet road passing the old parish church of St. John the Baptist in a delightfully dilapidated condition and often open (left). The motorway is now thankfully out of sight thus preserving the tranquil setting of this quaint hamlet where San Froilán had a hermitage as we enter:

2.2 km Ruitelán •**Albergue** *Pequeño Potala* private network* hostel (Luis & Miguel 987-561 322) on corner (right). Open all year with 34 beds in 3 rooms. Good facilities (no kitchen but shared dinner and breakfast offered) massage may also be available. There is a small shop and bar. Continue out of the village passing new posada rural •**El Paraíso del Bierzo** CR (987-684 137) to turn off <left (opposite bar and sign for La Faba) cross the Romanesque bridge over the río Valcarce into the village ahead **[1.1 km]**.

Albergue – *Pequeno Potala*

1.3 km Herrerías •Albergue *Miriam* a new private hostel opened in 2008 (Miriam 654-353 940) located on the left at the start of the village. Open all year with 20 places in bunk beds. Basic facilities and vegetarian dinner and breakfast provided in this renovated traditional village house. Other accommodation •**Casa do Ferreiro** CR & restaurant. Also café/bar

Albergue Herrerias – *Miriam*

Polin with shop opposite and local taxi José Lopez Barreiro (649-647 504). The ancient hamlet stretches lazily along the river, its name derived from the iron foundry whose furnaces have long since disappeared. This is the point where the Dragonte route (described next) rejoins the recommended route.

Alternative route [3] via Dragonte.

The route described here is was one of the ways that pilgrims used to traverse the Valcarce Valley. It is longer, with 3 deep river valleys to cross, and is waymarked as part of the GR-11 and is variously referred to as *Camino de los Franceses* or *Camino Dragont*e with the more discreet green and white circular walking plaques or the red and

white blaise predominating although the yellow arrow pops up occasionally. There are few facilities along the way and no accommodation until you reach Herrerías although you can take any of the roads down into the main valley and rejoin the other routes with their plentiful accommodation – see map.

It is the 'road less travelled' and on this account will appeal to those seeking a more contemplative way. It is very beautiful and, as yet, unspoiled. The distance from the albergue in Villafranca to Herreías, via Dragonte, is 26.1 km with an extra 8.3 km up to O'Cebreiro (total 34.4 km) in addition there is a total height climbed in the day of 1,900m (6,230 feet) so best plan to stay in Herrerías or, if accommodation is not available there then consider staying in Ruitelán or La Faba. Waymarking is not as obvious as on the main route and the paths beyond Dragonte are frequently overgrown by scrub vegetation, particularly the last stretch down into Herreíras, so only contemplate this route if you are fit, have a good sense of orientation and an instinctive nature when faced with unexpected options. Don't expect to get lost but allow some additional time in case you do and find you have to retrace some of your steps! Leave early in the morning and don't tackle it in the winter months when daylight hours are restricted or if the weather is bad or set to deteriorate.

1.0 km **Option point** at 1st Bridge (rio Burbia) on the outskirts of Villafranca (1.0 km from albergue [1]) veer <left and continue <left over the 2nd bridge (río Valcarce) at Hostel Mendez **[0.2 km]** and head over the old N-VI **[0.4 km]** by the A-6 tunnel (signposted Corullón) and turn up sharp right> **[0.4 km]** signposted Dragonte by a walkers notice board and map. This first section into Dragonte is all by steep asphalt road **[4.8]** but rewarded with splendid views back over Villafranca. Head up into and through the village of:

5.8 km **Dragonte [F]** (right) a welcome pilgrim fountain has been installed here. The path continues up (less steeply now) onto wide track keep straight on maintaining the contour as the track veers left in between quarry (left) and hill *La Corona* (right) to a high point on the track of 1,050m (3,445 feet) where, opposite a grove of trees down to the left of the track, we turn off right> [!] at GR-11 sign **[1.6 km]** onto narrow path through scrubland following a ditch around to our left and down to an asphalt road **[0.7 km]** which we follow for another **[0.7 km]** into:

3.0 km | **Moral de Valcarce** village **[F]** (no other facilities). Drop down through wooded valley to stream at bottom **[1.5 km]** where you may get wet but must turn right> [!] *before* derelict stone building to regain dry path in 30m the path now winds its way up (keep to larger of the tracks through the woods) to emerge by church **[0.8 km]** (formerly monastery and pilgrim hospice of San Fructuoso, viewpoint to rear) pass the access road (right) and up **[0.4 km]** into:

2.7 km | **Vilar de Corrales** isolated hamlet with drinking font **[F]** but no other facilities. Make sure water bottles are full before proceeding. Continue up veering right> **[0.3 km]** *Camino de los Franceses* off the main track and 100m later continue straight over tracks at the brow of a wide mountain shoulder and high point (1,055m). We now begin the descent into the second of the 3 valleys we have to cross. Turn off <left after 800m (main track veers right) to descend steeply [!] towards the open cast stone quarry below. The descent in not only steep but the narrow paths are confusing as the waymarks here may have been obliterated by the quarrying activity but

our destination, the valley floor, is obvious and you zigzag down as best you can. For general orientation fix your route by the village (San Fiz) visible on the opposite side of the valley. To add spice to an already exhilarating ride note that this is a blasting area *Zona de Voladuras!* Console yourself with the fact that many have passed this way before you and there will be others following! You finally join an access road into the quarry *cantera* **[2.6 km]** and make your way through the quarry itself (watch out for trucks). The dirt road now crosses the river onto the public road **[0.9 km]** where there are signs for the GR-1 *Ruta Wolfram* and *Ruta Verde* (be careful not to confuse the various local walking paths in this area). Turn right> along the asphalt road and take the turning <left 400m up for another 500m **[0.9 km]** into:

4.7 km | **San Fiz do Seo [F]** Church dedicated to Virgen de los Dolores (right) turn up left by small cantina (often closed) and make your way up through the village with **[F]** right at exit (make sure you have water for this next section before proceeding). The path now levels out – essentially we maintain the contour around the base of the hill on our right ignoring tracks that turn right up towards it continuing gently down at fork **[1.1 km]** passing beehives (right) all the way to the valley floor and over stream **[0.7 km]** before beginning our ascent up steeply for **[2.3 km]** towards Villasinde ignoring path down to the left Ruta Verde GR-1 to cross asphalt road into:

4.1 km | **Villasinde [F]** and bar (knock on door if closed – Celia will generally open). Note: from here it is possible to take the minor road down to the albergues at Vega de Valcarce (4 km all on asphalt) or if you are still feeling adventurous and there is sufficient light left in the day then head up and out of the village passing parish church before veering right uphill following GR11 signpost to pass between the rise *Teso Redondo* (left) and *Vilela* (right) towards the radio mast ahead visible on the horizon. Pass **[F]** (left) continuing up to crest the hill and join track to radio mast (right) **[1.6 km]** we turn <left on this track (Alto 1,002m) and keep this contour as it swings around to the right (ignore path signposted Ruta S.Julián up to the left). Shortly afterwards pass **[F]** and another radio mast appears

on the peak in front and at broken signpost **[1.0 km]** turn off <left to start our descent into the valley floor with the A6 viaduct and our destination Herrerías now coming into view in the middle distance. Up until this point the pathways had been reasonably well maintained and signposted but the path down to the valley floor is little used and requires effort to force through the broom and heather. The path at the top is steep and the broom maybe useful to hold to avoid slipping but be alert for the occasional bramble growing across the path that can act as a trip wire! If you are on course you will come to another walkers sign at a muddy section before the path begins to level out and becomes more obvious through woodland to cross over a small stream **[1.4 km]** down to a river where we turn right> into the village and the new pilgrim hostel **[0.8 km]** at:

4.8 km Herrerías to finally join the pilgrims coming up Valcarce for the climb up into O'Cebreiro – another demanding stage of 8.4 km and an ascent of 620m (2,035 feet). This will have been a very full day so secure a bed in Miriam's refugio (photo opposite) or Ruitelán (1.1 km further back) or try one of the several casa rurales in the area.

From **Herrerías Bridge** we wind our way through this quaint village (see p. 231 for facilities) that meanders alongside the river with its simple stone architecture. The fountain by the river was known as *Fuente de Quinoñes* linking it with the chivalrous knight who defended the Puente de Órbigo. We pass several bars and an old forge *A Casa do Ferreiro* and the even more distant English hospice *Hospital Inglés* at the far (western) edge of the village, a reference to the medieval English pilgrims who passed this way (a pilgrim chapel and cemetery were known to have existed here though the buildings are no longer discernible) Fill up the water flask and gird your loins for the final assault on the mountain ahead. Continue along the quiet asphalt road before turning off <left onto **path [2.0 km]** that drops down briefly to the valley floor where we start our steep ascent through delightful woodland, mostly chestnut *castaños* on a rocky path (slippery in wet) for **[1.1 km]** up into the pretty hillside village of:

3.1 km La Faba •Albergue parish house adjoining the church Iglesia San Andrés (left). Renovated by a German Confraternity and open April-October with 35 beds. All facilities and shaded parkland setting adjoining the church. This delightful hamlet has a small shop, bar and a house offering massage (and possibly a floor if you're spaced out after a massage). The path continues up and out of the village along a path lined with Spanish chestnut trees and splendid views back over the Valcarce valley to reach:

2.5 km Laguna de Castilla •Albergue private hostel (Roberto 989-157 392) with 15 places on mattresses in one large room and all basic facilities including a café/bar with outside tables. This tiny hamlet may represent the last outpost in Castille but it houses a wonderful example of a functional Galician *palloza* in the farmyard just behind the fountain [**F**]. These traditional structures built in the round with straw roofs can be visited in O'Cebreiro.

Just above Laguna we pass the first concrete marker post *K.152.5 OS Santos*. These markers will accompany us all the way to Santiago (the route has been changed since they were originally surveyed so distances are no longer accurate but they provide reassuring waymarks) and we arrive at the Galicia Frontera [**1.1 km**] a substantial marker records the fact that we are finally leaving the autonomous region of Castilla y León (provincia León) to enter Galicia (provincia de Lugo). The path continues through gorse and scrubland to skirt the stone wall that brings us the remaining [**1.2 km**] into:

2.4 km O'Cebreiro Iglesia one of the earliest surviving buildings on the Camino de Santiago welcomes you to its sheltered interior *Iglesia de Santa Maria Real* dating, in part, from the 9th century and the oldest extant church associated directly with the pilgrim way. O'Cebreiro (Pron: *Oh-thay-bray-**air**-oh*) another significant gateway on the camino has administered to the needs of pilgrims since the twilight of the first millennium. Santa María la Real is patroness of the area and her 12th century statue is prominently displayed along with the chalice and paten connected with

Santa María – *Chalice and Paten*

the miracle of O'Cebreiro *Santo Milagro* in which, 'a haughty celebrant of the mass, dismissive of a devout and humble peasant, saw the bread and wine turn into the body and blood of Christ as he offered them to the supplicant who had risked life and limb to attend mass in a terrible snowstorm – the statue itself was also said to have inclined its head at the miraculous event.'

The church also marks the resting place of Don Elias Valiña Sampedro (1929–1989) the parish priest who did so much during his life to restore and preserve the integrity of this route – it was his idea to mark the route with the familiar yellow arrow and it was largely as a result of his efforts that we walk the route today. His bust presides over the church square and many confraternities have placed their names on the plinth as a mark of their deep respect for his life and efforts on behalf of the modern pilgrim. He was also responsible for the restoration of the adjoining Hostal *San Giraldo de Aurillac* that is now run by members of the family. These handsome stone buildings

Don Elias Valiña Sampedro

originally formed part of the monastic settlement dating back to the 11th century when King Alfonso VI assigned their care to the monks of the Abbé de Saint Giraldo from France. Queen Isabella stayed here in 1486 on her pilgrimage to Santiago. Opposite the church is a museum in a renovated Palloza. It is now only a short walk past the several bars, shops and restaurants to:

0.3 km | **O'Cebreiro** •**Albergue** Xunta hostel (Edita Nuñez 660-396 809) situated on the western (furthest) end of the village on an exposed and elevated site above the main road. Modern purpose built hostel open all year with 80 beds and all facilities recently renovated. *[Next albergue: Hospital de Condesa – 5.5 km].*

Note on Galician Albergues: the regional government *Xunta de Galicia* has constructed modern purpose-built pilgrim hostels or converted former school buildings all along the route from here to Finisterre. This is one of the better examples of a rather uninspiring uniform design. These hostels can generally be identified by the stark white walls and the blue Telefonica kiosk outside. They all have reasonable facilities, such as ample hot showers and toilets, but kitchens are frequently out of commission or lacking in cooking utensils. The more cynical might point to commercial exploitation by local restaurants but forewarned is fore-armed and everyone needs to make a living – there is usually a restaurant close by, often run by the hospitalera.

Other accommodation. •**San Giraldo de Aurillac** HsR** (982-367 125) adjoining the church with popular bar and dining room. You need to book here also for the •**Santuario do Cebreiro** H* (982-367 125) above the adjacent bar and souvenir shop. •**Casa Carolo** CR (982-367 168) and •**Venta Celta** CR & Restaurante (Irenea 667-553 006) in the centre of the village while below on the main road is •**Mesón Anton** (952-151 336). O'Cebreiro has become a popular tourist venue as well as pilgrim halt – accordingly demand for beds can outstrip supply in the summer months so find a bed before celebrating.

GALICIA PROFILE: The Valcarce valley and O'Cebreiro provide a wonderful foretaste of the distinctive Galician culture that now awaits you. The mountains of Galicia are the first object in 5,000 km that the westerly winds coming across the Atlantic hit so you can expect an immediate change in weather with frequent rain showers and thunderstorms *lluvia y tormenta* and thick mountain fog *(see photo)* all feeding a maze of mountain

streams and deep river beds. The countryside is reminiscent of other Celtic lands with its small, intimate fields and lush pastures grazed by cattle with sheep, pigs, geese and chickens all foraging amongst the poorer ground.

Thick hot soups *caldo gallego* and rich vegetable and meat stews provide inner warmth from the damp. Nearer the coast, fish dishes such as steamed octopus dusted with paprika *pulpo a la galega* and shellfish *mariscos* will dominate. Local red wines with their coarser characters accompany most meals and help to fuel the inner glow. For more delicate whites to accompany scallops *vieiras* try the white Ribeiros or the incomparable Albariño. Round up your meal with local cheese and quince jelly *queso y membrillo* or the famous almond tart *tarta de Santiago*. If you are still feeling cold try the distilled grape skin *orujo* or its marginally more refined cousin *hierbas* mixed with local herbs. Stone granaries *hórreos* are *everywhere* storing the local harvest (primarily maize *maíz*) out of reach of rat and rain.

Galicia shares many historical and physical similarities with other Celtic regions particularly the west of Ireland. Too poor to provide much employment for its large family structures, emigration (particularly of the younger men) has cast it spectre across the region. Here, women drive the tractors or herd the oxen and seem to find time to do the cooking and tend the bars as well. Surprisingly you may find locals that now speak some English on account of having spent time working abroad (or while visiting children working in the UK or USA). If any doubt remains as to its Celtic past then the strident whirl of its bagpipes *gaita* should dispel them. The language *Galega* is still spoken by a substantial minority and understood by the majority while writers and poets such as Rosalia de Castro have helped preserve it more robustly than Irish or Scottish Gaelic. The most visible difference is in the spelling of place names and signposts where, for example, X now replaces J as in Xunta or Igrexa. *Céad míle fáilte!*

Galicia's material poverty has left her with an abundance of spiritual wealth and the region is generally at peace with itself and its traditions largely intact. While a strong Catholic faith overlays its earthy spirituality, its pagan past never totally faded. Deep respect, even veneration of the natural elements remains as evident as the elements themselves. *Finis terra* was, after all, the end of the ancient world – west of Finisterre was the 'Land of Eternal Youth' *Tir-na-nog* where the sun never set. Long before the tomb of St. James was discovered and before Christianity spread to these shores, pilgrims from all over the known world came here to witness the sun sink in the west – and to open to some transcendental reality that emphasised the temporal aspects of earthly life. The countryside ahead is full of the dolmens and mamoas of these earlier settlers who were deeply reverent in character and who handed down this earthy respect for the natural world. The wayside *cruceiros* add an air of solemnity to the path and are a reminder of the deep spirituality of Galicia that seems to have survived the consumer culture and materialism that has swept over much of the rest of Europe. Santiago de Compostela is the capital of the autonomous region of Galicia which is divided into the 4 provinces of A Coruña, Lugo, Ourense and Pontevedra. See *A Pilgrim's Guide to Finisterre* for a detailed account of the history and legends of this fascinating corner of Galicia – and try and make time to walk the route out to the end of the way and the world.

REFLECTIONS:

❏ **If you want the rainbow, you've gotta put up with the rain.** *Dolly Parton*

MAP 27 *163.4 km (101.5 miles) to Santiago de Compostela*

O'CEBREIRO – TRIACASTELA

▬▬▬	Path / Track	--- ---	14.2	---	*69%*
▬▬▬	Minor Road	--- ---	6.5	---	*31%*
▬▬▬	Main Road	--- ---	0.0		
Total km	**Total distance**		**20.7 km** (12.9 miles)		

Adjusted for climb   21.7 km (accrued ascent 200m = 1.0 km)

Alto ▲ High Point: Alto do Poio 1,335m (4,380 feet)

The Practical Path: Remember that, while this stage is only 20.7 kilometres and mostly downhill, most injuries are sustained going down (not up) so extra time and care is needed. There are several villages and drinking fonts along the way and (providing it isn't pouring rain) the most stupendous views in every direction. Early morning mists can give rise to the most astounding ethereal floating islands in the sky where hilltops appear above the clouds. These exotic experiences generally give way to clearer skies, as the sun burns the swirling mists away. Whatever time of year, be prepared for *any* weather, as the mountains, and particularly Galicia, can be very unpredictable. **Intermediate accommodation:** Liñares (3.1 km) – Hospital de la Condesa (5.5 km) – Alto do Poio (8.6 km) – Fonfría (12.1 km) – Biduedo (14.4 km).

❏ **The Mystical Path:** High places help lift us towards Higher Mind. At such heights, a wider perspective opens up to both the physical and the inner eye. What do you see, feel and hear from this elevated space? Do the angels incline their heads to listen to your prayers? Does the silence and peace in your heart allow the inner voice to be heard? Are you open to receiving a miracle and to seeing the inner rainbow – symbol of God's Covenant?

❏ **Personal Reflections:** *"... The deluge continues and not a break to be seen in the clouds in any direction. I ask myself was it serendipity that sent the brief shaft of light through the tiny church window bathing me in its warm rich glow; its light so strong I was momentarily dazed by it. I sense again that altered state, devoid of ego, and all the pain of yesterday has gone. I feel inspired to write a pilgrim guidebook and Don Elias Valiña Sampedro appears to have given me his authority and blessing and so I commit to it right here and now ..."*

Leaving the albergue take the main road out of O'Cebreiro and continue to:

3.1 km   **Liñares Iglesia San Esteban** a small hamlet that once grew flax *lino* for the linen trade, today we find a bar and •**Casa Jaime** CR (982-367 166).

SAMOS ①   ② SAN XIL

Berce **Priv.**[28]→ A A ←*Aitzenea* **Priv.** *[38]*
Complexo Xacobeo **Priv.** *[44]*→ A A ←*Oribio* **Priv.** *[27]*
Xunta [82] **Albergue [1] 3.1**→ A **TRIACASTELA**
(Pop. 900 – Alt. 675m)

Ramil

As Pasantes

Villoval   ←**3.2** **X-Cruce** *(Túnel)*

C ←**2.3** **Biduedo**
S. Pedro

Puesta del Sol

O

N

S

Salida del Sol

E

A ←**3.5** **Albergue** *A Reboleira* **Priv.** *[47]*
F
FONFRÍA
C

1,335m
Alto do Poio
Santa Maria do Poio H A ←**3.1** **Albergue** *del Puerto* **Priv.** *[18]*

Padornelo
S. Oxan

Sabugos

HOSPITAL de la CONDESA
A ←**2.4** **Albergue** *Xunta [20]*

Monumento do Peregrino m

Alto San Roque
1,270m

San Esteban 3.1→ ■ **LIÑARES**
Casa Jaime C

A-6

N-VI

Xunta [80] **Albergue 0.0**→ A

O'CEBREIRO
(Pop. 50 – Alt. 1,330m)

Pedrafita do Cebreiro

The path takes us past the ancient parish church and a short uphill climb to Alto de San Roque **[0.8 km]**. Here an impressive pilgrim monument looks out over the vast expanse of Galicia and its deep valleys. A path continues parallel to the road for **[1.6 km]** into:

2.4 km Hospital de la Condesa •Albergue *Xunta* hostel (Concepción Fonfría 982-161 336) Prominently located above the road (right) as we enter the village. Open all year with 18 beds and all facilities. The village once boasted a pilgrim hospital (hence its name) and was reputed to have been one of the earliest ever built for Christian pilgrims on the way to Santiago, but now the most notable remains are the interesting church with its stone roofed belfry and cross of Santiago aloft.

Albergue – Hospital

We rejoin the main road for **[1.2 km]** turning off right> down a minor road (signposted Sarbugos) for **[0.3 km]** before picking up the path again into Padornelo **[1.0 km]** with the recently restored chapel *ermita San Oxan* connecting this area with the Order of St. John. A short but steep climb **[0.6 km]** now brings us to the highest spot on the camino in Galicia:

3.1 km Alto do Poio 1,335m. (4,380 feet) •**Albergue del Puerto*** *Posada del Peregrino* (Remedios 982-367 172) Network* hostel open all year with 50 places (30 beds + 20 mattresses) beds. Good facilities (no kitchen) but Bar Puerto caters for evening meals and the breakfast trade is livened up with pilgrims from O'Cebreiro. On the opposite side of the road individual rooms available in •**Hostal**

Albergue/ Bar – Alto do Poio

Santa María de Poio (982-367 167). Rejoin the road for a short stretch before turning off right> onto a path above it all the way into:

3.5 km Fonfría another typical Galician village with •**Casa Núñez** CR (982-161 335) providing a welcoming bar and restaurant. Fill your flask from the cool waters of the *fons [fuente] fría* **[F]** after which the hamlet is named. Just outside the village up on the right is •**Albergue*** *A Reboleira* (Ángela 982-161 335) network* hostel in modern building with 40 places in 6 rooms including some for individual use. Good facilities (no kitchen) but meals available. Continue on track parallel to main road before turning off right> into:

Albergue – Fonfría

2.3 km Viduedo a rural idyll with its pequeño capilla de San Pedro and welcoming •**Meson Betularia** (982-367 172) serves meals and has rooms. Nearby is •**Casa Quiroga** CR (Isabel Riu 982-187 299). The path now begins to descend more steeply with wonderful views over the countryside to the west. Just after marker stone 132 we come to:

3.2 km Cruce Filloval cross the main road (or take the muddy underpass) and skirt Filloval before returning to the main road and then through As Pasantes and Ramil on the ancient camino worn down with the feet of countless pilgrims and local livestock, a classic stretch of *corredoira* – a narrow lane walled-in with granite. Soak up the peace as you meander above the wooded valley of the arroyo Roxino that flows down from Monte Oribio. This primitive way is guarded by a venerable oak and chestnut trees that offer shade all the way to:

| 3.1 km | **Triacastela** •**Albergue** [1] *Xunta* hostel (Jesús 982-548 087) situated on a green-field site to the left of the camino at the start of the village and overlooking the river. Imaginatively restored from traditional stone buildings with modern extensions. Open all year with 82 beds (14 rooms) and good facilities (no kitchen) but large lounge and extensive outdoor recreation area.

It is now 500m into the town centre to: •**Albergue*** [2] *Complexo Xacbeo* (982-548 037) new network* hostel directly on the camino adjacent to the bar / restaurant Xacobeo to which it is connected. Open all year with 44 places in modern extension to the rear with good facilities. Further along the camino is •**Albergue** [3] *Bercce do Camiño* (Consuelo Río Rubio 982-548 127) private hostel open all year with 28 places in 6 rooms. All facilities in this modernised terraced house adjoining Caixa Galicia. Back on the main road is •**Albergue*** [4] *Aitzenea* (Lucita Páez 982-548 076) popular network* open April – October with 38 beds (3 rooms). No kitchen but facilities include drink vending machine. Sympathetic conversion of traditional stone house by a Basque architect *(aitzenea is Basque for stone-house)*. Further up the main road is •**Albergue*** [5] *Refugio del Oribio* (Elvira Doval Pérez 982-548 085)

Albergue [2] *Complexo Xacobeo*

Albergue [4] *Aitzenea*

network* hostel in a modern building near the panadería. Open all year with 27 beds (2 rooms) and all facilities (no lounge). *[Next albergue: Samos – 11.7 km] or Alternative route: Calvor – 13.4 km].*

Other accommodation includes: •**García** Pr* Rúa Peregrino, 8. •**Casa Olga** (982-543 184) c/Rúa de Castro. At the lower end of town •**Hospedaje O'Novo** (982-548 105). •**Vilasante** Pr**(982-548 116) and opposite albergue [3] •**Casa David** Pr**(982-548105). The town has a variety of restaurants serving pilgrim menus.

TRIACASTELA town of the three castles, none of which survive (except on the coat of arms of the local council) an important stop for medieval pilgrims coming down off the mountain with several hospices and an extensive monastery (XIth stage in the Codex Calixtinus). It is no less an attractive stop today with a wide selection of bars, restaurants and hostels serving the increasing number of pilgrims passing through. The parish church is dedicated to Santiago and has an unusual 18th century tower on which is carved a relief of the three castles. Nearby are the quarries that provided the limestone used in the building of Santiago Cathedral. Medieval pilgrims would carry as much as they were able to the limekilns in Casteñeda (through which we pass during stage 31) and the pilgrim monument in the town square recognises this ancient tradition while acknowledging the rebirth of the camino – paying equal respect to both.

❏ **Happiness is a mystery, like religion, and should never be rationalised.**
———————————————————————————————— *G.K. Chesterton*

MAP 28 *142.3 km (88.4 miles) to Santiago de Compostela*

TRIACASTELA – SARRIA (via SAMOS)

	Path / Track	--- ---	12.9	---	*52%*
	Quiet Road	--- ---	11.1	---	*44%*
	Main Road	--- ---	1.0	---	*4%*
Total km	**Total distance**		**25.0 km** (15.5 miles)		

Adjusted for climb   26.0 km (accrued ascent 200m = to 1.0 km)
Alto ▲ High Point: Renche 690m (2,264 feet)

The Practical Path: When leaving Triacastela you must decide whether to go the southern route via Samos **recommended route [1]** or via San Xil the northern **alternative route [2]**. They both follow quiet country roads into Sarria. The San Xil route is shorter by 6.5 km but steeper and is supposedly the more traditional route but it now mostly follows an asphalt road. For this reason the southern or Samos route is the one recommended here and while it is longer it follows the delightful river Oribio. It also provides an opportunity to visit one of the oldest monasteries in Spain, the Benedictine monastery of Samos, which provides basic pilgrim accommodation. Be careful to distinguish the camino from local walks in this area that are waymarked *Senderismo de Sarria* as two of these walks connect with the Samos route, *Rutas de las Aceñas* and *de Aguiada a Samos* – indeed we walk part of the latter (in reverse) to rejoin the alternative route in Aguiada. Both routes are attractive and offer alternative accommodation along the way. **Intermediate accommodation** (distances from albergue [1]) Samos (11.7 km) – S. Mamed del Camino & Calvor (12.9 km) on alternative route.

———

❏ **The Mystical Path:** Will the winding river reveal her natural weir to you? The manmade example, that diverts water to the village mill, is no match for the beauty of this one. Will you rest awhile in the tiny Hobbit-like shelter whose entrance is shielded by the branches from the adjacent *castaño*? The unadorned beauty of this path remains largely undiscovered by officialdom. How long will it remain in its pristine state uncluttered by the trappings of man?

❏ **Personal Reflections** *"... The deepening silence of my journey coupled with a rare break in the downpour combine with the glorious Landscape Temple to create an overwhelming sense of well-being. I am entirely alone and yet I feel more connected to a larger way than at any other time in my life. The outer weather fades into insignificance as I open to an inner reality that seems more alive than anything on the level of form. My body is wet and cold for the umpteenth day in a row and yet I glow with an inner warmth as I sit under a dripping chestnut tree and contemplate the irrationality of it all. I am beginning to turn the conventional world on its head and everything suddenly becomes clearer. I feel at last I am turning towards Home ..."*

Xunta [40] **Albergue** 1.0

A

Lugo >

Cruce 2.7

i

A *A Pedra*

SARRIA
(Pop. 13,000 – Alt. 455m)

C-535

Carballal

San Pedro *do Camiño*

San Mamed del Camino

Albergue 1.4 → **A** ← 2.0 **Albergue**
Paloma y Leña **Priv.[30]**

Aguiada 3.2 → **Aguiada**

A ← 2.3 **Albergue**
Calvor *Xunta [22]*

río Sarria

LU-633

Aldea de Abajo ●

3.0 **Puente**

Casa Cines

C → **Pintín**

2.0 **Camino** *(río)*

† Texios

Furela 2.8 →

SAMOS

A ← 3.5 **Albergue** *Conv.[90]*

H

3.3 **Montán**

Alto do Ríocabo
920m ▲

Renche 2.5 →

San Cristobo 5.0 →

← 1.5 **San Xil**

Capilla S.Pedro → †

2.3
A Balsa

río Oribio

①

②

?

0.7 **Opción**
TRIACASTELA
(Pop. 900 – Alt. 675m)

O
Puesta
del Sol

N

S

E
Salida
del Sol

Xunta [82] **Albergue** 0.0 → **A**

Leaving albergue [1] in Triacastela proceed down through the town and at the far end we join the main road for decision time:

| 0.7 km | **Opción [?]** For **recommended route [1]** (via the monastery at Samos) we turn left out over the bridge. The road follows the river all the way to San Cristobo where we veer off right> just before the village:

| 5.0 km | **San Cristobo** traditional village occupying a lovely position on the bank of the river Oribio with its ancient weir and mill buildings. Cross over the river onto a delightful track that winds its way through mixed woodland following the meandering course of the río Oribio re-emerging onto the road at:

| 2.5 km | **Renche** with **[F]** and bar. Pick up a track and shortly before reaching Samos take a graffiti emblazoned tunnel under the road and continue down into the village (ignoring sign for *Samos por Freixo* which is 4 km *off* the route) into:

| 3.5 km | **Samos** the tiny village wraps itself around the enormous monastery in this peaceful river valley where time seems to stand still and the only thing in a hurry are the waters of the shallow Oribio rushing to join the río Miño. •**Albergue [1]** *Monasterio de Samos* (982-546 046) Benedictine hostel located to the rear of the main monastery building. Open all year with 90 beds in one

Samos Monastery & Rio Oribio

stark dormitory. Basic facilities only with no kitchen or lounge area. The simple austerity matches the surroundings and regular services take place throughout the day with Vespers at 19:30 in the chapel accessed also via a rear entrance. Regular tours of the monastery take place during the day. This is one of the oldest monastery's in the whole of the western world with one of the largest ground plans and cloisters in Spain. •**Albergue [2]** *Casiña de Madera* (653-824 546) new private hostel just outside the town beside the 1,000 years old cypress tree known as *La Capilla de Ciprés* and Capilla del Salvador 9th century. The hostel is open all year with 18 places and all modern facilities including a library and massage service. Other accommodation: •**Victoria** HsR* (982-546 022) on Rúa Salvador 4, opposite the albergue [1]. •**A Veiga** Hr* (982-546 052) on main road. Samos has several bars and restaurants.

We now follow the main road out of town (signposted Sarria) passing the roadside chapel in Teixos to look out [!] for the waymarks that direct us right> *up*hill. It is possible to follow the road all the way to Sarria at this point but the recommended route follows a delightful riverside walk to Aguiada (Calvor) on the alternative route.

| 2.0 km | **Camino** we now enter onto a gently undulating walk that follows the course of the tranquil river valley (this is also a local wayside walk) and while waymarks are somewhat obscure we basically follow the river to a sharp bend where the path crosses over and then back again just below the hamlet of Aldea de Abajo and:

| 3.0 km | **Puente** we continue over a small stream (tributary of the Río Sarria) all the way up to:

| 3.2 km | **Aguiada** where we join **alternative route [2]** coming from San Xil.

For alternative route [2] via San Xil at the option point (0.7 km from albergue [1] in Triacastela) turn right> and stay on the main road for **[1.6 km]** turning off <left for the **[0.7 km]** concrete access road into:

2.3 km   **A Balsa** pass the tiny chapel to Our Lady of the Snows *N. S. de las Nieves* (right) and continue up on a path through woodland for **[1.0 km]** to rejoin road **[F]** and scallop shell and continue by road for **[0.5 km]** into:

1.5 km   **San Xil** from here we begin the climb up and around alto do Riocabo (910m) the highest point of this day's stage and into:

3.3 km   **Montán** a path now brings us to Fontearcuda **[0.8 km]** (there is a short detour to visit the stone artwork at Mondaviega) continuing mostly on paths for **[2.0 km]** up into:

2.8 km   **Furela [F]** continue through the hamlet to Pintín **[0.8 km]** •**Casa Cines** (685-140 635) Pensión with 7 rooms and café/bar – proceed **[1.5 km]** to:

2.3 km   **Calvor** •**Albergue** Xunta hostel (982-531 266) in former school building located on the roadside. Open all year with 22 beds and all facilities. Continue to Aguiada **[0.5 km]** where the **recommended route** joins from the left.

A new pilgrim path has been installed alongside the road which we follow to:

1.4 km   **San Mamed del Camino** •**Albergue** new private hostel (Paloma y Leña 658-906 816) set back from the road and a veritable haven of peace. Open all year with 30 places (2 dormitories of 10 and 5 double rooms). Excellent modern facilities with dinner and breakfast available. Peaceful music fills the air and adds to a sense of calm. *¿porque no acqui?* Why not indeed! The path now follows the road through the hamlets of San Pedro do Camiño and Carballal all the way to the outskirts of Sarria.

Albergue – Paloma y Leña

2.7 km   **Vigo de Sarria** •**Albergue** *A Pedra* (José & Marta 982-530 130) private network* hostel, open all year with 15 places. All modern facilities in this recently restored period house. *Turismo* (982-530 099) helpful pilgrim advice centre with maps of the town and list of places to stay and walks and other activities in the area if you plan to stay an extra day. To get to the central pilgrim hostels and the old quarter proceed over the busy junction (rúa José Sanchez and Calvo Sotelo) into rúa

Albergue *A Pedra* & Turismo

do Peregrino that takes a wide curve to cross the río Sarria over puente Ribeira to turn right> in c/Benigno Quiroga and then <left by Spain's first specialist pilgrim shop *PeregrinoTeco* (982-530 190) where José welcomes pilgrims to come and browse books and equipment exclusive to pilgrims. Climb the ancient granite steps *Escalinata Maior* into the bottom end of rúa Maior, close to all amenities.

1.0 km   **Centro de Sarria** •**Albergue [1]** Xunta hostel (Maria Carmen Arias López 660-396 813) situated at the start of the old town at Nº 79 c/Mayor. Open all year with 40 beds and all facilities in a sympathetically restored period town house, lacking only an outside patio. Continuing up c/Maior at nº44 •**Albergue** [2] *O Durmiñento* (Raquel & Jorge 982-531 099) Private network* hostel open all year with 42 beds (dormitories + private rooms) and modern facilities including massage room *sala de masajes* (no kitchen) meals available. At nº57 •**Albergue** [3] *Internacional* (982-535 109) private hostel that opened its doors in 2008 to

Albergue [1] *Xunta*

offer 58 beds and all modern facilities including café and restaurant and lovely roof-top terrace. At nº31 •**Albergue** [4] *Los Blasones* (Aurora Gudín 600-512 565) private network* hostel open all year with 30 places in one dormitory and all facilities including a rear garden area. At nº10 •**Albergue** [5] *Don Álvaro* (Mónica López Castedo 982-531 592) private hostel open all year with 32 beds + individual rooms and all facilities including a pilgrim reading room with open fireplace off a pleasant patio garden. Just behind it in rúa Conde de Lemos, 23 is •**Albergue** [6] *Dos Oito Marabedís* private network* hostel (Adolfo 629-461 770) located in a modern terraced house with 19 places and all facilities.

Other accommodation: •**Casa Matías** Pr* (982-530 559) Calvo Sotelo,39 and at the far end of this main shopping street by the railway station •**Roma** H** (982-530 570) Calvo Sotelo 2, also nearby in c/Jose Antonio,39 is pensión •**Mar del Plata** (982-530 724). At the other end of town and price bracket is the modern hotel •**Alfonso IX** H*** (982-530 005) at rúa do Peregrino, 29 and more affordable •**Villa de Sarria** H* (982-533 873) on c/Benigno Quiroga, 49. The town has a wide selection of restaurants and bars with those around c/Maior offering pilgrim menus. A welcoming new pilgrim shop run by José •**Peregrino Teca** with extensive range of equipment, books and maps is now open directly on the camino at the start of the rua Maior.

Pilgrim Shop – *Peregrino Teca*

SARRIA with Celtic origins was a major medieval centre for pilgrims with several churches, chapels, monasteries and 7 pilgrim hospitals. The ancient atmosphere can still be felt in the attractive old quarter that climbs along the main street *rúa Maior* past Igrexa de Santa Mariña (*credenciales*) with its evocative pilgrim mural – on up to the ruined castle at the top *Fortaleza de Sarria*. The ancient convent *Mosterio da Madalena* has a fine plasteresque façade and leads down to the medieval bridge over the río Celerio (see next stage). The coming of the railway at the end of the 19th century pulled the town centre eastwards leaving the ancient *camino real* largely intact. Sarria is now a bustling modern town with a population of 12,000. It has become a major starting point for pilgrims with limited time but anxious to pick up a *compostela* at Santiago – starting from here will cover (just) the requisite 100 km to the cathedral which is the reason why there are so many pilgrim hostels in town. Pilgrims arrive via the busy bus and rail stations and from now on the route becomes crowded with the new arrivals. Many hostels provide a backpack *mochila* transport service. *Note:* Beware for any sign of resentment at such intrusion on 'my' camino – remember that many of the new arrivals may be nervous starting out and the last thing such a person needs is aloofness built on a false sense of superiority. A loving pilgrim welcomes all they meet along the path – without judgement.

SALIDA

Ponte Áspera →

río Celeiro

Camiño Francés

San Roque

Cementerio

Mosteiro da Madalena
(credencial)

Estación Ferrocarril

rúa José Antonio

Roma

H

Parque
Do
Bosque

Campo da Feira

Castelo (Ruinas)

Torre

rúa da Mercede

rúa do Castelo

† Cruceiro

Sarmiento

El Salvador A

Dos Oito Marabedis [20]

Don Álvaro [32] A

Meson Camiño Francés

Taberna Lopez

Los Blasones [30] A

Concello

O'Durmiñento [44] A

A **Internacional** [58]

† **Santa Mariña**
(credencial)

rúa Nova

rúa de Valvo Sotelo

Casa Matías
C

rúa Matias López

Estación de Autobuses
(Santiago via Lugo)

rúa Maior

A **Xanta** [40]

rúa Matias López

Escalinata Maior →

rúa Benigno Quiroga

Peregrino Teca (Equipamiento)

SARRIA
(Pop. 13,000 – Alt. 455m)

Oca Villa H

Ferreiro

rúa Diego Pazos

Río Sarria

Malecón

Campo do río

rúa de Valvo Sotelo

Río Sarria

H
Alfonso IX***

Rúa do Peregrino

O

Puesta
del Sol

S ——— N

Rest. Giovannino

i **Turismo**

A **A Pedra** [15]

Salida
del Sol

E

ENTRADA ↗

❒ **To err is human, to forgive, divine.** *Alexander Pope*

MAP 29 *117.7 km (73.1 miles) to Santiago de Compostela*

SARRIA – PORTOMARÍN

▬▬▬	Path / Track	--- ---	10.6	--- *46%*
▬▬▬	Quiet Road	--- ---	12.3	--- *54%*
▬▬▬	Main Road	--- ---	0.0	
Total km	**Total distance**		**22.9 km** (14.2 miles)	

Adjusted for climb   24.4 km (accrued ascent 300m = 1.5 km)
Alto ▲ High Point: Cruce / Mominetos (660m)

The Practical Path: Today's stage is spread equally between quiet country roads and natural pathways. Apart from the bare flanks around the Peña do Cervo at Momientos (above Portomarín) much of this stage is along tree-lined roads and pathways. So we have good shade from the sun or shelter from the driving rain. We will pass through many small hamlets that seem to blend seamlessly one into the next but few offer any facilities so bring some provisions. **Intermediate accommodation** (distances from albergue [1] in Sarria): Barbadelo (4.3 km) – Morgade (12.0 km) – Ferrerios (13.6 km) – Mercadoiro (17.5 km).

❒ **The Mystical Path:** Two ancient Orders occupied opposite sides of this river but their strongholds are long gone – buried under the floodwaters created by the dam to serve the insatiable demands of a new generation. We cannot live in the past and we try in vain to live with the idea of some future golden age. The only place we can truly inhabit is the present. The rest is fantasy – some painful, some pleasurable – both deceptive.

❒ **Personal Reflections:** *"… I reflect on the extraordinary revelation of the third secret of Fatima. We are all fallen angels struggling to find our wings so that we can fly back home to the Divine. If God is my Father what does that make me and, by extension, all my fellow brothers and sisters? We each share the same Identity and the same Inheritance. And so I come full circle, back to the place where I began and to the realisation that the only way out – is in. The only way off the mortal coil is through the total forgiveness of self, other and the world. That is why external authority must collapse. The Voice for God is within and urges each one of us, as children of one God, to become the authors of own awakening …"*

Leaving albergue [1] in Sarria head up c/Mayor past the church of Santa Mariña (right) with its interesting, if somewhat sombre, medieval pilgrim murals and past the town hall *Casa do Concello* (so called in Galicia as opposed to ayuntamiento in the rest of Spain) which has a small information office. Opposite is the popular pilgrim Taberna Lopez and towards the top of the street (left) is the 13th century Church of St. Saviour *Igrexa de San Salvador* that

río Miño

Xunta [160] →A

PORTOMARÍN
(Pop. 2,000 – Alt. 420m)

A A

2.1 **Albergues** *Mirador* **Priv.***[27]
Ferramenteiro **Priv.***[120]

C-535

Vilchá 3.3 →

Embalse de Belesar

río Miño

Parrocha

Loio †

Moutrás

Albergue 3.9 →A **Mercadoiro**
Jose **Priv.[20]**

LU-613

Paradela

río Loio

Cruce Momientos

Peña do Cervo

Rozas

Pena

Piedra F

Arroyo Ferrerios

Mirallos

Páramo
▲ *880m*

FERRERIOS A 1.6 **Albergue** *Xunta* [22]

Morgade 3.9 →C † *Capilla*
Casa Morgade • *km 99.5 !*

Brea

Casal

Lavandeira

Cortiñas

Peruscallo

Velante †

← 3.8 **Leimán/Pena**

C-535

F

Mercado de Serra

Casa Nova da Rente C

A *Casa Carmen* **Priv.[12]**

Santiago † A 3.1 **Albergue** *Xunta* [18]

BARBADELO

Vilei

río Celeiro

< Ourense

C-546

Ponte Áspera 1.2

Lugo >

C-546

SARRIA
(Pop. 13,000 – Alt. 455m)

A ← 0.0 **Albergue** *Xunta* [40]

O

*Puesta
del Sol*

S ——— N

*Salida
del Sol*

E

has a lovely Romanesque tympanum over the main door. Adjacent was St. Anthony's Hospice *Hospital de San Anton* (now courts of Justice) and here we turn right> to pass the ruins of the 13th century Sarria castle Fortaleza de Sarria (left) only one of the 4 original towers remains. The castle was destroyed during the uprising of the peasantry against the aristocracy in the 15th century known as the *Irmandiños*. We pass a stone *cruceiro* (right) with fine views back over the town and up past the country market *Campo da Feira* (left) which has existed here since the 14th century and down to the plasteresque façade of the Mosteiro da Madalena originally instituted in the 13th century, later coming under the Augustinian rule. We finally head down past the ruins of the Capela de San Lázaro making our way across the main road and over the río Celeiro at:

1.2 km | **Ponte Áspera** 'Rough Bridge' which describes its coarsely cut stone. A path now continues between the river and railway before crossing the line in the area known as San Miguel *Santi Michaelis*. The path then crosses a stream and climbs up through delightful ancient woodland to join the road in Vilei **[2.2 km]** for the remaining **[0.9 km]** into:

3.1 km | **Barbadello** Xunta •Albergue (982-530 412 Cruz González 686-744 048) another former school building open all year with 18 beds and all facilities. Opposite the albergue is the Romanesque *Igrexa de Santiago* with an interesting tympanum over the entrance door. The area is known locally as Mosteiro in reference to a monastery founded here as early as the 9th century. Behind the albergue is

Albergue *Xunta*

an 'outdoor' summer café and at the top of the road (200m) the popular •**Casa de Carmen** (Pedro Xosé Quintana 982-532 294) with pilgrim dormitory for 10 and several other private rooms. Home cooking available in this restored 17th century farmhouse with adjoining chapel of San Silvestre and outside terrace.

Continue along road through woodland to Rente with Casa Rural •**Casa Nova de Rente** (982-187 854) with 6 double rooms. We now find ourselves on delightful wooded pathways through ancient oak and chestnut groves to Mercado de Serra and just beyond the village **[F]** we continue on paths to cross the main Sarria to Portomarín road into:

3.8 km | **Peruscallo** with bar-restaurant and, being close to the main road and Sarria, one of the few villages in the area that has seen any modernisation. Off the route (1 km left) is another Romanesque Church at Velante. We now pass a series of tiny hamlets through Cortiñas and Brea and passing an official marker post indicating 99.5 km to Santiago, into:

3.9 km | **Morgade** •**Casa Morgade** (982-531 250) popular café and restaurant with rooms. Just beyond the village is a tiny stone chapel (now used as a source of pilgrim messaging) and we continue on a rough track down and through the Ferreiros stream. This is rural Galicia at her best; wet and green with the sweet smell and squelch of liquid cow dung underfoot. Narrow laneways with granite stepping-stones raised above normal flood levels and another gentle climb up to:

Casa Morgade

1.6 km Ferreiros Xunta•Albergue (Primitiva
Galloso 686-744 940). Open all year with 22
beds and all facilities in another schoolhouse
conversion set in a leafy glade. Ferreiros was
formerly known for its blacksmith tradition
from which its name is derived. Popular
pilgrim café on the corner. Continue down
the shallow river valley to Mirallos with café/
restaurant adjoining the Romanesque Church

Albergue *Xunta*

of Santa María de Ferreiros and just beyond it (also on the left) an ancient marker.
Proceed up along the road passing **[F]** and the hamlets of Pena, Couto, Rozas **[F]**
and the high point at Peña do Cervo (660m – fine views) after which we begin to
descend towards the río Miño and its reservoir through Moimentos into:

3.9 km Mercadoiro / Moutras •Albergue
La Bodeguiña (José 676-476 260) new private
hostel opened in 2008 with 25 places and all
facilities – part of the adjoining café-restaurant
with pilgrim menu in this delightful hamlet
with an official population of – one! Continue
through a string of tiny hamlets including
Moutras and A Parrocha and just off the route
to the left is the remote and beautiful valley of
Loio with the ruins of the Monastery of Santa
María de Loio – birthplace of the Order of
Santiago in the 12th century.

Albergue /Café *La Bodeguiña*

3.3 km Vilachá. We now follow the course of the road and make our way over
the modern bridge into Portomarín. The original bridge was of Roman origin
and joined the southern district of San Pedro with its links to the Knights of
Santiago with the northern district of San Nicolás headquarters of the Knights
of Saint John. The river formed a major strategic boundary and consequently
the area had a turbulent past. The steep staircase in front is part of the original
medieval bridge across the river Miño. These lead up to the arch and Chapel of
Santa María de las Nieves which, along with several other historic monuments,
were all removed to the high ground around Portomarín when the dam was built
across the river to create the Belesar reservoir in 1962. Climb the stairs in front
of you and turn <left into Rúa Chantada for the new albergues.

2.1 km Portomarín convenient •Albergue
[1] *Ferramenteiro* (Iván 982-545 362) a new
private network* hostel with 120 beds and
excellent modern facilities in this new building
overlooking the river. Measurements are shown
to and from this readily accessible hostel.

Albergue [1] *Ferramenteiro*

Albergue [2] *O Mirador*

Adjoining *Ferramenteiro* is •Albergue **[2]** *O
Mirador* (982-545 323) another new network*
hostel and pensión with great view over the
river and reservoir. Open all year with 27
places and panoramic bar and restaurant with
access also from the main square above.

The centre of the town and action is up at the top end ½ kilometre away. Continue up the cobbled main street *rúa Xeral Franco* with its handsome stone colonnades. Pass the tourist information (left) at the corner of the main square *Praza Conde de Fenosa* in the centre of which is the somewhat austere 12th century Romanesque church of San Nicolás, sometimes referred to as San Juan or San Xoán due to its links with the Knights of Saint John. It was painstakingly rebuilt from its original site now submerged under the reservoir and is ascribed to the workshop of Master Mateo who carved the Portico de Gloria in Santiago. At the back of the square are the handsome *Casa do Concello* and *Correos*.

A variety of cafés, restaurants and pensiones surround the square including •**Albergue** [3] *El Caminante* (Asunción López 982-545 176) private hostel located on c/Rúa Sánchez Carro. Open Easter–October with 48 places including private rooms limited facilities (no kitchen but microwave) and at the far end •**Albergue** [4] *Xunta* hostel (Tina Vázquez 982-545 143) carratera de Lugo. Open all year with 100 beds in 4 rooms and all modern facilities in this renovated (original) hostel. *[Next albergue: Gonzar – 8.2 km].*

Albergue [4] *Xunta*

Other accommodation: **Fonda/Café Posada del Camino** (982-545 081) in the centre square with restaurant (see photo) also nearby •**Taberna Pérez** (982-545 040) •**Pensión Manuel** Rúa do Miño. •**Villajardín** H* (982-545 200) Rúa do Miño, 14. •**Pensión Arenas** Pr** (982-545 386) Praza Condes Fenosa, 5. •**Portomiño** P (982-547 575) c/ Sánchez Carro, 23 and at the top end of town and price bracket: •**Pousada de Portomarín** H*** (982-545 200) adjacent to the attractive Parque Antonio Sanz and nearby Church of Saint Peter *Iglesia San Pedro* with fine Romanesque doorway.

REFLECTIONS:

❏ **The foolish man seeks happiness in the distance; the wise man grows it under his feet.** *J R Oppenheimer*

MAP 30 *94.8 km (58.9 miles) to Santiago de Compostela*

PORTOMARÍN – PALAS DE REI

	Path / Track	--- ---	11.5	---	*44%*
	Quiet Road	--- ---	14.0	---	*54%*
	Main Road	--- ---	0.6	---	*2%*
Total km	**Total distance**		**26.1 km**	*(16.2 miles)*	

Adjusted for climb   28.3 km (accrued ascent 450m = 2.2 km)
Alto ▲ High Point: Sierra Ligonde 720m (2,362 feet)

The Practical Path: A day of varied terrain as we start by skirting the reservoir *Embalse de Belesar* climbing up through woodland to play hide and seek with the main road before leaving it to climb the ridge beyond Ventas de Narón *Sierra Ligonde*, dropping down to Portos which offers us the detour to Vilar de Donas. Then comes a gentler climb around the side of Rosary Heights *Alto Rosario* to drop down finally to Palas de Rei. Prepare for an early start if you intend to take the detour to Vilas de Donas. **Intermediate accommodation** (distances from albergue [1] in Portomarín): Gonzar (8.2 km) – Hospital de la Cruz (12.7) – Ligonde (17.1 km) – Eirexe (18.4 km) – Portos (20.6 km).

❏ **The Mystical Path:** Will you make time to detour to this mystical resting place of the Knights of Saint James? Here effigies of the knights in their armour are watched over by the beautiful frescoes that adorn the walls of this sacred temple dedicated to Saint Saviour. A pilgrim must travel on two paths simultaneously. The tourist will look for the stone altar – the pilgrim an altered state. The one seeks sacred sites – the other in-sight. Will you make time today to detour into the inner mystery?

❏ **Personal Reflections:** *"... The incessant rain pounds down as heavy as when it started a week ago. The country is awash; roads have turned to rivers – rivers to torrents. I sat for a while at the base of the ancient oak and felt its solid support and in the same instant knew that my period of silence was ended. I don't know how long I been in this altered state, induced as much by physical exhaustion as any ecstatic revelation. And I don't know how long they had been there but they helped me to my feet and we embraced in love and respect for the experiences we had each invoked; 3 pilgrims from 3 different countries with 3 different languages but part of one family. I found it hard to speak after such a long spell of silence but I managed to say 'bless you' realising that with every breath I send out positive or negative vibrations. Regardless of outer conditions I can choose to send out love. Until that moment I had not noticed the ancient wayside cross silently witnessing this loving meeting of fellow pilgrims ..."*

Buen Camino Priv.*[41] **Albergue** 1.2 →Ⓐ

PALAS DE REI (Pop. 4,500 – Alt. 575m)

Ⓗ

Xunta [60]

Centro Deportivo Ⓐ← 3.9 **Albergue**

Xunta [80] Pavillón Os Chacotes

Rosario

Alto do Rosario

Brea

Mamurria

Vilar de Donas [2.3 km]

Valos

N-547

San Salvador

Casa A Calzada Priv. [10] **Albergue** 2.5 →Ⓐ

Portos

< Monterroso LU - 221

< Monterroso

Ⓗ *Pension Mesón*

EIREXE Ⓐ← 0.9 **Albergue**

Xunta [20]

Xunta [18] **Albergue** 3.6 →Ⓐ

LIGONDE

Lameiros

Sierra Ligonde 750m

■ Perrera

N-640

VENTAS DE NARÓN

O Cruceiro Priv*[25] **Albergue** 1.3 →Ⓐ

Ⓒ *Casa Molar Priv.[20]*

Xunta [22] **Albergue** 4.5 →Ⓐ

HOSPITAL

N-540 Lugo >

< Ourense N-540

Castromaior

Xunta [20] **Albergue** 5.2 →Ⓐ

GONZAR

Casa García Priv.*[20]→Ⓐ

O *Puesta del Sol*

S

N

Salida del Sol

E

□ Toxibó

Fábrica 3.0 →■

PORTOMARÍN (Pop. 2,000 – Alt. 425m)

Ⓐ← 0.0 **Albergue**

Embalse de Belesar *Pasarela*

Ferramenteiro* [120] Mirador*[27]

Leaving Portomarín return to the stairs of Our Lady of the Snows *Escalinata N. S das Neves* and turn right> to pass the petrol station and <left over the footbridge *pasarela* río Torres. We now make our way up through dense woodland around St. Anthony's height *alto San Antonio* to join the main road at:

3.0 km **Fabrica cerámica** where we cross over the road onto the modern *senda* before crossing back over again for the path into Toxibó. We continue parallel to the road and rejoin it **[F]** for the stretch into:

5.2 km **Gonzar** •**Albergue [1]** *Xunta* hostel (María Elisa Fente 982-157 840) bleak location on the main road but recently refurbished (see photo). Open all year with 20 beds and all facilities – the hospitalera lives next door.

•**Albergue [2]** *Casa Garcia* (982-157 842) new network hostel in beautifully renovated village house with central courtyard bar and restaurant (see photo). Open all year with 26 places including private rooms. On the main road is another café/bar and just beyond it we turn off <left onto minor road and then right> onto track before joining road into Castromaior (originally a Celtic castro) with its tiny Romanesque church of Santa María and a café. Continue through the village up to:

Albergue [1] Xunta *(above)*
Albergue [2] Casa Garcia *(below)*

4.5 km **Hospital de la Cruz** where the main road cuts rudely through this ancient village – its medieval pilgrim hospice no longer visible, but hospitality awaits us at the enterprising farmyard conversion (left) where *sopa caliente y bocadillos* are available from the obliging hostess and just beyond it restaurant El Labrador and then Xunta •**Albergue** (Digna 982-545 232) another conversion of a school building by the main road. Open all year with 22 beds in 2 rooms. All facilities. The main road is on a blind bend at this point (N-540 Ourense – Lugo cutting) but a minor road continues across to the next village.

1.3 km **Ventas de Narón** •**Albergue [1]** *Casa Molar* (Avenencio Fernández Rodríguez 696-794 507) an attractively renovated rural house with 22 places including 2 private rooms. Good facilities (no kitchen) but restaurant and bar.
•**Albergue [2]** *O Cruceiro* (Adelina Vázquez 658-064 917) new network* hostel open all year with 25 places good facilities (no kitchen) but restaurant and bar. The area was scene of a bloody battle in 840 between Moor and Christian but there is nothing here now to disturb the peace beyond pilgrim chatter in the 2 cafés and the tiny stone chapel *Capela de Magdalene* with picnic area adjoining. Now we start to climb the Sierra Ligonde to the highest point of today's route (720m) passing dog kennels *perrera* before dropping down to:

Albergue [1] Casa Molar *(above)*
Albergue [2] O'Cruceiro *(below)*

3.6 km **Ligonde** Xunta •**Albergue** [1] *Escuela de Ligonde* skilfully restored hostel with 22 spaces and all facilities. •**Albergue** [2] *Fuente del Peregrino* (982-183 752) Private hostel with 10 places and basic facilities – open summer only. Ligonde was formerly a significant medieval stop on the way. Charlemagne reputedly stayed here and it had a pilgrim hospice. The church is

Albergue [1] – Ligonde

dedicated to Santiago and has a Romanesque porch. We now follow the road down and across the río Ligonde passing Casa Mari Luz (bar/restaurant only) and up to the village of:

0.9 km **Eirexe** Xunta •**Albergue** (982-153 483) converted school building at village crossroads. Open all year with 18 beds and all facilities – keys with hospitalera María Paz. Also around the village green are: •**Pensión Mesón** and Bar-restaurant Conde Valdemar. Continue on quiet country road passing splendid 17th century wayside cross (left) by gnarled oak tree and the ancient hamlet of

Albergue – *Eirexe*

Lameiros with its diminutive capela San Marcos, through Portos to:

2.5 km **A Calzada - Detour** •**Albergue** *A Calzada* (982-183 744) new private hostel with 10 places in separate stone pavilion at the rear (see photo right) of the bar-restuaruant on the camino. Delightful peaceful gardens and picnic area.

Detour: Vilar de Donas recommended detour (4.4 km there and back) to this national monument and ancient seat of the Knights of Santiago. Closed Mondays and holidays (check with the albergue in A Calzada for opening times before proceeding there). The Church of El Salvador is primarily 14th century but its origins go back to the formation of a nunnery here in the 10th century (hence the appellation Donas). Its unique frescoes and stone effigies of the knights are hauntingly impressive.

Directions: Turn right off the camino (opposite A Calzada) along quiet country lane across the main road **[1.0 km]** (N-547 Palas de Rei – Lugo) passing rest area *área de descanco* (right) for remaining **[1.2 km]** to:

2.3 km **Vilar de Donas – Igrexa San Salvador**. Take time to soak in its ancient history and to savour its treasures lovingly attended by the knowledgeable guardian. Return the same way.

Vilar de Donas
tombs of the knights.

From A Calzada continue along pathways into and through the hamlets of Lestedo, Valos, Mamurria and Brea up to:

| 3.9 km | **Albergue / Alto Rosario** here the camino meets up with the busy N-547. On a clear day you can see the sacred peak above Santiago *Pico Sacro* and on entering the hamlet of Rosario pilgrims would start to recite the Rosary, hence the name. Beside the road is an old school building *Casa Peregrino* now thankfully abandoned in favour of the ultra-modern *Pavillón* just below it overlooking the wide recreation area. Xunta •**Albergue** *Os Chacotes* with 100 places in 2 enormous

Albergue – *Os Chacotes*

dormitories packed tightly with bunk beds. Good modern facilities – the design is so new they even invented a new description *Pavillón de Peregrinos*.

We now pass a holiday centre with timber clad bungalows and hotel Las Cabanas and the town sports stadium to enter:

| 1.2 km | **Palas de Rei** Xunta •**Albergue [1]** (María García 982-374 126) prominently located at main road junction in praza Concello, directly opposite the Town Hall. Open all year with 60 beds in 6 rooms and basic facilities – somewhat neglected but popular on account of its central position.

Albergue [1] *Xunta*

•**Albergue [2]** *Buen Camino* (982-380 233) new network* hostel in converted town house on the lower square. Open all year with 41 rooms and all facilities. *[Next albergue: Mato Casanova – 6.3 km].*

Other accommodation: Hostal •**Casa Curro** P* (982-380 044) Av. Ourense. Hotel •**Casa Benilde** Hr* (982-380 717) c/del Mercado. Pensión Bar •**Guntina** Pr* (982-380 080) on Travesia do Peregrino. The Av. de Compostela has a selection of pensions and hotels that includes: •**Vilariño** Hs* (982-380 152).

Albergue [2] Buen Camino

Palas de Rei stands directly on the way but little remains to remind us of its illustrious past. The Church of San Tirso has a Romanesque portal and scallop shell motifs are visible in the town. Today, it is an administrative centre with good modern facilities serving a population of 2,000. The regular Lugo – Santiago bus stops here and if you didn't take the detour to Vilar de Donas you can always share a taxi from at this juncture.

REFLECTIONS:

❏ **Walking, I am listening to a deeper way. Suddenly all my ancestors are behind me. 'Be still, they say. Watch and listen. You are the result of the love of thousands'.** *Linda Hogan*

MAP 31 *68.7 km (42.7 miles) to Santiago de Compostela*

PALAS DE REI – RIBADISO (ARZÚA)

▬▬▬	Path / Track	--- ---	19.3 ---	73%
▬▬▬	Quiet Road	--- ---	5.6 ---	21%
▬▬▬	Main Road	--- ---	1.5 ---	6%
Total km	**Total distance**		**26.4 km** (16.4 miles)	

Adjusted for climb   27.1 km (accrued ascent 150m = 0.7 km)

Alto ▲ High Point: Palas de Rei 605m (1,984 feet)

The Practical Path: Today we cross 6 shallow river valleys and a glorious 73% is on pathways mostly through woodland that helps to keep the noise of traffic down and energy levels up. Melide makes a good half way stop where you can try its renowned octopus dishes *pulpo Galega* for lunch if you are continuing to Ribadiso. If you intend to detour off the route to visit the magnificent Pambre Castle or the famous Pazo Ulloa you need to leave early in the morning. **Intermediate accommodation**: San Xulián 3.6 km – Mato-Casanova 6.3 km – Leboreiro 9.7 km – Melide 15.3 km.

❏ **The Mystical Path:** Will you see the tiny representation of Santiago in the flyover? He appears at the entrance and the exit, welcoming us and blessing us on our way. What does he represent to you and why do we follow his way? Is it to revere his relics that may lie in a silver casket two days ahead? Is that what brought you this far? Do you believe he chose to martyr his earthly body so we could venerate it? He has many names, but who was he really and what significance does he play in our story? What unknown hand beckons us to follow in the way of the true Master? Where will we find Him?

❏ **Personal Journal:** *"... Every moment of every day I sense my guides setting up situations for me to learn the next lesson. I have an image of adoring angels aching for me to learn through grace rather than grit. But the lesson will be integrated in perfect timing and with exquisite precision for the exact amount of sand required to produce the pearl. Not one grain too many, but, alas, not one grain too few. So my angelic escort set me up Oshio, just when I had lost my inner way and was confused as to my motivation. And he asks me three questions: each one a reminder of my reason for doing this pilgrimage and an invaluable aid to its accomplishment. How, in heaven's name, did they conceive of a Japanese Shinto grandfather to place on the earthly path of a lost Christian soul? ..."*

Xunta [48] A A
H **ARZÚA**
(Pop. 7,000 – Alt. 390m)

Río Iso

Tunél
N-547 **RIBADISO**
A 5.4 **Albergue** *Xunta [70]*

Portela

Castañeda

Embalse de Portodemouros

Río Boente

Boente 5.7 F H †
Os Albergue [10]

Raído

Puesta del Sol
O
Arroyo San Lázaro
S
N
Salida del Sol
E

Ponte de Penas

Carballal

A 1.8 **Albergue** *Xunta [130]*
H **MELIDE**
(Pop. 8,000 – Alt. 460m)

A Coruña >
C-540

† *Cruceiro Antigua*
H *San Pedro*
† **FURELOS**
Puente 3.8

Río Furelos

< *Ourense C-540*

Parque Empresarial

Disecabo

Muni.[20] **Lobreiro** 3.4 → A

Cornixa

Río Seco

Campanilla

Castillo Pambre

Porto de Bois
N-547

A CORUÑA

LUGO

A 2.7 **Mato-Casanova**
†

Pazo Ulloa ⌂

Casa Domingo **Priv.*** *[14]* A
Ponte Campaña Mato

SAN XULIÁN
Albergue 3.6 → A †
O Abrigadoiro **Priv.[12]**

río Pambre

Buen Camino **Priv.*** [41] **Albergue** 0.0 → A
Xunta [60] A
PALAS de REI
(Pop. 4,500 – Alt. 575m)

Leaving the albergue in Palas de Rei continue down the street past the monument and field of the pilgrims *Campo dos Romeiros* where medieval pilgrims gathered for the journey to Santiago and onto a path that avoids a short stretch of the main road which we cross and re-cross several times before reaching:

3.6 km San Xulián do Camiño with its tiny 12th century parish church and the welcoming •**Albergue** *O Abrigadoiro* (Minerva Gómez 676-596 975). Open all year with 16 places. No kitchen but dinner and breakfast available. The path continues down to the Rió Pambre that we cross at Ponte Campaña-Mato **[1.6 km]** and •**Albergue** *Casa Domingo* (Gonzalo & Ana 982-163 226) network* hostel open from May – October with 14 places in renovated farm-steading occupying a tranquil rural setting on the river. Good facilities (no kitchen but meals available). The route now climbs gently through ancient oak woods for **[1.1 km]** to:

Albergue *Casa Domingo*

2.7 km Mato-Casanova •**Albergue** (Mari Carmen 982-173 483) the last Xunta hostel in Lugo before we enter into A Coruña. Open all year with 20 places and all facilities. Directly on the road but in a quiet rural location surrounded by woodland. We proceed down the Pass of the Oxen *Porto de Bois* (scene of a bloody battle between warring nobility) and then up to Campanilla before crossing over the provincial border at an unsightly scrapyard in Cornixa.

Detour: Castillo de Pambre and **Pazo de Ulloa**. 2 km along the quiet country road we have just joined is the impressive 14th century Castillo de Pambre. Strategically situated on the río Pambre it has survived the advances of time and the Irmandiños revolt (the war in which the aristocracy were fighting the peasants rather than each other) but is currently engaged in a dispute between private ownership and public access. Unlike its counterpart in Sarria, the four corner towers and inner keep are still proudly standing. 2 km further still is the Palacio Villamayor de Ulloa one of the best-preserved Galician manor houses *Pazos* and setting for the novel *Los Pazos de Ulloa* by Emilia Pardo Bazán (only available in Spanish). Accommodation is available in •**Albergue Turístico** *A Bolboreta* (Montse 609-124 717) situated between the camino at Mato-Casanova and the castle. Bunk beds or private room and all meals available.

At Cornixa we join the N-547 briefly before picking up the paved pathway into:

3.4 km Leboreiro *field of hares* •**Albergue** (Petra Folla 981-507 351) basic (if colourful) municipal hostel adjoining the main road you may have to enquire locally for the hospitalera and key. Open all year with 20 places on mattresses with all basic facilities but only one w. c. The village itself is further on, just off the main road and retains a medieval atmosphere. 13th century Romanesque Church of Santa María with a lovely carved stone tympanum of Virgin and Child over the main door. The house opposite with armorial shield was formerly a pilgrim hostel donated by the wealthy Ulloa (*pazo*) family. We now cross the medieval Magdalena Bridge over the río Seco into Disicabo. The path continues up towards the main road and over a footbridge to join a mercifully short stretch of senda separating the N-547 from an industrial estate Parque Empresarial, where the Knights and Dames of the Way of St. James *Orde de Caballeros y Damas del Camino de Santiago* have erected a monument to themselves. We now make our way down through woodland to:

3.8 km **Ponte Velha – Furelos** magnificent medieval bridge over the río Furelos into the old village of Furelos with the church of San Juan, a Bar and taberna. No trace is left of the pilgrim hospice that used to adjoin the church (but a replacement hostel is planned). From here we begin the climb up to Melide through its rather haphazard modern suburbs. The route brings us to the main road opposite the Romanesque Church of San Pedro & San Roque beside its famous 14th century stone Cross reputed to be the oldest in Galicia *Crucero do Melide*, Christ in majesty facing us and Christ crucified on the reverse.

We now make our way up past the main square (left) to the busy cross roads *Ronda de la Coruña* and cross over into the old town. Here around the central square *Plaza del Convento* we find the austere parish church, Sancti Spiritus, formerly a 14th century Augustinian monastery. Opposite was the hospice de Sancti Spiritus that served the Jacobean pilgrimage. This is the point where pilgrims travelling down from Oviedo on the original pilgrim route *camino Primitivo* join the *camino Francés*. In the Casa Municipal is an interesting museum and displays of the traditional life of this part of Galicia *Museo Etnográfico*. It is now only a short walk down the rúa de San Antonio to:

1.8 km **Melide** attractive Xunta •**Albergue** (Concepción Amo Diaz 660-396 822) Rúa San Antonio close to plaza del Convento at the edge of the old town. Open all year with 130 places in 9 dormitories + summer overflow on mattresses. All modern facilities and outside patio area.

Other Accommodation: The central Hostal •**Xaneiro I** (981-505 015) on rúa San Pedro and its more modern counterpart •**Xaneiro II** Hs** (981-506 140) Av. de la Habana, 43. Hostales •**El Molina** on Rúa Rosalía and •**Estilo II** on c/del Progreso (981-505 153). •**Sony** (981-506 473) Lugar de Codeseira and the only hotel •**Carlos** Hr* (981-507 633) modern building on Av. de Lugo, 119.

MELIDE a prosperous administrative town with a population of 8,000. The old part follows its medieval layout with narrow winding streets with shops, bars and restaurants serving the regional speciality, octopus *pulpo*. One of the best-known speciality restaurants *pulperías* is Exequiel on Av.de Lugo on the way into town. Passing behind the albergue we make our way through the back streets down into the western suburbs of Santa María de Melide with its Romanesque church dating from the 12th century *Igrexa Santa María de Melide*. The interior is delightful with inspiring frescoes above the altar. We now leave the busyness of Melide and the N-547 (sign for San Martiño) and make our way across the arroyo San Lázaro (the remains of the leprosy hospice long disappeared).

Our way is now mostly by path that winds through shaded forest, oak and chestnut now increasingly giving way to eucalyptus and pine. We cross myriad river valleys during these final stages so our path is more arduous than the contour plans might suggest. *Ultreya!* Continue by Carballal and Ponte de Pena and across the río Raído and up through the village to:

5.7 km **Boente** Igrexa Santiago with images of the Saint. •**Os Albergue's Mesón** (Josefina Mariano 981-501 853) 10 places with basic facilities. Stone cross and drinking font **[F]** 2nd bar and restaurant on main road which we now leave through the underpass down into the steep Boente valley and up the other side to join minor road into Castañeda with the parish Church of Santa María. It was here that the pilgrims would deposit the limestone rocks they had brought from Triacastela to be fired for the lime used in the building of the Cathedral at Santiago. Shop and bar just off the camino also •**Casa Rural Milía** (981-515 241). From here we go around a wooded hill and across a raised pass over the N-547 through more woodland to pick up minor road down to the fine medieval bridge over the río Iso to:

5.4 km **Ribadiso** Xunta •**Albergue** idyllic location on the river Iso adjoining the medieval bridge. Open all year with 62 places + room for the differently-abled *minusválidos*. All facilities are provided (toilets located in a separate building) and pleasant space to relax on the riverbank (weather permitting). This is a wonderful reconstruction of one of the oldest pilgrim hospitals still in existence, with an award for environmental architecture. Bar and restaurant close by. *[Next albergue: Arzúa – 2.0 km]*.

Albergue & Río Iso

REFLECTIONS:

❏ **Let no one ever come to you without leaving better and happier.**

Mother Teresa

MAP 32 *42.3 km (26.3 miles) to Santiago de Compostela*

RIBADISO – ARCA DO PINO

	Path / Track --- ---	14.7 ---	*66%*
	Quiet Road --- ---	2.7 ---	*12%*
	Main Road --- ---	4.8 ---	*22%*
Total km	**Total distance**	**22.2 km** (13.8 miles)	

Adjusted for climb   23.0 km (accrued ascent 160m = 0.8 km)
Alto ▲ High Point: Palas de Rei 590m (1,935 feet)

The Practical Path: 2/3rds of today we walk on natural pathways with good shade offered by the ubiquitous eucalyptus. We start with a climb up into Arzúa and end with a climb around the alto de Santa Irene. In between we have a largely level path with just 3 shallow river valleys. **Intermediate accommodation**: Arzúa (2.0 km) – Santa Irene (19.1 km)

❏ **The Mystical Path:** The beautiful memorial to Guillermo Watt is timely. What plans have *we* made for our onward journey? Or are we too preoccupied with the dramas of this life to consider the next? To contemplate the impermanence of our earthly form can be revitalising, urging us to make every step a prayer for understanding, every breath a song of gratitude, every moment a chance to awaken from the dream that keeps us separate from our eternal Source.

❏ **Personal Reflections:** *"… The debate had become heated, the only seeming accord being that the problems that beset our world were real and worsening. She had remained silent but now took the rare moment of quiet to state with utter conviction, 'There is only one solution'. Her words struck a chord – what that might be? 'Allah' she replied. The response was so penetrating that we were completely silenced. We had been looking for solutions on the level of the problem – our human condition of fear. She was a Sufi devotee. I laugh at the paradox that it took a Muslim woman walking an outwardly Christian path to point out to us the deeper truth that lay beyond. Whatever name we choose to describe the ineffable is immaterial. The only way out of our dilemma, is inward through Love …"*

Leaving the albergue in Ribadiso proceed up to and through the tunnel under the busy N-547 and veer right> on the far side back up to the main road again which we follow all the way straight into Arzua passing café and hostal El Retiro **[1.6 km]** on the outskirts and another **[0.7 km]** to •**Albergue [1]** *Don Quijote* (981-500 139) (see photo) new network* hostel in

(PEDROUZO) **ARCA** O PINO

P Muiño pensión/bar ☎ 686 419 046
A Porta de Santiago **Priv.*** [86]
☎ 981-511 103
Xunta [126] **Albergue** 3.1
A

Burgo
H O Pino
C
Rua
río Burgo

SANTA IRENE
A ◄ 5.1 **Albergue** Xunta [36]
Santa Irene Priv.* [15] **Albergue** **A**

O Emplame
Alto de
Santa Irene

Brea

Ras

Oxen
Mesón La Equipa → **m** Guillermo Watt

◄ 2.6 **Salceda**

N-547
Boavista

◄ 5.3 **Calle**

Calzada

Ponte Ladrón
Pereiriña

Cortobe

Raído

Río Brandeso

Túnel 3.1 ◄

As Barrosas

H Suiza
río As Barrosas

Via Láctea Priv.*[60] **A**
Xunta [48] **Albergue** 3.0 →
Ultreia Priv.*[36]
Don Quijote Priv.*[50]
A
A Santiago Apostol Priv.*[84]
H
O Retiro

ARZÚA
(Pop. 7,000 – Alt. 390m)

Río Iso

N-547
RIBADISO

A ◄ 0.0 **Albergue** Xunta [70]

Puesta
del Sol **O**
S
N
Salida
del Sol **E**

modern terraced building on the left as we enter Arzúa on c/Lugo, 130. Open all year with 50 places in bunk beds with good facilities (no kitchen but meals available). Adjoining is •**Albergue** [2] *Ultreia* (Raquel 981-500 471) another new network* hostel in same modern block. Open all year with 36 places and all facilities with café serving breakfast. Directly opposite is the latest addition (opened in September 2008) •**Albergue** [3] *Santiago Apostol* (Inma 981-500 004). Open all year with 84 places and every modern convenience (including a lift to all floors!) and restaurant with pilgrim menu.

Proceed up to the centre of town and the Plaza Mayor **[0.5 km]** where we turn <left into rúa do Lugar and adjoining the Iglesia de Santiago y capela da Madalena **[0.2 km]** is:

3.0 km **Arzúa Centro** and Xunta •**Albergue** [4] *Río Vello* (Margarita Aramburu 981-500 455) restored hostel in traditional stone town house in convenient central location. Open all year with 46 places and excellent modern facilities. •**Albergue** [5] *Vía Láctea* (Borja 981-500 581) central location in c/Jose Antonio. Open all year with 60 places and all facilities including attractive terrace. Other accommodation: •**El Retiro** HsR* (981-500 554) Av. Lugo on the way in and further along

Albergue [4] Xunta

the avenue the newer •**Teodora** Hs** (981-500 083) and •**Rua** HSR** (981-500 139). Centrally located in more traditional accommodation on rúa Ramón Franco is •**Casa Frade** (981-500 019) and adjoining •**Casa Carballeira** (981-500 094). Also central •**Mesón do Peregrino** Hs* (981-500 830) while on the outskirts on the main road *carratera Santiago* is the modern •**Suiza** H** (981-500 862).

ARZÚA is the last major centre of population (7,000) before we enter Santiago. The untidy development of the modern town is mirrored in the haphazard layout of the older central part and waymarking is also irregular. Off the central square to the left is the original 14th century Augustinian Church *Capilla de La Magdalena* and nearby is the modern parish church dedicated to St. James with image of Santiago as both Moorslayer and pilgrim. The camino continues out through the old quarter of town down c/del Carmen (left of the main road) past fountain and over stream (site of San Lázaro hospice) and into ancient oak woods through As Barrosas meandering back to the main road (close to Hotel Suiza) where we take another tunnel:

3.1 km **N-547 Tunél** continuing over the río Raído through the tiny hamlets of Raído, Fondevila, Cortobe, Pereiriña and Ponteladrón whence we cross the arroyo Ladrón and up the far side through Calzada and into:

5.3 km **Calle** pretty village with traditional stone houses and café adjoining the river serving snacks **[F]**. The camino wends its way through Boavista and Alto where we head towards the main road at:

2.6 km **Salceda** stretching along the main road with a bar and a grocery shop and at the far end the Mesón La Equipa. The path now veers off right> (behind the restaurant) and enters a woodland path. Here, on the right, is a poignant monument to fellow pilgrim, Guillermo Watt, who died at this spot only a day away from his earthly destination.

The waymarking now becomes somewhat irregular as we play hide and seek with the main road continuing through Xen before crossing the main road into Ras and back again to Brea emerging finally in Emplame with restaurante Pau (pilgrim menu) at the crossroads. We now have an option to stay with the main road down into Santa Irene or to take the path right (recommended) through the dense eucalyptus woods that cover Alto de Santa Irene before arriving at pilgrim rest area and:

5.1 km **Santa Irene** Xunta •**Albergue** [1] (María José Rodríguez 660-0396 825). Open all year with 36 places and all facilities but directly on the busy main road. On the opposite side of the road (back 300m towards restaurante Pau) is:

Albergue [1] Xunta *(above)*
Albergue [2] Santa Irene *(below)*

•**Albergue** [2] *Santa Irene* network* hostel (Esther Calvo 981-511 000). Open all year with 15 beds and all facilities in this delightful small refuge set back from the main road with lovely rear garden. Named after the nearby 18th century Chapel of Santa Irene (an early Christian martyr).

Continue down the main road veering off <left into A Rúa **[1.5 km]** Casa Rural •**O Acivro** (981-511 316) with bar-cafeteria and meals available. At the entrance to the village there is an option to turn right for hotel-restaurante O'Pino (700m) up on the main road. To continue to Arca proceed through A Rúa over the arroyo Burgo now climbing up through eucalyptus onto the N-547. **Option:** To continue directly to Santiago cross the main road here into the eucalyptus woods ahead and continue into San Antón where the route below rejoins *or* for the albergue turn <left along the main road for [0.6 km] (not 200m as indicated on road!) up to:

3.1 km **Arca do Pino (Pedrouzo)** Xunta •**Albergue** [1] purpose built hostel (Obdulia Rendo 660-396 826). Open all year with 126 places and full range of facilities. The albergue is somewhat 'hidden' down behind the supermarket and Correo at the start of the town (left). On the opposite side of the road is the new •**Albergue** [2] *Porta de Santiago* (981-511 103) new private hostel in modern building in the main street just beyond the Veterinaria. Open all year with 86 places and all modern conveniences.

Albergue [1] Xunta *(above)*
Albergue [2] Porta Santiago *(below)*

Other accommodation includes: •**O Pino** H* (981-511 148) rúa de Arca. Pensión/bar •**O Muiño** P (686-419 046). •**Maribel** PR* (981-511 404) and adjoining •**Arca** on rua Os Mollados - all adjacent to the camino off Rua de Concello on the way out to Santiago.

Arca do Pino (Pedrouzo) is a modern satellite town of Santiago that straddles the busy N-547 with a variety of shops and restaurants. If you intend to make the Cathedral for the 12 noon pilgrim mass then you need to leave early.

❑ **He took Peter and John and James, and went up into the mountain to pray. And as he prayed, the fashion of his countenance was altered, and his raiment was white and glistening.** *Luke IX, 29.*

MAP 33 *20.1 km (12.5 miles) to Santiago de Compostela*

ARCA do PINO (PEDROUZO) – SANTIAGO

▬▬▬	Path / Track	--- ---	8.1 ---	*40%*
▬▬▬	Quiet Road	--- ---	7.6 ---	*38%*
▬▬▬	Main Road	--- ---	4.4 ---	*22%*
Total km	**Total distance**		**20.1 km** (12.8 miles)	

◣ Adjusted for climb 20.7 km (accrued ascent 120m = 0.6 km)
Alto ▲ High Point: Monte do Gozo 370m (1,214 feet)

The Practical Path: The first part of this last stage is through tall stands of the ever present eucalyptus. Make the most of their shade and the peace they exude. As we get nearer the city, asphalt and crowds begin to take over. Prepare yourself also for the long hike up to Monte Gozo, which, while still surrounded by eucalyptus, is all on asphalt road. **Intermediate accommodation:** Labacolla (9.9 km) – Monte do Gozo (15.5 km).

Note: Inevitably large numbers of pilgrims will be gathering. Many groups organise just this one-day in which to enter the city and so bus loads may join you from here on in. If you experience a rush of joy at ascending Monte do Gozo, praise be! We each create our own experience. However, it might be helpful to create an air of detachment. That way you will not set yourself up for euphoria nor for disappointment. If you are making for the pilgrim mass at 12 noon be prepared for the crowds – Santiago has become a very popular destination, so be patient. You will doubtless have to queue, perhaps for hours, to complete the traditional pilgrim routine on entering the cathedral: An alternative might be to find a quiet church or square in the city (there are many) to offer thanks for your safe arrival and then find a bed, have a shower, attend the pilgrim office and obtain your compostela. Meet with friends, have a drink and a celebration meal – then early the following morning when the cathedral is all but empty and quiet …

❑ **The Mystical Path:** Will you stay awhile and lose yourself in the tiny grove of holm oak, itself almost lost amongst the mass of alien eucalyptus? How appropriate that this grove should bear the Cross of James in the midst of such indifference. Will you stop in Lavacolla, whose waters were used in the ritual cleansing of pilgrims prior to entering the City of Saint James? Today the water is putrid but it is the symbolic purification that we seek so that we might glisten with the pure white light of Christ.

AP-9

Turismo ☎ *981-555 129* → **i** ← **4.6** **Catedral**

SANTIAGO DE COMPOSTELA

Semenario Belvis **A**

Fontiñas

Priv. [50] ☎ *981-575 438 Acuario* **A**

N-634

Roma

S.Lazarus

✝ *San Lázaro Santiago*

A *Residencia de Peregrinos (S.Lazaro) Xunta [80]*

Xunta [500]
Albergue **5.6** → **A**

Capilla S.Marcos ✝

Monte del Gozo ▲ 370m San Marcos

A-54

AP-9

TV

Casa de Amancio → **C**

N-634a

Capilla S.Roque ✝

H *San Paio*

Vilamaior

2.3 **Lavacolla** *(igrexa)*

San Paio

Ruta Jacobeo **H**

Garcas **H**

túnel

✝ **3.9** **San Payo**

Labacolla aeropuerto

✈ ✈

✈

A-54

A Pereira

Cimadevila

3.7 **Amenal** *(Túnel)*

N-547

N-634

ARCA O PINO
(PEDROUZO)
Xunta [126] **Albergue** **0.0** → **A**

P

A *Porta de Santiago*

❑ **Personal Reflections:** *"... I had walked the equivalent of one day for each year Christ spent on earth. Here I was on the 33rd day but I could find no joy on this hill amongst the crowd of pilgrims huddled against the driving rain ... As I entered the cathedral I realised I had failed in my purpose. But in that same instant I realised I had been searching in the wrong place. A sudden rush of joy enveloped my soaking body. I knew the answer lay where the world of things ended and the unseen world began and I knew I had to go there. Not tomorrow, but now. I hurried down the steps and out the city gate. I was alone but I had company. I did not know where I was going but I felt completely guided ..."*

Leaving albergue [1] in Arca turn <left on the main road into the town and turn off right> past the Casa Concello and the sports stadium and proceed into the dense eucalyptus forest and through the village of San Antón where we join the direct route (the one that bypasses the hostel in Arca) and head down into the río Amenal valley and village:

3,7 km **Amenal** */Túnel* cross under the N-547 and head uphill through Cimadevila to thread our way through the forestry area around Santiago airport. A dedicated pilgrim track alongside the motorway takes us down into a deep cutting at the end of the runway to cross over an access road down into.

3.9 km **San Payo** ancient hamlet with popular bar and restaurant *Casa Porta de Santiago*. We now enter the last recognisable stretch of the medieval 'Royal Way' *Real Camino* as we head uphill veering right> onto a natural path lined with remnants of the native deciduous woodland that once covered this land before eucalyptus was imported to fuel the pulp industry, head downhill into:

2.3 km **Lavacolla** */Igrexa*. Lavacolla is recognised today more for the name of the international airport than the place where medieval pilgrims came to wash *lavar* and purify themselves before entering the city. Modern Lavacolla now tends more to the business traveller than the pilgrim with its various restaurants, bars and commercial hotels •**San Paio** P* (981-888 205) on Lugar de Lavacolla. **Short detour** Capela San Roque (300m): If you continue down the steps past the bandstand you come to the little chapel dedicated to the pilgrim saint *San Roque* (right) and while it may be closed it has a covered portico and sits in a delightful grove of trees. A good place to shelter from the rain or sun and here you can perform your own purification ritual, although the traffic on the main road intrudes somewhat on its relative tranquillity.

The path now continues around the side of the parish church to cross over the access road to the airport (N-634a). Cross over a small stream and head steeply uphill along a dedicated pilgrim track into **Villamaior** and casa rural •**Casa de Amancio** (981-897 086) with bar and restaurant. Shortly afterwards we pass the TV Galicia HQ (right) and then turning <left at the camping ground opposite TV España studios into San Marcos with several bars and café. A short paved pathway now brings us to the charming capilla de San Marcos sitting in a small glade of trees and where, if it was not raining, medieval pilgrims first espied the cathedral towers giving rise to the name, Mount Joy *Monte do Gozo – Mon Xoi* in Galego. Today, a monument commemorating the visit of Pope John Paul II stands sentinel atop the hill and the view is now dominated by the Santiago sports stadium. Continue down to:

5.6 km **Monte del Gozo** Xunta •**Albergue [4]** *Monte do Gozo* (981-558 942) prominently located on this elevated site overlooking the city of Santiago. Open all year with a total of 500 beds in 20 separate blockhouses containing rooms with 8 beds in each. Good modern facilities including bar and restaurant + large canteen on the main plaza. The hill itself has been reshaped by the bulldozer to provide a vast leisure complex for the city. The sprawling dormitory and recreational buildings are the price of an ever-increasing demand for accommodation. The tiny chapel of San Marcos is the only thing left on the hill that gives any sense of history to this romantic sounding place. The route continues down the hill along Rua do Peregrino and down a flight of steps at the far end where we join the city traffic to pass over the A-9 autopista and railway and over the roundabout into the wide N-634 and the modern the city suburbs with the *Palacio Congresos y Exposicións* hall (left) and on the opposite side of the road (right – not well signposted 200m from roundabout) •**Albergue** [3] *Residencia de Peregrinos* just off rúa de San Lázaro (981-571 488) also operated by the Xunta and open all year with 80 beds (6 rooms) and all facilities with garden area to the rear.

Continue along the main road passing the ancient chapel of *San Lázaro Santiago* which stands as witness to the leprosarium that existed here in the 12th century, sufficiently far outside the medieval city walls to ensure contamination didn't spread inside. Continue towards the centre veering <left into rúa do Valiño and close to its junction with rúa Estocolmo (down to the left) is: •**Albergue** [2] *Acuario* Rúa Estocolmo, 2-b. (981-575 438). Private hostel run by the Asociación Xacobea Acuario. Open all year (excepting December and January) with 58 places in one dormitory. Good modern facilities including washing and drying machines (no kitchen but many restaurants in the area).

Continue down rúa das Fontiñas and Fonte dos Concheiros and over the ring road *Av. de Lugo* with the main bus station (right) and enter *Rúa dos Concheiros* named after the stall holders who used to sell pilgrim shells *conchas* and at the top we reach St. Peter's cross *Cruceiro de San Pedro* which heralds our arrival in the old city as the spires of the Cathedral now open up before us and we take the cobbled rúa de San Pedro to Praza San Pedro a tiny shaded square with Church of San Pedro (left). Opción [?] We are now only 900m from the main entrance to the cathedral and the likelihood is you will want to press on. However you have an option at this point to go directly to the main pilgrim hostel at the Seminario

Menor de Belvis •**Albergue** [1] only 800m off to your left. Depending on your time of arrival and intentions for the day you might consider going directly to the hostel from here (opens from 13.00 with lockers for backpacks) *Directions*: Turn left into Calzada San Pedro and rúa de Belvís around the walls of the convento de Belvís to the enormous edifice of the Seminario Menor which houses the main city hostel (see next page).

Albergue [1] Seminario Menor

Continue straight on to the famous Gate of the Way *Porta do Camiño* which gives access to the wonderful old medieval city. Up on the right and overlooking this main city entrance is the *Convento de Santo Domingo de Bonaval* which houses the Pantheón and the Galician museum, with the centre for contemporary Galician art opposite. There is also a relatively quiet park behind the convent buildings to refresh mind and soul from the rigours of city life. (See city map for directions to these and other places of interest). We now proceed up Casas Reais and Rúa das Ánimas into Praza de Cervantes (with statue to the writer) where we follow the right hand street lined with jewellers selling jet *azabache* (see later) Rúa da Azabachería into Praza da Inmaculada (also called Azabachería) down under the arch of the Pazo do Xelmírez into the famous:

| **2.5 km** | **Praza Obradoiro and Cathedral**. Take time to just *arrive*. We each experience different emotions on entering the Cathedral that range from euphoria to disappointment. Whatever your individual reaction – honour and accept it. Gratitude for safe arrival is a frequent response but if you are overwhelmed by the crowds why not return later when you feel more composed and the Cathedral is, perhaps, quieter (open daily from 07:00 until 21:00). Whether now or later and whichever door you entered by, you might like to follow the timeworn pilgrim ritual (amended) as follows:

[1] It is no longer permitted to place your hand in the Tree of Jesse, the central column of the Master Mateo's masterpiece Door of Glory *Portico de Gloria*. But you can stop and admire the incomparable beauty of this inner portico carved between 1166 and 1188 (the exterior façade was added in 1750). The Bible and its main characters come alive in this remarkable storybook in stone. The central column has Christ in Glory flanked by the apostles and, directly underneath, St. James sits as intercessor between Christ and the pilgrim. Millions of pilgrims over the centuries have worn finger holes in the solid marble as a mark of gratitude for their safe arrival (the reason why it is now protected by a barrier). Proceed to the other side and **[2]**

Pilgrims arrive at the cathedral

touch your brow to that of Maestro Mateo whose kneeling figure is carved into the back of the central column (facing the altar) and receive some of his artistic genius in the ritual known as head-butting the saint *Santo d'os Croques* – touch your forehead to his and receive some of his inspiration. Proceed to the High Altar (right) to ascend the stairs and **[3]** hug the Apostle. Perhaps lay your head on his broad shoulders and say what you came here to say. Proceed down the steps on the far side to the crypt and the reliquary chapel under the altar. **[4]** Here, you can kneel before the casket containing the relics of the great Saint and offer your prayer …

Pilgrim mass at 12 noon each day (doors may close 5 minutes before on busy days). The swinging of the giant incense burner *Botafumeiro* was originally used to fumigate the sweaty (and possibly disease-ridden) pilgrims. The ritual requires half a dozen attendants *tiraboleiros* to perform it and so became an infrequent event but is used increasingly during the mass these days. During 2004 the seating capacity was permanently extended from 700 to 1,000 so you might even find somewhere to sit but don't hold any expectations and remember – time itself is a journey.

Cathedral from Praza Obradoiro

REFLECTIONS: 'Time is the journey from ignorance to Gnosis. Time is imperfection longing to be the Good and progressively improving. Time is the relative reaching towards the Absolute.' *Jesus and the Lost Goddess.*' Freke.

_____
_____
_____
_____
_____
_____
_____
_____
_____
_____
_____
_____
_____
_____
_____
_____
_____
_____
_____
_____
_____
_____
_____
_____
_____

Four squares surround the cathedral and provide access to it, as follows:

Praza do Obradoiro. The 'golden' square of Santiago is usually thronged with pilgrims and tourists admiring the dramatic west facing façade of the Cathedral, universal symbol of Santiago, with St. James looking down on all the activity from his niche in the central tower. This provides the main entrance to the Cathedral and the Portico de Gloria. To the right of the steps is the discrete entrance to the museum. A combined ticket will provide access to all rooms including the crypt and the cloisters and also to the 12th century palace of one of Santiago's most famous individuals and first archbishop, Gelmírez *Pazo de Xelmírez* situated on the (left).

In this square we also find the beautiful Renaissance façade of the Parador named after Ferdinand and Isabel *Hostal dos Reis Católicos* on whose orders it was built in 1492 as a pilgrim hospice. Opposite the Cathedral is the more austere neoclassical seat of the Galician government and town hall *Pazo de Raxoi* with its solid arcade. Finally, making up the fourth side of the square is the gable end of the *Colegio de S. Jerónimo* part of the university. Moving anti-clockwise around the cathedral – turn up into Rúa de Fonseca to:

Praza das Praterías. The most intimate of the squares with its lovely centrepiece, an ornate statue of horses leaping out of the water. On the corner of Rúa do Vilar we find the Dean's House *Casa do Deán* now the pilgrim office (which issues the *compostelas*). Along the walls of the Cathedral itself are the silversmith's *prateros* that give the square its name. Up the steep flight of steps we come to the magnificent southern door to the Cathedral, the oldest extant doorway and traditionally the entrance taken by pilgrims coming from Portugal. The quality of the carvings and their arrangement is remarkable and amongst the many sculptured figures is one of St. James between two cypress trees. Continuing around to the right we come to:

Praza da Quintana. This wide square is readily identified by the broad sweep of steps separating the lower part *Quintana of the dead* from the upper *Quintana of the living*. Opposite the Cathedral is the high blank wall of the *Mosteiro de San Paio de Antealtares* (with museum of sacred art). The square provides the eastern entrance to the Cathedral via the Holy Gate *Porta Santa* sometime referred to as the Door of Pardon *El Perdón* that is only opened during Holy Years (the next in 2010). Adjoining it is the main entrance to the

Pilgrims during Holy Year

Cathedral shop that has several guidebooks (in various languages) with details of the Cathedral's many chapels and their interesting carvings and statuary and the priceless artefacts and treasures in the museum. Finally, we head up the broad flight of steps around the corner and back into:

Praza da Inmaculada (Azabachería) to the north facing Azabachería façade, with the least well-known doorway and the only one that *descends* to enter the Cathedral. It has the most weathered aspect, with moss and lichen covering its bleak exterior. Opposite the cathedral is the imposing southern edifice of the Mosteiro de San Martiño Pinario where the square in front can be a pleasant place to sit as it gets any available sun. The archbishop's arch *Arco Arzobispal* brings us back to the Praza do Obradoiro.

Check in at the •**Pilgrim Office** *Oficina del Peregrino* in the Casa do Deán adjacent to the Cathedral on Rúa Vilar at its junction with Rúa Gelmirez. There is a notice board here for pilgrims to leave messages. Providing you have fulfilled the criteria of a bona fide pilgrim and have walked at least the last 100 km, you will be awarded a certificate of completion *Compostela*. This may entitle you to certain privileges such as reduced entry fees to museums and discounted travel home. If you have not already made arrangements for your return travel *Viajes Viloria* have a travel kiosk on the ground floor with discounted travel within Spain. But check deals that may be available elsewhere and may prove cheaper than the special pilgrim discounted fares on offer and refer to the travel notes at the beginning of this guide.

Compostela

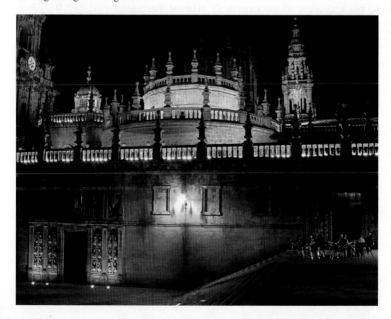

There are several *municipal* tourist offices serving the city. The main **Turismo** is on Rúa do Vilar, 63 (981-555 129). Another helpful office is located in the centre of Plaza do Galicia (981-573 990). Either will provide you with a full list of accommodation and things to do and see in Santiago and opening times of museums. For travel information within Galicia try the *regional* tourist office (opposite the Turismo) in Rúa do Vilar, 30–32 (902-332 010). Note: Reserve your accommodation as early as possible as rooms can be difficult to secure late in the day and the longer you leave travel arrangements, the more expensive they are likely to be.

Albergues: The major pilgrim hostel is 1 km east of the Cathedral in the •Albergue [1] *Seminario Menor de Belvis* (981-589 200) with main access via Rúa Trompas – a large and largely soulless hostel open all year with 177 places (depending on time of year). Lockers are now provided which has dealt with the petty theft problem. A new purpose built hostel to the rear is under consideration (planned for 2010 but more likely 2012). The other hostels at Monte do Gozo and in the San Lazaro area have already been described.

Other Accommodation: There are numerous hostels and hotels in every price bracket. Popular pilgrim haunts around the old historic central part include: *in the less expensive bracket* (from around €30+ for a single room and marked on the town plan attached) north/east of the Cathdral: •**La Salle** (981-585 667) Tras de Sta. Clara. •**Hostal Moure** Rúa dos Loureiros *Laureles*, 6 and adjacent at no, 12 •**Hostal Moure 2** both owned by the same family (981-583 637). Close by, more upmarket at Rúa do Hospitalillo, 8 we find •**Hotel Fonte de San Roque** (981-554 447) and •**La Campana** on Campanas de San Juan, 4 (981-584 850). •**Estrela** (981-576 924) Plazuela de San Martín Pinario and just below it •**Seminario Mayor** (981-583 009) summer only on Praza da Inmaculada. •**Pico Sacro** (981-584 466) Rúa San Francisco, 22 (opposite the side of the Parador) and adjacent to its more upmarket sister establishment •**Pico Sacro II**.

South/west of the Cathdral: •**La Estela** (981-582 796) Rúa Raxoi, 1 (some rooms with view of the cathedral). •**Hostal Barbantes** (981-581 077) Rúa do Franco, 3 (some rooms overlook the square). •**Santa Cruz** (981-582 362) Rúa do Vilar, 42. •**Hostal Suso** (981-586 611) Rúa do Vilar, 65 close to the tourist office, small rooms but popular bar on the ground floor and opposite at n°12 •**San Jaime** (981-583 134). Further on (just inside the city walls before Plaza Galicia) in Rúa Entremuralles are •**A Nosa Casa** (981-585 926) and the adjoining •**Hostal Mapoula** (981-580 124). Outside the 'walls' but adjoining the city park *Alameda* at San Clemente, 32 •**Hostal Alameda** (981-588 100).

In the middle/ upper price bracket (from €60+ single) •**Hotel Rúa Vilar** (981-557 102) at n° 12 or try one of the 4 *Pousadas de Compostela* the most central is •**Hotel Airas Nunes** (902-405 858) in Rúa do Vilar, 17 opposite the pilgrim office. •**Entrecercas** (981-571 151) Rúa Entrecercas. •**Costa Vella** (981-569 530) Porta de Pena, 17 with lovely garden patio (located close to the Moure hostels, run by the same family). No list would be complete without mentioning •**Hostal de los Reyes Católicos** in the Plaza Obradoiro (981-582 200). The oldest hotel in the world in constant use for that purpose and one of the grandest and by no means the most expensive. Call in for a drink on the terrace bar or try for one of the 3 free meals (breakfast 09:00 lunch 12:00 dinner 19:00 served to the first 10 pilgrims queuing for the privilege with a *copy* (not the original) of your *compostela* – humble exchange for transferring the buildings from pilgrim hospice to luxury hotel. If budget allows luxuriate in one of its rooms or take a meal in its atmospheric diningroom (the original carriage entrance).

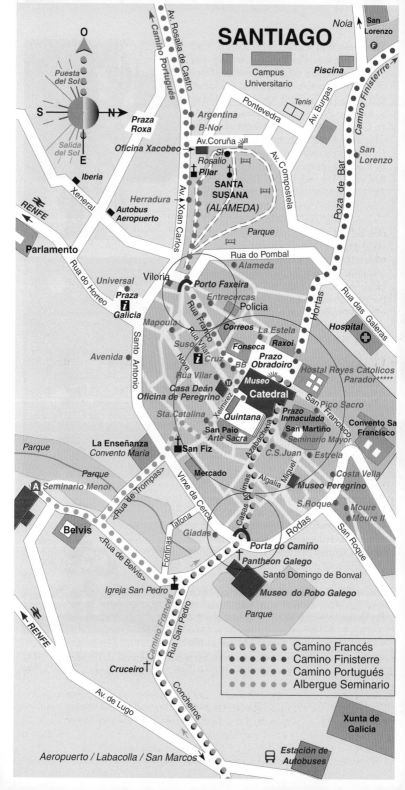

Museums and Parks: The crowds head for the *Museos Catedralicos* but try and make time for the pilgrim museum *Museo das Peregrinacións* in the Casa Gótica on Rúa de San Miguel dos Agros (off Praza de S. Martiño Pinario). Further away at Porta do Camiño (where we first entered the old city) is the Galician museum *Museo do Pobo Galego*, with artefacts and displays of Galician culture in the Convento do Bonaval. The adjoining church houses the remains of some of the illustrious sons (Castelao) and daughters (Rosalía de Castro) of Galicia *Panteón Galegos Ilustres* and behind we can relax in quiet park, a good place to reflect on our journey and where it might lead on from here. At the other end of town are the delightful shaded city gardens, the *Alameda*. Take a stroll up the Avenue of the Lions *Paseo dos Leónes* to a handsome statue of Rosalía de Castro and climb to the Igrexa de Santa Susana, hidden in the trees

Santiago is a wonderful destination, full of vibrancy and colour. Stay awhile and soak up some of the culture and atmosphere of this fabled city. The official literature for the last compostelan jubilee year *año jubilar compostelana* stated boldly on the front cover, 'A Road with an END' *Camino que tiene META*. That may be so – but it is not the end of the road.

Finisterre. Before you leave this corner of the earth why not visit the end of it *Finis Terra*. "… Finisterre is one of the great hidden treasures amongst the many Caminos de Santiago. Only a tiny proportion of pilgrims arriving at Santiago continue by foot to the end of the road. The way to Finisterre truly follows *the road less travelled by* and *that* may make all the difference. We need to search out the waymarks to the source of our own inner knowing. The light, while obscured, lies

hidden in our memory – it is no coincidence that the path to Finisterre ends at the altar to the sun *Ara Solis* and a lighthouse." From *A Pilgrim's Guide to the Camino Finisterre*.

USEFUL PILGRIM CONTACTS:

You may be able to obtain further information of the route and a pilgrim passport, record or *credential*, subject to membership from one of the English speaking organisations listed below. Allow several weeks to process postal applications.

UK: **The Confraternity of St. James**, 27 Blackfriars Road, London SE1 8NY (0044-[0]2079 289 988) e-mail: office@csj.org.uk / *www.csj.org.uk* the pre-eminent site in English with an on-line bookshop.

IRELAND: **The Irish Society of the Friends of St. James**. Based in Dublin, contact through their web site: *www.st.jamesirl.com*

U.S.A. **American Pilgrims on the Camino**. *www.americanpilgrims.com* *also:* Friends of the Road to Santiago *www.geocities.com/friends_usa_santiago*

CANADA: Canadian Company of Pilgrims Canada. *www.santiago.ca*

SOUTH AFRICA: Confraternity of St. James of SA *www.geocities.com/csjofsa*

TRANSLATIONS: *www.freetranslation.com/* or: *www.babelfish.altavista.com*

There are a number of additional web sites (in English) loosely connected with the Way of St. James or with the theme of pilgrimage as spiritual journeying that you may find helpful. These sites provide links with other organisations so you can explore and, hopefully, find information that resonates with you:

Alternatives of St. James *www.alternatives.org.uk* exploration of ways of living that honour all spiritual traditions. Based at St. James Church, London.

The Beloved Community *www.emissaryoflight.com* on-line courses in spiritual peacemaking and peace pilgrimages based in the USA.

Findhorn Foundation dedicated to personal and planetary transformation *www.findhorn.org* with daily reflections from 'Opening Doors Within.'

The Gatekeeper Trust devoted to personal and planetary healing through pilgrimage. *www.gatekeeper.org.uk*

Lucis Trust incorporating the Arcane School of spiritual education and meditation and World Goodwill *www.alicebailey.org*

Paulo Coelho *www.paulocoelho.com.br* also *www.warriorofthelight.com* with on-line news and reflections from Brazilian author of 'The Pilgrimage.'

Peace Pilgrim *www.peacepilgrim.com* audio and visual reflections of Peace Pilgrim's life and work.

The Quest A Guide to the Spiritual Journey. A practical home-study course for personal and spiritual discovery *www.nvo.com/thequest*

The Latest News from Santiago and the Caminos *www.santiago-today.com*

BIBLIOGRAPHY:

Some reading with waymarks to the inner path include:

A Course In Miracles (A.C.I.M.) *Text, Workbook for Students and Manual for Teachers*. Foundation for Inner Peace.

The Art of Pilgrimage *The Seeker's Guide to Making Travel Sacred*, Phil Cousineau. Element Books

Anam Cara *Spiritual wisdom from the Celtic world*, John O'Donohue. Bantam Books

A New Earth *Awakening to Your Life's Purpose*, Eckhart Tolle. Penguin Books

A Brief History of Everything *Integrating the partial visions of specialists into a new understanding of the meaning and significance of life*, Ken Wilber.

Care of the Soul *How to add depth and meaning to your everyday life*, Thomas More. Piatkus

Conversations with God *Books One, Two and Three*. Neale Donald Walsch. Hodder & Stoughton

From the Holy Mountain *A Journey in the Shadow of Byzantium*, William Dalrymple. Flamingo

Going Home *Jesus and the Buddha as brothers*, Thich Nhat Hanh. Rider Books

Loving What Is *Four Questions That Can Change Your Life*, Byron Katie. Rider

Handbook for the Soul *A collection of wisdom from over 30 celebrated spiritual writers*. Piatkus

The Hero with a Thousand Faces *An examination, through ancient myths, of man's eternal struggle for identity*, Joseph Campbell. Fontana Press

How to Know God *The Soul's Journey into the Mystery of Mysteries*, Deepak Chopra. Rider

Jesus and the Lost Goddess *The Secret Teachings of the Original Christians*, Timothy Freke & Peter Gandy. Three Rivers Press

The Journey Home *The Obstacles to Peace*, Kenneth Wapnick. Foundation for A Course In Miracles

The Mysteries *Rudolf Steiner's writings on Spiritual Initiation*, Andrew Welburn. Floris Books

Mysticism *The Nature and Development of Spiritual Consciousness*, Evelyn Underhill. Oneworld

Nine Faces of Christ *Quest of the True Initiate*, Eugene Whitworth. DeVorss

No Destination *Autobiography (of a pilgrimage), Satish Kumar*. Green Books

Paths of the Christian Mysteries *From Compostela to the New World*, Virginia Sease and Manfred Schmidt-Brabant. Temple Lodge

Pilgrimage *Adventures of the Spirit*, Various Authors. Travellers' Tales

The Pilgrimage *A Contemporary Quest for Ancient Wisdom*. Paulo Coelho

Peace Pilgrim *Her Life and Work in Her Own Words*, Friends of Peace Pilgrim. Ocean Tree Books

Pilgrim in Aquarius, David Spangler. Findhorn Press

Pilgrim Stories *On and Off the Road to Santiago*. Nancy Louise Frey.

Pilgrim in Time *Mindful Journeys to Encouter the Sacred*. Rosanne Keller.

The Power of Now *A Guide to Spiritual Enlightenment*, Eckhart Tolle. New World Library

Peace is Every Step *The path of mindfulness in everyday life*, Thich Nhat Hanh. Rider Books

Phases *The Spiritual Rhythms in Adult Life*, Bernard Lievegoed. Sophia Books

Sacred Contracts *Awakening Your Divine Potential*, Caroline Myss. Bantam

Sacred Roads *Adventures from the Pilgrimage Trail*, Nicholas Shrady. Viking

Secrets of God *Writings of Hildegard of Bingen*. Shambhala

Silence of the Heart *Dialogues with Robert Adams*. Acropolis Books

The Gift of Change *Spiritual Guidance for a Radically New Life*, Marianne Williamson. Element Books

The Reappearance of the Christ. Alice Bailey. Lucis Press.

The Road Less Travelled *A new Psychology of Love*, M. Scott Peck. Arrow Books

The Soul's Code *In Search of Character and Calling*, James Hillman. Bantam

The Prophet. Kahlil Gibran. Mandarin

Wandering Joy *Meister Eckhart's Mystical Philosophy*. Lindisfarne Press

Wanderlust *A history of Walking*. Rebecca Solnit. Verso

Who Dies? *An Investigation of Conscious Living and Conscious Dying*, Stephen and Ondrea Levine. Anchor Books

Whispers of the Beloved *The mystical poems of Rumi*. HarperCollins

RETURNING HOME:
Reflections ...

When, after a prolonged absence, friends and family remark, *'you haven't changed at all'* I am hopeful they are either blind or following some meaningless social convention. I have spent the last 20 years of my life with the primary intention to do just that – to change myself. One of the more potent aspects of pilgrimage is the extended time it requires away from the familiar. This allows an opportunity for the inner alchemy of spirit to start its work of transformation. It's not just the physical body that may need to sweat off excess baggage – the mind needs purifying too. Our world is in a mess and we are not going to fix it with more of the same. We need a fresh approach and a different mind-set to the one that created the chaos in the first place. Hopefully, this re-ordering of the way we see the world will quicken apace as we open to lessons presented to us along the camino and begin to understand that life itself is a classroom.

A purpose of pilgrimage is to allow time for old belief systems and outworn 'truths' to fall away so that new and higher perspectives can arise. We may also need to recognise that colleagues and partners at home or at work may feel threatened by our new outlook on life. Breaking tribal patterns, challenging the status quo or querying consensus reality is generally considered inappropriate at best or heretical at worst. The extent to which we hold onto any new understanding is measured by how far we are prepared to *walk our talk* and live our 'new' truth in the face of opposition, often from those who profess to love us. Christ was crucified for living The Truth.

These guidebooks are dedicated to the awakening of human consciousness. They arose out of a personal existential crisis and the urgent need for some space and time to reflect on the purpose of life and its direction. Collectively we live in a spiritual vacuum of our own making where the mystical and sacred have been relegated to the delusional or escapist. Accordingly, we live in a three dimensional world and refuse to open the door to higher dimensions of reality. We have impoverished ourselves in the process, severely limiting our potential. Terrorised by the chaotic world we have manifested around us, we have become ensnared in its dark forms. We have become so preoccupied with these fearful images we fail to notice that we hold the key to the door of our self-made prison. We can walk out any time we choose.

Whatever our individual experiences, it is likely that you will be in a heightened state of sensitivity after walking the camino. I strongly recommend that you do not squeeze your itinerary so you feel pressurised to rush back into your work and general lifestyle immediately on your return. This is a crucial moment. I have often witnessed profound change, in myself and others, only to allow a sceptical audience to induce fear and doubt in us so that we fall back to the starting point – the default position of the status quo. Be careful with whom you share your experiences and stay in contact with fellow pilgrims who can support new realisations and orientation. Source new friends and activities that enhance and encourage the ongoing journey of Self discovery.

If you feel it might be helpful, please feel free to email me any time at *jb@ caminoguides.com* – I cannot promise to answer all emails in writing but be assured they will all be noted and a blessing sent in return. I have developed great empathy and respect for my fellow pilgrims who have placed themselves on the path of enquiry. We are embarking together on a journey of re-discovery of our essential nature and opening up to knowledge of Higher Worlds. We have, collectively, been asleep a long time and while change can happen in the twinkling of an eye it is often experienced as a slow and painful process. It is never easy to let go of the familiar and to step into the new. How far we are prepared to go and how resolute in holding onto our new found reality is a matter of our own choosing.

Whichever choice you make will doubtless be right for you at this time. I wish you well in your search for the truth and your journey Home and extend my humble blessings to a fellow pilgrim on the path. The journey is not over and continues, as you will have it be, dedicated to the sacred or the mundane, to waking or sleeping. To help remind us of our true identity, I leave you with the following words of Marianne Williamson, distilled from A Course In Miracles and immortalised in Nelson Mandela's *freedom speech*.

Our deepest fear is not that we are inadequate.
Our deepest fear is that we are powerful beyond measure.
It is our Light, not our darkness, that most frightens us.

We ask ourselves, who am I to be brilliant, gorgeous, talented and fabulous?
Actually, who are you not to be? You are a child of God.
Your playing small doesn't serve the world.
There's nothing enlightened about shrinking,
So that other people won't feel insecure around you.

We were born to make manifest the Glory of God that is within us.
It's not just in some of us; it's in everyone.
And as we let our Light shine,
We unconsciously give other people permission to do the same.
As we are liberated from our own fear,
Our presence automatically liberates others.

Before a new chapter is begun, the old one has to be finished. Stop being who you were, and change into who you are. *Paulo Coelho* www.warriorsoflight.com

Stay in Touch:

The evolution of human consciousness is gathering apace, one manifestation of this is the increasing interest in taking time out to go on pilgrimage and nowhere is this more apparent than along the camino where facilities struggle to keep up with demand. Information garnered in one month may be out of date the next as old hostels fall prey to new building regulations while new ones open up. Paths are realigned to make way for new motorways and budget airlines suddenly announce new routes (or with the advent of 'peak oil' – closing some). Whilst great care has been taken in gathering the information for this guide it also requires feedback from pilgrims who have recently walked the route to enable it to stay fresh and relevant to those who will follow on after us. Your comments and suggestions will be gratefully received and used to provide up-to-date advice on the free 'updates' page on **www.caminoguides.com** so if you would like to offer something back to the route or simply stay in touch please e-mail me at:

jb@caminoguides.com

A tithe of all royalties from the sale of this book will be distributed to individuals and organisations seeking to preserve the physical and spiritual integrity of this route.